CBT for Appearance Anxiety

An evidence based approach produced as part of the research programme:

Identifying factors & processes contributing to successful adjustment to disfiguring conditions

Funded by: The Healing Foundation, in association with The Welton Foundation and the Worshipful Company of Tin Plate Workers

Written by: Alex Clarke, Andrew Thompson, Elizabeth Jenkinson, Nichola Rumsey, Rob Newell

and on behalf of the ARC consortium:

James Byron-Daniel, Roger Charlton, Sally-Ann Clarke, Diana Harcourt, Hayley McBain, Antje Lindenmeyer, Tim Moss, Stanton Newman, Krysia Saul, Eleanor Walsh, Paul White, Emma Thomas

With contributions from Heidi Williamson Jenny Barke and Esther Hansen

CBT for Appearance Anxiety

Psychosocial Interventions for Anxiety
Due to Visible Difference

Alex Clarke, Andrew Thompson, Elizabeth Jenkinson,
Nichola Rumsey and Rob Newell

WILEY Blackwell

This edition first published 2014
© 2014 John Wiley & Sons, Ltd

Registered Office
John Wiley & Sons, Ltd, The Atrium, Southern Gate, Chichester, West Sussex, PO19 8SQ, UK

Editorial Offices
350 Main Street, Malden, MA 02148-5020, USA
9600 Garsington Road, Oxford, OX4 2DQ, UK
The Atrium, Southern Gate, Chichester, West Sussex, PO19 8SQ, UK

For details of our global editorial offices, for customer services, and for information about how to apply for permission to reuse the copyright material in this book please see our website at www.wiley.com/wiley-blackwell.

Library of Congress Cataloging-in-Publication Data

Clarke, Alex, 1953–
    CBT for appearance anxiety : psychosocial interventions for anxiety due to visible difference / Alex Clarke, Andrew Thompson, Elizabeth Jenkinson, Nichola Rumsey, and Rob Newell.
      pages   cm
    Includes bibliographical references and index.
    ISBN 978-1-118-52343-8 (cloth) – ISBN 978-1-118-52342-1 (pbk.)   1. Anxiety disorders–Treatment.
2. Body image–Psychological aspects.   3. Disfigured persons–Psychology.   4. Cognitive therapy.
I. Thompson, Andrew R. (Andrew Robert), 1970-   II. Jenkinson, Elizabeth (Psychologist)
III. Rumsey, Nichola.   IV. Newell, Robert, 1954-   V. Title.   VI. Title: Cognitive behavior therapy
for appearance anxiety.
    RC531.C52 2013
    616.85′22–dc23

                                2013021913

A catalogue record for this book is available from the British Library.

Cover design by Nicki Averill Design & Illustration

Set in 10/12.5pt Minion by SPi Publishers, Pondicherry, India
Printed in Singapore by Ho Printing Singapore Pte Ltd

1   2014

In memory of Mr. Michael Brough,
Consultant Plastic Surgeon,
Royal Free Hospital, London

Contents

Foreword

The publication of this work represents the efforts of many people, it reflects the generosity of a few but it epitomises the vision of just one man.

Behind the principal authors of this seminal work, The Appearance Research Collaboration - the network of academics and practitioners who collaborated on the original Healing Foundation funded project – is the embodiment of how high quality medical research should be conducted; with the focus always on the patient and professional egos placed to one side.

An expert research team however, would achieve little without the selfless financial support of the Healing Foundation donors who supported the core research that has informed this publication. In particular, the very generous Trustees of The Welton Foundation and the officers and members of the The Worshipful Company of Tin Plate Workers. We are grateful that they shared our confidence in the quality and importance of this work.

The person whose life and contribution this publication most celebrates however, is Michael Brough. The inspirational, quiet, unassuming but pioneering plastic surgeon responsible for the establishment of the Healing Foundation. Following the King's Cross fire of 1987, it was Michael's recognition of the the dearth of evidence based treatments and support, both surgical and psychological, for survivors of major burns and other disfiguring conditions that has led in time to this work. It is fitting and certainly no coincidence that the lead author, Alex Clarke, was the first to fill the Clinical Psychologist role at the Royal Free Hospital that Michael fought so convincingly to establish.

This is the first major piece of work inspired by Michael Brough's vision. As his charity, the Healing Foundation, continues to grow, we expect it and the patient benefits it will bring, to be among the first of many that will forever be his legacy.

Brendan Eley
Chief Executive of the Healing Foundation

Preface

This guide has been written by clinicians and researchers working with adults. It is aimed at therapists working at levels 3 and 4, such as practitioner psychologists and nurses who are familiar with Cognitive Behaviour Therapy (CBT). We have included examples of level 1 and 2 interventions so that this provides a comprehensive guide to treatment options including online resources.

It has been produced as part of a major study funded by The Healing Foundation, which examines the factors and processes associated with adjustment to disfiguring conditions and has used these data to inform and develop the interventions described. This research is referred to as the Appearance Research Collaboration (ARC) research programme in this handbook, and a full summary of the findings is included as appendix A.

The aim of this guide is to use these research findings to pull together the common approaches to the psychosocial management of disfigurement or visible difference[1] and to present them in a way which refers back to our underlying theoretical model and allows evaluation of effectiveness. Since the main findings of The Healing Foundation study identify a key role for appearance-related cognitions in psychological adjustment, a cognitive behavioural approach to management has been outlined. There is increasing evidence of the effectiveness of CBT both in this area and closely related areas (social anxiety), and this approach is one that allows us to construct a systematic and standardized approach to intervention whilst addressing the complexity and variety of individual differences in our patients' presentation. The guide to intervention draws from different sources, predominantly from the Clark and Wells (1995) model of social phobia and Wells (1997) cognitive therapy for anxiety treatment manual. We are assuming a basic understanding of cognitive behavioural therapy. This book illustrates its application in appearance anxiety. Where basic skills are described, this is to show their relevance in this setting rather than to teach their use from scratch.

---

[1] Many terms have historically been used to indicate appearance which differs from cultural norms. These include 'disfigurement', 'disfiguration', 'deformity', as well as many others. Visible difference is a term which has more recently been used by a number of researchers and user groups. We use this term as far as possible throughout as we regard it is as more socially neutral than many of the alternative terms.

This book is very clearly focused on adults and the management of appearance concerns and disfiguring conditions in an adult treatment setting. We are aware of the need to develop a similar resource for children, but although we have included some material on transition and examples of both young and older adults, this is not a book about managing appearance concerns for children or their families. Similarly, although disfiguring injuries often result from trauma, the specific management of trauma and Post-Traumatic Stress Disorder (PTSD) is a specialist field with good resources, and we have therefore made a decision not to duplicate that material here.

Clinical examples have been used, but we have endeavoured to disguise and change identifying factors and we have combined elements from many different patients. None of the completed examples are therefore 'real' patients, and any resemblance is due to the similar presenting problems for many people.

During the revision stage of the manual, there was increased focus on the cosmetic surgery industry as a result of the Poly Implant Prosthèse (PIP) breast implant scandal. The resulting Keogh review being carried out by the Department of Health in the United Kingdom is likely to make recommendations about regulation of practice including psychological screening. For this reason, we have included examples of screening patients requesting cosmetic treatments such as rhinoplasty. We are aware that there are few resources available for clinicians working with what is likely to become a more common referral.

We hope that there will be something here for all practitioners to draw from, even those using other therapeutic approaches. We hope this is of benefit for all practitioners in this field, particularly for those newly qualified or new to the management of 'visible difference'. Above all, we hope that this book will provide the opportunity to standardize treatment approaches and therefore allow systematic evaluation of psychological management of appearance anxiety.

Professor Alex Clarke on behalf of the Appearance Research Collaboration.

1

Background, Clinical Problems, Common Presentation and Treatment Considerations

Chapter Outline

CBT for Appearance Anxiety: Psychosocial Interventions for Anxiety Due to Visible Difference, First Edition.
Alex Clarke, Andrew Thompson, Elizabeth Jenkinson, Nichola Rumsey and Rob Newell.
© 2014 John Wiley & Sons, Ltd. Published 2014 by John Wiley & Sons, Ltd.

Whether present at birth or acquired later in life, a visible disfigurement can have a profound psychological impact on those affected (Rumsey & Harcourt, 2004, 2005; Thompson & Kent, 2001). Difficulties include adverse effects on body image (Newell, 2000), quality of life and self-esteem and shame (Kent & Thompson, 2002; Turner et al., 1997). Macgregor (1990) and others have argued that visible disfigurement comprises a 'social disability', since in addition to impacting on the thoughts, feelings and behaviours of those affected, it also affects the reactions of others. Social encounters can present many challenges, including meeting new people, making new friends, unwelcome attention such as staring, audible comments, teasing and unsolicited questions (Robinson, 1997). Research to date has focused predominantly on the difficulties and distress resulting from disfigurement. Rumsey et al. (2002) reported levels of anxiety, depression, social anxiety, social avoidance and quality of life were unfavourable in a third to a half of a sample of 650 consecutive out-patient adults attending hospitals for treatment of a wide range of disfiguring conditions. However, not all are equally affected. A proportion adapts positively to the demands upon them and either relegates their visible difference to a relatively minor role in life (Rumsey, 2002) or uses it to good advantage (Partridge, 1990).

There is a consensus amongst researchers and practitioners in the field that individual adjustment is affected by a complex interplay of physical, cultural and psychosocial factors (Clarke, 1999; Endriga & Kapp-Simon, 1999; Falvey, 2012; Moss, 1997a; Rumsey & Harcourt, 2004, 2005). However, what is very clear is that people affected by a disfigurement do have to contend with a range of reactions from others, many of which may be subtle and automatic (Grandfield et al., 2005). This is centrally important as the processing of information in people with a visible disfigurement is likely to be primed by the threat posed by the automatic reactions of others and such priming will activate normal bodily threat mechanisms. Awareness of this assists in normalizing the responses. That said, there is a high level of individual variation. Some factors clearly contribute to distress, yet others appear to 'buffer' a person against the stresses and strains of living with a visible difference. Some researchers have developed models of the processes involved (see for example, Kent & Thompson, 2002; Newell, 2000; White 2000). However, in most cases these have been condition specific, based on evidence drawn from small samples, and problem focused. Whilst models may help to organize collective thinking, they have the greatest clinical value where they focus on the identification and clarification of those factors which have the potential to be amenable to change through psychosocial support and intervention – either as an adjunct, or where appropriate, as an alternative to surgical and medical intervention. The Appearance Research Collaboration (ARC, funded by the Healing Foundation) has derived a cognitive model of adjustment based on previous research (see Figure 3.5, section 'The ARC Framework of Adjustment to Disfiguring Conditions', Chapter 3), and further developed it using data from both community and clinical samples (Thompson 2012).

In addition to emphasis on appearance-specific cognitive processes highlighted in the current research programme, previous research has indicated that a range of physical, treatment-related, socio-cultural and some other psychological factors are implicated in adjustment. Readers are referred to Moss (1997a), Clarke (1999), Newell (2000), Kent & Thompson (2002), Rumsey and Harcourt (2004), Moss (2005), Ong et al. (2007), and Thompson (2012). However, a brief resumé of the factors identified in previous research as the 'likely suspects' affecting adjustment is offered below. The findings of the ARC research programme are expanded in Chapter 3 of this guide.

Physical and Treatment-Related Factors

These include aetiology, the extent, type and severity of the disfiguring condition, and the treatment history of each individual. Contrary to the expectations of the lay public and many health care providers, the bulk of the research, clinical experience and personal accounts written by those affected, demonstrates that the extent, type and severity of a disfigurement are not consistent predictors of adjustment, although the visibility of the condition has been shown in some studies to exacerbate distress (Moss, 2005; Ong et al., 2007; Rumsey & Harcourt, 2004; Thompson & Kent, 2001).

Socio-Cultural Factors

Socio-cultural factors are particularly important as there is a fundamental human motivation to be connected with one another and the nuances of how these connections operate are dictated by social and cultural conventions. Cultural factors influence the core beliefs that people share about the meaning and consequences of disfiguring conditions. Social and cultural factors therefore provide a context in which adjustment takes place and are often influenced by demographic factors such as age, developmental stage, gender, race, and social class as well as the broader cultural milieu, religion, and parental and peer group influences. Research has also established that the media can play a role in creating and exacerbating the pressures on those distressed by their appearance although the impact of media and other socio-cultural factors varies between individuals (see Halliwell & Diedrichs, 2012; Prichard & Tiggemann, 2012 for review). Early experiences of attachment and of being accepted are likely to be particularly important in sensitizing individuals to the perceived threat posed by a disfigurement (Kent & Thompson, 2002), and this should be fully explored as part of the history and formulation building during therapy.

Psychological Factors and Processes

Factors included in this category include the structure of a person's self-esteem and self-image (e.g. the weight given to the opinions of others and to broader societal standards), a person's personality/disposition, characteristic attributional style, coping repertoire, perceptions of social support, levels of psychological well-being (e.g. anxiety, depression) and social anxiety, feelings of shame and the perceived noticeability of their visible difference to others (see Moss & Rosser, 2012a, 2012b for review). Again, it is important to consider that such factors are intimately associated with, and shaped by, socio-cultural factors. They can be broadly categorized as affective (relating to feelings), cognitive (relating to thoughts) or behavioural (relating to behaviour), and are, on the whole, more amenable to change than physical, treatment-related or socio-cultural factors.

Body Image Disturbance

In addition to those people with a disfiguring condition visible to others, there is a second group for whom their concern is related to self-perception, or a perceived problem or deficit in their appearance. Body Dysmorphic Disorder (BDD) is described in the *Diagnostic and Statistical*

Manual of Mental Disorders, Fourth Edition (*DSM-IV-TR, 2000*) under somatoform disorders, and is defined as a preoccupation with an imagined or slight defect in appearance, which cannot be better explained in terms of an eating disorder (such as Anorexia Nervosa) or a disfiguring condition.

Many commentators have expressed concern about a diagnostic category which is dependent on the observation and judgment of an observer rather than the experience of the individual. An experienced plastic surgeon is likely to use a different normative scale from someone who is influenced primarily by the norms of their peer group. The definition also suggests that someone with a very obvious disfiguring condition should be excluded from this diagnosis; yet there are some people in this group for whom the high levels of preoccupation and concern are very characteristic of BDD.

For all these reasons, in our opinion, and contrary to the categorical *DSM-IV-TR* definition, BDD represents the extreme end of a continuum which can arguably be anchored at the opposite pole by a 'normal' preoccupation with appearance, dress and dissatisfaction with appearance. In clinical settings, body image disturbance is often present in disfiguration independent of cause or severity, and may be most evident in the more objectively 'minor' disfiguration group. The perceived mismatch between actual and ideal (how they ought, should or used to look) can result in considerable preoccupation, checking behaviour and anxiety in the absence of actual negative social reactions from other people. (See Price (1990) for discussion of this mismatch in mediating challenge to the integrity of body image.) Indeed, reassurance seeking from others that 'they look okay' serves to maintain anxiety, probably by maintaining focus on the perceived threat (Veale et al., 2009).

The results of the ARC research programme have reinforced the clinical observation that people also present with multiple concerns, or with a specific 'highlighted' problem in the context of other concerns about appearance. For example, excess skin following weight reduction is often described as 'ageing' and it is important to recognize that the 'normative' concern with appearance that is evident in the general population means that there is often a multiplicity of issues underlying appearance cognitions. Further, the ARC study demonstrated that people with a disfigurement might be more concerned about other unaffected areas of their bodies (such as the size of their stomach or buttocks), so it would be inaccurate to assume that the simple anatomical location of the disfigurement may be the prime source of concern.

Clinical Problems and Presentation

All examples are based on real clinical examples referred to people working in psychological therapies, attached to general hospital services, including plastic surgery. Names and identifying details have been altered. In the brief vignettes in the box below, the range and complexity of appearance concerns are illustrated. This is to provide an overview for those new to this area of work and briefly indicate both the similarities of concerns (e.g. the worries about the reactions of others and the impact of unusual appearance on self-esteem), and also the importance of individual differences (e.g. the meaning of the disfigurement for that person). More in-depth examples are provided through the book to demonstrate treatment approaches, with the major treatment focus in Chapter 7.

Example 1

Geraldine has a small skin graft on her nose following treatment for facial cancer. An artist, she finds the change in her appearance devastating although she accepts that it is relatively minor. She is puzzled by her own response to what she can see is a relatively minor change but is seeking revision of surgery to try to achieve symmetry.

Example 2

Jack has a congenital condition which includes an absence of an ear on one side. Although he has undergone ear reconstruction with a good result, he is still anxious about the appearance of his ear and has avoided cutting his hair or going swimming. He continues to wear a hat pulled low over his head.

Example 3

Eve has had surgery to remove facial cancer which has left her with a visible disfigurement, including loss of her nose. She is overcome by this and cannot envisage ever leaving the house again. She confines herself to her bedroom. Her husband seeks help from the doctor and is told that there is nothing that can be done; 'she just has to learn to live with it'.

Example 4

James has an industrial injury and loses his dominant thumb. He hates the appearance of his hand and is fearful of others seeing it. He has very marked episodes of dissociation, flashbacks of the injury and his mood is low. His doctor lectures him about people who learn to use their feet to write and use cutlery. He tells him he is making too much fuss and should get back to work immediately.

Note that James presents with symptoms characteristic of post-traumatic stress disorder (PTSD) as well as appearance concerns. Managing the impact of trauma is the priority at this point. Hand injuries may also cause pain and this can impact on mood and ability to manage the treatment regimen. Again we would recommend pain intervention as a priority.

Example 5

Pauline has small breasts. She feels that these single her out from her peer group and describes herself as a freak. She has identified breast augmentation as a means of improving her self-confidence and allowing her to undertake her hoped for training as a beautician.

Pauline has breasts which objectively fall within the normal range, but which she perceives to be abnormal. Her own experience of her appearance is very similar therefore to someone who is worried by a disfiguring condition, and for whom this perception results in appearance anxiety. Unfortunately she is likely to be perceived as vain and her concerns dismissed as 'purely cosmetic'. She is heavily invested in appearance choosing a career in this field.

Example 6

Mark is a builder who has lost a finger in an accident with a Stanley knife at work. He is very distressed by the appearance of his hand, keeping it in his pocket. He anticipates that he will never get a girlfriend because his hand is off-putting and disgusting. He is very angry both with himself and his employer.

Example 7

John has had surgery for a facial palsy. He had a good result but still has a noticeable palsy when he smiles. He presents with a very low mood, finding it hard to cope at University and feeling that his peers treat him differently and that he is unable to fit in.

Example 8

Peter lost an eye as a child, and the resection means that he is unable to wear an eye patch. He is now at University where he feels that his obvious facial disfigurement limits his opportunity to socialize and in particular to meet girls. He describes himself as 'always the one going home on his own'. He has low self-esteem and self-confidence and perceives his appearance to be limiting his opportunities for the future both socially and for employment. He is becoming increasingly socially avoidant.

Example 9

Lucy has a breast asymmetry. She presents requesting surgery and becoming very upset in the consultation. She feels like a freak, having been for a bra fitting where the assistant has told her: 'you need to see a doctor my dear, you are deformed'.

Example 10

Jenny has burn scarring affecting 80% of her body. In the past, most people with the severity of her injuries would have died, but advances in burn care mean that she and other people like her now survive. She presents with a chaotic lifestyle, drinking and smoking heavily with a low mood and has difficulties managing the physical problems resulting from her original injury. Managing her temperature in the absence of sweat glands is a particular challenge. When she goes out she experiences high levels of staring and comments from other people, including frequent questions about the cause of her scarring.

Example 11

Veronica presents with scarring on both wrists resulting from self harm as a teenager. She wants these scars removed as they are reminders of an unhappy and difficult time in her life, and she finds them difficult to explain when other people ask her about them.

Example 12

Bryony has had a cycling accident resulting in significant scarring and contour changes to her legs. She is unable to look at the scarring, retching and sweating if she catches sight of her appearance during dressing changes.

Example 13

Sean has acne and also a stoma following surgery to treat Crohn's disease, he is depressed and rarely leaves the house except to weight train. He misuses steroids. He sees himself as 'disgusting' and is unable to see how life could be different without reversal of the stoma and treatment of the acne.

Example 14

Gillian is a softly spoken shy 20-year-old, who appears much younger than her age. She has severe psoriasis. She tends to avoid swimming and covers the affected areas of her body. She has not had an intimate relationship and she describes herself as lacking confidence in her job. She has several very close friends, but she has not told any of them about her skin condition or shown them it, for fear that they would see her differently and might not wish to be friends with her.

Example 15

Frank suffered an industrial accident that left him with severe crush injuries to his leg which was eventually amputated. The rehabilitation team report that he is 'de-motivated' and hostile. He has stopped socialising and ended the relationship he had prior to the accident. He says he is furious towards his employer as he believes the accident could have been prevented. He talks of having 'flashbacks' and describes spending hours ruminating on how his appearance has 'changed for the worse' and how they (his employers) have 'finished him'.

Note that whilst Frank describes having 'flashbacks' formal assessment suggests that he is describing intense rumination about the consequences of the accident rather than having dissociative episodes of re-living it, and consequently the primary issue is adjustment following limb loss.

Example 16

Jeff suffered a road traffic accident where he sustained severe damage to his arm resulting in it being stiffened and the muscle wasting. He has returned to work and driving and attempts to socialize as much as he can and is continuing to spend time with his family and children. However, he says that he has to 'bully himself along' and he can't really believe why his wife is sticking with him as he now looks 'old and odd'.

Example 17

Mark has had alopecia since childhood, during which time he was bullied; now in his 40s, he no longer fears teasing or bullying, yet he describes feeling 'different' and is unable to leave home without wearing a hat or a hooded sweatshirt, and he will not answer the door unless he is wearing a hat. He says that people have commented on him wearing a hat but he believes that he 'just can't do without it'. His reliance on wearing a hat or hooded sweatshirt has detrimentally affected his occupational opportunities and in his last job he received a written warning for not adhering to the expected dress code. Following this he described losing his confidence and feeling unable to work.

Example 18

Michele has had cancer of the mouth and had extensive reconstructive surgery. She does have some facial scarring and palsy and she now feels less attractive to her partner and feels unable to continue to associate with her friends who 'always talk about appearance'. She says her mood fluctuates between rage and sadness.

Example 19

Peter has Moebius syndrome and has no facial nerves, meaning that he is unable to smile or use his face to express emotion. He is very frustrated by the behaviour of other people who often treat him as though he has learning disabilities.

Common Features in Referral

Visibility of Condition

The first thing that is clear from the examples above is that all these people locate the source of their difficulties in their appearance, or the change in their appearance, and all have sought or considered medical intervention as a solution. Some have completed their treatment, sometimes for a life-threatening condition, but are still preoccupied and disabled by the appearance change. Objectively, there is a considerable range in degree of visible difference when rated by an observer. For some, the problem may need to be pointed out, whilst others may have features which are habitually concealed by clothing. For some, the appearance difference has been lifelong and for others acquired as a child or adult. For all, the level of preoccupation is high and the 'problem' is perceived as significantly distressing and disabling. This is the core issue that the group have in common, and the reason that they are appropriate for referral and/or treatment of appearance anxiety. Severity does not predict distress (Moss, 2005; Ong et al., 2007), and those with a more minor objective disfigurement may have equal or higher levels of distress than those with greater objective visible difference, although they will very often have been told that their distress is 'out of proportion' to their appearance. Some have more than one disfiguring condition and it is not necessarily the thing that is most obvious to other people which is the one that causes most concern. Importantly, the lack of a clear relationship between visibility to others and levels of distress is confirmed in the ARC research programme.

Thus, psychological treatment approaches focus on managing the impact of the condition (anxiety, the preoccupation and worry, altered and avoidant behaviour, etc) rather than changing the condition itself, sharing the same goals for treatment as psychological interventions across the range of chronic health conditions.

Shame

As long ago as 1963, Goffman described shame as central to the experience of stigma and yet the concept of body shame has received less attention than body image. Clinicians widely acknowledge body shame as a commonly occurring issue in some people living with a disfigurement that drives avoidance and safety behaviours (Gilbert & Miles, 2002). A distinction has been drawn between internal and external shame, where external shame describes the experience of perceiving oneself to be 'disgusting' or unattractive to other people, whilst internal shame describes perceiving oneself to be shameful (Gilbert & Miles, 2002; Kent & Thompson, 2002). Internal shame may be accompanied by marked parasympathetic response (see below). Whilst internal and external shame tend to occur together, they may occur independently. Thus, individuals may comment that although they know that other people do not notice or respond to their appearance, they have strong feelings of revulsion or disgust about themselves (internal shame), whilst others may feel that although other people have issues about their appearance, personally they are not ashamed of their appearance, but they maybe nevertheless worried by anticipated negative reactions of others. The concepts of internal and external shame are closely related to the idea of felt and enacted stigma and the processes involved with all these concepts may act independently of objective appearance (for a full discussion see Gilbert & Miles, 2002; Thompson, 2011, 2012).

The Meaning of Visible Difference

Linked with shame, the meaning that people place on unusual appearance is important to understanding its impact. For example, people commonly believe that their disfigurement labels them as 'deformed, freakish, ugly or unattractive'. Often surgeons are reluctant to carry out procedures which objectively 'worsen' appearance; however, even when the objective visibility of a scar is increased, this may sometimes be successful in reducing anxiety when it is the means of altering the meaning and therefore the anticipated stigmatizing from others (see Example 11). This points to the need for careful assessment of motivation for treatment seeking and for being clear about the nature of people's thoughts about the perceived disfigurement. A psychological intervention may similarly focus on modifying the meaning of scars, for example, as evidence of strength, resilience, and survivorship rather than signs of weakness, or of having had a disease such as cancer.

The Experience of Loss

Many people describe the impact of visible difference in terms of loss or bereavement. The process of grief for the loss of appearance and for the undamaged self is not dissimilar to the process of mourning in other kinds of loss. It is important to recognize that this applies equally to those who have acquired disfigurement and to those with a congenital or longstanding condition. Loss of the idealized or never experienced self has as great a potential to impact on the individual as loss of the previous self. Loss also impacts at the level of perceived loss of opportunity; not only loss of appearance but questions about opportunities for the future. 'Will the same life opportunities be there? Will I be able to do the same job? What about relationships? Will other people find me attractive? Will I find a sexual partner? Do I need to compromise because I am not like other people?' Like bereavement in other settings, there may be periods of intense emotion, anger and sadness (Bradbury, 1996). Timing of a structured intervention needs to take account of this emotional response. Evidence for management of distress after trauma supports a model of information provision followed by treatment within the first 4 weeks following trauma (see National Institute for Health and Clinical Excellence (NICE) guidance) using a standardized approach. Although no clear evidence based recommendations can be made for a similar model in managing appearance issues, clinical experience suggests that a period of simple acknowledgement of loss and legitimizing of concerns as a first step before social skills intervention, or further specific focus on managing visible difference (Clarke, 1999).

Physiological Responses

Whilst the level of preoccupation and concern is usually high, physiological responses vary considerably. Some people dislike the visible difference but can look at and touch it, allowing them to participate in self-care behaviours (Gaind et al., 2011). However, others exhibit considerable physiological arousal including bradycardia, sweating or nausea. This may be because they are repelled or disgusted at the sight or sensation of their own body, and show pronounced disgust responses, or tachycardia because of anxiety. An acquired visible difference may also be a trigger for intrusive recollection of a traumatic event that is likely in turn to result in hyperarousal and avoidance.

Culture

Appearance is valued differently in different cultures and there may be a particular premium placed on appearance for women. In addition, beliefs about illness are known to be linked to psychosocial adjustment and beliefs about conditions affecting appearance may well vary according to culture and ethnicity. Understanding the meaning of altered appearance and the explanations and beliefs within the relevant culture is essential to formulating the problems and planning treatment. (For a good review of these concepts see Falvey (2012) and Habib and Saul (2012).)

One of the ARC studies examined British Asian women's experience of the depigmenting skin condition, vitiligo (Thompson et al., 2010, and summarized in the Appendix). Like other participants with vitiligo from other ethnic backgrounds, the respondents described feeling different, and reports of stigmatisation were not uncommon. However, the experience of stigmatisation was associated with subtle cultural values related to the role played by appearance in status, and myths linked to the cause of the condition. The condition was perceived as affecting marriage prospects. Cultural nuances as to how stigmatisation operates are also reported in one of the other ARC studies that explored community views of disfigurement (Hughes et al., 2009). Therefore, whilst the original ARC model included consideration of social and cultural factors, the need for further emphasis on this emerged as a result of the findings of the ARC studies and consequently a fourth element that specifically highlights the role played by social and cultural influences has been recently added to the ARC model and is given consideration in guiding the interventions described in this handbook (see Thompson, 2012).

Gender

There is a prevailing belief that appearance-related issues have a bigger impact for women. However, this research programme has identified considerable levels of distress in male participants which, for some, results in high levels of hostility and enacted aggressive behaviour. Similarly, in an audit of 300 facially disfigured patients referred to the Royal Free Hospital over a 5-year period (Cordeiro et al., 2010), male patients were significantly distressed by both objective and perceived facial changes, with no evidence that women comprised a less well-adjusted group. Where male concerns about appearance have been framed as related to the muscular ideal, this evidence identifies facial issues as highly relevant in male groups. It may therefore be important to challenge the beliefs of other health professionals or family members that male patients are not appropriate for treatment or 'should not be making so much fuss about things'.

Age

There is a similar belief that older people are less worried about appearance. The ARC research programme has found supporting evidence for lower levels of distress in older group. However, there is considerable variability in this population; some older people have very high levels of concern about their appearance. Age should not, therefore, be used as a criterion for referral or access to psychological services. Children may have particular problems with teasing and bullying in schools and this is often cited as the reason for surgical intervention at a young age. Unfortunately, this approach anticipates a problem which may not arise, and there is an interesting ethical debate around the question of whether or not it is appropriate to intervene before a child is old enough to consent to significant surgery, on the basis of problems anticipated by parents.

Expectations of Treatment

Most people with concern about their appearance will present to clinicians with a request for a physical treatment, commonly surgery – increasingly laser or dermatological techniques. Others will present to clinicians following treatment for some other condition that has resulted in an iatrogenic change in appearance (such as following colorectal or breast surgery). The lay understanding of surgical procedures is often very poor and may be driven by commercial marketing. Patients tend to have unrealistic expectations of surgery to ameliorate scars, the appearance of scars after treatment and the fact that scarring is inevitable after surgery. Indeed many people are referred for 'scar removal'. Information is often drawn from reality television shows and magazines. General practitioners in the United Kingdom do not have plastic surgery included in undergraduate training and may often be under the same misapprehension as patients (Charlton et al., 2003). Therefore, despite advice to discuss plastic and reconstructive procedures with a primary care physician (Department of Health, 2007), these may be a source of misinformation. For this reason, many potential clients can be angry or disappointed since they have identified a solution to their problem that is impossible to provide. Some people also present after surgery that has failed to meet expectations for the same reasons, or that has resulted in unexpected changes in their appearance. There is also emerging evidence from the health psychology literature that procedures that are predominantly sought for quality of life gains have a higher risk for associated postoperative dissatisfaction (Elkadry et al., 2003). This research suggests that whilst clinicians traditionally target reduction of symptoms or functional improvement, patients target secondary lifestyle changes, which may be only indirectly related to the intervention. For example, change in the shape of a feature may be perceived by a surgeon to be correction of asymmetry, but for a patient it may be the opportunity to have a relationship. Where a relationship fails to materialize, dissatisfaction is attributed to the procedure or the surgeon, or both.

Association of Physical Change with Psychological Outcome

Most people with appearance-related problems associate their well-being, self-confidence and self-esteem with appearance. Expectations of outcome for treatment are commonly phrased in these terms. However, evidence from studies of outcome following cosmetic procedures suggests that higher satisfaction is related to expectations of physical rather than psychological change (Sarwer and Crerand, 2004; Sarwer et al., 2006). For this reason, an early emphasis on identifying exactly what will change physically and how much it will change is important for patients about to undergo physical treatments. Similarly, it is helpful to frame psychological goals in more concrete ways that can be measured and are more evident. Thus 'improve self-confidence' can be described in terms of consequent behaviour change, for example, go out with my friends, remove concealing clothing, change job, etc.

Where there is a very visible difference in appearance, people often report high levels of social intrusion with staring, comments and questioning commonplace (Partridge, 1990). Surgery is often seen as the solution to managing the behaviours of other people driven by the assumption that if the appearance difference is minimized, then social situations will no longer be anxiety provoking. However, as a raft of research literature has indicated, an appearance closer to the social norm does not necessarily make traversing the social world easier, indeed many people with unremarkable appearances find social situations difficult. Viewing appearance changes (rather than cognitive and/ or behavioural change) as a means to fix social relationships including problems with intimacy, should be identified as an ineffective solution and be challenged during assessment.

Fix It Solutions

The myths about medical interventions include a common perception that surgery and medications can 'fix' a problem and that less-than-optimum outcomes are the result of lack of expertise, 'something gone wrong' with a procedure, or rationing of resources. Since patient-centred goals and expectations of outcome are predictive of satisfaction with treatment, preparation for any intervention should include eliciting expectations and helping the patient to modify them where necessary. It is also helpful to elicit expectations of the treatment setting. Many people are unaware that they will see different doctors rather than have continuity of care and that the length of stay will be short in most hospitals. Paradoxically, very small changes in appearance are often much harder to achieve than significant change, and it can be hard for people to understand that heart transplant is possible whilst scar removal is not.

Treatment Considerations

Clinical health psychologists are familiar with the challenges of framing health-related problems in psychological terms (e.g. in pain management, management of chronic conditions and disability). Formulating an appearance-related problem in psychological terms and making this accessible to the patient has the additional challenge that a patient often presents when the perceived ideal treatment is either unavailable or has failed. Psychological solutions can be seen as second best.

A key goal for an assessment is evidence from the patient that the therapist has listened and has understood the problem. This is described more fully in the section on assessment, where standard techniques of reflecting back, questioning and summarising are used to help frame a psychological formulation. Attempting to reassure by commenting on the objective appearance of the patient is almost always unhelpful. Many people report doctors and other therapists commenting that 'it is not that noticeable'. This is perceived as evidence that the problem has not been understood – or as one patient put it 'they just don't get it'. People with body image issues often ask therapists how noticeable their feature is. Encouraging the patient to examine whether this is a helpful question is a better way of dealing with it than offering an opinion, and is also an early 'taster' of what treatment might entail. Most people accept that there is no answer that is reassuring – either it is very noticeable, or the therapist is perceived to be 'trying to make me feel better'. Framing appearance as unimportant is another potential pitfall, especially with younger people. Sayings such as 'you can't judge a book by its cover' or 'beauty comes from within', 'personality is more important than appearance' are all messages which are contradicted by the social context in which people exist. All the evidence, to which the patient has access and their own experience, is to the contrary. Appearance is actually very important in determining how people appraise each other, and suggesting that it is not makes it harder to work with people for whom appearance has a very high premium. Again, such non-specific and stereotyped attempts at reassurance demonstrate to the patient that the therapist has not understood the nature of their problem.

Later on in treatment, examining the role that appearance plays in people's lives may well form part of therapy in the context of examining components of self-esteem. The role of behaviour in creating a positive impression will also be considered as part of the skill set of someone managing an unusual appearance. But entering an early debate about the value of appearance is not helpful in an assessment.

Formal psychometric assessment using scales such as the Derriford Appearance Scale (*DAS24*; Carr et al., 2005) is helpful not only for quantifying the level of distress and the associated avoidance behaviour but also for reinforcing the idea that the therapist is trying to understand the problem. It is also very useful in identifying tangible treatment goals. Simple idiosyncratic psychological measurement tools including visual analogue or ordinal scales of noticeability and worry, which can be recorded on a daily basis to provide information about the process of change, are excellent practice-based tools (see section 'Core Clinical Dataset', Chapter 4). High scores on both are predictive of psychological distress. It is also helpful to be able to formulate treatment goals in terms of reducing worry or preoccupation, since most people will accept that it would be helpful for them to be less worried or preoccupied by their condition.

For a psychological intervention to be effective, the patient must be able to identify goals for change that are achievable and perceived to be important. People need to feel ready for change, and goals must be structured so that they are easily understood and agreed to be manageable. Intervention may start by working on these aspects of a client's motivation, readiness for change and perceived self-efficacy in the therapeutic partnership. Formulation of appearance-related problems in terms of psychological management is not intuitive to people outside a psychological setting. Even other health professionals commonly perceive such an intervention to be a non-directive general counselling intervention. The idea that psychology is about changing how a problem is understood and modifying behaviour to reduce disability needs constant rehearsal. For this reason, it is helpful to summarize the formulation and goals for treatment at the beginning of each session – eliciting these from the patient as they become more familiar with the model (see treatment plans in Chapter 7). This is equally important whether working within a systematic CBT framework or simply providing social skills training. It is also useful to ensure that the patient's support network is also familiar with the model of treatment being offered. This will decrease the likelihood of well-meant but ineffective advice, and distracting 'helpful' articles cut out of newspapers about magical new physical and psychological treatments.

Finally, it is important to think about the therapist. To what extent will the appearance of the therapist impact on the course of treatment? Unlike most therapeutic settings where little is known about the therapist, appearance, the central focus of therapy, is immediately apparent. Race, ethnicity, wearing make-up, colouring hair, choice of clothing, visible piercing or body hair, having a visible disfigurement, body shape and size, all have a different meaning in the context of working with body image concerns. This is particularly important because patients may habitually make social comparisons that may in turn trigger self-criticism. For example, someone who is worried about the appearance of a specific feature will tend to make comparisons with the same feature on other people. There is a bias amongst those with visible difference who experience difficulties toward 'upward' comparison (i.e. studying people who have an 'ideal' or 'better' version of that feature) rather than downward comparisons with people who are perceived to have a 'worse' feature (see Halliwell & Diedrichs, 2012). This tends to maintain the idea that the feature is substandard or unacceptable. Sometimes patients may bring these issues up themselves, and when they do it is helpful to explore the processing associated with them. Or this might be covertly addressed by checking how the patient feels about working with the therapist. Occasionally, the therapist may encounter outright resistance stemming from envy associated with perceived differences in appearance.

Similarly, people beginning work in this area should consider the way their own body image or appearance-related concerns may impact in their work with patients. High levels of disgust sensitivity (which can be screened and treated via an exposure programme) can also make it more difficult to work comfortably with people who have significant wounds. Similarly a therapist with a very high investment in their own appearance will need to be aware of the way this impacts for different patients. Addressing the needs of those who experience psychological difficulties leads to consideration of a broad range of factors affecting the individuals themselves and also affecting the general management of the treatment process. These considerations are explored in more detail in the remaining chapters.

2

A Stepped-Care Approach to Psychosocial Intervention

Chapter Outline

CBT for Appearance Anxiety: Psychosocial Interventions for Anxiety Due to Visible Difference, First Edition.
Alex Clarke, Andrew Thompson, Elizabeth Jenkinson, Nichola Rumsey and Rob Newell.
© 2014 John Wiley & Sons, Ltd. Published 2014 by John Wiley & Sons, Ltd.

The previous chapter provides an introduction to the problems of visible difference and appearance anxiety. Clinical examples illustrate the range of problems that people encounter. However, the majority of psychological support is provided by the health professional team, such as nurses, surgeons and doctors rather than a psychosocial specialist. It is important not to deskill those professionals who have the most interaction with people as part of their care. Specific psychological interventions can be successfully provided by non-specialists, and even a complex problem can sometimes be significantly impacted by a relatively brief intervention. Kleve et al. (2002) report a mean of three attendances for treatment and positive results from a large number of one stop interventions in their cohort, for whom a single focused and practical session proved adequate. For this reason, it is important that the apparent complexity of a problem does not threaten to deskill the many health professionals who work with populations who have disfiguring conditions or altered appearance. Clarke and Cooper (2001) clearly demonstrated that whilst clinical nurse specialists lacked confidence in their ability to support people with disfiguring conditions, they delivered a psychosocial intervention very effectively when provided with resources and basic training. This comprised social and coping skills training with systematic exposure (see Chapter 5) Therefore, readers providing intervention at level 3 and 4 may wish to consider implementing this framework with health professional colleagues as a means of increasing access to first-line treatment. Similarly, more generalist readers should note that effective intervention does not always entail specialist intervention. The stepped-care model provides a framework both for actual interventions and for supporting decision-making about when further referral is necessary.

Stepped-care models, now part of routine practice in many settings, including cancer and primary mental health care, provide an approach which facilitates the psychosocial care of patients by providing a role for everyone in the care team. Level 1 intervention refers to the provision of a sympathetic and caring environment in which people are treated with dignity and respect, encouraged to ask questions and provided with relevant information. Whilst all team members are involved at this level, more complex interventions (level 4) would be delivered by specialists with additional training. A similar approach is illustrated by the PLISSIT (Permission, Limited Information, Specific Suggestions, Intensive Treatment) model in sexual health, used here because it offers the advantage of an acronym which aids recall.

The PLISSIT Model

Table 2.1 illustrates a stepped-care framework. (For those delivering level 1 and 2 interventions, Chapter 5 describes these interventions.) (Annon, 1974).

Level 1: Permission

The first level – permission – is a particularly important concept since observers often worry about whether it is appropriate or not to address issues relating to appearance; the model provides a framework in which a direct approach is encouraged. Permission also applies to both sides of the interaction, in which both patient and health professional are encouraged to ask questions about psychosocial issues. Enquiring about appearance may also serve to normalize that distress associated

Table 2.1 Stepped-care framework for interventions to promote psychosocial adjustment in appearance concern.

Level of intervention	Description	Example of intervention	Health professional background
Level 1	Permission	Sensitive exploration of psychosocial concerns	All health practitioners including General Practitioners, Practice Nurses, and Psychological Well Being Practitioners (PWPs) and professional health care helplines.
Level 2	Limited information	Written information, recommended websites and contact details for support groups. Answering basic questions about visible difference	All health practitioners working with target groups including doctors and nurses in relevant specialties
Level 3	Specific suggestions or interventions	Social skills training, dealing with staring, comments and questions. Managing social situations proactively	Individuals with relevant training and with access to supervision such as: Clinical Nurse Specialists, Occupational Therapists, Maxillofacial Technicians, Support Groups
Level 4	Intensive treatments	Cognitive behaviour therapy aimed at identifying and modifying maladaptive appearance schemas	Clinical Psychologists, Cognitive Behavioural Psychotherapists

with living with a disfigurement and clinician interest can also show acceptance which can strengthen the working relationship.

We have recommended that all patients should develop a response to answering questions about their appearance, which manages curiosity by providing a minimal amount of information (Coughlan & Clarke, 2002; Rumsey et al., 2002). In practice, this means that all practitioners are responsible for raising questions about appearance:

Example 1

How are you coping with these changes in your appearance?

People tend to be very curious about others. Have you had a lot of questions from other people?

Have you got a good answer to questions about your face/hand, etc?

Has anyone else seen the scar? What does your husband/partner think about it?

Sometimes it is hard to work out when to tell people about your scar, particularly when it is hidden. Have you thought about this? How do think you might approach it?

These kinds of questions are often very helpful in identifying patients who are socially avoidant. A 'good' answer is one which demonstrates that the person has thought about the situation and has a plan, or is clearly not distressed about the likelihood of this kind of intrusion. A response that suggests the patient is hoping no one will notice, or is planning to stay at home 'until all this is sorted out', or 'is putting life on hold until I look completely normal again' should be a trigger for offering further information.

Level 1 training can be delivered as part of a simple study day or via written information available to health professionals. However, it is also essential that pathways are in place for referral where it is evident that people are having significant problems in addressing some of these issues.

Level 2: Limited Information

If health care professionals are to ask about appearance, then they must have an idea about how to manage the responses that they get. Perhaps the biggest barriers to asking about emotional reactions are the lack of training to deal with the response and/or lack of access to someone else who can help.

Resources such as details of support organizations or website addresses provide a Limited Information response by giving useful information that can help an individual feel that they are not the only one who is experiencing such concerns. Changing Faces[1] leaflets, or other resources produced to specifically address this area by charities such as the Vitiligo Association can also be provided via a patient library or via the book prescription scheme. As a basic minimum, anyone who has an unusual facial appearance should be encouraged to have an answer to the question:

What happened to your face?
Chapter 5 provides details of examples of how this might be managed, but the goal is to try to elicit a response from the individual that is personal to them and fits within their usual interpersonal style – rather than to provide a 'stock answer'.

It would be reasonable for all health professionals to deliver the first two levels of this stepped approach after minimal training.

Level 3: Specific Suggestions

At this level of intervention, the health professional is providing more guided help towards a specific problem. This has been framed as a 'target stressors' approach – building strategies for managing commonly reported problems. This approach is greatly facilitated by the use of Changing Faces information resources. Condition-specific resources are also available from other charities; for example the Psoriasis Association has a wealth of accessible information on its web pages (see section 'Sources of Support').

As a minimum, this level of intervention would require an assessment and identification of the goals for change (see section 'Goal Setting' in Chapter 4), the design of a strategy to achieve this goal,

[1]   Changing Faces is a major user-led organization for people with visible difference and actively promotes awareness of visible difference, including the provision of information.

and ideally monitoring of effectiveness and a further assessment to evaluate the outcome. The section on social skills training gives examples of working in this way (Chapter 5).

Clinical nurse specialists, occupational therapists, maxillofacial technicians, and psychological well-being practitioners are ideally placed to deliver a psychosocial intervention at this third level of the PLISSIT model, although this approach is also of use to the wider medical team, including medical practitioners. The training days for health professionals at Changing Faces have included this tier for health professionals working in head and neck cancer, and other training events have been provided by the authors of this handbook. Supervision from staff with level-three training, such as clinical psychologists or practitioner health psychologists, should be available.

Computer-based interventions such as Face IT, developed by Bessell et al. (2012), are a recent addition to psychological treatment and the evaluation of this approach indicates that it shows promise. Face IT could be part of an intervention provided by a non-specialist, but has been evaluated as part of a package where it is supervised rather than standing alone. It could also be a very useful addition or first step to an intensive treatment offered by a psychologist. It offers the enormous advantage that the intervention can be completed remotely.

Level 4: Intensive Treatment

This final level of intervention relies on specialized training in psychological therapy. The Cognitive Behavioural Therapy (CBT) model outlined in Chapter 6 should be delivered by someone with a relevant qualification in psychology or accredited further training in CBT.

This stepped-care model suggests that a non-psychologist can provide the first three levels of intervention to include behavioural approaches to managing problems of visible difference. They must be provided with additional training; resources and appropriate clinical governance arrangements should be in place to ensure supervised practice. These levels of intervention can be effective when there is:

- Good agreement between objective and subjective assessment of visibility
- Clear evidence of intrusion from other people with concrete examples
- Inadequate social skills, particularly poor eye contact
- Visible safety behaviours – baggy clothes, hats and camouflage, unkempt appearance
- Inability to deal comfortably with staring and questions about appearance
- Preoccupation with appearance, which is situation specific rather than constant.

An intensive intervention provided by a specialist psychologist/CBT therapist is more appropriate when there is:

- Clinically significant levels of anxiety and depression
- A substantial mismatch between subjective and objective ratings of visibility of the appearance concern
- Multiple appearance-related concerns
- Past history of, or current, body image concerns

- Shame proneness or very high levels of fear of negative evaluation in the absence of concrete examples of stigmatization ('no one actually says anything but I know what they are thinking' or 'it doesn't matter what they think, I know I'm ugly')
- High frequency of checking, particularly in the form of reassurance elicited from other people or dependence on others
- Complicated safety behaviours such as using internal mechanisms that create attentional bias (for example high levels of social comparison)
- Preoccupation with appearance is continuous (for example continued rumination or self-monitoring/appearance checking)
- High levels of anticipatory anxiety and post-event analysis.

The skills for providing this stepped-care approach are further developed in the following chapters together with a more formal description of the rationale for and delivery of a cognitive behavioural approach.

3

Models and Frameworks

Expanding the Conceptual Approach to Managing Appearance-Related Distress

CBT for Appearance Anxiety: Psychosocial Interventions for Anxiety Due to Visible Difference, First Edition.
Alex Clarke, Andrew Thompson, Elizabeth Jenkinson, Nichola Rumsey and Rob Newell.
© 2014 John Wiley & Sons, Ltd. Published 2014 by John Wiley & Sons, Ltd.

Whilst we advocate the use of a framework to guide treatment, we place emphasis on the use of individual Cognitive Behaviour Therapy (CBT) case conceptualization or formulation, particularly in working with complex presentations. Kuyken et al. (2009) describe case conceptualization as follows: 'a process whereby therapist and client work collaboratively, first to describe and then to explain the issues a client presents in therapy'. 'Its primary function is to guide therapy in order to relieve client distress and build client resilience' (p. 3). Case conceptualization should draw from evidence-based theory but enables the development of a bespoke individualized treatment approach to be designed and avoids some of the problems of drawing on one model (Thompson, 2012).

Explanation for Choice of Therapeutic Approach

There are many choices of therapeutic intervention. This book is not intended to provide an exhaustive description of all the different ways in which a psychosocial specialist might work with the problems outlined in Chapter 1. Our focus is on a cognitive behavioural framework, because interventions of this type allow us to integrate the findings of the Appearance Research Collaboration (ARC) research study and have been informed by the evidence-based therapeutic approaches to social phobia with which appearance anxiety shares many features (see later). Both are underpinned by a cognitive behavioural model. However, it is useful at this point to review the different models and frameworks which have helped us to develop our therapeutic work for people with disfiguring conditions, to see the evolution of our understanding and how the models have evolved from a basic behavioural 'target stressors' approach. While we acknowledge the extensive literature on body image (Cash, 2007; Cash & Pruzinsky, 2002; Cash & Smollack, 2011) which examines this multifaceted concept largely in a normal population, we are confining our discussion to research on visible difference and social anxiety. It is also important to acknowledge the social and cultural changes that have informed our thinking. Starting from a position in which most of the people we worked with had disfiguring conditions (i.e. objective conditions which created a visible difference in appearance), we are all aware of a growing perception of abnormal appearance in people whose objective appearance falls within the normal range. Appearance anxiety may therefore be associated with a disfiguring condition or arise because of a perceived shortfall between an ideal and objective appearance. Understanding the cognitive processes that underpin this growth in appearance anxiety is one of the drivers for our focus on CBT.

Behavioural Approaches: Fear Avoidance and Social Skills Training

In response to the King's Cross Fire in 1989, the charity Changing Faces was launched by James Partridge, whose experience of his own burn injury had led him to the conclusion that modifying his own behaviour was the best way of influencing the thoughts and behaviour of other people. In summarizing this, Partridge described a negative feedback loop in which an aggressive or uncertain response to negative behaviour from the observer resulted in unsuccessful social encounters marked by social avoidance. He proposed that the individual could be instrumental in promoting a positive response by a change in their own behaviour, and that this would then facilitate social interaction (see Figure 3.1).

The behavioural management of disfiguring conditions is derived in part from this practical approach based on patient experience, and partly from the academic work of Rumsey and colleagues.

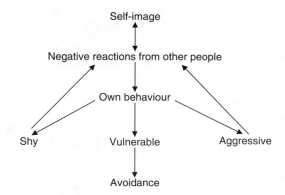

Figure 3.1 The negative feedback loop. Clarke 1999. Reproduced with permission from Taylor and Francis. http://www.tandfonline.com/doi/abs/10.1080/135485099106270

In a series of controlled analogue studies using methodological techniques from social psychology (see Bull & Rumsey, 1988, for a full description), research demonstrated a reciprocal breakdown in social encounters where a person with a disfigurement used avoidance strategies to disguise appearance. These included poor eye contact and posture, hand over mouth, and also lack of verbal strategies for putting the other person at ease. Thus, it was behaviour and poor social skills rather than appearance that caused the problem, and work from completely different origins drew the same conclusions.

Combining resources, Rumsey and Partridge designed a social skills programme, delivered over 2 days in a group format, to people who had contacted the charity Changing Faces. This was evaluated at the end of the intervention and at 6 months follow-up with very good outcomes in terms of reduced social anxiety and avoidance. At 6 months, people had not only maintained change but had further developed their skills in social situations. Despite criticism that there was no alternative treatment control and that this was a select group, this study suggests the social skills and positive coping skills training may be effective (Robinson et al., 1996).

A similar behavioural approach was described by Newell using parallels from the treatment of people with phobic anxiety resulting in social avoidance. Newell proposed his fear-avoidance model as an explanatory framework for understanding the problems of disfiguring conditions (Figure 3.2). His work concentrated on using the principles of anxiety management and graded exposure to habituate the anxious response, eliminate avoidance and promote social-interaction behaviours (Newell 1999). Newell and Clarke (2000) reported a favourable response for this approach delivered in written format in a controlled study of people with self-identified facial visible difference.

We can think of three levels of cognitive behavioural case conceptualization: Level 1 is concerned with clarification of the presenting issues in cognitive behavioural terms; Level 2 is concerned with cross-sectional analysis of the triggers and maintenance cycles and Level 3 is concerned with identifying the role of longitudinal factors or predisposing factors. Newell's model looks beyond the presenting and cross-sectional levels that maintain the avoidant response, and acknowledges the role for historical (longitudinal) dispositional factors and life events. In this sense it can be seen as a first attempt to acknowledge the complexity of individual case formulation in the development and maintenance of social avoidance. However, Newell's model does not describe the nature of longitudinal factors or indicate how these might need to be considered in treatment; rather the emphasis in

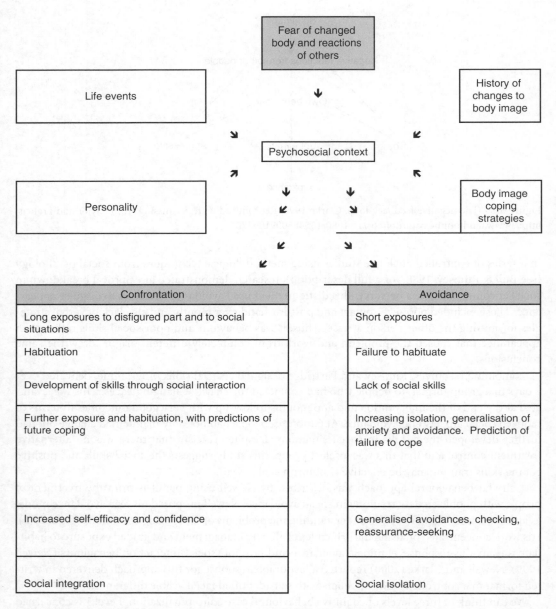

Figure 3.2 A fear-avoidance model of psychosocial difficulties following disfigurement. Newell 1999. Reproduced with permission from John Wiley & Sons, Ltd.

Newell's model is essentially a behavioural one, focusing on reducing an anxious response by repeated prolonged exposure to a feared stimulus.

The advantage of a behavioural approach to treatment is that it is systematic but relatively formulaic and can be delivered by nurses, psychological well-being practitioners, or other health professionals with specific but short-term training. Thus, Clarke and Cooper (2001) investigated the training needs of specialist nurses in head and neck cancer and designed an intervention that they could use for rehabilitation with patients. This deals with answering questions about the condition, managing other people's uncertainty and practical management of a visible difference and disability, as described in the previous chapter. Outcome data demonstrated that nurses perceived themselves to be more skilled and modified their practice to include psychosocial interventions (e.g. encouraging the patient to answer questions from other people) which was then used effectively by patients (Clarke, 2001).

Techniques used in behavioural approaches may also be used in cognitive approaches, but with a different rationale. For example, exposure (see Chapter 4) is used as a core component of intervention in behavioural treatments with the aim of eliciting a fear response and habituating the resulting anxiety. The same approach using a hierarchy of problem situations may be used in a cognitive programme, but with more emphasis on modifying the affective state and providing a behavioural experiment, which encourages the reattribution of beliefs and schema modification.

Building an Evidence Base

In recent years, research focusing on the utility of these models in clinical practice has grown to a small number of empirical research studies which help inform best practice in the assessment and treatment of appearance-related anxiety for adults with visible differences. Existing published quantitative studies evaluating the effectiveness of interventions were independently, critically evaluated using a systematic reviewing process by Bessell and Moss (2007). Of the 12 studies which met the inclusion criteria, 5 studies within their review evaluated CBT-based approaches with this patient group (Fortune et al., 2002, 2004; Kleve et al., 2002; Newell & Clarke, 2000; Papadopoulos et al., 1999). Collectively, the studies suggest CBT based interventions can be beneficial to patients well-being measured in terms of favourable change in anxiety, depression, social anxiety, quality of life, self-esteem and appearance-related anxiety and avoidance. These studies had good ecological validity, with real patients attending either private or National Health Service clinics as participants and the interventions under study used by clinicians in the field. However, partly due to the applied nature of these studies, they lacked methodological rigour. As concluded by Bessell and Moss, caution should be applied to concluding that these studies provide definitive evidence for the recommendation on CBT as an effective intervention for this patient group.

Nevertheless, coupled with the burgeoning evidence base for the use of CBT with people with anxiety disorders, social avoidance and body image disturbance, the evidence built so far seems to point clinicians to cognitive behavioural therapy as an appropriate and potentially effective therapeutic intervention for many patients. Indeed, cognitive behavioural approaches are widely used by health care professionals working with people with visible differences to good effect, including the authors of this book. However, a greater number of good quality research studies testing its effectiveness in meeting patients needs is still required, and clinicians interested in this area are urged to consider using valid and appropriate measurement tools to document and share findings within the research and clinical community to help further understanding of what works for whom and in what context. Everyone working in this area in a clinical capacity can provide evidence of the effectiveness of a psychological approach using case history data; although there is considerable scope for better analysis of single case data. Given the problems of randomised controlled trials (RCTs) in this field, systematic case study designs provide a real opportunity to add to the evidence base using methods which have a strong tradition in psychological research and can provide details not only about the clinical significance of change, but the process of change. For example, patients commonly anticipate that behavioural change will follow mood change:

> If I felt better about my appearance, I could socialise more.

An alternative assumption might be:

> If I can socialise successfully and more often, I will feel better about my appearance.
>
> (This is a good example of a testable hypothesis. One way of helping someone to modify their beliefs would be via a behavioural experiment in which they rated their preoccupation with their appearance after regularly attending a specific social activity. Because anticipatory anxiety is often high and leads to social avoidance, people are often surprised to find that the reality is much more manageable than they had expected. This additional information can be added to modify the formulation as above)

This latter view is consistent with the evidence for the value of behavioural activation in mental health. A series of case studies based on daily recording of mood and hours spent outside the house will provide evidence of the temporal sequence of these factors in a way that RCT cannot.

Cognitive Approaches: Comparison of Appearance Anxiety and Social Phobia

A review of treatment approaches to body image concerns more widely (such as in relation to Body Dysmorphic Disorder) and approaches to the treatment of social anxiety and social phobia, suggests common features in presentation and opportunities to draw on these related fields. The importance of models of social anxiety was commented upon by Thompson and Kent (2001) in their review, and the interventions described later in the manual draw upon the approach developed by Clark and Wells' (1995) model of social phobia and Wells' (1997) *Cognitive Therapy for Anxiety Treatment Manual*.

Appearance-related anxiety is excluded from existing versions of diagnostic classification systems (e.g. the *Diagnostic and Statistical Manual of Mental Disorders: DSM-IV-TR*), but patients presenting with the problems outlined in Chapter 1 share many of the characteristic features of 'anxiety disorders'. In addition, there are many overlaps with dominant cognitive models such as Clark and Wells' (1995) model of social phobia. An understanding of the similarities is helpful in formulating problems and treatment plans, particularly for those patients where there is a mismatch between objectively measured minor disfigurement and high levels of preoccupation and social avoidance. However, it is always essential to strive for an individualized formulation of the specific presenting problems.

Clark and Wells (1995) propose a cognitive model of social phobia (Figure 3.3). The processes which are hypothesized to take place in a feared situation are illustrated in this model (reproduced with permission).

Clark and Wells propose that social phobia is characterized by a high need for positive evaluation by others and strong beliefs about an inability to achieve this. The model illustrates the mechanism in which the assumption of failure is triggered by a social event with the focus of attention directed internally onto processing the self as a social object rather than externally onto what is actually happening. The model also explains the maintenance of the phobia, since exposure to social situations will activate

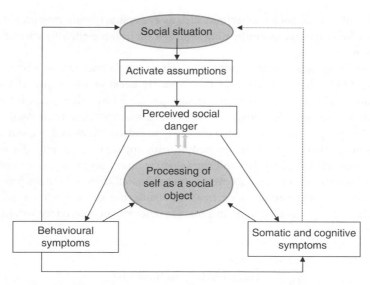

Figure 3.3 A cognitive model of social phobia. Clark and Wells 1995. Reproduced with permission from Guilford.

a pathway which reinforces rather than extinguishes the response. According to this account, simple exposure treatments which do not consider cognitive factors may therefore be ineffective.

Unlike other forms of phobia where the feared response rarely happens, (e.g. panic attacks leading to fainting or loss of consciousness), social anxiety may trigger the visible behaviours that the individual fears (e.g. hands shaking, sweating, stammering). These responses themselves become sources of anxiety and threat because they are perceived as highly noticeable to others, which may result in feelings of shame, embarrassment and negative self-evaluation. The resulting behaviour may also be perceived as less relaxed, eliciting less positive behaviour from others and reinforcing the fear. Everyday behaviours such as eating and drinking in public (hand shaking) or speaking (dry mouth, stammering) are all behaviours on which people can form judgments about others and at which they can therefore fail.

This model is very useful in explaining what may happen in social situations for someone with an unusual appearance. Like social phobia, the social situation may activate assumptions that observers will scrutinize appearance and make comments about it. Although appearance is not included within the classification of social phobia, presentation of the self can be conceived as a 'performance'; thus people are judged on physical attractiveness, weight, make-up, hair and clothing, such that failure or negative evaluation can result simply by walking into a room. Feared responses such as staring, comments or questions from others quite frequently occur for people with a visible difference, so that like social phobia, the feared outcome becomes a reality and people maintain a level of vigilance or anticipation of questioning with each new person that they meet.

Other similarities with social phobia are the marked shift in attentional focus from the social environment to a detailed monitoring and observation of one's own behaviour, which then interferes with social interaction (for example, holding the head at a certain angle, keeping hair over a facial lesion). Like the use of self-focused attention to construct an impression of themselves, which people may then attribute to others, an overestimation of the extent to which a feature is evident to other people can lead both to a preoccupation with the impact of that feature on others and misinterpretation of normal social behaviour, such as eye contact being interpreted as staring. For both groups, this feeds apparently confirming information into the anxious schema and maintains maladaptive behaviour.

Since this processing bias is maladaptive, it is important to understand why it is maintained. Clark and Wells (1995) have argued that this is partly because social situations provide very little unambiguous information about how we are perceived by others, and for most people, a perception that we are regarded positively is derived mainly from their own perceptions of positive worth. For people living with social phobic type presentations and, we would argue on the basis of the results of this programme, for people with appearance anxiety, the fear of negative evaluation becomes self-fulfilling through the selective attention to negative events or negative interpretation of neutral events such as eye contact. Thus all the component processes in Clark and Wells' model have a potential relevance in considering the experience of disfigurement and in formulation of the development and maintenance of social anxiety secondary to altered appearance.

Use of Safety Behaviours

Like social phobia, appearance anxiety is characterized by the use of protective behaviours, which Clark and Wells (1995) have termed 'safety behaviours', developed as a means of avoiding negative evaluation. Just as fear of hand tremor may lead someone with social phobia to avoid holding a glass, or filling it only partially, the use of hats, make-up, hair-styles or beards, or even holding particular stances, are common attempts to minimize or disguise visible differences in appearance. People may carefully select venues with subdued lighting or choose to sit on a particular side of someone so that a profile or other supposed defect is less visible. Extreme social avoidance can include going out only at night or choosing a job in a setting where there is likely to be less interpersonal interaction (e.g. security guard, long-distance lorry driver). Features that are normally hidden by clothing can become a problem in intimacy where people worry about how to keep a body area hidden. Avoiding looking at one's own body can become extreme so that people may shower wearing bathing suits and refuse to touch or look at themselves. Maintaining breast size is achieved by stuffing a bra or even in extreme situations by repeat pregnancy to maintain breast fullness.

The underlying core belief for many people with appearance anxiety is that their appearance is abnormal, that they are therefore abnormal, substandard and 'a freak' and that they are disgusting. They experience internal shame and assume that 'if they know what I really look like' external shame in others will be enacted by expressions of disappointment, disgust and ultimately rejection. Safety-seeking behaviours are therefore seen as protective because they prevent a negative response from other people; these anticipated responses could be a glance, simple question, an expression of disgust or horror, walking away, telling other people 'the secret' and other actions which 'expose' the hidden source of shame. If enacted, these responses would confirm the underlying core beliefs and reinforce a negative schema built around a sense of worthlessness.

Unfortunately, safety-seeking behaviours are often themselves problematic, partly because they may draw attention to, rather than disguise, a feature, but more importantly because they remove the opportunity for unambiguous feedback from others, thus maintaining an underlying fear of negative evaluation. Success in a situation (no one notices or mentions appearance) is attributed to the safety behaviour rather than to positive regard from others. Safety-seeking behaviours may also themselves be shameful, feeding back into the core belief of being a disgusting or unacceptable person, for example, the use of make-up by men and fear of discovery, or use of repeat pregnancy and termination to ensure breast fullness.

Maladaptive safety-seeking behaviours in appearance anxiety are a major problem and an important focus for intervention.

Example 1

Sarah sustained facial scarring from a smashed windscreen in a car accident. Although a relatively minor injury when viewed objectively, she became convinced that people were staring at her, forming negative evaluations about her and avoiding her. She described very clearly what she perceived as 'uneasy' glances and behavioural avoidance in shops and on buses. This experience supported a core belief that she was 'spoiled' or 'deformed' and that any attention was negative. In exploring this further, it became clear that she had put in place a number of safety behaviours. She was wearing a baseball cap pulled low over her forehead and avoiding eye contact. So that this 'fitted' with what she was wearing, she stopped wearing skirts and switched to jeans and boots. Combined with her height, her attempts to avoid eye contact and conversation, she could easily be perceived as threatening.

This information was used to begin to develop a formulation of the presenting problems and factors that maintained them (Figure 3.4). This was refined and modified as she underwent treatment.

Clothing and camouflage are very commonly used safety behaviours. They present particular challenges because of their intermittent reinforcement value. For example, a large baggy jacket covering scars on the arms, breast asymmetry or abdominal laxity may 'work' in the winter when everyone wears a coat, but will single out an individual in summer when everyone wears a T-shirt. For this reason, treatment schedules should, where possible, include maintenance follow-up sessions during the summer months.

Anticipatory and Post-Event Processing

Anticipatory anxiety is high in appearance-related anxiety, as with social phobia. Prior rehearsal of a social event may start considerably in advance though the selection or purchase of new clothing. Inability to wear the same items as a peer group (e.g. strappy tops or low-cut clothing), inability to obtain the correct size in popular chain stores or to find a bra that fits may contribute to unfair and self-critical underlying schemas (strong core beliefs that may be difficult to alter) such as 'I am a freak, I am not normal'. This will then lead people to derive assumptions or attitudes ('I am not as good as everyone else, I can't do what they do, I need an operation to make me look the same') with the result that they will see themselves as excluded from the behaviour associated with peer group membership. Like earlier studies, (Gamba et al., 1992; Ramsey & O'Reagan, 1988), the ARC research programme has confirmed that an additional problem for appearance anxiety is anticipated intimacy and the disclosure of a feature which is usually disguised. This frequently triggers a set of assumptions

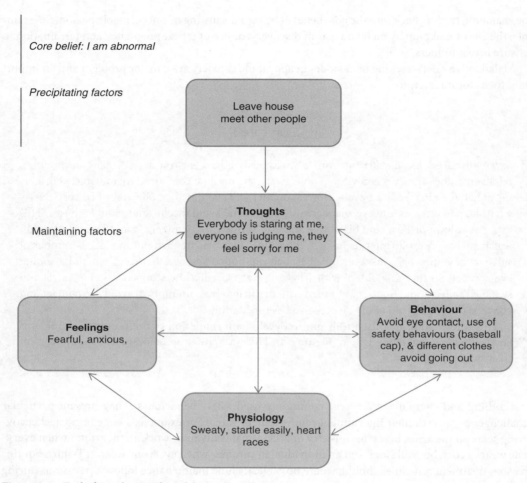

Core belief: I am abnormal

Precipitating factors

Leave house meet other people

Thoughts
Everybody is staring at me, everyone is judging me, they feel sorry for me

Maintaining factors

Behaviour
Avoid eye contact, use of safety behaviours (baseball cap), & different clothes avoid going out

Feelings
Fearful, anxious,

Physiology
Sweaty, startle easily, heart races

Figure 3.4   Early formulation of Sarah's avoidance behaviour.

about rejection that are not tested, but avoided, and which are therefore maintained. In the context of clinical practice, it is very common to find a gradual withdrawal in the form of a reverse hierarchy, with intimacy first avoided; then one-to-one situations with potential partners avoided; followed by social situations in which potential new partners may be present, until social situations are avoided altogether. If the goal is intimacy and this is seen as unachievable, then the steps toward it are gradually eliminated too. This can result in extreme isolation and low mood (see Working with CBT Level 4, Example 5, Chapter 7 for an example of working with someone to manage fears of intimacy).

Anticipatory anxiety about a feature being noticed or stared at is common. People report 'hypervigilance' or scanning other people for evidence of a negative reaction. Because normal communication involves close attention to the other person via sustained eye contact, people can make incorrect attributions that someone has noticed or is staring, particularly when a condition is not particularly noticeable to an observer. This attribution is easily followed by further 'mind reading' or development of further incorrect assumptions and feelings, for example that the observer is repelled or shocked, when most people are simply curious. This pattern of thinking is very common and frequently recognized as relevant, as it is introduced into the formulation as part of the cycle of maintaining factors (see Example 1). However, people vary enormously in terms of the flexibility of their thinking about alternative explanations. Where some very easily see how a hypothesis about the explanation of another person's behaviours can be self-sustaining through biased selection of confirming evidence, other people find it hard to let go of the idea that they 'know' what other people are thinking. Reference to early social psychological experiments such as those carried about by Strenta and Kleck (1985) can be helpful in thinking about this.

In this study, actors had make-up applied to mimic a port wine stain or facial scar. They were asked to report anything unusual about the behaviour of other people. They reported heightened self-awareness and intrusive behaviour from others including staring and behavioural avoidance. A second group of actors were made up in the same way but unknown to them, had a solvent rather than fixative applied which removed the disfigurement. Despite an unremarkable appearance, they reported the same intrusive behaviour from other people as the first group. This finding can be explained either in terms of false attributions, (biased selection of neutral behaviour to support expectations of a negative response), or in terms of subtle behaviour change in the actors, for example, avoiding eye contact, change in posture, etc., which paradoxically attracts attention from others. This is consistent with other studies which confirm altered behaviour rather than appearance as the source of discomfort in social encounters.

Acknowledging and managing anticipatory anxiety early in treatment is important. An explanation of the nature of physical symptoms of anxiety is a simple and important initial intervention. Relaxation strategies can be helpful, particularly in managing physiological changes such as heart racing, tremor and churning stomach when confronting a feared situation. Attentional training exercises are useful, for example, practice in sustaining attention to one source whilst ignoring another and then switching, (a simple example would be reading with the radio on). Mindfulness techniques such as close attention to sensory stimuli (colour, smell, texture) can be practiced in everyday situations (on the bus, walking through the park) before applying in social situations. Learning to focus on the other person in an interaction can also be a simple technique aimed at disrupting over focus on the self. Developing ways to answer questions in a variety of ways can promote confidence, self-efficacy and perceived control over the situation. Exposure to feared situations without developing some coping tools early on is likely to simply confirm the belief that social encounters are embarrassing and awkward, which will increase rather extinguish anxiety. Reassurance should always be given that the application of such techniques takes practice and confidence tends to grow with practice as with the acquisition of any new skill.

Of course for people who have a very visible condition, there is a high probability that others will notice and will stare or ask questions. This reality should never be ignored and actual incidents of stigmatization should be assessed. This has treatment advantages since the feared situation is enacted and can therefore provide the basis for practicing responses and behaviour change. Because the observer response to appearance is variable for people with less noticeable conditions, treatment may take longer (operant learning theory also tells us that intermittent reinforcement schedules result in longer latency until the undesired target behaviour (avoidance) has been extinguished). But questioning can take different forms and often catches people off guard. The observer often waits until initial social contact has been made and this can be interpreted as 'not having noticed'. When the question comes, it can be seen as an 'ambush' and is often not answered well. This then leads to post-event preoccupation and re-evaluation of the situation.

Example 2

Ann had a facial palsy as a result of an acoustic neuroma, resulting in a lack of mobility on one side of her face. In the middle of a conversation with a woman at a Christmas party and well into a discussion of her daughter's progress in her piano lessons, the woman suddenly leaned closer to her and said 'I think you are so brave dear, coming out when you look like that'. Ann described herself as caught off guard. Because there had been no warning of this remark and even though she interpreted it as supportive, she was embarrassed and unable to frame a suitable reply. She found herself ruminating about this incident, going over the ways she could have handled it and her social avoidance of similar situations temporarily increased.

Where a situation has gone badly, it is often characterized by embarrassment on both sides, confirmation of negative evaluation by others and a sense of failure. Because what happened confirms the anticipatory fear, people tend to remember it very clearly with many details preserved (such as the exact words or phrases used by others) and rumination leads to recall of similar events which resulted in similarly unhelpful outcomes. Lack of anticipation that things will go well, means that positive outcomes are less salient and are not as well recalled. Thus, it is a list of 'disasters' which tends to be constructed with stronger conviction of social inadequacy and corresponding overestimation of the frequency with which similar events are likely to occur. Attribution style is also important, with a tendency for self focus to result in internal attributions for neutral or ambiguous responses, whilst positive feedback is attributed externally. (When things go well it is something to do with the situation or other person; when things go badly it is my fault.) Fortunately, most patients can acknowledge that there are many situations which have positive outcomes and are receptive to the idea that negative outcomes tend to be selectively recalled. This can be demonstrated by reference to other forms of behaviour that the patient is encouraged to recall, or by behavioural monitoring as a homework task. Again, the combination of anticipatory anxiety and 'post mortem' preoccupation are characteristic of social phobia.

The Role of Assumptions and Schema in Appearance Anxiety

Although many people with appearance anxiety do have an appearance that lies outside the norm, it is often their cognitive interpretation of themselves and their potential relationships with others that maintains their anticipatory anxiety and drives unhelpful safety behaviours and other compensatory coping strategies. Clark and Wells (1995) identify three categories of dysfunctional assumption in relation to social phobia:

1. Excessively high standards for social performance. Thus, the need for everyone's approval and exceptionally high standards of performance are similar to the beliefs that everyone should look their best, skin conditions will not be tolerated by others, judgments are made on the basis of appearance, 'no one will speak to someone who looks like me', 'no one will want to have a relationship with someone who has less than perfect looks'. These assumptions are supported by

upward comparisons with perceived role models (in magazines, other media, with a previous 'undamaged' self) with an appearance that is unachievable by most people.

2. Conditional beliefs concerning social evaluation take the form of, for example, 'if people knew what I really looked like they would not like me', 'if I had not spent 5 hours getting ready no one would have spoken to me', 'if there had been any other men there, they would never have wasted their time with me' and similar beliefs characterized by the assumption that what other people might think about me is therefore the truth about me.

3. Unconditional beliefs about the self are more varied. Clark and Wells (1995) observe that in social phobia, people can usually distinguish between how they feel when they are with other people who they know well, such as friends and family, and people who they are meeting for the first time and who are therefore perceived to be evaluating them. People with a visible disfigurement also commonly confirm that anticipation of the first impressions formed in new social situations is the most challenging. As in social phobia, many would agree that there would be no problem if they were on a desert island away from the rest of us. However, it is also common for people to maintain core beliefs that they are 'abnormal' or 'not the same as other people' by making comparisons with an 'ideal self', informed either by external comparisons or by an internal comparison with a previous (pre-injury) appearance. For them, it is their own negative evaluation of their appearance, independent of others' perception, which maintains their preoccupation. For this group, the theme of negative automatic thoughts is more to do with loss and self-devaluation (i.e. characteristic of depression rather than focused on the anxiety or danger-related themes which characterize negative automatic thoughts in anxiety). It is important to note that whilst the majority of patients with appearance-related concerns present with marked anxiety particularly in social settings, they may also be depressed.

Summary

In summary, the cognitive model of social phobia suggests that the problem persists because people are not attending to what is really happening in social situations, are building up safety behaviours which prevent unhelpful beliefs being disconfirmed and using their own impression of themselves as the main evidence that other people regard them in a negative way. Applied to people with an abnormality of appearance, whether objectively visible or not, the parallels lie in the lack of attention to what is really happening and preoccupation about the assumptions that the other person is making about them. Similarly, it is the comparison with the ideal or ought self rather than the responses of other people that are used to provide evidence for being viewed in a negative way. Progressive social avoidance is used to protect, but ultimately it cuts people off from the social environment and the opportunity to learn positive and pro-social coping skills.

Of course there are some real differences between disfigurement and social phobia. Particularly in conditions that are noticeable to others, the reality is that some people do react in a negative fashion or in a way that requires managing by the individual with a visible difference. Use of camouflage, make-up, hairstyles and clothing can be seen as safety behaviours, but they are also useful everyday coping tools. Indeed, one important aspect of psychological intervention is helping the individual to distinguish between inappropriate use of such tactics (which serve to maintain unhelpful cognitions and anxiety) and appropriate use (which encourages confrontation of fears and hypothesis testing).

Therefore, in the management of appearance-related anxiety, we can try to integrate the relevant findings from this parallel field of research and clinical intervention for social phobia into our existing models. We can also use the extensive experience of working with people who are visibly different in our clinical practice and finally we can use the data from the ARC research programme, to refine and further develop the models which underpin our therapeutic approach. The following section summarizes the ARC research (see Appendix A for full details), before describing the fully integrated framework.

Deriving a Cognitive Behavioural Treatment Model: Identifying Factors and Processes Contributing to Successful Adjustment to Disfiguring Conditions

Working Framework of Adjustment to Disfiguring Conditions

The ARC research programme investigated the factors and processes which had been suggested by previous research to contribute to adjustment to disfiguring conditions. In order to conceptualize a working model of adjustment, the team of researchers and clinicians reviewed the existing evidence and drew up a framework to guide the programme of research. This was an evidence based but also a pragmatic process in which there is inevitable bias. Selection of factors is constrained to some extent by the availability of robust measures. For some factors which were thought to be theoretically important, new measures were devised and standardized for this study. Similarly, clinicians working with the patient group over many years were keen to include factors which are seen commonly in people presenting for treatment, even where there is no significant literature, for example, anger and aggression. We also needed to operationalize concepts which we could integrate into therapy, both to inform formulation and to underpin the therapeutic techniques being used. It is highly likely, nevertheless, despite being a large and experienced research group that other people would have included other concepts and chosen different measures, and it is important to point out that our findings are inevitably constrained by these choices. Choosing the primary outcome measure required considerable thought, because appearance anxiety can be considered either as a process or an outcome measure. Having settled on the outcome measure, it was then important to ensure a wide range of process measures to ensure suitable independence, otherwise, the regression analysis will inevitably result in positive findings. The final choice of the Derriford Appearance Scale was made on the basis of its widespread use in clinical practice, its focus on feelings, beliefs and behaviours and therefore its relevance to a CBT model, and its potential value as a measure of change during the pre- and post-treatment periods.

The quantitative measures/questionnaires were completed by 1265 participants from the community and outpatient clinics across a number of UK cities. The data resulting were used to investigate the relationships between the components of this framework for predicting well-being and distress in people with disfiguring conditions.

The ARC Framework of Adjustment to Disfiguring Conditions

Within this framework (Figure 3.5), the process of adjustment to visible differences is viewed as having three different facets. The first is the predisposing factors such as demographic characteristics, socio-cultural setting and family environment, which are implicated in the development of core

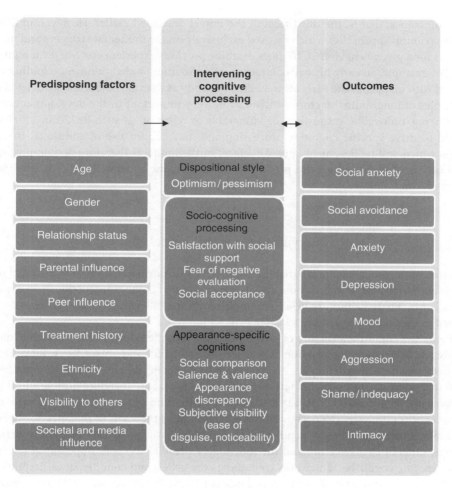

Figure 3.5 Working framework of adjustment to disfiguring conditions.

beliefs about the self, and distress or resilience to distress related to appearance. The second is the intervening cognitive processes which are used to process appearance-related information and maintain the overall appearance schema. The third facet is the outcomes that can result from having a visible difference/disfigurement, both those associated with well-being and distress.

Predisposing Factors

This facet of the model includes demographic factors, previous treatment history and also the more generic societal and media influences which have a pervasive influence on attitudes to appearance generally. Whilst theoretically important, it is easy to overlook these factors. From the therapeutic perspective, the focus in CBT is the intervening cognitive processes, the second facet of the model, which are modifiable and therefore provide the focus for interventions which can improve outcomes, that is, the third facet of the model described earlier. However, unlike tradi-tional behavioural approaches which focused exclusively on the immediate triggers and maintain-ing factors for a given behaviour, CBT does examine previous experience as a determinant of core beliefs. For example, an early history of attachment difficulties or abandonment, childhood abuse associated with inappropriate early awareness of the body as a sexual object and associated shame, are examples of longitudinal factors which may be very important in the development of a core belief of being 'unlovable', 'disgusting', or vulnerable to rejection. If such beliefs or schema exist, they tend to drive specific cognitive processing and may call for use of additional therapeutic strategies which will be described later. This facet of the model is therefore very important both theoretically in understanding the predictors of adjustment and practically, in treatment, by informing formulation.

Intervening Cognitive Processing

This section of the model includes variables that describe 'dispositional style' or factors that relate to all beliefs and behaviour as well as those specifically implicated in the construction of an appearance related schema. These factors are briefly summarized in the following. Clinical application will be illustrated in the case examples (see Chapter 7).

A schema is a cognitive structure or generalization about the self and others which allows us to assimilate and understand information. A schema will both guide and organize new information. As experiences are encountered, they are assimilated into an existing schema which then may be modi-fied and shaped to accommodate this new knowledge. Schemas are therefore flexible and shaped by new experience. However, schemas can also be maladaptive and rigid. In more severe cases of anxi-ety disorder, it is ultimately the content of the schemas that is the focus of therapeutic intervention with the aim of identifying the core entrenched beliefs that drive assumptions about the world being dangerous, others being rejecting and the individual's inability to cope. Appearance schemas are therefore specific cognitive frameworks containing core beliefs and conditional assumptions about appearance and the impact of this on self and others (Altabe & Thompson, 1996). For example, the core belief 'I am deformed' might lead to the assumption 'if anyone sees what I look like they won't want to know me'. This will be maintained by selective data gathering via the different cognitive processes outlined in the following. The aim of therapy is to help the individual to process informa-tion in a more flexible way to consider alternative explanations and to ultimately modify the schema and revise the rigidly held beliefs about the self. Therapy in the case of an objective visible disfigure-ment will also need to focus on the management of others' reactions, and there is a balance between addressing the often exaggerated beliefs held by the individual whilst acknowledging that prejudice still exists and needs managing.

Dispositional Style

Optimism/pessimism: The role of optimism/pessimism in adjustment has been suggested as an important protective factor in coping with chronic health conditions (Reich et al., 2010). Within the framework they are highlighted as a potential buffer to psychosocial distress associated with living with disfigurement. Therefore, dispositional optimism and pessimism were investigated in the research programme to examine their role in adjustment. The word 'dispositional' should not suggest an unchangeable attribute but rather an enduring style. A behavioural explanation proposes a pattern of selective attention to negative information which reinforces the belief that 'something bad will happen' or 'I am never going to be good enough', etc. Negative automatic thoughts are a central tenet of CBT and learning to challenge the immediate assumption of failure rather than success or simply a neutral position, is a common feature of all CBT interventions. 'Seeing the world through rose tinted spectacles' is a good lay summary of dispositional optimism and like the other factors in this facet of the model, it is modifiable via attention to the thinking bias.

Socio-Cognitive Processing

Social support is a strong predictor of psychological adjustment across long-term conditions generally. This has been found to be the case in earlier studies into adjustment in disfigurement and highlighted again in the ARC research programme. Again, this is a subjective concept, the predictor being the perception of social support as adequate or not, rather than the amount or type of support from others. Good social support provides not only a practical structure for social interaction but impacts at the level of self-esteem and self-worth. The irony in appearance-related problems is that because people avoid contact with others, they remove themselves from the opportunity to have the kinds of relationships which we know to be influential in producing positive appraisals about appearance. Therefore, much of the goal for intervention is about increasing the opportunities for social interaction and the strength of social networks.

Where there is an opportunity to involve a friend or partner as co-therapist in some or all of an intervention, this can be seen as a strategic way of increasing social support. Goals must be negotiated, but additional feedback from behavioural experiments, prompting to complete homework and back up 'in the field' are helpful inputs into treatment and reduce kindly meant but dismissive messages ('It doesn't bother me what you look like'). Examples of where this might be helpful would be in early exposure as part of a behavioural experiment. It might be easier to go out with someone else rather than alone in the first steps to assess anticipated attention to appearance or asking questions. It is very important to have a plan. If the therapeutic partner becomes very angry at unwanted attention or answers a question in a way that has not been agreed, then this can have an unhelpful impact.

Example 3

Following surgery for facial cancer, Jane was very self-conscious about her appearance but also very tired. She had withdrawn from her usual activities becoming increasingly avoidant. Formulation suggested a core schema in which control or loss of control was central and which had been strengthened by the cancer diagnosis. 'Going to a social event' generated assumptions about lack of control over peoples questioning, being able to leave the event if she felt tired, etc. Involving her partner to help her develop an answer to questions, but also an answer that he should use: 'why don't you ask Jane'? helped her to feel that she could resume control and prevent people discussing her. Similarly, the couple agreed that if she felt tired and suggested leaving, he would support that rather than try to persuade her to stay.

Another important example that can inform formulation is checking out with others rather than making assumptions about appearance.

Example 4

Joanna disliked the post-pregnancy appearance of her body after having twins. Her breasts had become smaller and less 'full' and she described her abdomen as much less firm and also covered with stretch marks. Her assumption that she 'looked awful' was maintained by comparison with pictures of 'celebratory new mums' in magazines but also with pictures of her own pre-pregnant self. She withdrew from intimacy with her husband on the basis that he would find her appearance equally off-putting. Joanna was set the homework task of discussing this with him. He was relieved to talk to her and whilst acknowledging that her body had changed, confirmed that this had no impact for him in terms of finding her attractive, and indeed that he felt even more warmly towards her as the mother of his children. Joanna was able to re-evaluate the assumptions underpinning her avoidant behaviour and to re-establish their sexual relationship.

Fear of negative evaluation is a commonly measured cognitive variable in social anxiety research and is predictive of social anxiety and avoidance in a variety of social settings, not necessarily concerned with appearance. The use of safety behaviours is associated with the drive to pass unnoticed, not to draw attention, etc., and there appears to be a strong attributional bias with attention being automatically classified as negative per se rather than negative because of its evaluative component or the associated beliefs or behaviour of the observer. Intervention can therefore explore alternative explanations for attention. Its relevance to appearance-specific situations has, however, been emphasized in the ARC research programme. Clinically, it is of great relevance both to appearance that is visible to other people, but especially with appearance that is normally hidden by clothing and needs to be disclosed in intimate situations where people feel at their most vulnerable.

Example 5

Jack described himself as very self-conscious about his facial scarring. He had had acne in his 20s, and now in his 30s although no longer experiencing active disease had visible scarring. His assumptions that other people regarded him negatively were supported by his perception that other people stared at him. Jack was set a homework task to obtain more data about the behaviour of other people. After his session in the clinic he walked back to his office through a park. He was asked to count the number of people that he passed and to note how many of them appeared to stare at him.

At his next appointment, the homework task was reviewed. Jack had passed 100 people and 1 person had stared at him. He then smiled, and said that this person had first smiled and then come up to ask him directions. Jack was able to modify his thinking about other people viewing him negatively given his experience that of all the people in the park that day he had been selected as looking the most approachable. This accidental behavioural experiment allowed us to reformulate his problems and to help him to be more flexible in his thinking about other people's assumptions.

Social Acceptance

Negative evaluation feeds strongly into the assumption that 'other people's assessment of me is the truth about me'. If other people regard me in a negative way then this must be correct and I sit outside an 'acceptable social and cultural norm'. It is not surprising that the concept is so aversive and associated with high levels of fear. Appearance is the most immediate form of information about other people in social encounters and underpins social media such as Facebook. The enormous success of this social media illustrates the premium that people place on social networks, where images proliferate via photos taken at all social events. Our current research on appearance illustrates a growing focus on 'how I look' as a determinant of self-worth in younger and younger age groups. Many young people now look to cosmetic surgery as a means of changing their appearance to meet a social norm which is 'more acceptable'. Social acceptance is also a driver of cultural practices which modify appearance such as hair removal (see Falvey, 2012; Halliwell & Diedrich, 2012).

Appearance-Specific Cognitions

Social comparison processes: Social comparison sounds self-explanatory. The extent to which people rate their own self-esteem and self-worth is with reference to an identified norm or peer group. Similarly, the way that people judge their own appearance is influenced by the prevailing 'norms' of appearance evident in their own social context. This will include peer groups, cultural norms, and increasingly international norms promoted by global access to, usually Westernized, images. Some images will also be air brushed or composite images that present an idealized form. However, there is a difference between comparing oneself with other people and deriving an 'idealized' appearance with reference to cultural norms resulting in *appearance discrepancies* (Thompson et al., 2010). Social comparison processes contribute to an 'ideal' or 'ought' self, but this mechanism is often not clear to patients. Most will reject the idea that they compare themselves with other people:

> This is not about what other people look like – I might look much better than some other people; this is about me – how I feel about myself

Here, the primary focus is on an earlier appearance – before the accident, before pregnancy – or on an ideal self never achieved. This is not necessarily an attractive or exceptional appearance, more usually an ordinary or unremarkable appearance characterized by 'fitting in' or anonymity and marked by a strong sense of lost identity or discordance between perceived and internalized body image. ('I am not supposed to look like this'; 'This is not me'.) The link with social comparison is less immediate here; whilst earlier or 'ought' appearance may have been derived with reference to social norms ('I used to look okay', 'I'm not asking to be a movie star') immediate appearance is compared with that of an earlier or imagined self.

A further problem in a clinical setting is that discussion that invites comparison with other people can be inferred as a comparison with other patients (some of whom, in a specialized centre, may have very visible injuries). 'I feel terrible taking up your time when I know I'm not as bad as those people out there'. Downward comparisons of this kind, interestingly, are not universally helpful, and are often distracting, reducing self-efficacy 'I feel completely useless when I see what other people are coping with' and this supports the hypothesis that it is the internalized self which is providing the sense of discordance for a significant group of patients. However, others find it more helpful to learn about the strategies that other people use to cope. Our experience, reinforced by the equivocal results of our research programme, is therefore that working with the concept of social comparison processes sometimes but not always has a place in intervention.

Attributional style refers to the tendency to locate the explanation for an event either internally (with reference to one's own behaviour) or externally (with reference to events outside one's control, which may include the behaviour of other people). In the earlier section on social phobia, the tendency for self-focused attention to result in internal attributions for neutral or ambiguous responses was noted, with positive feedback attributed externally. In lay terms, when things go well you credit other factors and when they go badly you blame yourself.

In terms of working with patients, this is an intuitive idea, people 'get it' and can think of examples so that it lends itself well to challenging beliefs and behavioural experiments.

Salience and Valence: In the body image literature, the terms salience and valence are equivalent to body image investment (salience) and body image evaluation (valence). For the ARC team, salience of appearance refers to the importance that people place on their own appearance in terms of influencing their self-concept. In clinical settings this equates to preoccupation or to how much they think about it and may relate to how much they underplay other aspects of themselves. High salience may relate to internalized family/societal values and as such may be learnt early in life and it is not unusual for people to describe coming from a family where appearance is held in high esteem. Salience is not static; it may vary, for example, during the summer when fewer clothes are worn, the opportunity to use clothing as 'safety behaviour' is reduced and other people's appearance is also more obvious, inviting comparison. Similarly, salience is often more important for people who work in situations such as hair salons where they are surrounded by mirrors and the focus of everyone around them is on appearance. High salience may also be evident if there are common intrusions about appearance – staring, comments and questions, in new situations where appearance invites scrutiny or where there is excessive checking of appearance, all of which provide constant feedback about appearance. Where appearance is very highly valued, other aspects of life can be viewed as though through a 'filter' of 'what I look like', with a very high impact for people with conditions that alter appearance in a negative way.

Valence refers to the positive or negative beliefs that people have about their appearance. They may value their own appearance very highly or be very critical of their own appearance. Appearance will be valued differently by different people and by the same individual at different times of their life or in different situations. Evidence from studies with general populations indicates that 'what I look like' is the biggest component to judgments of self-worth for adolescent females, and even primary age children modify behaviour in the classroom (not putting up their hand to answer a question) if they feel they don't look their best (Lovegrove, 2002).

In terms of appearance anxiety, distress is likely to be highest for someone who values appearance very highly (high salience), is working in a setting where appearance has a high premium (e.g. working in fashion), but who feels that their own appearance fails to meet their ideal (low to moderate valence). In terms of promoting adjustment, modification can be achieved either by:

- moving the individual's perception of their appearance towards their ideal via reduction in upward comparisons with inappropriate images
- reducing the salience of appearance to self-concept (e.g. by increasing the value of other attributes or aspects of personality (see Chapter 6))
- reducing the immediacy of appearance-related stimuli and the context whereby appearance is highly valued (e.g. change of employment).

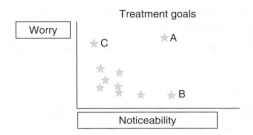

Figure 3.6 Noticeability and worry graph.

Subjective Visibility – Ease of Disguise and Noticeability: Typically, patients will focus on changing their objective appearance as a means of reducing noticeability. The impulse is therefore towards disguising a feature through make-up or clothing, or permanent change through surgery or other medical treatments. However, the ultimate goal is to reduce distress. Thus, whilst those involved in delivering traditional interventions will identify the treatment goal as movement from right to left along the horizontal axis, the ultimate goal is movement from high to low down the vertical axis. A cognitive intervention aims to reduce worry and preoccupation – move down the vertical axis – without reference to the objective noticeability of the condition.

In the hypothetical situation illustrated above (Figure 3.6), patient A rates noticeability and worry as high. Patient B rates noticeability as high but worry as low, and is therefore unlikely to be seeking treatment (or treatment is being sought for him/her by relatives). Patient C has a high level of preoccupation but recognizes that objective noticeability is low. Patient A may respond favourably to a treatment that reduces the noticeability of the condition, or to an intervention which reduces preoccupation. For patient C a psychological intervention is indicated.

In practice, the association between noticeability and worry tends to be maintained throughout treatment. Thus, interventions that reduce noticeability also reduce worry – but interventions that reduce worry also reduce perceived noticeability. (This makes intuitive sense given that preoccupation with appearance leads to hypervigilance and over-inclusive attributions about other peoples' behaviour.) This diagram is a useful device in the sharing and explanation of the cognitive model during formulation and to other health professionals.

Outcomes

Social Anxiety and Avoidance

The ARC research programme selected social anxiety and avoidance (as measured on the Derriford Appearance Scale (24), DAS24) as primary outcome measures. The pattern of anxiety leading to gradual withdrawal from social interaction has been described in many previous studies using both qualitative and quantitative data. Previous research and the results of the ARC research programme stress the impact of an unusual appearance in social interactions, and psychological interventions commonly focus on increasing social interaction and reducing anxiety as the goals for treatment.

Social skills are important in facilitating the individual's ability to develop a series of strategies with which to manage the challenges of unusual appearance in the day-to-day setting. These techniques are linked with approach rather than avoidance, and aimed at facilitating the reciprocal nature of social interaction. In terms of intervention, a substantial part of therapy is framed around the concept of learning these skills, behavioural practice and building up a range of skills in a systematic way, and using this change in behaviour to modify the appearance schema and other determinants of self-concept.

Anxiety, Depression and Mood

These are included as separate outcome measures. Whilst there is usually a strong correlation between social anxiety and generalized anxiety in the study population, this is not necessarily apparent, particularly where the appearance-related problem is not visible to others.

In general, visible difference is associated with higher levels of anxiety than depression, an interesting finding which has been replicated in many studies (Clarke et al., 2012; Cordeiro et al., 2010; Rumsey et al., 2004).

Anger/Hostility/Aggression

Whereas social anxiety and avoidance are often included as outcome measures, aggression has not been included in most previous studies. However, clinical experience demonstrates that some people respond to perceived intrusive reactions with hostility and aggression (Thompson & Broom, 2009). Anecdotally, this appears to be a problem particularly for men and may reflect a gendered response to managing interpersonal challenges. In the model in Figure 3.5, anger/aggression is represented as an outcome that may result when the individual is unable to develop a positive coping response, and is included within this study as an important outcome measure.

Shame*

Bodily shame is experienced where a value judgement (negative) is attached to appearance either by the individual (internal shame) or perceived to be attached to appearance by others (external shame). Shame is a powerful affect that tends to drive self-criticism and even self-attack and leads to avoidance and subjugation behaviours.

Internal and external shame often coexist, but not invariably. Thus, someone may be self-critical and unaccepting towards their own appearance but know that others do not or are not bothered by it (high internal but low external shame). Equally, someone may believe that others will have a negative perception of their appearance but they themselves accept their appearance (high external but low internal shame). However, high internal shame tends to be related to high external shame, as perceiving oneself to be 'unattractive' tends to lead to assuming that others will too.

Interventions targeting shame can focus on a range of things but addressing self-criticism and building a capacity for self-soothing and for self-directed compassion tend to be key (see treatment examples in Chapter 6).

*In efforts to contain the size of the participant pack, shame was not directly measured in the Healing Foundation study, but it has been discussed elsewhere as an important component of adjustment (Kent & Thompson, 2002; Thompson & Kent, 2001).

Intimacy

This was introduced as a new measure as relational difficulties are commonly reported by people with some form of visible difference. Concern about when to disclose a disfiguring condition often preoccupies people with scarring normally hidden by clothing and understandably may lead to preoccupation and concern about intimacy and rejection.

Psychological Well-Being

As in earlier studies, the ARC research programme demonstrated a significant group of people who are well adjusted to their disfigurement and for whom psychological well-being is not negatively impacted. This focus on resilience provides an important alternative conceptual basis for understanding how people manage the challenges of unusual appearance, and one that is less pathologizing than a focus on 'problems' and difficulties. Measures of positive and negative affect were therefore included as outcomes in the ARC research programme and also have relevance in clinical settings.

In addition to a large-scale cross-sectional study, the ARC research programme included studies using a variety of quantitative and qualitative methodologies exploring a variety of topics including longitudinal change, the impact of visible difference in other ethnic groups, and other aspects of adjustment to appearance including positive adjustment (Egan et al., 2011). These studies are described fully in Appendix A, but the findings are summarized briefly in the following text, since we draw on these findings in the treatment examples.

The ARC Research Programme Findings

The ARC programme was a 3-year research programme designed to identify and investigate the psychosocial factors and processes contributing to successful adjustment to disfiguring conditions, with particular emphasis on those aspects which are amenable to change. (A full discussion of the different studies is provided in the Appendix A.)

Aims

- To clarify the psychosocial factors and processes which contribute to variation in adjustment in people with visible disfigurement.
- To use the results to inform the development of packages of support and intervention.

The Studies

- A large survey of 1265 participants with visible differences from a variety of causes.
- A further survey following up 360 participants over 9 months.
- An interview study following up 26 participants in depth after 9 months.
- Nine smaller studies looking at emerging issues in greater depth.

Summary of Findings

Overall: Whilst many people in the study described coping well with their visible difference, there were considerable numbers who met accepted criteria for psychological disturbance. It is important to acknowledge that many people manage well, since this is the logical reason for developing a tiered or stepped-care approach to treatments, that is, whilst some people will be helped by intensive approaches, there are many who will benefit from simple interventions or indeed manage well on their own or with the help of their friends and families.

- *Community versus Hospital*: Levels of distress and the need for support are considerable within both the community and hospital samples, suggesting unmet need in both settings.
- *Age*: The overall picture suggests that the impact of concern about appearance decreases with age, but the variation in the sample suggests that concern about appearance is not simply the preserve of the young.
- *Gender*: Levels of social anxiety and avoidance, anxiety and negative affect were higher for women but the effect sizes were small. A significant number of men also scored above clinical cut-offs on some of the outcome measures. There were no significant differences in depression and aggression and levels of positive affect were higher for women. There is therefore no justification for the common perception that visible difference is less significant for men than women and this is consistent with other recent research evidence.
- *Visibility to others*: The findings here are mixed. Sixty-five per cent of the sample indicated concern about parts of the body normally visible to other people such as face and hands. However, the regression analyses demonstrate that a lack of visibility to others was associated with higher levels of distress. This suggests problems with intimacy and the disclosure of areas of the body normally covered. This finding is supported by evidence from a nested study looking at intimacy from which it is clear that some people have very high levels of anxiety associated with the perception that sexual attractiveness depends on an ideal appearance of the body. For a sizeable proportion, the results also reflect concerns about weight and, for some, these override the problems of disfigurement.
- *Multivariate nature of adjustment*: The measures chosen as outcomes in the ARC framework were significantly correlated, supporting the view that adjustment is multi-factorial. In the regression model for social anxiety and social avoidance as measured by the DAS24, the factors contributed to an impressive 66% of the variance. This compared with 30% for positive affect and aggression, 45% for negative affect and 46% for both anxiety and depression.

Grouping the factors together allows us to make the following conclusions about the impact of clusters of factors on outcome as follows:

- *Dispositional style*: (optimism/pessimism) has a strong effect on many of the outcome variables including depression, anxiety, aggression, negative affect and to a lesser extent, appearance-related social anxiety and avoidance.
- *Social-cognitive processes*: Perceived social acceptance and social support are protective with those describing isolation or perceiving their appearance to restrict their membership of a peer group, reporting lower levels of adjustment.
- *Anxiety and aggression*: There is clear association between anxiety and aggression. This may be because the root of both of these problems is fear, particularly of negative evaluation. This is a new finding with considerable impact for the design of interventions.
- *The role of appearance-related cognitions*: Their role is complex, and can be debilitating, but it is clear that appearance schemas are derived from factors which are amenable to intervention, and this provides strong support for the utility of CBT interventions. The results of this study support previous tentative findings that the appearance concerns of people both with and without

disfiguring conditions contribute to a range of processes including beliefs about the way that other people form impressions based on appearance and how this impacts on perceptions of the self. The way that people process information about appearance contributes to levels of adjustment. These factors are not new in the psychological literature but have not been clearly demonstrated in the field of appearance until now. They include a propensity for those with appearance concerns to interpret ambivalent stimuli as appearance related and negative and to preferentially attend to evidence that supports a negative interpretation of their own appearance. The cognitive processes of valence and salience of appearance issues in processing information and the discrepancy perceived between the self and social norms were shown to play a significant part in the regression models. This makes intuitive sense: an unusual appearance will impact less on adjustment if appearance is less highly valued than other factors that make up self-concept. Similarly, where appearance is highly valued, cognitive biases in how information about appearance is retrieved and assimilated within an appearance schema will lead to a self-reinforcing cycle where appearance information is more frequently acknowledged, processed and employed in processing and interpreting the world.

Key Messages from the Research Programme

- Adjustment to disfigurement is very variable, and, whilst many are well adjusted, there are also high levels of distress.
- Relationships between adjustment, age, gender and other demographic features are equivocal.
- The role of cognitive processes and interactions in mediating adjustment is clear.
- The media, society and culture contribute to pressure on those vulnerable to appearance concerns.
- Given the considerable variation in response to visible difference, support and intervention should be available at a range of levels of intensity to meet various levels of need.
- Findings of the research programme support the need for interventions which seek to address unhelpful appearance-related thoughts and social behaviour.
- Continuing campaigning and publicity efforts are required to modify attitudes within society and offset the effects of the media and culture.
- Important research remains to be done into key areas raised by the programme, particularly measurement and intervention.

Implication of These Findings for Design of Interventions

These findings stress the need to focus intervention on the unhelpful cognitions and beliefs that lead to poor adjustment. Behavioural approaches have tended to view adjustment as dependent on a lack of familiarity with the tools and skills which facilitate communication, particularly where a disfigurement is highly visible. However the ARC findings explain the way in which people understand the world and interpret information differently according to cognitions about appearance. Anxiety about appearance shares many common features with social phobia in that the world is perceived to be threatening with rules about social performance in which comparisons with others can quickly lead to the perception of inadequacy or inability to cope. In the same way that someone shy may make upward comparisons with someone who is socially skilled, those with appearance anxiety

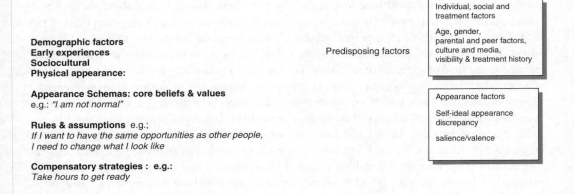

Demographic factors
Early experiences
Sociocultural
Physical appearance:

Appearance Schemas: core beliefs & values
e.g.: *"I am not normal"*

Rules & assumptions e.g.;
If I want to have the same opportunities as other people,
I need to change what I look like

Compensatory strategies : e.g.:
Take hours to get ready

Predisposing factors

Individual, social and
treatment factors

Age, gender,
parental and peer factors,
culture and media,
visibility & treatment history

Appearance factors

Self-ideal appearance
discrepancy

salience/valence

Triggering events: e.g. *social activities*   Precipitating factors

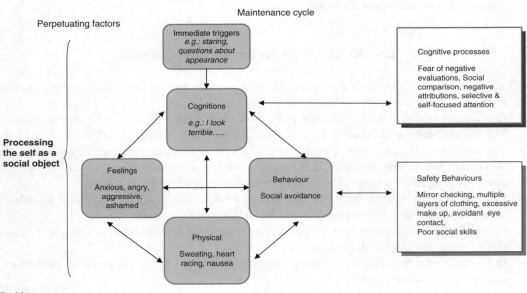

Maintenance cycle

Perpetuating factors

Immediate triggers
e.g.: staring,
questions about
appearance

Cognitions

e.g.: I look
terrible.....

Cognitive processes

Fear of negative
evaluations, Social
comparison, negative
attributions, selective &
self-focused attention

Processing
the self as a
social object

Feelings

Anxious, angry,
aggressive,
ashamed

Behaviour

Social avoidance

Safety Behaviours

Mirror checking, multiple
layers of clothing, excessive
make up, avoidant eye
contact,
Poor social skills

Physical

Sweating, heart
racing, nausea

Problems
Eg: *"Can't have a relationship"*

Resilience & Strength   Protective factors
Social acceptance and social support
General dispositional style (optimism)

Figure 3.7 Integrating the cognitive model of social phobia and ARC research findings into a CBT template.

make upward comparisons with those who appear to fit an idealized norm (or a younger or premorbid version of themselves) resulting in appearance discrepancy. For both groups, there will be a tendency to avoid situations where their 'defects' are exposed to the scrutiny of others, with the result that opportunities to test out competing explanations or to develop coping skills and revise underlying maladaptive beliefs are limited. Social support and a more positive optimistic dispositional style will be protective.

The way that appearance schemas are developed and maintained suggests the utility of CBT approaches. The maladaptive schema is explored and challenged through a gradual reduction in safety behaviours and modification in attentional processes, with the aim of promoting positive and adaptive schemas. The following framework integrates the cognitive model of social phobia, behavioural concepts and social skills with the ARC findings to provide a template for a cognitive behavioural formulation (Figure 3.7).

This structure will be used in the following chapters as a basis for describing treatment examples, with example formulations and therapeutic techniques linked to these cognitive processes.

Summary

The results of the ARC research programme have provided good evidence in support of a model linking cognitive processes to adjustment to disfiguring conditions and appearance anxiety. The rationale for extending the basic social skills and behavioural techniques of therapy to incorporate more cognitive approaches to intervention is therefore supported by the study as well by the evidence from related fields.

4

Clinical Assessment

Chapter Outline

CBT for Appearance Anxiety: Psychosocial Interventions for Anxiety Due to Visible Difference, First Edition.
Alex Clarke, Andrew Thompson, Elizabeth Jenkinson, Nichola Rumsey and Rob Newell.
© 2014 John Wiley & Sons, Ltd. Published 2014 by John Wiley & Sons, Ltd.

Eliciting the Problem

Although assessment is often thought of as primarily an information-gathering exercise, in practice it is also an intervention that provides opportunity for normalization and for raising morale. In addition, it is helpful to begin socialization to the therapeutic approach by punctuating the assessment sessions with summary statements that steer the individual towards a cognitive behavioural explanation. Thus, where an individual makes a statement which allows the emphasis to be put on beliefs about appearance, it is useful to explicitly comment on this. This makes the final formulation of the problem more accessible and less of a surprise for an individual who has not previously considered their problems in these terms. The following examples drawn from assessment sessions illustrate this.

Example 1

(After basic introductions)

T: Would you like to tell me something about your concerns about your breast and what has triggered your request for surgery now?
    I have got one breast bigger than the other and it is really getting to me
T: In what way do you mean?
    I can't do things with the children like take them swimming or go to the beach.
T: What would happen if you tried to do these things?
    I would feel really terrible as if everyone was looking at me
T: How strong is the feeling that everyone is looking at you?

Very strong. I feel as if everyone is staring. I know it sounds stupid – they probably aren't. There are people far worse; my cousin has the same problem even more obviously and no one takes any notice of her and it doesn't seem to bother her, but I don't feel like that. I feel as if everyone is looking at me. I just…. I don't know…

T: Well, it doesn't sound stupid, but it seems what you are saying is that being on the beach or going swimming feels very uncomfortable for you. Part of you knows that people are not staring, because you can see that they take no notice of other people who are worse, like your cousin – but it FEELS as if all eyes are on you.
    Yes that's it.
T: So it seems as if the problem is less to do with what other people are doing or what you actually look like, and more to do with how you FEEL, if you are in these situations.
    That's right.
T: Good that's helpful, I understand that now. Can you give me some more examples of things that you find difficult?

Example 2

T: You have said that everyone is staring at you and doing a double take when they meet you for the first time. How does that make you feel?
It makes me feel terrible, as if I am a freak. I just want to be normal so that I can stop being so uncomfortable.

T: Can you give me an example of the last time you felt like this?
Yes, I was standing in a queue at the airport and this chap kept turning round and looking at me. I couldn't get away, because I didn't want to lose my place.

T: What happened then?
I got more and more uncomfortable and then he turned round again and asked me what happened to my face.

T: How did that make you feel?
It was awful. I felt humiliated. I didn't know what to say. I ended up mumbling something about the dog.

T: What did he do?
He just shrugged and turned round again.

T: How did that make you feel?
Even worse. He didn't even say he was sorry about the dog or anything.

T: So he made you feel small and discounted. Is that right?
Yes. I just want to have surgery so it stops happening.

T: Let me see if I have this right. Since the dog bite, you find people tend to notice and stare and then ask you what happened?
Yes.

T: And is this humiliating because other people seem to think it is okay to ask you lots of questions and stare at you and this makes you feel angry or degraded?
Yes.

T: So it's not just that people stare and ask questions, is it the fact that these questions make you feel angry and humiliated that is so difficult.
Yes that's right.

T: I see. I understand. Can you give me another example of this kind of situation?

As the examples given indicate, these framing statements punctuate the assessment and can be drawn together in the formulation (see figure 4.1) and explanation of the nature of treatment.

It is useful to put together several examples and refer back to earlier examples so that the assessment becomes a process of guided discovery with the patient connecting each example, such as, for example, as given earlier in Example 1.

Ah ha. I see what you are saying. If I didn't let it get to me, like my cousin, it wouldn't be as big a problem.
T: That's right.

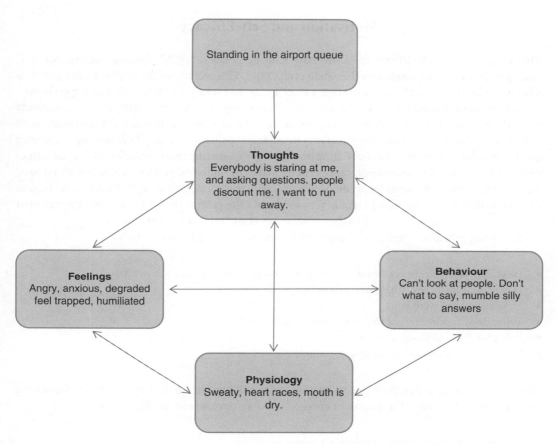

Figure 4.1 Developing the framework for maintaining factors from the first assessment for Example 2.

Summarizing

Punctuating the assessment session with summaries helps to show the therapist has listened, and can be one vehicle for demonstrating empathy. Crucially, it is also a vital part of socializing the individual into the therapeutic approach. Finally, putting forward a summary also invites a patient to correct the therapist if necessary so that misunderstandings do not occur. In these ways, summarizing demonstrates the collaborative approach inherent in Cognitive Behavioural Therapy (CBT). Summarizing is particularly useful in the following situations:

- In a one-to-one consultation or at the start of a session when the content of a previous session is revisited
- As a means of clarifying confusing or lengthy input, particularly with multiple issues
- When the patient has completed what they want to say
- If you are unclear about the information that is being given
- At the end of the session when plans for homework are being made.

Motivation and Self-Efficacy

This section is modified from the University College London (UCL) training package for self-management of chronic conditions (Newman et al., 2008). This section will be helpful for practitioners working at levels 1–3, and those working at level 4 may find it helpful for teaching or supervision.

It is important to assess motivation for behaviour change as part of the assessment process, particularly when the patient is being introduced to a cognitive formulation or where they perceive alternative ways of managing the problem. For example, trying to implement a CBT approach to managing disfiguring conditions whilst someone is on the waiting list for surgery is usually more difficult and may be unsuccessful. Changing beliefs about appearance is perceived to be unnecessary if the problem is 'about to be fixed'. For this reason it is sensible to complete physical interventions before psychological input begins, or to be within a programme where it is very evident to the patient that physical interventions offer only a partial solution. Confidence in their own ability is also critical for participants.

Identifying potential barriers to change can be achieved through the questions:

- How easy/difficult do you think it will be for you to carry out this behaviour?
- Have you done other things like this in the past?
- How successful were you?
- What do you think might make it easier for you now?
- What kind of help might you need?
- Is there someone who can help you to do this?

Bandura (1997) discusses people's expectations of behaviour change in health settings suggesting that people tend to assess three components of the behaviour and outcomes

1. What would happen if no behaviour change takes place?
2. What is the outcome of a given behaviour likely to be?
3. What is the extent to which the individual feels able to carry out the behaviour (this is often discussed in terms of self-efficacy or self-confidence)?

Self-efficacy is highly predictive of successful behaviour change, and low self-efficacy can be modified. Bandura outlines four approaches:

- *Direct experience of mastery.* In practice this means planning goals in simple steps so that they are easily achievable and people go through the experience of success early on. This is an important way of operationalizing the Appearance Research Collaboration (ARC) findings about the protective value of dispositional optimism. For people who are worried about appearing conspicuous, even the activity of coming to sessions is a success, particularly where it involves use of public transport and social exposure. Thus, anyone who is being seen for assessment is already likely to have overcome a problem that they have found difficult and has therefore achieved an early first success which can be reinforced and introduced into formulation to challenge assumptions about being ineffective or unable to change behaviour. A successful event can have a profound impact and this should not be surprising in that it effectively disproves what might be a long-standing hypothesis about being ineffective or incapable.

Example 3

Kieran had a congenital condition causing a visible facial disfigurement. His social skills were basic with poor conversation skills. However, his car broke down one night and he successfully talked to the mechanic who came to fix it by using the strategies we had worked on for starting and maintaining a conversation. He considered the things he might have in common with the car mechanic and decided to ask him about cars, with the result that they talked successfully whilst waiting for a breakdown van to arrive. This very early success allowed Kieran to substantially revise his assumptions about being unable to do things that others appeared to find easy.

- *Indirect or vicarious experience.* Bandura suggests that observation of mastery in other people is helpful. This needs to be presented in terms of a specific behaviour and not a behavioural style. There are several well-known role models, such as Simon Weston, who often are referred to spontaneously. However, this is usually in terms of, 'I could never be like Simon Weston. I think he is marvellous but I could never do that'. Patients are observing the whole 'Simon Weston package' rather than isolating a behaviour which they can emulate, hence, 'I cannot be like Simon Weston, but I can learn to answer questions about my appearance by using the same strategies that he uses' is an effective way of using a positive role model to increase (rather than decrease) self-efficacy. Examples that other patients have found helpful can be useful here, although it is important to present a range of ideas so that the patient can identify something that sounds concordant with their personality.
- *Verbal persuasion.* This is helpful in conjunction with the previous two approaches. Identifying other situations in which someone may have high self-efficacy modifies attributions such that it is the situation which is labelled problematic rather than the individual's behaviour. For example, someone who identifies themselves to be 'a good mother' can be introduced to the idea that they must be very capable and confident about the parent role. It can also be persuasive to illustrate CBT using examples from similar patients who were just as uncertain about their own capabilities in the first instance.
- *Management of mood states.* 'Stress' or anxiety can impact negatively on self-efficacy. It can therefore be helpful to plan goals, achievable at a time when there are no competing activities, for example, postponing an intervention so that someone is not in the middle of moving house, job or relationship. Helping people to manage their mood will make behaviour change appear more achievable. It might be very helpful to begin a therapeutic intervention by teaching skills such as relaxation training, distraction or anger management at the outset in the same way as we may teach strategies to deal with staring and asking questions.

Readiness for Change

The concept of readiness for change lies at the heart of the Trans-theoretical model (Proschaska & DiClemente, 1984). This model proposes a process underpinning behaviour change which has been found to be helpful in thinking about the steps that precede, predict and accompany behaviour change.

Proschaska and Diclemente propose five potential stages in the process of planning and effecting behaviour change:

- *Precontemplation*: not performing a behaviour and not intending to do so
- *Contemplation*: not performing a behaviour, but considering doing so
- *Preparation*: planning to perform the behaviour with some partially successful attempts
- *Action*: performing the behaviour regularly, but for less than 6 months
- *Maintenance*: performing the behaviour regularly for more than 6 months.

Different beliefs underpin each stage. For example, it is likely that at the early stages, the perceived costs of carrying out a given behaviour outweigh the benefits, whilst at the later stages this balance is likely to have reversed. Although, the stages suggest unidirectional movement, the research evidence is equivocal, and in practice, people move in either direction between stages, and in some cases may miss stages out altogether. Nevertheless, the concept of readiness for change is useful, and has been operationalized in health promotion settings using techniques derived from motivational interviewing (MI). The individual is introduced to the concepts within the Trans-theoretical model and asked to locate their own position with respect to the particular behaviour, for example, change in eating, weight loss, exercise and smoking cessation. In the context of working with people who have visible differences, MI techniques are useful in identifying potential barriers to change, identifying potential resources to help with change, goal setting and timing for interventions.

Rollnick et al. (2002) distinguish between different kinds of behaviour change intervention. The first, **brief advice**, tends to occur in opportunistic settings, for example, eliciting information and offering advice about smoking in a nonrelated medical consultation. In the context of appearance, this is how we might describe the advice given by a nurse about managing staring or questions from others, as part of a routine dressing change. **Behaviour change counseling** involves many of the skills of motivational interviewing including open questions and reflecting back information elicited, with the goal of providing a nonjudgmental discussion of changes that the individual may wish to consider. An example might be to ask questions about tanning as part of a routine dressing change after excision of a skin cancer. The aim is not to advise the patient to stop the behaviour but to provide an opportunity for themselves to reflect on their practice. **Motivational interviewing** would take this conversation a step further by selectively responding and reflecting back information to increase discrepancy between beliefs and diminish resistance to change. For example:

> Mary has had a small mole removed from her back. She is very anxious that this may be a melanoma. The histology is benign. Whilst her stitches are being removed the nurse uses the opportunity to talk to her about her anxiety about a cancer diagnosis and her very tanned appearance. He selectively reflects back statements which show that she is aware of the risks of tanning and the discrepancy between her repeated tanning appointments and her fear of cancer.

> In this example the nurse is responding to the cancer diagnosis. Suppose however, she had been concerned about the appearance of the scar when she went swimming? In this situation the nurse might share an experience of his own about scarring and give brief advice about nonavoidance, perhaps eliciting an example of another occasion when she had faced an anxiety-producing situation that she was attempted to avoid. This could be an everyday experience such as speaking in public.

This example is chosen to illustrate a common misunderstanding of motivational interviewing. MI is not and was never intended to be a stand-alone behaviour change technique. However, it is a useful tool in thinking about the timing of an intervention aimed at behaviour change and is often used to work with an individual to help them to identify the barriers to making a change. It is also a useful way of exploring valued directions or principles that can be useful in formulation.

Measurement Tools

Baseline measures are important to monitor change and measure outcomes. However, the measures used should relate to the underlying theoretical model in the case of research, and in the clinical setting, to the formulation of the problems with which a patient presents.

Measures have been developed in three broad research areas: body image, appearance and disfigurement, condition-specific research. In addition, there are a plethora of scales which measure generic psychological constructs which are relevant in both clinical and research settings. The following list is not exhaustive, but includes those scales which have been found to be particularly reliable and responsive to change.

Generic Measures of Psychological Constructs (as used in the ARC Study)

Dispositional Style
Optimism: To assess levels of optimism, a shortened four-item version of the Life Orientation Test-Revised (*LOT-R*; Scheier & Carver, 1987) was used. Responses were on a four-point Likert scale, ranging from 1 (strongly agree) to 4 (strong disagree). Total scale scores range from 4 to 20 with higher scores indicating a more optimistic outlook. The scale is designed to be viewed as measuring a continuum, with no 'cut-offs' for optimism or pessimism.

Social Networks: The scale utilized was a shortened four item version of the Short Form Social Support Questionnaire (Sarason et al., 1983). The quantity responses were considered primers and were not included in the analysis. Quality ratings ranged from 1 (very satisfied) to 6 (very dissatisfied), potential total scores range from 4 to 24, with higher scores representing greater satisfaction with their social network.

Feelings of Acceptance: To assess feelings of social acceptance, two items with a seven-point Likert scale ranging from 1 (not at all) to 7 (completely), assessed the extent to which the respondent felt accepted by their social group and society in general. Potential total scores range from 2 to 14, with higher scores indicating higher levels of acceptance.

Fears of Negative Evaluation: The Brief Fear of Negative Evaluation (FNE) scale (Leary, 1983) examines whether concern about other people's opinions regarding themselves is a characteristic of the individual. Twelve items are presented and participants are asked to score each statement from 1 (Not at all characteristic of me) to 5 (Extremely characteristic of me). Potential total scores range from 12 to 60 with high scores indicating a greater fear of negative evaluation. The authors cite adequate psychometric properties, with high levels of internal consistency ($\alpha = 0.90$), a 4-week test–retest reliability with a student population yielding a 0.75 reliability coefficient and acceptable levels of construct validity.

Social Comparison: The social comparison scale is a brief version of the Gibbons and Buunk (1999) Iowa–Netherlands Social Comparison measure (INCOMM). The scale measures frequency of social comparisons. Participants were asked to complete the scale in reference to their appearance and responses range from 1 (strongly disagree) to 5 (strongly agree) with higher total scores indicating a higher frequency of engagement in social comparison. Potential scale scores range from 11 to 55. The scale has good internal consistency (alpha = 0.83) and concurrent validity ($r = 0.88$). The authors also cite adequate test–retest reliability for 4 weeks and 1 year yielding correlation coefficients of 0.71 and 0.60, respectively. It should, however, be noted that the results of the ARC research programme suggest that the possibility of developing a measure more specifically tailored to appearance-specific comparisons should be explored (refer to Appendix A).

Positive and Negative Affect: The Positive and Negative Affect Schedule (PANAS; Watson et al. 1988) assesses how a respondent rates how they have felt over the past week in relation to a number of positive and negative emotions. Two subscales of negative (NA) and positive affect (PA) are a summed score of 10 questions. Scores for each subscale range from 10 to 50 with higher scores indicating greater identification with those feelings. The authors report convergent validity with several measures of affective disorder (Beck et al., 1961; Derogatis et al., 1974; Spielberger et al., 1970). The measure demonstrates adequate internal consistency ($\alpha = 0.80$ for PA; 0.85 for NA).

Anxiety and Depression: The Hospital Anxiety and Depression Scale (HADS; Zigmond & Snaith 1983) is a valid and reliable 14-item self-screening questionnaire for depression and anxiety in patients with physical health problems. For measures of mood, the scale scores range from 0 to 21, with higher scores indicating greater levels of anxious or depressed mood. A score of 0–7 for either subscale is regarded as being in the 'normal' range, a score of 8–10 is suggestive of the presence of moderate levels of anxiety or depression and a score of greater than 11 indicates 'caseness', a high likelihood that a person would be diagnosed to be suffering from clinical anxiety or clinical depression.

Literature reviews of the HADS (e.g. Bjelland et al., 2002) have found that the HADS has consistently shown adequate internal consistency over a range of studies, including those that have been translated into languages other than English. The measure also has good concurrent validity when compared to a range of other anxiety and depression scales ($r = 0.60–0.80$). In addition, the HADS has been used to good effect in previous studies with patients with facial disfigurements (Martin & Newell, 2004).

Anger/Hostility: The Refined Aggression Questionnaire (RAQ) (Bryant & Smith, 2001) is a brief version of Buss and Perry's (1992) Aggression Questionnaire and has been found to have similar robust/good psychometric properties (Bryant & Smith, 2001). This RAQ scale uses 12 items to assess whether aggressive behaviour is characteristic of the respondent, with responses ranging from 'strongly disagree' to 'strongly agree'. Divided into four factors (physical aggression, hostility, verbal aggression and anger), each factor has an individual score with lower scores representing lower levels of that particular type of aggression. Potential total scores range from 3 to 15 (after appropriate item score reversals).

Measures of Psychological Constructs Specifically Related to Appearance

DAS59 & DAS24; Social Anxiety and Social Avoidance

The Derriford Appearance Scale Short Form (*DAS24*; Carr et al., 2005), is a 24-item version of the *DAS59* (Carr et al., 2000) and is a measure of social anxiety and social avoidance in relation to appearance. It has been widely used in research related to disfigurement in the recent past. Norms derived from UK populations, also exist. Total scores range from 11 to 96 with lower scores representing low levels of social anxiety and social avoidance. It has adequate internal consistency ($\alpha = 0.92$), test–retest reliability ($r = 0.82$), concurrent validity with the *DAS59* ($r = 0.88$) and convergent validity with measures of anxiety, depression, social avoidance, social distress, fear of negative evaluation, negative affect and shame ($r = 0.45$).

CARVAL, Valence of Appearance

The CARVAL (Moss & Rosser 2012b) is a six-item valence questionnaire that measures how positively or negatively a participant evaluates their own appearance. Responses range from 1 (strongly disagree) to 7 (strongly agree) with higher total scores indicating a more positive self-evaluation of their own appearance. Potential scale scores range from 6 to 36. The scale has recently demonstrated good internal consistency (alpha $= 0.89$) and very good test–retest reliability with a student population at 3 months ($r = 0.95$).

CARSAL, Salience of Appearance

The CARSAL (Moss & Rosser, 2012b) measures the extent to which appearance is part of a person's working self-concept or how important it is to a person (salience). Responses range from 1 (strongly disagree) to 7 (strongly agree) with higher total scores indicating appearance forming a greater part of one's self concept. Potential scale scores range from 6 to 36. The scale has recently demonstrated good internal consistency ($\alpha = 0.86$) and good test–retest reliability with a student population at 3 months ($r = 0.89$).

PADQ, Physical Appearance Discrepancy

The PADQ (Altabe & Thompson, 1995) distinguishes the discrepancy between how a person perceives they look and how they or their significant others would ideally like them to look ('ideal' discrepancy) and how they ought or should look in relation to duty, responsibility, or obligation ('should' discrepancy). A large 'ideal' discrepancy is associated with feelings of disappointment, dissatisfaction, shame and embarrassment due to unfulfilled desires and a belief they have lost esteem in the opinion of others. A high 'should' discrepancy is associated with fear, feeling threatened, resentment and guilt, often due to the belief that they have transgressed the moral standard of either themselves or significant others. The two subscales of 'ideal' and 'should' discrepancy consist of four items each, with responses ranging from 'not at all different' to 'extremely different', and yielding a potential total score for each subscale ranging from 4 to 28, with a higher score indicating greater discrepancy.

The following measures may also be useful in working with this patient group.

Measures of Body Image

Body Image Quality of Life Inventory
The Body Image Quality of Life Inventory (BIQLI) (Cash & Fleming, 2002) was developed and empirically evaluated with 116 college women. A 19-item assessment tool, it has good internal consistency and examines a range of body image behaviours including eating and weight management. It converges significantly with other measures of body image evaluation including body image investment.

Appearance Schemas Inventory
The Appearance Schemas Inventory (ASI-R) (Cash et al., 2004) assesses body image investment (salience) or the psychological importance that people place on the appearance of the body. Two related constructs are included: (i) self-evaluative salience, or the importance of appearance to self-worth and (ii) motivational salience, the extent to which the individual is motivated to maintain or change their appearance. The ASI-R has been used in normal populations and with eating disorders.

Measures of Psychological Constructs Specifically Related to a Condition Type

Head and Neck Cancer
See Pusic et al. (2007) for a useful systematic review of quality of life scales which have been validated for use in head and neck cancer.

The BREAST-Q
The Breast-Q (Pusic et al., 2009) is a 91-item (and therefore somewhat lengthy to complete) patient-reported outcome measure to assess the impact of breast surgery (breast reduction, augmentation and reconstruction after cancer). There are six different dimensions: overall outcome, satisfaction with breasts, process of care, psychosocial wellbeing, physical wellbeing and sexual wellbeing. With pre- and postsurgery scales, it was developed using Rasch methodology and has excellent psychometric properties.

Dermatology Quality of Life Index
The Dermatology Quality of Life Index (DQLI) (Finlay & Khan, 1994) is a practical questionnaire technique for routine clinical use. Standardized on 200 patients with different skin diseases and with good psychometric properties, it records the impact of skin diseases and their treatment on day to day life.

Patient Scar Assessment Questionnaire
The Patient Scar Assessment Questionnaire (PSAQ: Durani et al., 2009) is a 39-item patient-reported outcome measure with five dimensions: scar consciousness, scar symptoms, scar appearance, satisfaction with scar appearance and satisfaction with scar symptoms. It has good psychometric properties.

Skindex
Originally a 61-item patient-reported outcome measure (PROM), Skindex (Chren et al., 2001) has been refined into a 29-item scale with good psychometric properties. It has three core dimensions: symptoms, emotions and functioning

Cosmetic Procedure Screening Questionnaire
The Cosmetic Procedure Screening Questionnaire (COPS; Veale et al., 2012) is designed as a screening measure for Body dysmorphic disorder to be used in cosmetic procedure settings. It can also be used to assess severity of symptoms. It is also available in a slightly different wording as a measure of body image.

Body Dysmorphic Disorder (BDD)

A number of questionnaires have been developed to aid the assessment of BDD and these may be useful in assessing the benefits of receiving surgery in situations where the objective disfigurement is mild or not noticeable. However, these questionnaires have some limitations and should not be used alone as the sole factor in deciding whether or not to pursue medical treatment (see Cororve & Gleaves, 2001).

Body Dysmorphic Disorder Questionnaire
Body Dysmorphic Disorder Questionnaire (Phillips, 1996) is a screening measure for BDD which is widely used and has excellent psychometric properties. Standardized on a general population, it has been used in cosmetic surgery and psychiatric settings.

Cosmetic Procedure Screening Questionnaire
The Cosmetic Procedure Screening Questionnaire (COPS; Veale et al., 2011) is designed as a screening measure for Body dysmorphic disorder to be used in cosmetic procedure settings. It can also be used to assess severity of symptoms. It is also available in a slightly different wording as a measure of body image.

Core Clinical Dataset

Clinical intervention depends on record keeping and behavioural monitoring, and there are distinct advantages in being over- rather than under-inclusive in terms of baseline measures. Scales like the *DAS24* have high face validity in addition to their strong scale and psychometric properties. These measures can also stimulate and facilitate discussion. Many people report relief that their difficulties are shared by others, particularly those who have encountered previous therapists unfamiliar with body image problems, demonstrably, the typical expression voiced by patients when reading the items is: 'this is me – this is exactly what I do'. In any clinical assessment, people often have an over-whelming emotional response when being asked about their problem, perhaps even being surprised at being asked. This is particularly common when people have not had an opportunity to talk about it before. In practical terms, this surprise or emotional reaction may also make it hinder an individual's ability to describe the course and impact of their problem. Thus, measurement tools have the additional function therefore, of ensuring that the assessment has been thorough. Scope for people to add additional comments if they have failed to mention something important, or more commonly, cannot remember whether they mentioned it or not, is available.

Appearance concern can also affect intimate behaviour and relationships, and people are often reluctant to spontaneously volunteer such information about this area of their life. However, people do tend to provide information about intimacy and relationships if they are directly asked. A scale to measure the impact of appearance concerns on intimacy is currently being developed as part of the ARC research programme to address these behaviours, and the use of this measure may well facilitate the discussion of this topic.

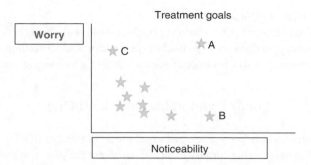

Figure 4.2 Noticeability and worry graph. 'A' has ranked their appearance as highly noticeable and is worried about it. 'B' ranks their appearance as noticeable but is not particularly concerned. 'C' is very worried about their appearance but acknowledges this is not particularly noticeable to others.

All the scales discussed can be used to provide repeated assessments and consequently can be used to measure progress. In practice, simple noticeability and worry scales have a high correlation with both the *DAS24* and HADS scales and such idiographic measures lend themselves well to recording change in each session:

How noticeable is your condition to other people? (0–10, where 0 is not noticeable and 10 is very noticeable)
How much do you worry about it? (0–10).

Worry is clearly linked to appearance anxiety and our experience in clinical practice is that noticeability is strongly correlated with worry. This can be understood in terms of the anticipation of negative evaluation from others feeding back into anxiety and stimulating safety behaviours and avoidance:

The worry and noticeability scales provide a particularly useful visual analogue of change when plotted against each other as given in Figure 4.2.

Regular Subjective Measures of Frequency for Events, Thoughts and Feelings

The measurement of subjective units of distress (SUDs) is easily understood by patients practicing behavioural experiments, and daily recordings of behavioural measures such as 'number of hours spent outside the house' are very simple measures and responsive to change. These feature as a helpful way of collecting relevant data throughout the treatment process, as well as a powerful source of reinforcement for patients. (Collecting data only at the beginning and end of treatment provides no information about the process of change – whether incremental or characterized by sudden shifts, for example, when a strategy becomes mastered or associated with a key achievement.)

Patient-reported outcome measures (PROMS) are becoming increasingly important in NHS settings and in addition to monitoring process from session to session, a full collection of data is important at the final session. As a minimum, assessment of the *DAS24* and HADs, with additional scales (e.g. an aggression scale) where relevant are recommended. Specific reporting of goal achievement is also important where goals have been set (see following text).

Goal Setting

Goals should be simple and achievable but also challenging enough for someone to see that they are making progress. They should be negotiated rather than imposed so that they are perceived to be relevant, and patient-defined goals are vital to assessing the progress of treatment and providing relevant accurate feedback to both patient and therapist. Moreover, goal-setting provides an opportunity for collaboration and socialization to the therapeutic model. Eliciting people's expectations and intentions about specific goals is a way of working out whether each specific goal is appropriate, for example by asking the individual:

- How likely is it that you will carry out this behaviour? (0–10)
- How likely is it that you will be successful? (0–10).

Where scores are very low, further collaboration may be needed to arrive at an attainable goal. Other useful goal measures include desirability, difficulty and progress:

- How much difference would achieving this goal make to your life? (0–10)
- How difficult is this goal for you currently? (0–10)
- How much progress have you made towards achieving this goal (0–10).

All these types of goal measurement offer therapeutic opportunities in themselves, as they allow the therapist to address issues of:

- Perceptions about self-efficacy and the likelihood of success
- Relevance of the goal and impact of the problem on the patient's life
- Provision of feedback and reinforcement for attempts already made to address the problem.

The SMART Acronym

The SMART acronym is a useful guide for goal formulation. Goals should be:

- **S**pecific
- **M**easurable
- **A**chievable
- **R**elevant
- **T**ime limited.

Distinguishing between short- and long-term goals is vital. People often fail at behaviour change because long-term goals are too distant in the future, how they are to be achieved is not clear and the steps to achieve them are not specific. In contrast, short-term goals are highly specific and describe the desired behaviour in detail. Efforts should also be made so that they are achievable from the person's current status.

Examples of goals for someone with socially avoidant behaviour, resulting from visible disfigurement, might be:

- *Long-term goal*: Socialize more with other people.
  (Vague, nonspecific and not achievable from this point).
  N.B. Interestingly, advice from other people is often couched in these terms.

That is, 'You just need to get out more, get a life, stop worrying', etc, which is impossible for the individual to achieve without some short-term goals set out towards achieving this.

- *Short-term goal*: Write down a clear response to the question: 'What happened to your face'? Practice this twice.

(Specific and achievable within week 1)

All sessions should begin with feedback about the previous week's goals. Successes should be reinforced and difficulties investigated, with goals being renegotiated. In the context of behavioural experiments, any result provides important feedback. For this reason, the only way in which a person can 'fail' in a CBT intervention is by not attempting the behaviour or by not coming to appointments.

Carrying out a behaviour that has less-than-ideal consequences provides important information, and for this reason, the phrase 'No such thing as failure only feedback' is a useful one. For this reason it is important to link short-term goals to long-term goals and to make sure the patient is clear about the link. In this given example, the therapist might seek from the patient an explanation of how being able to answer specific questions about their face is important in enabling them to get out and meet people. It is also useful to negotiate at any one time, a series of short-term goals of differing difficulty. Patients do not necessarily share therapists' views about the positive results of negative experiences, and ensuring that there is always an achievable short-term goal enhances engagement with more difficult experiments.

Challenges in Treatment for Appearance-Related Problems

Introducing a Biopsychosocial Model

Clinical health psychologists generally face considerable challenges in providing formulation of health problems, which are based on a biopsychosocial, rather than a medical model. Chronic pain management is a good example of a setting where the therapist is working with a patient to provide a formulation of their pain, which enables an increase in activity and reduction of disability. In the same way that people may take some time to understand that treatment does not involve 'fix-it' solutions, which 'take away' the pain, people with appearance-related concerns may take some time to appreciate that they can manage their appearance without 'fix it' solutions that alter their appearance. This applies equally across the range of appearance-altering conditions from those who worry about small breast size to people with anxiety about an objective disfigurement (see treatment examples in Chapter 7).

Depending on the referral route, the psychological approach to managing problems with appearance may also be perceived as a 'second best' alternative. Most people who are treated for appearance concerns will do so having first sought medical intervention. Some of these patients will have been disappointed by the outcome or limitations of treatment. Many will have drawn their knowledge of these interventions from sources which stimulate overoptimistic expectations of outcome (e.g. scarless healing). Even people who understand the formulation of the problem in psychological terms may still seek out potential new 'cures' on the Internet, or maintain a pattern of seeking additional surgical opinions.

Referrals from other health professionals may indicate a similar lack of familiarity with the limitations of surgical procedures. Since GPs do not do plastic surgery training, it is not surprising that they do not have a comprehensive knowledge of the risks and complications or surgical procedures. This may inadvertently reinforce the patients' expectations.

In mental health settings, there is an increasing evidence base that psychological approaches to management provide the most effective intervention for mild to moderate presentations of common mood disturbance (see NICE guidelines for anxiety and depression: www.NICE.org.uk). Sharing such information with patients can help raise morale – 'I appreciate that it feels as if nothing can change unless it's fixed, there is now substantial evidence that psychological treatment can reduce anxiety and depression associated with long-term conditions to the point that such treatment is recommended by the Department of Health'.

Treatment 'buy-in'

Factors that are helpful in motivating people to work within a psychological model are:

- *Easy access to services.* A multidisciplinary service provides the opportunity to meet people at the same time that they are referred for a surgical opinion. This is invaluable in reinforcing the importance of a psychological approach. Even where a full assessment cannot be made, it provides the opportunity for the psychologist to frame the approach rather than someone less familiar with it. Feedback from patients often stresses the importance of meeting someone at the outset, 'I probably would not have come back if I had just been sent an appointment'. However, if not available, the following approaches are helpful.
- *Written information.* A generic leaflet or website address, describing the service offered and providing a simple explanation for a psychological approach, provides a reinforcing message for people to take home and counteracts any misrepresentation by other health professionals. Similarly, information about managing common problems (e.g. staring), although usually provided later in treatment, is sometimes helpful for people who have difficulty understanding what is being proposed, or where time is limited, in demonstrating that the therapist understands the kinds of problems that someone is experiencing.
- *Examples of other patients treated.* Presenting examples of similar problems with good outcomes can be helpful. However, it is important to stress to new patients, that most people engaging in a CBT programme in this setting are sceptical to begin with. Indeed, it is helpful to encourage people to voice their scepticism and to actively encourage people to disclose if they feel the approach is not working. Periodically seeking such feedback provides opportunities for heading off therapeutic ruptures and dropout.
- *Examples of relevant research.* Illustrating the role of psychological factors in patient experience is often facilitated by providing examples of relevant research studies (e.g. Strenta & Kleck, 1985). This particular study illustrates the role of expectation in obtaining confirmatory information about an (inaccurate) hypothesis – 'everybody is staring at me because of my appearance'. It has the additional benefit that it neatly illustrates the CBT approach, of setting up an experiment to test a hypothesis. Finally, the implications of the study should also be very easily understood. Nichola Rumsey's work, which illustrates the importance of behaviour in influencing judgements about other people in first encounters, is also a good introduction to people demonstrating why psychology is important in managing a visible difference in appearance (Bull & Rumsey, 1988).
- *Initial goal setting.* People do not need to fully adjust their expectations about treatment in a first session. The goals are to get them to come back so their problems can be better understood, to have a detailed formulation developed and a treatment plan outlined. A helpful goal for a first session is to suggest that people consider the possibility that a psychological approach may be helpful. Rather than rule it out completely, most people are prepared to take away literature to read and to make a further appointment, particularly if they have had the chance to discuss the approach with a behaviour specialist in the clinic.

5

Social Skills and Coping Strategies

Chapter Outline

CBT for Appearance Anxiety: Psychosocial Interventions for Anxiety Due to Visible Difference, First Edition.
Alex Clarke, Andrew Thompson, Elizabeth Jenkinson, Nichola Rumsey and Rob Newell.
© 2014 John Wiley & Sons, Ltd. Published 2014 by John Wiley & Sons, Ltd.

The use of social skills and coping strategies is underpinned by a 'target stressor' or behavioural model as outlined in the previous chapter. These techniques are useful both as part of a level-4 intervention delivered by a Cognitive Behavioural Therapy (CBT) specialist, but also as part of a simple 'target stressors' approach as delivered at levels 1–3 of the stepped-care model. For example, Clarke and Cooper (2001) reported that clinical nurse specialists after training identified themselves as able to deliver psychosocial support for people with disfigurements. The development of strategies to answer questions about appearance was a central part of this training. This chapter is therefore primarily intended to inform intervention for practitioners providing support at levels 1–3, although practitioners working at level 4 will also find these approaches helpful to integrate into CBT psychotherapy.

Conceptually, a target stressors approach is underpinned by classical behaviour theory where the repeat exposure to an aversive stimulus results in gradual extinction of an anxious or avoidant response. The modification of underlying cognitive processes is not a target for change within this model, although in clinical practice, providing support to change behaviour typically also leads to some degree of change at a cognitive level.

In a CBT model, behaviour change is related to recognition of and systematic challenge to the unhelpful thinking styles that maintain maladaptive core beliefs and the underlying schemas. Maintenance of behaviour change is therefore dependent on change in the underlying beliefs, and the therapist is continually helping the individual to link back to and revise core beliefs and assumptions.

Example 1

Geraldine has very severe burn scarring resulting from a house fire. The scarring is visible all over her body. One of the practical problems she has is keeping cool in the summer since she cannot lose heat though her skin via sweating. The easiest thing is to swim. She does so several times a day when it is very hot. She knows that people notice her scarring and sometimes ask about it. She has therefore developed some good answers to questions, which give a minimum of information, but satisfy other people's curiosity. 'I know I am unusual, and I understand that people are curious, but I don't intend to tell them my life story'. Geraldine is confident, successful and good fun to be with. Her appearance is not a barrier to living a full life.

This is the goal for all our patients, developing good social skills, taking the lead when other people seem uncomfortable and allowing for the fact that curiosity is inevitable when confronted with something new. These are all positive ways of adjusting to a visible difference. For many people, an introduction to these principles is enough. Supported by written materials, this can be adequate in providing a basis for building up a set of skills or tools suitable for different situations. Kleve et al. (2002) reported a mean of three sessions being required for patients referred to a specialist outpatient Appearance Centre (OUTLOOK) following injury or disfigurement. This reflects the very high number of one-stop interventions, and although many people will need a longer intervention described in the following chapter, others very quickly adapt, particularly where they already have good social skills.

Staring, Questions, Comments and Loss of Anonymity

Staring by others is commonly reported. The human brain has evolved to take note of anything that is unusual or outside our experience. Babies and children are constantly gazing at objects and people as they build up a picture of the world. Madera and Hebl (2012) report that attentional bias results in peoples concentration being drawn to a disfigurement in a way that leads them to recall fewer facts relating to what the person with a disfigurement said. This suggests that coding an unusual image takes longer and explains the subjective experience that people maintain gaze in a way which is experienced as intrusive. Most of us will notice, or do a 'double take', when we see someone who looks unusual. It is important to note that, in the majority of instances, this 'curiosity' is an automatic response without a value judgement. However, it can feel like a problem, if it is accompanied by comments, questions or a whispered aside to a companion.

Questions are common. Curiosity is often followed by the impulse to ask more. 'I hope you don't mind me asking – but what happened to you'? There are not many people with a visible difference who are unfamiliar with this response from other people. Choosing how to answer is important in maintaining a sense of control and determining whether the encounter is going to be a positive one.

Comments directed to the person or about them to others are often infuriating even if kindly meant. 'I think you are so brave dear, coming out when you look like that' is designed to be reassuring, but can feel like (and sometimes is) patronizing and unhelpful. 'People like you should stay at home' is understandably experienced as a negative evaluation.

Loss of anonymity is one way of summing up this experience. Most people underestimate the luxury of being able to walk down a crowded street and know that no one will take any notice. The sense that we stand out, and that others notice us or pay us special attention can be uncomfortable. Note that people whose faces are well known, who have become celebrities, often complain about this kind of intrusion. Attention does not have to be negative to impact in a negative way – it simply needs to be unsolicited or outside individual control. This fear is extremely common for most people with a noticeable disfigurement and may lead to social avoidance. In any event, the loss of anonymity is burdensome and may be particularly so when an individual has not developed a series of quick comments to address such social intrusions.

Note also, that for many people with body image concerns, it is the anticipated fear of standing out, of appearing unusual or even 'ugly' that preoccupies them and prevents them from fully participating in social activities. For someone with a visible disfigurement, the fear that someone will notice is often enacted. People do notice, they are curious and they do ask questions. But what we need to do to help our patients is to help them to see that this is manageable. In treating people with a visible difference, we work on the basis that intrusions have a high probability of occurrence and that learning to manage them is the most successful form of coping. Mastering these skills is not difficult – Robinson et al. (1996) demonstrated substantial gains in social skills in a 2-day group workshop with social anxiety reduced, and these gains were maintained at 6 month follow-up.

Making the Most of Appearance

One common mistake people can make in response to altered appearance is to think that because they have a visible difference it is not worth bothering with other aspects of appearance. But people do make assumptions based on appearance, and if people perceive a strong message that people have written themselves off, they rapidly lose interest. Modifying appearance is a tool that everyone uses to express their mood and identity. Choosing the 'right' clothes for an interview or to fit in with a peer group are simple ways of promoting social inclusion. Good grooming is often perceived as a proxy for being well organized and efficient. The message that 'it is the inside that counts' is a naïve approach to success in societies which are becoming more competitive and have the means to change appearance.

So – people DO need to have their hair cut or styled regularly. They DO need to dress in a way that is appropriate for their lifestyle. Wearing appropriate clothes, looking tidy and ensuring that they do not have food spilt all down them is important. Personal hygiene should be good. Making an effort to fit into the peer group will prevent people being positioned as an outsider. In this context, it is important to note that sometimes clothes or make-up designed to be helpful or to disguise a feature can have the opposite effect. Baseball hats and hoodies may be particularly unhelpful in certain contexts as UK society associates them with aggressive behaviour and people can easily look threatening, especially if wearing them is associated with poor eye contact. Similarly, wearing very large jackets in the summer draws attention to people rather than disguising problems and unskilled use of camouflage creams can make a facial disfigurement more, rather than less, obvious. (See section 'Manipulating Safety Behaviours' in Chapter 6 for more details.) Finally, it should be noted that poor grooming can be seen as avoidance behaviour in just the same way as physical avoidance of social situations or the use of other safety-seeking behaviours. Neglecting grooming displays at least two avoidance responses: behavioural avoidance through trying to make the self less noticeable and cognitive avoidance through a pretence that appearance is not important. As well as emphasizing the positive aspects of appropriate grooming, the therapist needs to explore the cognitions which are involved in poor grooming. The same comments apply also to the discussion of posture, smiling, eye contact and verbal behaviour in the next sections.

Developing a Positive Approach to Visible Difference

Posture, Smiling and Eye Contact

Posture
How people stand is important. If they tend to look down and away from people, their behaviour is not open and inviting. Role play and practice of walking in a relaxed and upright way can begin within a session and then can be practiced at home. Involving partners or friends in this kind of approach can make the exercises seem less onerous, provides support and prompts to tackle more challenging goals.

Smiling
Sometimes when people have a facial condition, their face either moves asymmetrically (more on one side than the other), or for some people without a facial nerve at all, they are unable to smile or try to avoid it. People tend to be unaware that other facial features are important in smiling and that by restricting the mouth they are also failing to give a positive message with their eyes. Using film, homework where they observe smiling on television or providing an educational session of how the facial musculature works, can all encourage people to reduce the attempts not to smile. Using other forms of communication – commenting on the situation or using touch can be additional ways of signaling pleasure for those without any form of facial movement. For those with other forms of facial disfigurement, smiling can be used to reassure others in a social situation. Since, from the observer's perspective, much of the problem in visible disfigurement is focused on the reciprocal inhibition of social behaviour, simply smiling provides a first step towards positive engagement with others.

Eye Contact

Eye contact is a vital component of communication with others. It is used to signal interest, as an indicator of listening, and of whose turn it is to speak in a conversation. Avoiding the gaze of others will always come across as negative, because it gives a clear signal of reluctance to engage in any kind of contact with them. It is very easy to misinterpret other people's gaze as intrusive – staring at the disliked feature – when in fact people are simply trying to engage attention. There are many books and information resources about improving social skills. Changing Faces publish information and run workshops, and have a website (http://www.changingfaces.org.uk) where additional information can be downloaded (see section 'Sources of Support', Chapter 10).

Developing Verbal Skills

Learning to Have a Conversation

People often describe the fear of going blank in social settings – being unable to think of what to say. It is more likely to happen as a result of self-focused attention and a preoccupation with how others are responding – whether they have noticed or are about to comment on appearance – rather than listening and being actively involved in the content of what people are saying. Learning to focus on the other person can therefore bring multiple benefits – it breaks the cognitive self-attentional bias and at the same time shows interest in the other person which encourages positive interaction.

Developing verbal skills is a matter of practice, but there are some simple things that will help. First, it is helpful to develop skills for listening. What do other people talk about in different settings? The easiest place to start is at work or in a situation where people have lots in common with colleagues or are with a group of people that they know well. Asking people about themselves is a very productive way to get a conversation started. So asking if people live nearby, what they do for living, if their children go to the local school and similar questions are all ways of initiating a conversation. Similarly, topical subjects are things that other people will have a view about. The result of the latest big football match, the election, price of petrol, or news headlines are good places to start, in order to get used to practicing conversing and focusing outwards.

It can be a good idea to identify something about the other person that can be used as a question if there is a pause in the conversation. So, noticing if someone is wearing a particular piece of jewellery or an interesting tie is worth doing. T-shirts often have slogans or flags or something on which people can comment. If someone looks brown they may well have been on holiday. (Note that in this situation, people are responding to something about an individual that is unusual and therefore an opportunity for getting them to talk about themselves.) Trying to help people to use the same tactic – using appearance as an opportunity for social interaction – is a useful demonstration that comments about their own appearance are not necessarily negative, but simply an effective socialization strategy.

Answering Questions About Appearance

Questions from other people are likely and are typically related to curiosity and not necessarily indicators of negative evaluation. However, it is helpful if people can learn to take control and do not feel trapped into giving away more information than is comfortable. Telling 'the whole story' to other people is not necessary.

Developing a three-step approach to answering questions about appearance can involve graded amounts of information from an answer that gives enough information to close down questioning to an answer that gives the full medical history. For example, consider answering the question:

Q: What happened to your face?
A: I was in a house fire. It started at 2.00 in the morning and the first thing I remember is waking up and all the heat and the noise. My mother ran into the room...etc.

This kind of answer is full, detailed and often lengthy. Its relevance in new or short encounters is minimal. Yet interestingly, for people who worry about answering questions about their appearance, it is often the only one they ever use – with the result that they feel conspicuous and as if their private life is an open book to anyone who wants to know. Not surprisingly, they dread that opening line 'I hope you don't mind me asking, but...'

The second answer is the complete opposite. It is a simple response which closes down the questioning firmly, whilst giving very little or no detail:

Q: What happened to your face?
A: That's a long story. I'll tell you about it sometime.

Or

A: It was years ago – you don't want to hear all about that.

Together with a firm eye contact and a smile – both these answers work superbly at turning off the questioning. They are particularly effective if attention is then switched to the questioner, for example:

Q: What happened to your face?
A: That's a long story. I'll tell you about it sometime. I hear you've just come back from America. How long were you there?

The third way of answering the question is to give a more general response – about the condition rather than about the individual. For example:

Q: What happened to your face?
A: I was injured in a fire. Luckily, now that smoke alarms are available, injuries like mine are far less common.

It is useful to get patients to write down some of these alternatives, and work with them to use the examples to develop personalized responses that apply to their own situation. Flashcards can be used to encourage out-of-session practice which should generally be set up in a graded fashion. With graded practice, people are able to take much better control of the social encounter. There are no right and wrong answers, although some answers tend to invite more questioning. For example, look at these answers to the question:

Q: Why are you wearing that scarf on your head?
A: I have my reasons!

Or

A: I've had a small operation and I am keeping the stitches covered.

The first answer invites all kinds of speculation about what is under the scarf. The second answer gives a very simple explanation. Any further questioning can be managed with the 'turn off the questions' approach described.

Answering children's questions is very straightforward. They say exactly what they think, but are equally happy with a simple explanation:

Q: Why have you got a funny arm?
A: It's because I was burned in a fire. So don't play with matches will you?

Sometimes humour can be helpful. However, this has to be congruent with the individual's self-perception and habitual social behaviour. If they do not usually use humour, then this will come across as awkward and contrived. It is always worth exploring but only if people are comfortable with the idea that they are in control and that this is about laughing together and not being laughed at.

Tom, who is in his early 20s, was recently asked how he had lost a finger. To which he responded, 'it wouldn't fit up my nose so I cut it off!'

This is a great reply! It made the questioner laugh, gave nothing away and made Tom feel comfortable and in control. As people become more confident and as they develop their own answers, there will be certain favourites that are used again and again, and then some new ideas that are added in. The aim is to have them 'on the tip of the tongue' – hence the benefit of practice. Sometimes people can feel ambushed by the question that comes in the middle of a conversation about something else, but provided they have an answer ready, the situation can be managed positively.

Managing Staring

Sometimes it is easier to answer questions than to be in a setting where someone is staring, but does not ask. Often when they get into conversation, the curiosity will pass. People often become firm friends with others without ever discussing why one of them has a visible difference and over time it simply becomes insignificant. However, sometimes the staring can be very intrusive. Sitting on a bus or tube with a pair of eyes, which keep drifting back to your face is annoying. A firm stare back is often very effective. Or a question:

Have we met before? You seem to be trying to remember who I am.

An aggressive response, though sometimes tempting, is not usually helpful.

Distraction is another very easy way to focus away from the situation. A newspaper or book to read, particularly if it can be held up to interrupt the staring is helpful. A 'shoe review' in which the individual estimates who has the most expensive trainers or exotic sandals is a simple distraction. Visualization methods to imagine shrinking down the person into a tiny little figure or putting them into a different context (in their pyjamas) are all strategies which allow people to feel more in control of the social situation. As they develop a portfolio of responses which are practiced and are successful in social situations, so social anxiety and avoidance is reduced.

For people with severe social anxiety, simple distraction and visualization are less likely to be successful. They may well have used such tactics in the past and found them ineffective as they amount to a kind of avoidance which actually may *increase* anxiety. For these patients, focusing on the external situation and applying coping tactics which enable them to remain in the situation and reframe it are more effective.

Changing Faces (see section 'Sources of Support', Chapter 10) is a very good resource for more ideas about managing staring, comments and questions. In addition to written information, they have a website and video materials and are developing online interactive programmes, which help with remote practice of different social situations before exposure in vivo.

Putting it into Practice

The key to being successful in managing the social intrusion consequence of a visible difference is to take a proactive approach to social situations, work on developing social skills and then practice them in a graded way. For example:

> Eileen had been bitten by a dog and had a very visible 'v' shaped scar on her cheek. She was a very stylish woman in her 30s who liked clothes and make-up and was devastated by this change in her appearance. She stopped work, stayed at home and became increasingly depressed. Her greatest fear was that if she went out, someone would notice her face and ask about it.

Treatment started with developing some answers to questions. Eileen settled on a very simple answer:

Q: What happened to your face?
A: I was bitten by that Alsatian at number 32.

Having decided on this tactic, a 'hierarchy' of fared situations was constructed as in Figure 5.1, and subjective units of distress (SUDs) were recorded using a 0–1 scale.

Eileen very quickly managed number 1. She then spent a week going up to the shop and back every day but without going in. Gradually, her SUDs score dropped and her anticipatory anxiety about what would happen if she went into the shop got less. She then went in and picked up a paper and came home. She repeated this twice more and then went up to number 3 and so on.

10	Go back to work
9	Go to the supermarket
8	Go out with the family at the weekend
7	Invite a good friend back to the house for tea
6	Go to the corner shop and browse for groceries
5	Go to the corner shop and ask for a newspaper
4	Go the corner shop, pick up a paper and offer a £5 note
3	Go the corner shop with exact money for paper so I don't have to speak
2	Walk to corner shop but don't go in
1	Fetch the milk bottles in from the front step

Figure 5.1 Development of a hierarchy of feared situations for behavioural exposure.

Eileen successfully completed this treatment and went back to work, but there is an interesting addendum to Eileen's story. When she got to number 6, she waited patiently in the queue rehearsing her answer to the question she was expecting – and nothing happened. In the end, she got so tired of waiting that she pointed out her dog bite herself.

> What do you think of this then? I was bitten by the dog at number 32!

The shop keeper had noticed, but had politely refrained from asking. But taking control of the situation had lessened Eileen's anxiety that she felt able to introduce the topic of her face to a stranger. She described this as being very different from how she imagined herself to be at the start of her treatment.

Taking the Initiative in Social Encounters

Responding to staring and questions with well-rehearsed responses is a very effective, but ultimately reactive strategy. Being proactive in social settings provides a heightened sense of self-efficacy and strengthens control beliefs. Examples of this approach include:

- walking positively into a room rather than waiting for another to make the initial overture
- opening a conversation rather than waiting for others to start
- introducing the subject of a disfigurement in a casual way if the conversation allows it.

For example:

> You are looking very brown – have you been on holiday? One of the problems with a skin graft is keeping out of the sun.

This invites a question, but in a way which is controlled.

A similar setting is interviews. Where people believe that their appearance is preventing them gaining employment, then they might manage other people's expectations as follows:

> You will notice I have a condition which affects my face. I have developed my social skills to help manage this and I think you will find I am very good at putting other people at ease.

Or

> I have a facial condition, but this is a long-standing issue and does not mean that I will need time off for hospital appointments.

Humour too has its place:

> You will notice that I have a visible difference. The great advantage of this is that people can always remember who they spoke to.

Managing Anger and Developing Assertiveness

Anger

Within the model developed by the Appearance Research Collaboration (ARC) research programme (Figure 3.5, section 'The ARC Framework of Adjustment to Disfiguring Conditions', Chapter 3), anger is represented as an outcome which may result when the individual is unable to develop a positive coping response and may also be understandable where someone has experienced humiliation.

A common trigger for an angry response may be the perception of being stared at or comments being made by other people. Sometimes it is very clear that people are the subject of unwanted attention. At other times, ideas of self reference may arise when cognitive errors lead to incorrect attributions for other people's behaviour.

> Jeff has a facial port wine stain which is immediately visible to other people. He is often asked what it is and is aware of the gaze of other people. He describes himself as growing more and more angry in social situations: 'I just know what is coming and I feel it welling up in me. People make a comment and I just swear at them and storm off'.

Jeff is anticipating a response from other people for which he has no effective coping strategy. This can create a sense of helplessness. The behaviour of others is making him feel that he does not fit in, is not part of the peer group with which he identifies, and has fewer choices than others in terms of relationships and job opportunities, resulting in less control and feelings of helplessness about his life. As he grows more anxious, he is likely to attribute behaviour such as normal social eye contact as negative, and he may respond angrily either to a real or imagined intrusion. As an alternative to anger, responding assertively is a positive coping response, which maintains a high level of self-efficacy and perceived control. However, it is very easy to overdo an assertive response and impact in a negative way. For example:

> Peter has a distinctive facial appearance following a repair of a craniofacial condition and he also has alopecia [hair loss]. As he walked into the pub to meet friends, a group at the bar began to look his way and then mutter amongst themselves. Peter heard the word 'slaphead'. He walked straight over to them and asked them who they were looking at. A scuffle followed, after which he was ejected from the pub.

Thompson and Broom (2009) reported in their qualitative study of people who identified themselves as coping well with intrusive reactions that some of their male participants saw violence as acceptable where they interpreted others reactions as deliberately humiliating. For example Frank, who had significant facial scarring, and who viewed himself as not being 'bothered by' others' reactions, stated that if other men were rude, then 'Ten minutes later he's got his head in the urinal and I'm...peeing down the back of his neck'.

There is some suggestion in sociobiological research that masculinity is enhanced by facial scarring and it is very common for young men in particular, to perceive a facial scar as evidence that someone has been in a fight (they may have been, but not necessarily as the aggressor) and for this to act as a stimulus to demonstrating their own toughness. Anticipating this kind of attribution and intervening proactively before a situation escalates can be achieved through developing assertive approach behaviours rather than angry or avoidant ones. There may also be gendered cultural biases operating in relation to beliefs of some patients, as to how as a male one should deal with other men that are verbally rude.

Contrast the response of Peter and Frank, described earlier, to that reported by James Partridge in his book, *Changing Faces: The Challenge of Facial Disfigurement*:

> James walked into a pub to meet his brother at a point mid-treatment when his appearance was very unusual. As he pushed the door open, several people glanced over to see who had come in, and there was a noticeable decrease in ambient noise level as people paused mid conversation, startled by his appearance. James's response:

> Good evening everyone. Not looking my best tonight I am afraid

> This is an example of an assertive coping response in which James maintained control.

Interestingly, this is also a good example of using humour to diffuse a tense situation. Humorous responses, where the individual is comfortable with this device, are extremely helpful. In exploring this as an idea with people, it is important to distinguish between being laughed at by other people (where there is no control) and using humour as a proactive strategy where there is a high level of control. Described in terms of internal and external shame, a humorous response is a clear demonstration of positive self-esteem and self-efficacy and a lack of internal shame. Described in lay terms, other people feel at ease and take their cue from the patient. If he or she appears to be at ease, then they are likely to feel at ease too.

A firm statement delivered calmly, not shouted, is an alternative strategy, thus:

> 'Do you realise that you are staring at me?' is an assertive version of:

> Who do you think you are looking at?

> I've noticed you are looking at my face, I don't mind, but I'd rather you ask if you have a question, I have a skin condition that means I lose the colour, it's not contagious, do you need any more information

Generating these two different responses is ideally done by describing a hypothetical situation and asking the patient to give examples of how they might respond. Using real examples is perfect if they can remember any. Some people are so avoidant or anxious about social situations that they find it hard to think of any responses. In this situation it can be helpful to use examples that other patients have generated. Listing examples and asking the patient to order into categories; helpful or not, helps to overcome reluctance to contemplate the situation. In the example described earlier, most people sorting these alternatives are able to predict a positive outcome from the first alternative compared with the second.

Teaching the difference between assertiveness and anger involves a focus on both verbal and nonverbal skills. A confident statement needs to be delivered with firm eye contact and upright posture. Distance from other people is important, with close contact easily interpreted in terms of threat. Gestures such as finger pointing or raised fist need to be identified and managed. In addition, tone of voice is important and either of the given examples could be said in an aggressive way, so it may also be important to role-play tone and delivery style.

Walking into a room in a positive way is a very clear assertive response. Rather than lingering at the door waiting for someone else to make an approach, social skills exercises can address ways of making an initial approach to others.

These are very practical exercises with high face validity. Role play and practice in the treatment sessions can be followed with graded exercises as homework. Group interventions are also particularly useful ways of delivering social skills interventions, particularly as individuals can be encouraged to share responses they have found that work.

Anger may also be a problem, but may be only indirectly related to appearance. For example:

> Hayley is her mid-thirties and has recently undergone surgery to her abdomen. The abdominal wound has been slow to heal with her torso remaining very sore. Since returning home, she describes herself as 'having a very short fuse'. She and her partner have had blazing rows 'about nothing at all'. Both of them feel puzzled and upset about her change in her behaviour. In particular, Hayley is worried that if she continues to lose her temper with him, he will leave her. She is referred asking for help in controlling her anger.

In this situation, the triggers for the anger are unclear, and as a first step, Hayley kept a detailed diary of angry outbursts. As is common in behavioural monitoring, there were no examples of anger in the first few weeks, but gradually a pattern emerged in which anger was triggered by petty domestic incidents and then rapidly escalated into an intense rage with objects being thrown, screaming and complete loss of control. The treatment path for Hayley is illustrated in Chapter 7, because although social avoidance is a more common outcome, anger may also be an important determinant of lack of psychological adjustment to an altered appearance and is modifiable using generic anger management techniques which will be described.

Managing Intimacy

One intriguing finding from the ARC study was the level of appearance concern for people with a non-visible difference (i.e. normally hidden by clothing). In previous studies we have reported the higher impact of conditions which affect the face and hands (i.e. areas which are visible to others). However, clinically, it is the experience of the authors that patients who rely heavily on clothing or camouflage are using these as safety-seeking behaviours, and typically report high levels of anxiety and avoidance of intimacy or exposure to others. Major and Granzow (1999) and Smart and Wegner (1999) have suggested the 'Preoccupational Model of Secrecy' to describe the possible negative impact of over reliance on concealment associated with the threat of the stigma of being discovered and/or fear of revealing the stigma. Moss (2005) and Rosser (2008) have also highlighted the complex nature of the relationship between visibility and adjustment. Many people report safety behaviours such as undressing in the dark, wearing concealing clothing in bed and attempts to avoid intimacy. Often partners are bewildered about this level of avoidance but attempts to reassure can be interpreted as a lack of understanding. In extreme examples, people can withdraw sequentially from any social interaction: 'if I can't expose my body, I can't have an intimate relationship; therefore, it is pointless socializing with people and going out at all'.

Disclosing a Disfiguring Condition to a Partner

There are two aspects to disclosure. Someone may choose to disclose a disfiguring condition in the sense of providing a partner with an explanation for keeping an area covered (verbal disclosure), for example, keeping a bra on day and night. (It is interesting in clinical practice to find that many people, with or without a disfiguring condition, dislike nakedness even in front of a long-standing partner.) Or verbal disclosure may be a preliminary to preparing the partner to look at the area of concern (physical disclosure). Exposure without preparing a partner results in variable responses. Some people are completely unconcerned, others respond with curiosity or sympathy and others can be shocked. This is the least successful strategy because the outcome for the individual is not within their control and is unpredictable.

People have very different experiences of surgical wounds or disfiguring injuries. There is a surprisingly high prevalence of people who believe that scars can be 'removed' and that any scarring can be 'fixed' via surgery. In general though, people have a conceptual understanding of what a surgical scar is, so questions will usually be about the cause of the scar, how it was acquired, how it was treated or whether it hurts. Burns scarring or scars causing contour abnormalities are less familiar as are some dermatological conditions in which there can be assumptions of contagion.

Disgust emotions have recently been explored by Shanmugarajah et al. (2012) as an alternative explanation for avoidance responses in disfiguring conditions. They demonstrated that variable sensitivity to disgust in the general population results in differing responses to disfiguring conditions. Those with higher disgust sensitivity gave a higher rating for disgust when viewing images of disfiguring conditions. This would explain the variable response that people with a disfiguring condition experience in disclosing to a partner for the first time. (It also provides an interesting general explanation for why meeting people for the first time can result in variable, sometimes highly negative responses.) Moreover, disgust and fear responses are very similar, at least physiologically, and negative responses to visible differences may thus have a large fear component. In order to prepare for disclosure successfully, we often help the patient to think about ways to open the conversation and whether to use pictures of other similar conditions. This is one way that they can help their partners to understand the problem before they see it.

Preparation should also consider the problem of anticlimax. When someone is very distressed by their own appearance or considers it extremely abnormal, it can be as upsetting that others are not as worried by it as they are. Messages indicating that 'it is not that bad', about 'making a fuss about nothing' or a response that indicates that a partner had expected something much more significant, need to be anticipated. They can be interpreted as reassuring or equally, as unfeeling. Generally the message that 'no one else is going to be anything like as interested or worried about your appearance as you are' is supported in practice, provided there is a loving and supportive relationship. It is not true of abusive relationships where the opportunity to taunt someone about appearance provides another opportunity for bullying.

Before even considering disclosure to others, people should be comfortable with looking at and touching their body themselves.

Steps towards managing intimacy include:

- Checking the sources of appearance norms. Appearance may be within the normal limits but mismatched to ideals as opposed to norms of appearance. (For example, inverted nipples are as common as left-handedness. Yet, women who have not seen others with inverted nipples may believe themselves to be abnormal, and for some this may lead to appearance anxiety. Similarly, use of images from pornography has led to an increase in young women who believe their labia to be too large, but who have absolutely normal adult female bodies.)
- Working with the patient to consider ways in which the body area can be described. For example, careful use of language to avoid value judgments. Skin can be smooth or ridged, loose or tight, pale or dark but not disgusting, deformed or ugly.
- Reducing avoidance of the body area and increasing self-care. For example by massage, use of body lotions, deliberately looking at the avoided area in the bath.

- Examining the distinction between 'norms' of behaviour, for example, not everyone enjoys being naked even during intimacy and use of safety behaviours (One might find it congruent with personal norms to be naked, but be afraid to do so).
- Considering timing and style of disclosure.

Pauline had a mastectomy for breast cancer. Rather than use breast prostheses, she chose to have a prophylactic mastectomy on the nonaffected side. A tall and confident woman in her 50s, she received lots of invitations from potential partners. Her strategy was to disclose very early in any relationship. She would do this by looking for a very early opportunity to contextualize disclosure, for example,

> Talking about your colleague's illness prompts me to tell you that I had a mastectomy two years ago but I am absolutely fine now.

An alternative is to deliberately comment on the other person's appearance as a means of introducing the topic:

> You do look well! I used to love sunbathing but I have skin grafts which are quite extensive and I have to keep them out of the sun.

Another patient used the compliment about her shirt to introduce the topic of her psoriasis

> Thank you – yes I love this shirt. I have difficulty buying clothes because I have a skin condition which can sometimes be quite sensitive.

All these responses are different but they all promote the idea that the individual feels positive about themselves and aims to demonstrate that this is not something a potential partner should be concerned about. But often people do not feel positive in this way. As part of therapy, it is also worth discussing the fact that many people have areas of their body that they dislike and try to cover – especially in front of other people. So disclosing this to someone else is actually a pretty normal behaviour and likely to be understood, for example,

> I have lost a lot of weight recently and feel rather sensitive about the skin folds I have around my abdomen

> I am rather embarrassed about the skin grafts on my back.

Summary

Developing good social skills is often a sensible starting point if it is clear that people are not managing social situations effectively. For some, this kind of approach is very effective and a brief intervention with some simple goals based around skills acquisition, exposure and practice is adequate to achieve significant behaviour change.

For those where there is evidence of heightened preoccupation and maladaptive appearance-related beliefs or extreme body image disturbance with ritualized checking, social skills and exposure may be a necessary, but not sufficient intervention. The following chapters set out a more comprehensive approach to complex problems of appearance and body image anxiety.

6

Cognitive Behavioural Therapy

Chapter Outline

CBT for Appearance Anxiety: Psychosocial Interventions for Anxiety Due to Visible Difference, First Edition.
Alex Clarke, Andrew Thompson, Elizabeth Jenkinson, Nichola Rumsey and Rob Newell.
© 2014 John Wiley & Sons, Ltd. Published 2014 by John Wiley & Sons, Ltd.

Techniques in Cognitive Behavioural Therapy

Cognitive and cognitive behavioural interventions are not formulaic. The treatment for one individual may be very different from that of another with a similar problem, but will share a similar format. Thus, the number of treatments is highly variable. Kleve et al. (2002) report a mean of three sessions in treatment at OUTLOOK at Frenchay Hospital, but with a big range. Practice at the Royal Free Hospital suggests a more variable mean time frame and the sessions outlined subsequently range from brief interventions to a 10–12 session intervention. The focus on record keeping, practice and homework will be shared however long the intervention; the underlying model is the same and certain techniques are likely to be common to most programmes. Over the course of treatment, the emphasis will move from eliciting the problem and sustaining beliefs, challenging these beliefs through reviewing the evidence (often through behavioural experiments, usually involving entering situations which trigger fear) and modifying maintaining schemas by reformulation on the basis of new evidence. This is illustrated in the examples. The model is constantly revisited throughout treatment.

Many different techniques are used to support this approach. The following is not an exhaustive list, but common cognitive therapy techniques are briefly illustrated using examples of working with patients who have appearance-related concerns.

Socratic Dialogue

This section draws on a similar section in Wells (1997). Socratic dialogue is a means of questioning which makes as much use of open questions as possible. By avoiding questions with 'yes/no' answers, the individual is encouraged to provide more detail of the feelings, beliefs and behaviour which underpin the problem. Use of exclusively open ended questions can appear interrogative, so occasional use of clarifying statements, as described later, can allow the questioning to continue but break up the process in a way which is experienced as more comfortable. It is particularly important in working with concerns about appearance that the therapist focuses on the individual's ideas and beliefs. Most patients with appearance-related anxiety have had the experience of being told that 'you look okay to me'. There is an unfortunate common presumption, unsupported by all the evidence, that severity and psychological distress are related. Thus, someone with a significant difference in appearance is 'expected' to have problems whilst someone with an objectively small difference may frequently be described as being treated as having concerns 'out of proportion with the injury'. This means that family friends and some clinicians try to reassure about appearance without fully exploring the reasons for the concern. People will therefore be told that they look normal or unremarkable or are making a fuss. Clinicians may say that they cannot alter a scar surgically because they are focusing on the size when it is another aspect of the scar which is the focus of concern (see later). Socratic dialogue is therefore helpful not only in the context of a psychological intervention, but also within the clinical consultation when exploring the expectations of someone seeking medical or surgical procedures.

The following example demonstrates the way in which this questioning approach gradually focuses in on beliefs about 'being alone':

In both the given examples, there is strong underlying fear of being excluded, not belonging to the peer group and identifying appearance as central to this group membership. See figure 6.1 for an example of how the patient and therapist started to formulate the problems into a Cognitive Behavioural Therapy (CBT) template using this information.

Example 1

T: Can you think of the most recent time when you felt anxious about your appearance?
     Yes, it was at the weekend when I went to the theatre with two friends.

T: How did you feel?
     I felt awful.

T: Can you tell me more about that feeling?
     I felt big, enormous, as if I was standing out.

T: What is bad about standing out?
     Everyone will look at me.

T: If everyone is looking at you, why is that bad?
     Because I know what they are thinking. They think I look like a man.

T: If everyone was thinking that you looked like a man, how would that make you feel?
     I would be ashamed, embarrassed and self-conscious.

T: What would be bad about those feelings?
     They make me feel bad as if I am letting my friends down.

T: What did you do when you had these feelings at the weekend?
     I went and stood by the bar so that I was leaning against something.

T: What would have happened if you had stayed with your friends?
     Probably nothing, but I would have felt more obvious. I hate the feeling of standing out. I want to be like everyone else.

T: What does it mean for you to stand out? It sounds as though this about feeling different. Is that right?
     I hate the idea of being different….

T: What happens to people who are different?
     They end up all alone…

Example 2

T: What is the thing you dislike most about the scar?
     I just hate it.

T: Are there any aspects of the scar that you hate more than other things?
     I hate all of it.

T: There are lots of different things about the appearance of a scar. Some people worry about the size or the colour, for some people texture or the feeling of the scar is important….
     The colour.

T: Can you describe the colour?
     It is horrible, disgusting and revolting.

T: It sounds as if it is easier to describe how the scar makes you feel rather than what you see if you look at it
     I can't look at it.

T: What is the worst thing that would happen if you looked at it?
     It would make me cry.

T: Why would it make you cry?
     Because it would make me feel small and horrible.

T: What would other people think if they saw it?
No one ever sees it.

T: If someone else was to look it, what is the worst thing that could happen?
They would think I was disgusting.

T: If someone thought that about you – that you were disgusting, what would that mean?
It would mean I was unacceptable – no good.

Demographic factors: *42 year old single female*
Early experiences: *parents favour sibling*
Sociocultural: *ethnic group prizes appearance in women*
Physical appearance: *endocrine disorder, hirsutism, overweight*

Predisposing factors

Individual, social and treatment factors

Age, gender, parental and peer factors, culture and media, visibility & treatment history

Appearance schemas: core beliefs & values
e.g.: *"I am different, not feminine"*

Rules & assumptions e.g.;
Unless I look feminine I will be alone

Compensatory strategies: e.g.:
Try to make a special effort

Appearance factors

Self-ideal appearance discrepancy

salience/valence

Triggering events: e.g. *Social activities:*
going to the theatre

Precipitating factors

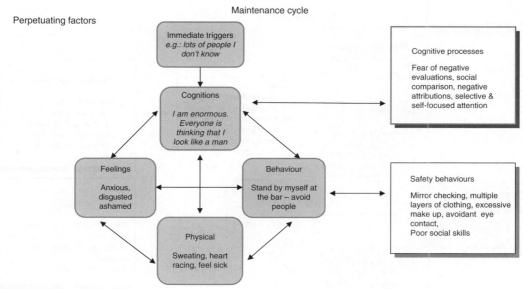

Perpetuating factors

Maintenance cycle

Immediate triggers
e.g.: lots of people I don't know

Cognitions
I am enormous. Everyone is thinking that I look like a man

Cognitive processes

Fear of negative evaluations, social comparison, negative attributions, selective & self-focused attention

Feelings
Anxious, disgusted ashamed

Behaviour
Stand by myself at the bar – avoid people

Safety behaviours

Mirror checking, multiple layers of clothing, excessive make up, avoidant eye contact,
Poor social skills

Physical
Sweating, heart racing, feel sick

Problems
Eg: *"Can't mix socially with other people"*

Resilience & strength
Good sense of humour
Several good friends

Protective factors

Figure 6.1 Using the CBT template to begin formulation for Example 6.1.

Eliciting Negative Automatic Thoughts

Cognitive therapies are built on the premise that anxiety is maintained by negative automatic thoughts, which are triggered spontaneously in response to perceived threat. Negative automatic thoughts are appraisals or interpretations of events which maintain a system in which fear is overestimated and the individual's ability to cope with it is underestimated. Wells (1997) distinguishes between negative automatic thoughts related to the appraisal of fear (primary thoughts) and those related to escape (secondary thoughts). Patterns in the way events are interpreted can be identified by reviewing the evidence for a particular belief and then considering alternative competing explanations.

One way of eliciting these thoughts is achieved by questioning about homework, recent experience or a specific memorable episode. Consider this extract from the treatment of a 22-year-old man with a pigment disorder, objectively unlikely to be visible to others. Figure 6.2 shows how this information is added to the formulation.

T: You have told me that social situations are particularly difficult because everyone stares at you. Can you give me an example of this happening to you recently?
     Yes, I had a really bad day on Saturday.
T: Tell me about it. What were you doing?
     I had agreed to meet my mates in the pub. I did not really feel like going, I knew I would feel uncomfortable.
T: Great, it's good you are entering these situations even though you thought it would be uncomfortable. Tell me how it felt.
     Just – really anxious, just hoping no one will notice.

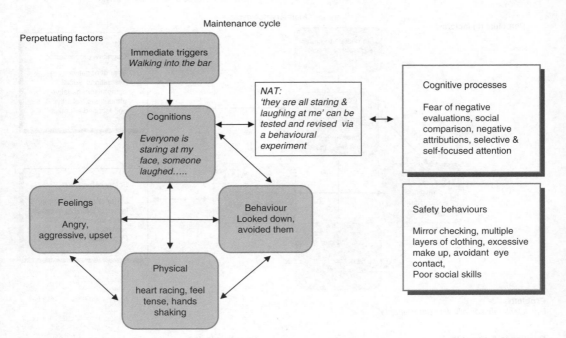

Figure 6.2   Adding to the formulation to demonstrate how thoughts can be challenged.

T: What happens when you feel like that? What do you do?
Just try not to look at anyone – just try to avoid looking at them.

T: So what happened when you went in?
I could see my mates at the end of the room, so I had to walk right past this group of lads at the bar...I could see one of them look right at me then he turned and said something to his mate and they all laughed.

T: How did this make you feel?
Really angry and upset. I know he was looking at my face...I went over to my friends, but the whole evening was ruined...

T: Let me just stop you there for a moment. So you walked into the room. As you walked in, someone at the bar turned and looked at you. Then he said something to his friend and he laughed.
That's right.

T: Why do you think that he looked at you?
Because of how I look.

T: How strongly do you believe that? (1–100%)
I'm sure – 100%.

T: I wonder if there is another way of looking about this situation. Are there any other reasons that people might look up as someone comes into a bar?
Yes...yes...I suppose if they were waiting to meet someone themselves.

T: How possible is it that this group were waiting for someone else?
It's possible...

T: So it's possible that he looked at you, because he was expecting someone else, not because of how you look.
I suppose so.

T: So let me ask you again, how strongly do you believe that he looked at you because of how you look?
I see what you are saying. I still think he did though so...70%

T: So there is a chance that he glanced at you, because he was waiting for his friend...If this was true, how would you feel about him looking?
I wouldn't care then – it's not about me.

T: So is it that what made you upset was not what he did, it is what you thought about the reason he did it – how you interpreted it?
That's right.

T: So, can you think of a way in which you could check this out if it happens again?
I'm not going to ask him!

T: You could ask him, but I agree that is quite confrontational...how else could you check out whether someone is waiting for a friend?
I could see what happened next.

T: So next time, you could think about an alternative explanation for what happened and you could check out if you were right.

Variations on this theme, of interpreting a glance as evidence of staring (at a real or imagined defect), are extremely common and predictive of maladaptive responses such as anger or social avoidance. In this example, the patient is very quick to acknowledge the negative automatic thought and to generate an alternative explanation. Often people are much more rigid in their thinking and more work is necessary to establish that a thought is not a fact. Similarly, people often find it difficult to report negative automatic thoughts, either because these thoughts are themselves aversive or because their attention is focused on many things during problem episodes (e.g. physical symptoms of anxiety, scanning for escape routes). One way to increase the ability to identify negative automatic thoughts and help generate alternative explanations might be to use a behavioural experiment. We might propose that the patient observes and records the behaviour of other people when someone comes into the room. Record-keeping is very important, since this information can then be used to reevaluate the belief that other people look up because they are staring at his face.

Unhelpful Beliefs Record Form

An unhelpful beliefs record form can be used to record the events that happened, identify the negative automatic thought which is triggered and recognize the link between thoughts and feelings.

We would usually begin by helping someone to identify the negative automatic thought and the frequency of occurrence (see figure 6.3).

The next step would be to generate some alternative ways of thinking about the problem. In the given example, the patient can generate the alternative explanation that everyone looks up when someone new walks into the bar. This allows him to modify his belief that everyone is staring at his face to introduce some flexibility in his thinking: it is possible that there could be another explanation. Figure 6.4 shows how the form is modified to capture this information.

What if the person in the described scene had been someone with a significant facial difference? In this situation, the probability of being stared at as he walks into the pub is very high. In this case, more emphasis on a behavioural management approach would have been used, developing skills and strategies for managing intrusive behaviour around staring as in Chapter 5 (e.g. look up and smile rather than down and away), as well as tolerating and reducing the levels of anxiety associated with the situation. The Faceit online computer programme (Bessell et al., 2012) would be another systematic method for learning and practicing some of these social skills without the need to attend one-to-one sessions.

Negative Automatic Thinking Styles Associated with Anxiety

The example given previously illustrates the common thinking style of 'jumping to conclusions'. It is a pattern of thinking that we all do from time to time when we are nervous but often becomes a habitual style of thinking where there is an exaggerated sense of threat and in such cases it serves to maintain the underlying unhelpful core belief such as being unlovable. Most of us would be able to generate competing explanations for our automatic thoughts. The aim of identifying negative automatic thoughts (NATs) is to become aware of patterns, to build a habit of examining alternative explanations and to move the emphasis onto the underlying beliefs, with the aim of gradual cognitive restructuring. With appearance-related concerns, common examples of styles of NATs include overgeneralization, personalization, catastrophizing, mind reading, jumping to conclusions, and self-criticism. Examples are given in Table 6.1.

Where somebody has real difficulties in generating competing explanations, it can be useful to provide other clinical examples. This can be done via reference to the research literature – again the Strenta and Kleck (1985) experiment is extremely helpful. Distancing the situation so that there is a general

Date	Situation	Emotion	Automatic thought
	Describe situation leading to unpleasant emotion *Everyone looks up when I walk into the bar*	Type of emotion (e.g. sad, angry ashamed, disgusted, anxious) *Angry, aggressive*	*They are looking at my face*
		Intensity of emotion 0–100 100%	Intensity of thought 0–100 100%

Figure 6.3 Unhelpful Beliefs Record (UBR) Form

Date	Situation	Emotion	Automatic thought	Alternative thought	Outcome	What else could I do?
	Describe situation leading to unpleasant emotion	Type of emotion (e.g. sad, angry ashamed, disgusted, anxious)		Is there another way of looking at it?	Type of emotion	
		Intensity 0–10	Intensity of thought 0–10	Intensity of alternative 0–10	Intensity 0–10	

Figure 6.4 Unhelpful Beliefs Record (UBR) Form

Table 6.1 Triple column technique. The following examples are drawn from clinical cases.

Automatic thought Strength of belief 0–10	Cognitive processing (unhelpful thinking style)	Alternative belief Strength of belief 0–10
Everyone is starting at me	*Overgeneralization*	Some people may be curious about my appearance: others are more interested in their own concerns
When people talk about plastic surgery it is because they have noticed my unusual appearance	*Personalisation*	People often talk about things they have seen on television
Now that I look like this I shall never be able to get a job	*Catastrophising*	People are employed because of their skills and talents not because of what they look like
No-one has actually asked me about my appearance, because they are too polite, but I know what they are thinking	*Mind reading*	I am very ware of my appearance but other people my not notice
I am hideous, disgusting, horrible, horrible, horrible, no one will want me	*Self-criticism*	I have a skin condition its part of me but not all of me I can be kind, loving, and others will see that too

discussion rather than a personal one helps the individual to start using logical deduction in a situation which is less anxiety provoking. Even further removed would be a discussion of a completely neutral example. For example, generating possible explanations for why someone may not be able to sleep allows a discussion of multiple different explanations from environmental (noisy) to work related (on shifts), disease related (depressed), life event (worried about a specific problem), etc. The goal is to help the individual to start generating other explanations rather than for the therapist to provide them. This can then be refocused on to the target problem. Sometimes, there is a persistent problem which suggests a very rigid schema, and early experiences then need more discussion. It is not uncommon to find that there is a history of persistent bullying, domestic violence or child sexual abuse. It would then be necessary to establish that the individual is currently safe, and to encourage the patient to address such issues as primary goals using a trauma-focused approach, in line with NICE guidelines (NICE, 2005).

Triple Column Technique

This is a common tool for identifying patterns in cognitive processing. The negative automatic thought is recorded, level of belief is rated and type of processing is identified. Finally, an alternative explanation is recorded that may focus upon consciously switching out of the processing style or acknowledging its role in maintenance of the problem (Burns, 1989) (Table 6.1).

Pie Charts

Pie charts are a very clear way of presenting competing explanations (Figure 6.5). Will has pigmentation under his eyes which gives darker hue to his skin when compared with the rest of his face. He reports frequent comments that he looks tired and teasing about staying up too late, drinking too

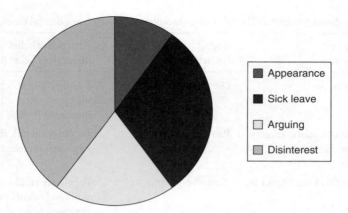

Figure 6.5   Charting different explanations for dismissal using a pie chart.

much, etc. He believes that people avoid him because of their assumptions about the cause of his visible difference. Using the given pie chart, we developed different explanations for his recent dismissal from work were generated, and a probability calculated for each:

- My appearance 10%
- Repeated sick leave 30%
- Arguing with the customers 20%
- Not interested in the job 40%

This enabled Will to reduce the strength in the belief that his employers 'did not like the look of him' from 90% to 10% and to attribute the likely cause of his dismissal to his behaviour at work.

Manipulating Safety Behaviours

Use of safety behaviours is common in appearance-related concerns and includes disguising features with clothing, make-up, facial hair and hairstyles. Cling film, blue tack and superglue are also used less frequently to flatten or reduce the prominence of a feature which is perceived to stick out. Repeated pregnancy has been recorded as a means of maintaining breast size. Carrying a large bag or sitting with a large bag on the lap conceals abdominal concerns. Social avoidance or careful choice of seating position and lighting are common. All these behaviours can be targeted for change, but it is clearly very important that the patient understands the link between these safety behaviours and maintenance of anxiety rather than its reduction. The goal is to reduce the behaviour so that anxiety is reduced (through habituation and revision of negative automatic thoughts), and there is the opportunity to develop positive adaptive behaviours.

Anxiety management techniques

As a first step, it is useful to consider anxiety management techniques such as relaxation training. It can be very hard for some people to even contemplate the possibility of reducing safety behaviours which have become a way of life. Using a hierarchy in the same way as in a systematic desensitization approach is a way of tackling things at a speed the patient can tolerate and learn from.

Example 1

Jeff was very preoccupied by mild gynaecomastia. Although his minor breast development was within normal limits, he felt that everyone would notice and comment on it. He developed the practice of wearing multiple layers of clothing including a tight fitting vest which was worn under everything. In the summer he was uncomfortably hot. Because he also felt unable to wear swimming trunks he disliked being on holiday with his family.

A hierarchy was drawn up to be used on holiday. The advantage here was that he could begin by practicing well away from anyone who knew him. The lowest item on the hierarchy was to walk along the beach first thing in the morning wearing a T-shirt but without his vest. Once his anxiety reached a manageable level, he moved up to repeating this at midday when many people were about. Again, once he mastered this, he was able to try the early morning trip by himself without any top at all. He reached the point that he could swim with his children without the need to cover up. These gradual steps were practiced in vivo with the use of visualization, relaxation and breathing techniques to help him control his physical symptoms. Although he still disliked his chest, he was able to dismantle the safety behaviours which had become a real problem.

Fran, described subsequently, had relied on clothing to cover her scars and had become frustrated about the restrictions in what she could wear. She was very highly motivated to change.

Example 2

Fran always wore high necked tops and jumpers to disguise her burn scarring. Like the previous examples, Socratic questioning indicated a fear of external shame, with other people commenting on her appearance or 'feeling disgusted' by what they saw. Fran had never exposed her scars and had not identified a form of reply which she could use if she was questioned about her appearance.

Target, Tools, Troubleshoot, Test

Clarke (2001) suggests a four 'T' algorithm to help devise a behavioural experiment. This is similar to the prepare, expose, test and summarize (PETS) protocol in Wells (1997). This approach acknowledges the need for most people who have a visible disfigurement to develop strategies for managing the curiosity of others by having an answer for questions. This approach therefore adds a 'social skill' component labelled 'tools' (see Chapter 5 on Social Skills, for examples). This algorithm also recognizes a common tendency to catastrophize and builds in a troubleshooting component so the chances of not carrying out the experiment are reduced and that the patient feels that there is a backup plan:

Target: Identify belief and explore supporting evidence. Design experiment and present rationale

Tools: Identify any strategies that will be helpful (e.g. ways of explaining the condition to others that reduce and redirect attention)

Troubleshoot: Examine individual's beliefs about what may go wrong 'what's the worst that can happen?' and generate response that facilitates engagement in 'Test'

Test: Exposure, monitoring and reformulation.

Using this framework, Fran examined her beliefs about scarring:

> A behavioural experiment was designed to test the assumption that other people would respond in an unfavourable way if they knew what she looked like.
>
> TARGET: Fran chose a wedding in another country at which to wear a dress which revealed her scars. (Beginning with a venue which is removed from the usual social context is often perceived as easier, because the costs of failure are perceived as lower).
>
> TOOLS: She then worked on a reply to likely questioning, which gave a simple explanation, but then employed distraction to limit further questions.
>
> TROUBLESHOOT: She increased the likelihood that she would wear the revealing dress by packing only this and no alternatives.
>
> TEST: She carried out the experiment, recorded the results and reformulated her beliefs (see Figure 6.6):

Fran was able to change her behaviour consistently on the basis of this experience and started wearing clothes that she liked at home and at work regardless of whether her scars were visible to others.

Results of this kind of experiment can be fed into a reshaping of the schema that is supporting assumptions and beliefs, as follows.

Here, vertical arrows are used to provide a diagram of how the schema can gradually be modified (Figure 6.7).

Cost–Benefit Analyses

In the given example, Fran identified a situation in which she felt able to test out her new behaviour for the first time. For many people, the idea of challenging safety behaviours seems counterintuitive – they have been doing them for years and they are sustained, because they are perceived to be successful. These are the patients who commonly respond that they 'can't' when a behavioural experiment is suggested. In addition to teaching anxiety management techniques, motivation to participate and perceived self-efficacy can be increased by generating a cost–benefit analysis. This is can be elicited by use of two columns as given in the following text, in which the advantages and disadvantages of a given behaviour (or a cognition) are listed. For example,

> Sarah had multiple facial scars after a car accident where her face collided with the car windscreen. She wore a baseball cap pulled low over her face to limit eye contact when she went out. Because she also wore jeans and big boots, the combination created a rather threatening impression.

Date	Situation	Belief and strength 0–10	What really happened	Strength of original belief 0–10
November 21	At my friend's wedding in the Caribbean. I wore a sun dress with thin straps. My scars were really visible. I worked out what I would say when asked, 'I was burned when I was a child by a kettle. How do you know Pete?' (the groom)	Everyone will stare at my scars. I will be asked by lots of people. Feel very on edge. 10/10	No-one seemed to notice. I suppose, because everyone was wearing the same kind of thing, I realised I would have stood out more in my usual kind of dress. In the end, someone asked me right at the end of the evening and I burst out laughing 'Thank goodness you have asked. I am supposed to practising answering this question and no-one has mentioned it'. I was surprised by how easy it was.	1–2/10 People were much more focussed on the wedding

Figure 6.6 Beliefs framework

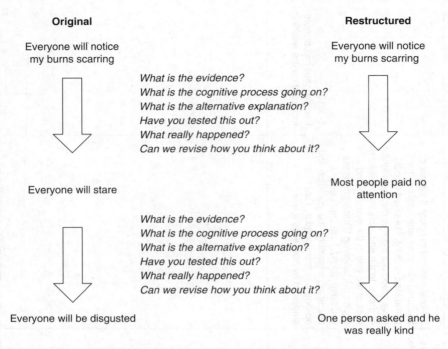

Figure 6.7   Vertical arrow restructuring (Wells, 1997). Reproduced with permission from John Wiley & Sons, Ltd.

Advantages of my hat	Disadvantages of my hat
People can't see my scars I can't see people looking at me I feel safe	I look threatening People avoid me People can't communicate with me because they can't see my face I can't wear my usual clothes I don't feel myself in jeans and trainers I am worried I will have to take it off if I go inside I am not allowed in Wetherspoons

Figure 6.8   A cost–benefit analysis for wearing a baseball cap.

Sarah found the idea of removing her baseball hat 'impossible'. She completed a cost–benefit analysis to help her work out the advantages and disadvantages of her behaviour (Figure 6.8).

Clearly the idea is to generate more disadvantages than advantages. Where the number is similar, weightings can be used to illustrate the point. For Sarah, the safety behaviour was successfully challenged in steps first removing her hat when she was alone at home and then substituting a fluffy beret which was less concealing and removed the perceived threat to other people.

Some Techniques for Dealing with Appearance-Related Self-Criticism and Shame

Living with a visible difference may be associated with feelings of shame, particularly when someone has internalized the negative reactions of others (see Example 6.1 in Chapter 6). This is at its most obvious when a patient vividly describes early experiences of being rejected, bullied, or ostracized on the basis of their appearance and they display a rigid acceptance of such reactions as merely representing 'how it is'. For example, John Storry (1997) has written about his own early experiences of living with a congenital disfigurement as follows:

> I will always remember the look on his [his father's] face. It is a mixture of bewilderment and derision. He cannot equate deformity with intelligence. He is unable to accept my deformity. I feel that he is ashamed of me... I think it is impossible to develop an attractive personality with a damaged face. (cited in Lansdown et al., 1997, p. 31, 33)

Shame may also occur following disfigurements acquired later in life, arising from a sense of being 'spoiled' (Goffman, 1963), particularly where there are preexisting schemas that place emphasis on the importance of appearance over and above other aspects of identity (Thompson & Kent, 2001).

Therefore, persistent experiences of appearance-based rejection, particularly if expressed by significant others, are likely to lead to the development of negative appearance-related schemas such as 'I'm unlovable', and consequently there will be an anticipation that others will reject the self (i.e. external shame). However, as described earlier, there may also be rejection of the self or the appearance of the self, and individuals may describe powerful feelings even 'self-disgust' associated with beliefs that their bodies are 'ugly' or 'hideous'. Such a schema will drive cognitive processing and typically results in avoidant-type coping and subjugation and may cause severe appearance-related distress in the form of both anxiety and depression. Body shame then involves both externally focused fears of being judged unattractive and internally focused self-evaluations. Self-criticism and self-attacking cognitive processing is characteristically associated with shame and the recognition and addressing of this processing style is crucial in intervention.

Paul Gilbert has pioneered the development of a variation of CBT that focuses on developing compassion as a method for addressing shame-based difficulties – compassion-focused therapy (CFT). (See, for example, Gilbert, 2009, 2010.) Compassion involves the ability to empathize and care about the difficulties of others and also oneself (self-compassion).[1]

> Reena has vitiligo which is highly noticeable upon her darker skin. She was bullied at school and now, in her late 30s, she still sees herself in a self-critical fashion as a 'freak'. She reports that people in the Asian community in which she lives don't really understand the condition and assume it has arisen because of things she has eaten or must have done in a prior life. She believes that she is not marriageable and has been prompted by her family to hide her vitiligo from potential suitors. She has felt safer seeking relationships with people from a different ethnic background and when in a relationship tends to subjugate her own needs and has consequently had several relationships where she has been taken advantage of or been abused.

Sensitive exploration with Reena using the approach described earlier revealed marked self-criticism. This was present much of the time but in its most intense form involved her locking herself into the bathroom with a mirror and berating herself for lengthy periods of time. This self-criticism and the specific behavioural routine of locking herself in the bathroom was difficult for her to disclose (for further fear of being judged) and was also difficult to let go of, as this processing style, whilst destructive, also served a function for her in the sense of her feeling as if she was appropriately punishing herself for her perceived physical flaws and the impact of these on others.

Assessment revealed that self-criticism often followed a stressful event where Reena perceived something had gone wrong particularly in her relationships with others. Initially, Reena was simply asked to monitor the occurrences of self-criticism and the functional role played by self-criticism was thus identified by functional analysis and built into the formulation described.

Functional Analysis of Self-Criticism

Therapists and clients alike may fail to recognize the power of the self-criticism and also the threat-based function that it may serve, and both of these things can make it difficult to change. The following two examples shows how the power and function of self-criticism can be identified and thus recognition of this can be built into the formulation and become a target for cognitive restructuring and a rationale for developing self-compassion.

Identifying the power of self-criticism

T: (Examining the unhelpful beliefs record which reveals an episode of self-critical rumination following having had an argument with her ex-partner about access to the children). So we spoke last week about how the self-criticism triggers very painful feelings and on this occasion it was triggered by an argument?
Yes, but it's funny because I know I was right but by the time I'd got home I just felt terrible and I locked myself in the bathroom and started looking in the mirror and saying those things to myself and I just couldn't stop – I feel stupid now

T: It sounds like you are being self-critical about being self-critical.
Yes, I suppose I am

T: It sounds like it an easy thing to be triggered, particularly when something is going on with your relationships. It sounds like when it is triggered it's pretty awful
Yes

T: I wonder if we can try and work out why it is so difficult to stop it once it starts but this will involve thinking about it and I realise that may be upsetting.
OK, if it's going to help, it is a problem

T: OK, we can stop if it gets too upsetting. Could you think back for a moment, and try to in your mind to hear the self-critical thought or voice… really try to get in touch with it. Can you hear it?
Yes

T: What does it sound like?
It's horrible

T: It's horrible, and how does it sound, loud, soft, or….
It's strong sounding

T: Would you be able to talk to it
No, it's, it's like shouting

T: If it were a person what would it be like?
Horrible, horrible, shouty, big

T: OK, let's stop there… what are your thoughts after doing that?
I don't know how I'd be able to stand up to it, but I can see it's like a bullying thing

T: Yes, that sounds like a useful description – a bully that needs addressing. But like all bullies it's hard to stand up to and we may have to think about how to come at it from a different angle, perhaps by developing another voice that of a helper, an inner helper.
I can't imagine how I'd do that.

T: There are a variety of techniques that we can look at using, that you can learn to use that can help to develop a sense of self-compassion.

Reena was later provided with support in learning to use compassionate self-imagery, so as to begin to build her capacity for self-compassion (see the following exercise: compassionate self imagery). Recognition of the bullying nature of the self-critical processing style was also important in focusing attention on the role it played in maintaining the problem.

Identifying the Function of Self-Criticism
As well as recognition of the power of self-criticism, it is important to see if this processing style also has a function, for example stemming from a belief that there is a need to punish the self for not having a good enough appearance, or pushing the self to achieve to compensate. Whilst this is not always the case, where this is occurring, it is important to identify the underlying belief as otherwise the ability to tackle self-criticism can be hindered:

T: Last time we spoke about the bullying nature of self-criticism and how hard it is to stand up to it, but I also wonder if we could talk about it some more to see if there are any other reasons why when you get caught up in it, it's hard to stop.
OK

T: OK, let's think back to the last time it happened (looking at the unhelpful belief record).... you'd just got back after the argument with your ex, and you felt that feeling that triggered off locking yourself in the bathroom, let's suppose that the self-criticism just went, what would that be like?
Great! But I can't imagine it would, it's like I have to do it, when I feel like that.

T: Have to?
Yes, it's like I don't know, it's like I deserve it, I know it doesn't make sense saying it out loud like that, especially after we spoke about how bullying it is, but it's like I have to hurt myself

T: OK, it sounds like you have surprised yourself saying that?
Yes

T: So let me see if I understand, there's almost a belief that you deserve to be bullied?
It's weird it like I need it, it's like with my skin being like this, ugly, means I have to be punished, because I'm not good enough.

T: Have to be punished? I think that's an important belief for us to know about, as it's likely to make it hard to stop the self-criticism and we might need to look at challenging that in its own right, looking at the fairness of it – would it be something you said to someone else with vitiligo for example?
No, no, never!

T: Perhaps we can look at this belief in a little more detail, examine its fairness to you, what would those that love you say, for example?
My family don't like the vitiligo, but they wouldn't agree that I should be punished… they know it's not my fault

Once the belief behind the function of the self-criticism is revealed this can then become an active target for cognitive restructuring. In addition, its ability to sabotage dealing with the self-critical thinking style can be noted, monitored, and challenged.
Exercise: *Compassionate self-imagery* (adapted from Gilbert, 2010, with permission)

There are a variety of practical exercises that have been developed to help build the capacity for self-soothing and becoming compassionate and accepting towards the self. Imagery techniques, as in the following example, can be used to create a sense of self-compassion that can be used to build capacity to challenge appearance-related self-criticism.

The rationale for this exercise can be stated as moving the focus away from appearance onto other inner human qualities (such as kindness) that will enable the development of self-acceptance. The following script is adapted from a recent study with people with the skin condition psoriasis (Muftin, 2013). 'We are going to be focusing on imagery because we know that *what* we imagine can have powerful effects on our bodies and our minds. For example, if there are things that we are anxious about and we imagine something frightening happening to us, this will stimulate our anxiety system. On the other hand, if we focus on something we are looking forward to – say imagining a happy holiday – this will give us a little buzz of excitement. So imagery then affects our feelings, thoughts and our bodies.

Compassionate imagery can work in the same way – if we focus our minds on kindness and caring, this will affect our feelings and stimulate our bodily processes in particular ways. In fact, we know from research that if we focus on feelings of caring and being cared for, this can have a range of beneficial effects on our minds, feelings and bodies. So we will imagine what it would feel like if we have great kindness, wisdom, confidence, authority and really want to be helpful and supportive. You will be invited to practice imagining having these qualities. You will be invited to notice what it feels like when you imagine your compassionate self having these qualities and try to bring that more into your life so as to tackle the appearance-related self-criticism.

1. First, sit comfortably when you are unlikely to be disturbed for a while.
2. Now take a straight posture and focus on your breathing, with the air coming in through your nose down gently into your diaphragm and out through your nose again. Remember that this is breathing slightly deeper and slower than you would breathe normally; notice the feeling of your body slowing down.
3. Relax your facial muscles. Then allow your mouth to turn upwards into a slight smile until you feel it is comfortable, a warm and friendly smile. Remember, as we go through the exercise you may find your mind wandering. Do not worry about that – just gently and kindly bring it back onto the task we are doing.
4. Now like an actor getting into a role and a character we are going to use our imagination to create an idea of ourselves at our compassionate best. So, for a moment think about the qualities you would like to have if you were a deeply compassionate person.
5. Remember it doesn't matter if you don't feel you are or are not a deeply compassionate person – the most important thing is to imagine the qualities of a deeply compassionate person, and that you have them.
6. Let's spend 30 seconds on imagining these qualities.
7. Now we're going to focus on some very specific qualities of compassion. We will start with the quality of kindness and your desires to be helpful and supportive. Focus on your motivation and desire to be compassionate and to contribute to others being free from suffering, being happy and prospering.
8. Hold your compassionate friendly facial expression and also consider the tone of your voice, how you would speak in a compassionate way.
9. So for the next 30 seconds gently and playfully imagine that you have great kindness and desires to be helpful.

10. Notice how you feel when you imagine yourself like this – when you imagine having these desires and feeling these desires in you.

11. Other key qualities of compassion, which make it possible to act with kindness, are the qualities of confidence, authority and maturity. So imagine you have confidence and authority – feel that in your body posture. Notice how you feel when you imagine yourself like this and an authority with confidence.

12. So holding your compassionate friendly facial expression and also the warm tone of your voice, think about how you would speak in a compassionate way, how you would move in the world, how you would express this confidence, maturity and authority. So for the next 30 seconds, gently imagine yourself as this confident, calm, strong and compassionate authority.

13. Compassion of course has wisdom in it too. So now focus on imagining yourself having wisdom, having learnt much from your life you can use this wisdom. Imagine yourself as open, thoughtful and reflective. Hold to your compassionate friendly facial expression and also consider your warm voice tone, imagine yourself expressing wise thoughtful insightfulness. So for the next 30 seconds imagine yourself as a wise, thoughtful and insightful compassionate person.

From these three qualities come others, such as generosity, forgiveness and playfulness, as well as concern and a commitment to be helpful.

1. Now to develop this practice, imagine that you are looking at yourself from the outside. See your facial expressions, the way you move in the world, note your motivations to be thoughtful, kind, helpful and wise. Hear yourself speaking to people, note your compassionate tone in your voice.

2. See other people relating to you as a compassionate person. See yourself relating to other people in this ideal compassionate way that you are developing.

3. So for the next 30 seconds playfully and gently enjoy watching yourself being a compassionate person in the world and others relating to you as such.

As you develop your practice, you can imagine yourself having all those qualities you have been practicing, so that when you focus on activating your compassionate mind or compassionate self, you will have a sense of the kind of mind and self you are wanting to become. The more you practice slowing down and imagining being this kind of person in the world, the more easily you may find you can access these qualities in you and the more easily you will find they can express themselves through you.

This technique is not necessarily easy to learn and it is advantageous to record yourself doing it with the client and to give them the recording to practice. As with all out-of-session tasks, making an explicit plan to practice and recording the outcome of practice is essential to success.

Summary

This is clearly not an exhaustive review of techniques used in CBT, but common approaches used in appearance-related anxiety have been illustrated. The way in which the techniques fit within the structure of an individual intervention is illustrated in Chapter 7.

7

Planning Treatment and Sessional Guides

Chapter Outline

CBT for Appearance Anxiety: Psychosocial Interventions for Anxiety Due to Visible Difference, First Edition.
Alex Clarke, Andrew Thompson, Elizabeth Jenkinson, Nichola Rumsey and Rob Newell.
© 2014 John Wiley & Sons, Ltd. Published 2014 by John Wiley & Sons, Ltd.

Introduction

In this chapter, case examples are used to illustrate psychological intervention using the stepped care framework as shown in the following text. One example each for level 1 are included for completeness and used as teaching examples, but most examples are for higher intensity work.

The examples are drawn from a range of conditions, but this does not imply that these particular conditions are always managed at this level; clearly it is the psychological impact and extent of the associated problems which indicates the level of intervention.

Working at Level 1 (Table 7.1)

Example 7.1

Reg is 65 and has clearly sun-damaged skin after a lifetime of working in mining in Australia and Africa. He has had a series of basal cell cancers on his scalp which have been treated by surgical removal and skin grafting. This leaves a scar after every procedure. He visits his GP for regular assessment of his blood pressure for an unrelated condition.

His GP asks him about his skin cancer and checks to see that no new lesions are present.

At this point, it would be easier to ignore any appearance issues. Reg is 65 and male. Is it likely that he will be concerned about what he looks like? The answer is that we don't know until we ask. As Rumsey has stated, 'appearance concerns are not the preserve of the young'. As he is examining the skin, the GP raises the subject:

GP: There are no signs of any new lesions and it is all healing up very nicely. Do you find people are curious? Have you had many questions from other people?
   Oh I never take my cap off
GP: That's interesting. What about indoors?
   I take it off at home - mind you I put it back on if someone comes to the door. I used to walk down to the pub – but they have a 'no hats' rule, you know, because of the young

Table 7.1 Stepped care framework for interventions to promote psychosocial adjustment in appearance concern.

Level of intervention	Description	Example of intervention	Health professional background
Level 1	Permission	Sensitive exploration of psychosocial concerns	All health practitioners including General Practitioners, practice nurses, professional health care helplines (such as NHS direct)
Level 2	Limited information	Written information, recommended websites and contact details for support groups. Answering basic questions about visible difference	All health practitioners working with target groups including doctors and nurses in relevant specialties
Level 3	Specific suggestions or interventions	Social skills training, dealing with staring, comments and questions. Managing social situations proactively (e.g simple advice on exposure and behavioural experiments). Level 2 interventions with more complexity/intensity	Individuals with relevant training and with access to supervision such as: Clinical Nurse Specialists, Occupational Therapists, Maxillofacial Technicians, Support Groups
Level 4	Intensive treatments	Gognitive behaviour therapy aimed at identifying and modifying maladaptive appearance core beliefs and schemas. Level 3 interventions with more complexity/ntensity	Clinical Psychologists Cognitive Behavioural Psychotherapists

> chaps in baseball hats and they made me take it off. I was pretty embarrassed - to be honest I don't go out as much I did.
>
> GP: I can understand that was embarrassing. I can see that would make you feel conspicuous. What are you doing with yourself during the day then?
>
> Not a lot. Everything seems a bit of an effort
>
> GP: You know, you aren't unusual. Quite apart from the cancer, changes to what you look like can take some coming to terms with.
>
> Not at my age, surely?
>
> GP: At any age. Whether you're male or female – doesn't matter, and the cause doesn't matter either. The effect is the same. Because you feel self-conscious you tend to stop doing the things you have done for years and before you know it you can start to feel very down…does that sound familiar? It does to be honest…
>
> GP: Would you like to know more about it? I know that there are some very good organisations that can provide more information…

All the GP is doing here is raising the issue in a sensitive way. He has provided brief acknowledgement of the challenge of appearance change and stressed that Reg is not unusual. The goal here is to help him understand that his response is not abnormal. Notice too that Reg has been making assumptions that because he is older he 'ought' not to be concerned. It is very unlikely that he would raise these issues himself unless he is prompted – and yet the beginnings of a pattern of social avoidance are there. Maintaining social networks is a protective factor for good mental health and well-being at all ages. This GP has not put any pressure on Reg – nor has he intervened to provide specific coping strategies. But by raising the question, he has helped Reg to acknowledge legitimate concerns and to do something about them. A sensitive GP might well end the consultation with something like:

GP: Well, perhaps next time I see you, we could check up on how it's going from the social side?

(Reg followed up the consultation by accessing the Changing Faces website and obtaining supportive literature.)

Working at Level 2 (Table 7.1)

Example 7.2

Jacqui is a 32-year-old lady with scleroderma. This is a multisystem autoimmune condition which can cause facial 'tightening' as part of the changes in the underlying connective tissue. People experience functional problems such as difficulty opening their mouth wide enough for dental hygiene and eating bulky foods. There are also characteristic changes in facial appearance. Jacqui has an outpatient appointment to follow-up treatment she is having with fat injections to increase facial mobility. The clinic nurse is examining the injection sites:

NURSE (N): This is all looking very healthy. No sign of infection. It is a little bit more swollen on this side but generally I think it is settling down well. What do you think?
            It's okay
N: You sound a bit disappointed
    Well to be honest…the swelling is a nuisance - and I thought it would make more of a difference. I suppose I had been building my hopes up for such a long time…
N: Well that's understandable. What do other people think? Your friends and family?
    They are great but sometimes I think they are trying to reassure me to make me feel better about myself…
N: It sounds as if you sometimes feel quite down about things
    I am okay most of the time – when I am working and things I tend not to think about it. But then if I am getting ready to go out and I'm thinking will anyone notice my face…
N: Do you find that people notice? What do they say?
    It is not what they say – it's more that I think they are looking and then I get embarrassed and anxious. Sometimes I even put off going out if my face is swollen.
N: Don't forget that we all look at faces when we meet people for the first time especially – and when we are trying to have a conversation with them. People quite often ask our patients about their appearance - it just curiosity. Have you got a good way of dealing with staring or questions? What do you do?
    I just hope they won't notice…

N: you might feel more relaxed if you have an answer up your sleeve. We usually find that people say this is really helpful…for example, your face is still slightly swollen this side. So it is quite likely someone might ask you 'have you hurt it?' Perhaps you could say something like:
'no I have had some hospital treatment but its settling down now. It doesn't hurt'
What do you think? It might be better to be ready than hope they don't say anything.
I'll think about it…

N: In a way, the swelling gives you an opportunity, because you've got a chance to practice whilst your face looks different. It'll also give you feedback on how you can cope with the anxiety you mentioned. It's a good idea to get out into the places that cause anxiety if you can, so you can prove to yourself you can cope with it. Let me finish this and then I will give you some information. We have got a good booklet but you might find some of the information on the website even more helpful…

The nurse here is aiming to provide limited information and advice. She decides to suggest one answer to questioning because the temporary swelling for this lady means that there is a higher probability that she will experience social intrusions. However, she does not go on to a systematic intervention aimed at building social skills as at level 3.

In both the level 1 and 2 examples here, the health professionals are providing holistic care. They are exploring concerns about appearance and using basic counselling skills (a combination of summarizing, open questions and reflecting back) and the opportunity of a 'teachable moment' to provide basic support. This is not adding to the time they are already spending with their patient because they have a clear pathway in place for onward support and they are aware of the boundaries for that they are trying to achieve. Busy health professionals are unwilling to raise questions for which they cannot provide some kind of answer in terms of treatment options or resources. However, once these are in place, they are in the best position to screen for problems and to provide early information and advice. See Appendix A for further resources.

The importance of providing these simple interventions cannot be overemphasized. Acknowledging the legitimacy of concerns and development of coping skills can help prevent the patterns of social avoidance which take longer to overcome once they are firmly entrenched.

Working at Level 3 (Table 7.1)

Example 3

Dan is an engineer. He lost a finger in a DIY accident at home. He attributes this to preoccupation with another problem when he was laying a floor. Momentary lack of attention to safety instructions meant that a circular saw slipped and took off his finger. He has a very neat amputation at the second knuckle. Although he is pleased with the appearance of his finger, he is concerned about the way other people respond to him. This is how his treatment with the psychologist was managed.

Session 1

Structure Outline

Eliciting the problem
Begin to form problem list and treatment targets
Introduction to model
Early formulation
Outline of potential timeframe – need to attend

First homework assessment questionnaire completion, etc.

T: I understand that you have had an accident and lost part of your finger. Would you like to tell me about any problems that this is causing you since you left hospital?
Yes. The problem is about work. I have to do presentations and I am worried about what people will think about my hand.

T: What do you think about it?
I think it is fantastic! I think they made a brilliant job of it. I have hardly got any scarring, it is not painful and I am learning to use a keyboard with it – I can't thank them enough.

T: What makes you think that other people will be worried about it when you are not?
It had not occurred to me, but then a colleague told me that I had upset someone when giving a presentation. He asked me if I had noticed, and to be honest, I hadn't. But now I am thinking, what if other people are upset? I have to do presentations in my job, and if I say I can't do them I am worried that this puts my job at risk.

T: I see. Apart from this colleague at work, are you aware of anyone else who is worried about the appearance of your hand?
Well, I notice sometimes that people look at it and do a double take.

T: Why do you think that they do that?
I think they are wondering what happened to it.

T: I think you are probably right. Have you checked that out at all by asking them?
No, I couldn't do that.

T: What would happen if you did that?
I just – I'm quite shy. I don't think I would be comfortable doing that.

T: What if someone asked you about your hand directly? What would you say then?
I don't know. I just hope that they won't ask. I try to keep my hand under a newspaper or something when I am on the train.

T: So let me summarise what you have told me. You have had an accident and lost your finger. You are very pleased with the outcome. It looks neat, is not painful and you are able to use it pretty well. But, there is a problem with other people. You are worried, because you are aware that other people notice it and sometimes that they are shocked by it. Is that right?
Yes.

T: Well, let's think about the strategy of hiding your hand first of all. It is very natural to try to conceal something, but it is quite hard to hide your hand. I wonder if you have found that?
Yes, I must admit that sometimes I forget and then sometimes I see people looking at it.

T: When that happens what do you do?
I don't really know, just look away…

T: Does that work? Do you find that this is helpful?
Not really. I feel as if I want to change seats. I wish I could find a different way.

T: One of the things that happens in this sort of situation is that everyone feels uncomfortable. You feel uncomfortable, because your hand has been noticed. The other person feels uncomfortable, because he has been caught staring. A good way of diffusing this is with a comment that demonstrates that you feel okay about it – after all, you have told me that you are very happy about its appearance.
Yes...

T: So showing that you feel okay will put the other person at ease. You could look at him and smile...
But then he might ask me...

T: Yes, he probably would, so you need to be ready with an answer. Can you think of something that might lighten the situation a bit? Humour often works very well. Can you think of something that might make him smile?
(Shakes his head.)

T: It has to be something that you feel comfortable saying – I was thinking of another patient with a similar injury who said something along the lines, 'Just adding to the DIY statistics!!!'
Oh!!...I see what you mean. Actually, that sounds just like me. Is it okay if I write that down?

T: I think you will find that being ready to manage other people's responses makes you feel a little more in control of the situation and is better than waiting for something to happen, or feeling that other people are uneasy. Also, the more often you don't conceal your hand and make that response, the easier it gets, the less anxiety-provoking. Bit like any other aspect of a presentation, really.
Yes I think I could do that. Do you think it would be okay at work?

T: I think it would be a good idea to try it out in other situations to see how comfortable you feel and whether there are other things you can say which sound like you. Then once it just trips off the tongue, think about using this at work. What you are looking for is a very clear statement that you feel okay about your hand and if other people are not okay, then that is their problem, not yours.
I see what you mean. I had not thought about it like that...

Dan was then introduced to a simple monitoring form and set the target of practising this response on the journey to work. A second appointment was arranged for 4 weeks' time.

At his second session his homework showed that he had used the strategy of commenting about DIY when he caught someone looking at his hand. This had produced a range of responses from a smile to a conversation about DIY. There had been no negative outcomes.

He also reflected on the idea that if his hand was not a problem for him, then he was not responsible for the way other people felt. This reattribution was very helpful; in fact he felt very indignant about the fact that he had assumed a responsibility for other people. He shifted this belief 100%.

In contrast to the previous example, this provides a good example of a one-stop intervention. The key points are:

- Some people can very quickly grasp the principle being discussed and apply this in their own situation. This patient was very significantly preoccupied and disabled by his beliefs about the response of other people. He was able to reduce this preoccupation 100% with one session plus focused practice.
- Sometimes it is very useful to use examples from other patients. This may not always end up as the statement used ultimately, but it gives an idea to people who can't immediately grasp the principle and provides a basis for a quick behavioural experiment.
- Relevant literature with an appointment letter is a very good way of giving permission to raise something else and therefore of triggering the main concern for the individual. This is particularly important because appearance-related issues are often poorly understood by those referring for psychological input.

This is a good example of an intervention, which might be offered by a health professional without a specialized psychology or CBT background, after a relatively brief period of appropriate training. An alternative is the use of computer-assisted intervention such as the FaceIT program.

Working at Level 3 Using FaceIT (www.faceitonline.org.uk)

Bessell et al. (2010, 2012) have developed an online programme designed to deliver a level 3 intervention for people with appearance concerns related to disfigurement. This has been assessed both for user effectiveness (Bessell et al., 2010) and clinical effectiveness (Bessell et al., 2012) when supervised by a health professional. The programme (and a similar programme for children, YPFACEIT (Williamson et al., 2012) is currently being developed as a stand-alone resource.

The programme consists of eight modules, each of which takes about 1 hour to complete, and outcomes include standardized measures of mood and appearance concern:

- Introduction to visible difference
- Non-verbal communication
- Verbal communication
- Goal setting
- Cognitive restructuring
- Social skills and anxiety management
- Exposure therapy
- Summary

Content of the modules is based on that described throughout this book.

Bessell et al. (2012) reported good user acceptance of the programme at all ages and even for people unused to using online resources. Outcomes indicated significant improvements with people continuing to report reduced anxiety at 6-month follow-up. The programme provides a very valuable additional resource and can be delivered by a non-psychology health professional under supervision. Future evaluation will report on the programme's effectiveness when used as a stand-alone resource.

Working at Level 4 Using CBT

Planning Treatment and Sessional Guides

CBT Session Guidelines
A typical course of CBT will last from 10 to 12 sessions of 50 minutes. Early sessions are focused on understanding the presenting problem using the conceptual framework presented earlier (see Table 7.1). Although the formulation of the problem will constantly be revised on the basis of evidence gathered during treatment, the earlier sessions should focus on assessment and sharing the formulation with the patient, together with goal setting and clear discussion of requirements with respect to record-keeping, homework and regular attendance. Later sessions will be focused on consolidation and maintenance. Wells (1997) suggests this timeline (see Figure 7.1).

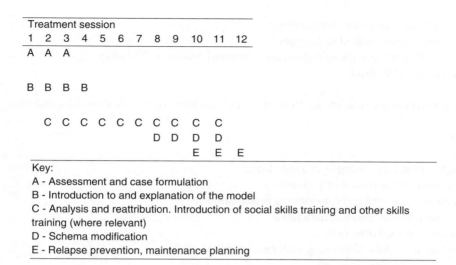

Key:
A - Assessment and case formulation
B - Introduction to and explanation of the model
C - Analysis and reattribution. Introduction of social skills training and other skills training (where relevant)
D - Schema modification
E - Relapse prevention, maintenance planning

Figure 7.1   A suggested time frame for treatment sessions (Wells, 1997). Reproduced with permission from John Wiley & Sons, Ltd

Each treatment session also has its own structure but always starts with a review of homework and agenda setting for the session. The content of the agenda varies according to stage in treatment but will usually cover the following (derived from Wells, 1997). For those with a visible disfigurement, development and practice of social skills may form part of the sessions.

1. *Review of homework*
   - Review self-report data (DAS24, HADS, noticeability and worry, specific target measures)
   - Reaction to written information
   - Feedback from thought monitoring
   - Results of mini experiments
   - Problems with homework
2. *Identification of Negative Automatic Thoughts (NATs)/assumptions and implementation of cognitive and behavioural reattribution, for example*:
   - Recent difficult events
   - Questioning the evidence
   - Behavioural experiments
   - Labelling cognitive/thinking processes
3. *Discussion of the emerging role of thoughts and behaviours on formulation, for example*:
   - Effect of safety behaviours
   - Role of avoidance in preventing disconfirmation
   - Influence of danger appraisals on behaviour
   - Effect of negative thoughts on emotion
4. *Setting new homework*
   - Identifying unhelpful thought record
   - Exposure and dropping safety behaviours
   - Mini surveys

- Attention and distraction strategies
- Compassion-focused techniques
- Specific coping skills answering questions and dealing with staring

5. *Summary and feedback*

Mapping this on to the timeline for treatment, session plans might look something like this:

Session 1
Assessment
Eliciting the problem – using Socratic dialogue
Begin to form problem list and goal setting
Noticeability and worry graph/beginning formulation
Evidence for internal and external shame
Magic wand – valued directions
Explanation of model – illustrating with case examples
Introduction to relevant research
Outline of potential timeframe – need to attend

First homework assessment questionnaire completion, etc.

N.B. Therapist homework – find out about condition, timeline and treatment (if unfamiliar with the particular condition with which the patient presents, it is helpful to understand as much as possible).

Session 2
Review data – identify particular high scores
Feedback observational data by therapist (social skills)
Set agenda – assess other factors motivation, readiness for change
Self-efficacy
Introduction to social comparison processes
Salience and valence (pie chart)
Magic wand – valued directions
Restatement of formulation
Therapeutic buddy (consider asking a friend to support treatment)
Homework
Summary and feedback

Session 3
Review of homework and reformulation
Set agenda
Introduction to behavioural monitoring using rating scales
Role of self-focused attention
Review of evidence in context of model

Introduction to NATs
Homework
Summary and feedback

Session 4
Review of homework and reformulation
Set agenda
Role of self-focused attention
Strategies for attentional training
Classifying cognitive errors
Reattribution of beliefs
Safety behaviours
Design behavioural experiments
TTTT – introduction to answering questions
Homework
Summary and feedback

Sessions 5–8
Review of homework
Set agenda
Strategies for attentional training
Symptom-focused reattribution
Feedback from behavioural experiments
Development of personal coping approaches
Homework
Summary and feedback

Session 9–11
Review of homework
Set agenda
Symptom-focused reattribution
Feedback from behavioural experiments
Schema-focused reattribution
Preparation for ending
Homework
Summary and feedback

Session 12
Review of homework
Set agenda
Reformulation
Relapse prevention
Follow-up planning
Outcome measures
Summary and feedback

Clinical Examples

Example 7.4

Jane has Bell's palsy. This arose spontaneously in pregnancy. She was offered no treatment and told that it would resolve itself. She was referred when her son was 1 year old with continuing preoccupation with her appearance. She wanted to return to work, but felt unable to do so because her job involved facing the public. Her doctor had told her that 'there was nothing anyone could do and she had to learn to live with it'.

She presented as a young woman with her hair scraped back off her face and no make-up or jewellery. She was entirely dressed in black clothing. Her facial palsy was objectively noticeable particularly when her face became animated, but she tended to look down when this happened. Her eye contact was initially poor, looking away and holding her head at an angle with the non-affected side facing.

Session 1

(After basic introductions)

T: Would you like to tell me something about your concerns about your face and what has triggered your request for this appointment now?

I have got this condition called Bell's palsy. I was pregnant and everything was going fine and I just woke up one day and one side of my face had stopped working.

T: What did you think about that? Had you ever heard of this happening to anyone else?

No…I couldn't explain it. I was really concerned that I had an infection and that the baby might have got it, so I went to the doctor – and he couldn't really explain it either. He told me not to worry and that it would get better in a few weeks.

T: Did it change at all?

No – nothing happened, and then when I went to see the specialist he said it was too late and there was nothing anyone could do. He said I just had to learn to live with it.

T: So you were told it would get better – but it didn't – and now there is apparently no treatment. How does that make you feel?

Really, really angry. No-one is interested – and it's my face. I am only 26 and I look as if I have had a stroke…

T: What does that mean for you – if other people think you have had a stroke?

I don't know – they stare and feel sorry for me.

T: Can you give me an example of what you mean?

Yes, me and my friend went shopping for the baby. We went for a cup of tea and were talking about how much everything cost. Then this woman offered to pay for us. She said she wanted me to help…

T: Did she say why?

No, I just assumed she felt sorry for me – I was so surprised. I suppose she thought I was a single mum – I don't know, but I think it was because of my face. I didn't really say anything, but afterwards I couldn't stop thinking about it. I am sure she thought she was being kind, but it made me feel terrible.

T: It is an interesting idea – that someone feels sorry for you…it is certainly an unusual thing to do. What if you are right and she feels sorry for you? What would that mean?

It would mean that she is sorry because I look ugly – I can't smile any more. I am not the person I was before. People are sorry for me and I can't stand it…I look miserable all the time and I'm angry with everyone, even my partner–especially him.

T: What do you think he feels about that?

I know he doesn't understand. He's very good – he says it doesn't make any difference to him, but it should do. He doesn't know what it feels like; I can't stop thinking about it…

T: So it sounds as if this is very difficult for you. Everyone else – the doctor, your partner is saying it is a pretty trivial problem, but for you it has changed the way other people see you and how you see yourself – and you are angry and preoccupied by it. So this has been a big change – just when you want to be thinking about the baby.

Yes, that's exactly right. I can't imagine how I can cope – I don't want to cope! I just want my face to be like it was before.

T: Let us imagine for a moment, that we have a magic wand. We can't change the appearance of your face, but we can think about how you would like life to be different for you. Can you tell me how your life is different? What might you be doing. How would your day-to-day life be different?

I would feel more confident about myself…

T: (interrupting) Exactly, but let's just move away from how you feel to what you do…if you felt more confident, what could you do that you are not doing at the moment?

NB: The distinction between feeling and behaving is very important in goal setting. People often slip back to talking in terms of feelings and prompting, even if this means interrupting, which maintains the focus on specific targets for change.

Well, I would be back at work for a start…

T: That is a very good example (writes down following maintenance cycle on a white board) (Figure 7.2).

The first session then continued in the same way, to elicit problems and identify further goals for treatment, including use of formal measurement. For example, Jane rated the visible difference in her appearance as 8/10 and her preoccupation and worry as 10/10 (Figure 7.3).

Jane rated the visible difference in her appearance as 8/10 and her preoccupation and worry as 10/10. The formulation of her problem was then developed further as in the following text and summarized in the template (see Figure 7.4):

T: You have described to me the way that this condition has impacted on your life. It suddenly appeared without explanation and you are aware that other people notice it and make assumptions about you that are not true. You are aware of people staring, making comments and asking questions and you feel conspicuous and as if you stand out.

Not surprisingly, this makes you feel unhappy and preoccupied with your face. You also feel angry because you can't find any way of changing this situation. You tend to avoid doing the things you used to enjoy, because you feel anxious when you meet other people. You would like to go back to work, but you feel your appearance is stopping you. Like many people in your situation you have taken steps to protect yourself. I have noticed in this assessment that to start with, you tended to look down or hide your face, but you stopped doing that as you relaxed. This is what we call safety behaviour – it makes you feel more comfortable, am I right? [Jane nods] But it actually makes it harder for other people to talk to you when they can't see your face. It is much easier for us to communicate when we can each see each other's eyes…

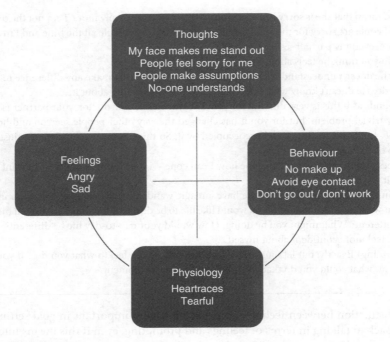

Figure 7.2   Triggering event: woman in shop offers to pay for tea.

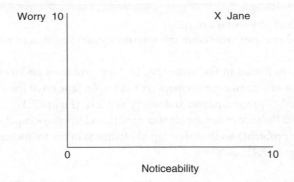

Figure 7.3   Noticeability and worry graph.

I think we should start off by identifying the things that you can do which can help you to manage other people – like the woman you described – in a way that allows you to feel in control. Some of this will be really practical – like working out some good answers to questions about your face or deflecting the attention away from you to other things. If we can reduce the amount that your face interferes in your day-to-day life, then we can also reduce the amount that you think about it and worry about it. Does that make sense? So, we have the same goal as a surgeon might have, to enable you to do all the things that you would like to do in your everyday life, but we are going to do it a different way. Can you see what I mean?

I can understand that it might be okay for other people, but to be honest with you, I can't imagine I could ever accept the way I look…

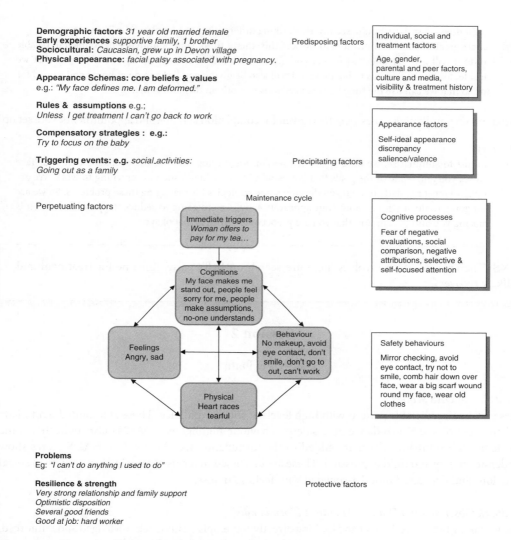

Demographic factors *31 year old married female*
Early experiences *supportive family, 1 brother*
Sociocultural: *Caucasian, grew up in Devon village*
Physical appearance: *facial palsy associated with pregnancy.*

Predisposing factors

Individual, social and treatment factors

Age, gender, parental and peer factors, culture and media, visibility & treatment history

Appearance Schemas: core beliefs & values
e.g.: *"My face defines me. I am deformed."*

Rules & assumptions e.g.;
Unless I get treatment I can't go back to work

Compensatory strategies : e.g.:
Try to focus on the baby

Appearance factors

Self-ideal appearance discrepancy salience/valence

Triggering events: e.g. *social activities:*
Going out as a family

Precipitating factors

Maintenance cycle

Perpetuating factors

Immediate triggers
Woman offers to pay for my tea…

Cognitions
My face makes me stand out, people feel sorry for me, people make assumptions, no-one understands

Feelings
Angry, sad

Behaviour
No makeup, avoid eye contact, don't smile, don't go to out, can't work

Physical
Heart races tearful

Cognitive processes

Fear of negative evaluations, social comparison, negative attributions, selective & self-focused attention

Safety behaviours

Mirror checking, avoid eye contact, try not to smile, comb hair down over face, wear a big scarf wound round my face, wear old clothes

Problems
Eg: *"I can't do anything I used to do"*

Resilience & strength
Very strong relationship and family support
Optimistic disposition
Several good friends
Good at job: hard worker

Protective factors

Figure 7.4 Using the CBT template to begin formulation for Jane.

T: I think that is very understandable at the moment; in fact I would say that most people can't quite see how they are going to feel differently about themselves at this early stage. However, the good thing about this way of working [CBT] is that we have done lots of research and have good evidence that this approach is effective. If I think of all the people I have seen over many years, I would say that most people start off pretty sceptical – but if we start by making some simple changes, then they begin to see change happening and build on these early successes. Let me give you an example…[relevant case example]. Does that ring some bells for you?

N.B. See section on motivation. Verbal persuasion is used here, via the example of another patient challenging perceived low self-efficacy.

Yes it does – I still can't quite see myself thinking differently, but I would really like to try.

T: That's great. If you feel motivated to work at this, then I think your confidence in yourself to be able to do it will grow stronger as we get going…so you need to attend regularly at the times that we decide, for say 10 sessions to begin with. I will also be giving you tasks to do at home and record for me so that we can use the time between sessions to work on this too. Is that okay?

Questionnaires and rating scales were then given for completion at home and appointments were set up.

Summary

T: So just to summarise, we have spent this session identifying some of the problems that your face causes you and some of the goals that you would like to achieve, such as returning to work. We are going to meet regularly to help you develop some strategies for managing these problems. So we are not going to do anything about your appearance, but we are going to reduce the problems that it is causing you and the amount that you are preoccupied by it. Is that okay?

NB: Therapist research involves literature search on Bell's palsy, timeline for treatment and likely recovery.

Session 2

Review Data

Discussion of DAS Scores

These fall in a predictable pattern with high levels of social avoidance. These are pointed out to Jane and the role of social avoidance as a safety behaviour highlighted. DAS24[1] also indicated some problems with intimacy, which are added to the formulation (see Figure 7.5). HADS scores show moderate anxiety and mild depression. These are discussed in terms of anticipatory anxiety in social situations and depressed mood associated with feelings of loss.

Feedback Observational Data by Therapist (Social Skills)

Jane is making better eye contact and looking directly at therapist. This is acknowledged and reinforced.

Set Agenda

Motivation, readiness for change and self-efficacy.

Introduction to Social Comparison Processes

Therapist discusses the way in which appearance is linked with success in media messages. Jane is asked to comment on her own appearance, hair, choice of clothing, etc. 'Write off thinking' (e.g. 'Now I look like this, no point in dressing nicely'). Examine counterarguments – how do other people

---

[1] The DAS24 is very helpful in introducing the problems of appearance anxiety as many people have never disclosed their concerns before and are particularly reassured by the examples of social avoidance included on the scale.

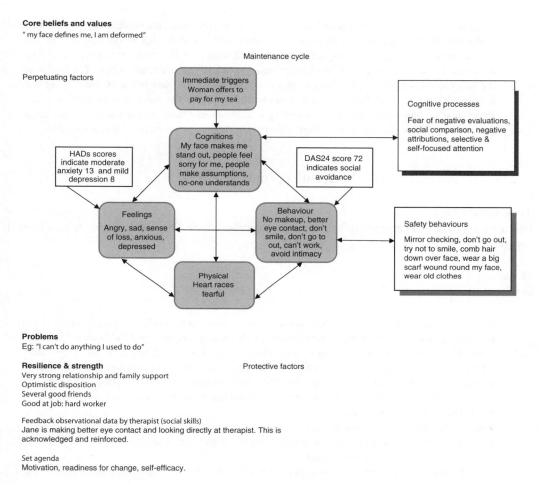

Core beliefs and values
" my face defines me, I am deformed"

Maintenance cycle

Perpetuating factors

Immediate triggers
Woman offers to
pay for my tea

Cognitive processes

Fear of negative evaluations,
social comparison, negative
attributions, selective &
self-focused attention

HADs scores
indicate moderate
anxiety 13 and mild
depression 8

Cognitions
My face makes me
stand out, people feel
sorry for me, people
make assumptions,
no-one understands

DAS24 score 72
indicates social
avoidance

Feelings
Angry, sad, sense
of loss, anxious,
depressed

Behaviour
No makeup, better
eye contact, don't
smile, don't go to
out, can't work,
avoid intimacy

Safety behaviours

Mirror checking, don't go out,
try not to smile, comb hair
down over face, wear a big
scarf wound round my face,
wear old clothes

Physical
Heart races
tearful

Problems
Eg: "I can't do anything I used to do"

Resilience & strength   Protective factors
Very strong relationship and family support
Optimistic disposition
Several good friends
Good at job: hard worker

Feedback observational data by therapist (social skills)
Jane is making better eye contact and looking directly at therapist. This is
acknowledged and reinforced.

Set agenda
Motivation, readiness for change, self-efficacy.

Figure 7.5   Reformulation.

regard me? Pie charts are used to develop idea of different attributes by which others are valued. Compare self and best friend. Elicit strength of belief that appearance of her face is the most important thing about her. Reduced from 80/100 to 10/100 since the last session.

Restatement of Formulation

T: We have thought about the way that this condition suddenly appeared without explanation. You are aware of people staring, making comments and asking questions and you believe that this makes you conspicuous – as if you stand out and that other people make incorrect assumptions about you and sometimes may feel sorry for you.

Not surprisingly, these beliefs make you feel unhappy and preoccupied with your face. You feel anxious about meeting people and depressed that this has happened to you. You can sense your heart racing at times and at others you feel tense or tearful. You have also changed your behaviour You have stopped using make up and have changed your hair, you avoid looking at people so they can't see your face and you have noted on the questionnaires that your relationship with your partner is affected. You have not yet started work which you would like to do. But we can also see that you have made some changes since last time. You are not hiding your face from other people and your eye contact is better and I am finding it much easier to talk to you as a result of that. You have used the way you think about your friends to alter the belief about your face being the main thing that defines who you are – and this makes it easier to understand to the way that your partner thinks about what has happened…so now we are going to think of some more ways in which we can change this pathway so that think and feel differently and how this can help you to achieve your goals…

Elicit Patient Understanding

Therapeutic Buddy
Discuss ways in which partner can help her with the programme. She decides to invite him to next session.

Homework
Behavioural experiment:

T: Remember earlier we talked about how the way you dress might be a safety seeking behaviour? I'm going to suggest we make an experiment to see whether it might be more helpful to dress as though you didn't believe there was anything wrong with your face. This would help us to see at least three things: whether your belief that you can't dress like that is true; whether the assumption that you are less safe if you dress like that is true; and whether your belief that you can't tolerate the anxiety you associate with dressing like that is true. I'm going to ask you what you believe you could do towards that between now and next time.
Well, I could start to wear make up again
T: Excellent, and can I suggest clothing somewhat like you used to dress before?
Well, I could wear a dress when I go out.
T: Great, I can tell you think it might be difficult, but let's look at it at this stage as a kind of fact finding task. Now, how often do you think you could do these things?

Record-keeping.
Summary and Feedback

Session 3

Jane's partner has come with her.

Review of Homework and Reformulation

Jane is dressed in bright coloured t-shirt and wearing make-up. Posture and eye contact are normal. She appears more relaxed and smiles more. Review of homework; she has been wearing clothes she had from before her pregnancy and has left off the scarf. Review the chart. She has had some compliments from family members. Rating of preoccupation with appearance is 7/10. Partner confirms that she is less depressed and more positive. Jane explains the model to her partner.

Set Agenda

Introduction to behavioural monitoring using rating scales. Jane has already kept simple record of what she wears every day. Now this is extended to reducing safety behaviours and building level of activity by going out more.

Introduction to Answering Questions About Her Face

She generates a statement she is happy with.

Role of Self-Focused Attention Discussed

Strategies are focused upon what is happening and not on how she feels. Her partner is recruited to help her. In social situations he agrees to stay with her and help with conversation. If anyone asks him about her face, he has an answer too, which she agrees with.

TTTT

Setting some goals for the week. Troubleshooting using 'what if?' questions. Review of evidence in context of model.
Introduction to NATs

Homework

Go with husband to the zoo with baby. Record using DBR form.
Summary and Feedback

Session 4

Review of Homework and Reformulation

She has been to the model village and added extra activities herself. Records show that she is aware of people looking at her. A child at the model village asked his mother 'why does the lady have a wonky smile?' She used her practised answer and ended up chatting to the mother about pregnancy. She felt very positive about her response. Her partner is very supportive and pleased. Her self-efficacy rating is higher. She is able to describe the model. She says that she can see herself making progress but still anxious about getting back to work and feels very conspicuous 'writing scripts' about what people are thinking (see Figure 7.6).

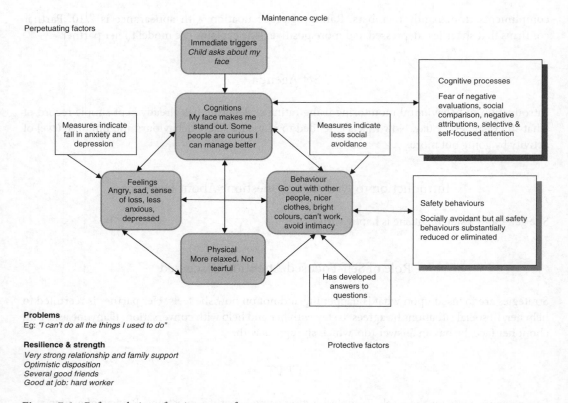

Figure 7.6 Reformulation of maintenance factors.

Set Agenda

Role of Self-Focused Attention
Experience that everyone is staring is discussed in the context of the Strenta and Kleck (1985) experiment (see Section 'Anticipatory and Post-Event Processing' in Chapter 3).

Revisiting NATs, classifying cognitive processing styles and reattribution of beliefs are all discussed using the Strenta and Kleck (1985) model:

- *Safety behaviours*, social avoidance and social skills are illustrated through her own change in safety behaviours (e.g. lack of eye contact). Role of avoidance in preventing disconfirmation is illustrated in this context.

Reattribution of Beliefs

'My appearance is responsible for how people respond to me versus my behaviour is responsible for how people respond to me'.

Design Behavioural Experiments

TTTT – further steps to answering questions and dealing with staring.

Homework

Increase social activity:
Monitor perceived staring using triple column technique. Generate counterarguments.
Go to local toddlers group with baby.
Go to the hairdresser.
Summary and Feedback

Session 5

Review of Homework

Social activity: Lots of examples, including general everyday activities, going to the supermarket and meeting friends. She is aware of people looking at her and feels anxious and upset. Explore the thinking biases that underpin her feelings and examine alternative explanations and reattribution in terms of curiosity. She identifies a pattern of 'all-or-nothing thinking'; if one person notices, this triggers other thoughts about noticeability, 'never' getting back to work, never meeting her ambitions for herself, etc. She is able to identify this pattern herself.

Toddlers group is difficult. She did not know anyone, found it difficult to get started with talking and is preoccupied with what other people were thinking. Eventually someone asked about her face halfway through a conversation about nursery schools – she felt ambushed and did not answer as she had planned. 'I went on and on about it until the poor woman looked bored stiff'.

T: Do you think that it is possible that boring people is something that we all do from time to time?
    I suppose it is possible – yes
T: So just because occasionally people are not interested in what we are saying doesn't mean that everyone is always going to feel the same way

This discussion went on to discuss the concept of mind reading and the temptation to use the other persons behaviour as evidence that we 'know' what they are thinking.

Because Jane felt disappointed, she did not complete the final homework task of hairdresser. Discussed in terms of social avoidance and inability to disconfirm her fears.

Set Agenda

Focus on homework as feedback and planning for next steps. Reassurance about zig-zag line in progress, eliciting reminders of other successes from the patient. There is no such thing as failure, only feedback. What needs to change in order to visit hairdresser?

Strategies for Attentional Training

Focusing on here and now and conversation skills.

Development of Personal Coping Approaches

Further ways of managing visible difference include being proactive, taking control and shutting down questioning, which becomes intrusive.

Homework

Continue self-monitoring of activities with record of NATs and cognitive processing styles.
Go to the hairdresser.
Summary and Feedback

Session 6

Review of Homework

She arrives with new hairstyle! She used approach strategies to talk to hairdresser about softening her hair and explaining palsy. She suggests that this is the way she can manage presentations at work. Rather than wonder if anyone has noticed, she can point out the difference in her face. She has worked out a way of incorporating humour into her explanation, having read the information from Changing Faces. She says that this 'sounds like the old me' speaking. She is much closer to husband, with no problems with intimacy and spontaneously talks about going back to work.
   Set Agenda

Measure Noticeability and Worry

Worry is now down to 3/10 and noticeability down to 6/10. She is surprised that as she thinks about her face less, she feels it is actually less noticeable to other people.

Reattribution of Beliefs

Appearance is important, but I can control the way people relate to me through the way I present myself and how I can behave. She rates self-esteem as much higher and 'feels more confident'.

Feedback from Behavioural Experiments

She can identify cognitive processing styles and is aware of starting a chain of thinking. She says to herself, 'DON't START!' when she recognizes mind reading.

Development of Personal Coping Approaches

Has three different ways of answering questions.

Homework

Continue to build of previous homework and add phone work – ask to come and see Human Resources (HR).
Summary and Feedback
She is very positive about treatment and feels she has 'turned a corner'.

Session 7

Review of Homework

She has an appointment with HR this week.

Set Agenda

Focus on preparation for interview and managing questions about her face. Reattribution of anxiety emotions – 'everyone is nervous at an interview'. Prepare statement for how she will talk about her face at the interview. Feedback from behavioural experiments: has been to 'work do' with partner. Dealt with one question. Most people did not even notice – 'too busy with their own issues'.

Schema-Focused Reattribution

How important is her appearance in achieving what she wants to do? 'Important in terms of how I present myself and the impression people form of me – but I can control that most of the time'. She spontaneously says that she understands now what her partner was saying when he said it was not important. It is important, but it is no longer the most important thing because it does not affect the things that she and the people important to her really value – it does not devalue her.

'I am not just my face. My face is different but that does not make me abnormal'.

Preparation for Ending

Plan for ending in four sessions.

Homework

Preparation and recording HR interview.
Summary and Feedback

Session 8

Review of Homework

She went to see HR. She discovered that they had anticipated her moving to a different job – 'less face-to-face contact'. She said that she did not need to consider this and negotiated a part-time return to her old job. 'Over the moon'. Never thought I could do it. Explained that she feels this condition has given her more insight into other people's problems. Met lots of friends whilst she was there – all very positive about having her back.

Schema-Focused Reattribution

Discussion of her underlying assumptions about appearance and its importance. She is able to make links between the differences in how she and her brother were treated, 'my mum always told me I was pretty but for him it was more about being a clever boy' – so as I child, I suppose I just assumed that is why she loved me. I have never really thought about this until now…but now I can see that… and I feel really lucky…because I have lots of people who care about and love me and it's not about my face….

Planning for Ending

She has been offered an early start back at work and feels that she would like to get on with this. The sessions are shortened. The last one next time is to focus on maintenance.

Homework

Review previous homework diaries and identify any areas she would like to review.

Session 9

Homework

Reviewed diaries. Re-read Changing Faces literature. Has added a 'shut down' response to questions: 'I'll tell you all about it sometime – but I want to finish these e-mails if you don't mind so I can get off a bit early today'.

Agenda

Keeping it going. Traffic lights: identifying a return to old patterns of thinking. Revisit her notebooks and challenge NATs. Accept having 'bad days'.

Final completion of rating scales and outcomes. Noticeability is now 4/10. Worry is 1/10. DAS24 and HADS are within non-clinical range.

One more session is booked at 6 months.

Outcome

Jane returned to work and was promoted within 6 months of returning. She had planned to be part-time but found that her son settled easily into a routine with a nanny and added extra days. Similarly, she had planned to work mornings only to begin with but found that she was less tired than she had thought and went into a normal working day pattern almost straight away.

Jane was followed up 2 years later. Her positive behaviour change had been maintained and she described herself as 'absolutely fine now', able to deal with other people's curiosity and less self-conscious about her facial appearance (see Figure 7.7).

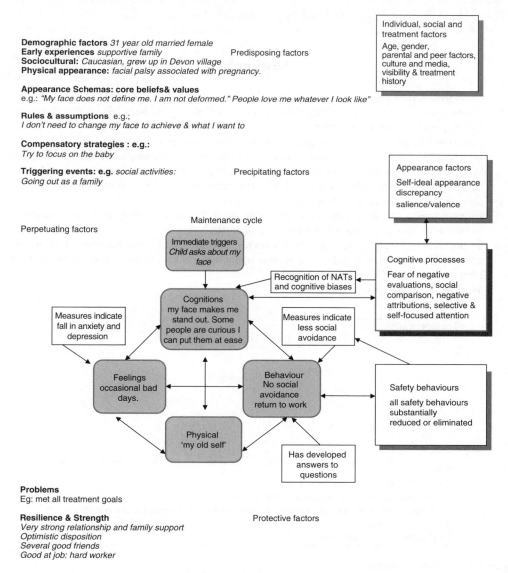

Demographic factors *31 year old married female*
Early experiences *supportive family*   Predisposing factors
Sociocultural: *Caucasian, grew up in Devon village*
Physical appearance: *facial palsy associated with pregnancy.*

Appearance Schemas: core beliefs& values
e.g.: *"My face does not define me. I am not deformed." People love me whatever I look like"*

Rules & assumptions e.g.;
I don't need to change my face to achieve & what I want to

Compensatory strategies : e.g.:
Try to focus on the baby

Triggering events: e.g. *social activities:*   Precipitating factors
Going out as a family

Individual, social and treatment factors
Age, gender, parental and peer factors, culture and media, visibility & treatment history

Appearance factors
Self-ideal appearance discrepancy
salience/valence

Perpetuating factors   Maintenance cycle

Immediate triggers
Child asks about my face

Recognition of NATs and cognitive biases

Cognitive processes
Fear of negative evaluations, social comparison, negative attributions, selective & self-focused attention

Measures indicate fall in anxiety and depression

Cognitions
my face makes me stand out. Some people are curious I can put them at ease

Measures indicate less social avoidance

Feelings
occasional bad days.

Behaviour
No social avoidance return to work

Safety behaviours
all safety behaviours substantially reduced or eliminated

Physical
'my old self'

Has developed answers to questions

Problems
Eg: met all treatment goals

Resilience & Strength   Protective factors
Very strong relationship and family support
Optimistic disposition
Several good friends
Good at job: hard worker

Figure 7.7   CBT template for Jane at completion of treatment.

Example 7.5

Deirdre has excess skin following gastric banding to treat morbid obesity. She has lost 100% of her excess body weight, losing a total of 10 stone from her maximum of 20 stone. She has successfully modified her diet, eating frequent small portions, and she has identified the foods that she can no longer eat. She is no longer taking medication to manage diabetes, and her blood pressure is normal. She is able to do more activities with her children and has no regrets about the surgery. However, she has been left with excess skin on her abdomen. She presents as a fashionably dressed woman wearing jeans stuffed into long leather boots and a loose top. She has long hair and is wearing make-up and jewellery (see Figure 7.8).

Session 1

(After basic introductions)

T: Would you like to tell me something about your concerns about your body and what has triggered your request for this appointment now?

I have lost 10 stone and now I have got all this extra skin everywhere – it's really awful

T: Were you expecting this? Do you remember discussing it when you were thinking about the original surgery?

Well yes I remember them saying 'by the way you might get some extra skin afterwards' but I didn't realise that it would be as bad as this. I wasn't prepared for the impact it would have on me

T: Can you tell me more about that and how it affects you?

It's just horrible. The thing is that I look okay with my clothes on. I'm getting loads of compliments but that is because people don't know what is underneath

T: So you had this life changing surgery which has had a brilliant result – you have lost all this weight and gained lots of health benefits. Everyone is saying that you look fantastic, but you know about what is underneath. Does that sound right?

Yes that's it – it looks just…. Horrible.

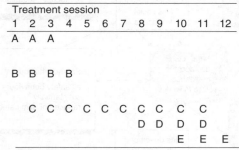

Key:
A - Assessment and case formulation
B - Introduction to and explanation of the model
C - Analysis and reattribution. Introduction of social skills training (where relevant)
D - Schema modification
E - Relapse prevention, maintenance planning

Figure 7.8   Treatment timeline.

T: Now, to help me understand the problem, I want you to imagine that you have just had a shower and you are looking at yourself naked in the mirror…
     (interrupting)…I never to do that…I can't look at myself….

T: Well let's just try to imagine that you are doing it. It might help if you close your eyes and just imagine yourself at home. Look at yourself in the mirror and tell me what you can see.
     It's just…it is not me…all this skin…(starts to cry)….

T: It is obviously very upsetting for you. Take your time…. Can you tell me how you are feeling? What is the emotion when you look at yourself like this?
     It's just…it makes me feel sick …it's disgusting.

T: So when you look at your own body you feel sick and disgusted. Is that right?
     Yes…and if I feel like this, what about other people? I've split up from my partner because I couldn't let him near me. And now I have met someone new and I can't let him near me. How could I ever let anyone else look at me when I look like this?

T: Let me see if I've got this right. You avoid looking at yourself because you feel sick and upset – you used the word disgusted – by what you see. So it sounds as though you are living a double life where everyone admires and congratulates you about how you look – but it is as if you have this shameful secret about what you really look like underneath…Yes, that's just it….

T: And if other people were to see – what would happen?
     I wouldn't let them see. I can't.

T: What about your children?
     Well, yes, they have seen – when I get out the bath. Sometimes they poke my tummy…. But they just say 'what's all that skin, Mummy?' which makes me feel worse that even they notice

T: So they notice and they are puzzled – because it looks different. But they don't sound as if they are upset by it. Is that right?
     No, I suppose…they actually laugh and say it feels squidgy….

T: So I am wondering if it is possible for something to look different but not necessarily to be horrible. Do you think that is possible?
     Well, not to me…

T: I am wondering about other people – say, your new partner.
     Well if I don't feel good about myself, I am never going to be able to show him

T: What might happen? What would be the worst thing that could happen?
     Well he would take one look and…I couldn't…

T: What might he do?
     He would think what I do. I can imagine the look on his face.

T: So he would be disgusted…What would that mean?
     It would mean that I have lost him. I am on my own again. I have ruined my body. I am finished.

T: That thought is pretty devastating. Let me see if I can summarise what you have told me. You have been through an enormous change and you have worked very hard to achieve it. Your whole appearance is different. You have said that people walk past you in the street because they don't recognise you. You speak as though you have a whole new identity – you have worked hard and have achieved something that you have been trying to do for years. So that is something you could be feeling really good about. But it has come at a big cost. And what makes it worse is that you daren't tell anyone about it. You have this big secret that you are ashamed of because actually believe that you are hideous and disgusting and if anyone really knew they would run a mile…
     Yes…yes that's it

T: So the only thing to do is to keep up the secret. Hide what you really look like and keep your partner at arm's length. But that also means no real relationship. So the solution has become part of the problem; either way the fear is that you will be all alone
     Yes, I'm only young. I don't want to be alone. I can't imagine how I can cope – I just want to cut if off me….

T: Let us imagine for a moment, that we have a magic wand. We aren't going to change the appearance of the skin, but we can think about how you would like life to be different for you. Can you tell me how your life is different? What might you be doing? How would your day-to-day life be different? Well I would be able to have a sex life for a start…And I could stop wearing all these layers. I could take the children swimming

T: Good let's make a list

The first session then continued to elicit problems and to identify further goals for treatment.

Deirdre's assessment of herself on noticeability and worry was plotted onto the graph (see Figure 7.9), whilst additional psychometric measures were put together for completion after the sessions (for this patient: DAS24 and HADs plus a measure of intimacy).

She rated the visible difference in her appearance as 10/10 and her preoccupation and worry as 10/10.

The formulation of her problem was then developed further as in the following text and summarized in the template:

T: You have described to me the way that this excess skin has impacted on your life. Although you were expecting some redundant skin – you actually put it very well – you said 'I was not prepared for the impact it would have on me'. It gets in the way, you can't bring yourself to look at it because it makes you feel physically sick and disgusted; so just at a time when you have worked so hard and everyone is so complimentary it is if you have just swapped one problem for another

Not surprisingly, this makes you feel really frightened and unhappy and completely preoccupied by trying to keep it all a secret. You avoid doing the things you would like to do – particularly being intimate with your partner but also things like taking the children swimming. This is because you think that everyone else is going to feel the same way as you do, disgusted, when they look at you – although we discovered that your children don't feel this way. You wear certain clothes which hold the skin tightly and looser tops to hide it, all of which adds to the sense of shame and having a secret which might be discovered.

You are not alone in this reaction. Many people who have this operation experience excess skin and are surprised, just as you have been, by the impact it has for them. But like you, the behaviour you put in place to protect yourself – we call them safety behaviours – like not touching or looking at

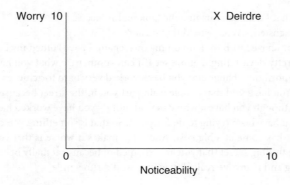

Figure 7.9   Noticeability and worry graph.

The noticeability and worry graph is completed during the first session because it is quick and provides some immediate data to inform the preliminary formulation. It is also very useful in explain the goals for treatment and the rationale of the CBT approach.

your body - start to become more of a problem than the skin. So we can make significant changes – and we do – to people's lives if we can help them to manage the skin in other ways.

What I am going to do is put this all together in a diagram, or model, so we can see how it all fits together. Some things we can change and some things we can't. But working this way helps us to concentrate on the things that we can change and to work out whether the things that you are doing to help you might be having the opposite effect – or whether there is anything else that you can instead which might be more helpful. If we can reduce the amount that your skin interferes in your day-to-day life, then we can also reduce the amount that you think about it and worry about it. Does that make sense? So, we have the same goal as a surgeon might have, to enable you to do all the things that you would like to do in your everyday life, but we are going to set about it a different way. So for example, we want you to be able to look at yourself in the mirror and wash and touch your own body. Well I am grateful for you trying to help me – but it is the skin that is the problem. If I can't get rid of it I don't see how any amount of talking about is going to help…but I've got to do something….

T: I know it is not easy to understand to begin with, but we will keep coming back to this model and reminding ourselves of what the problems are and what keeps them going. At the same time, you recognise you have to do something, and that is a great first step. I think most people only really start to believe that they can make changes once we start to succeed. Like many new things, it is something you have to experience for yourself. So if you feel motivated to work at this, then I think your confidence in yourself to be able to do it will grow stronger as we get going…so you need to attend regularly at the times that we decide, for say 6 sessions to begin with. I will also be giving you practical things to do at home and record for me so that we can use the time between sessions to work on this too. Is that okay?

Questionnaires and rating scales were then given for completion at home and appointments set up.

Summary

T: So just to summarise, we have spent this session identifying some of the problems that your skin causes you and some of the goals that you would like to achieve, such as touching at and looking at your own body, taking the children swimming and being able to have an intimate relationship. We are going to meet regularly to help you develop some strategies for managing these problems. So we are not going to do anything about your skin, but we are going to reduce the problems that it is causing you and the amount that you are preoccupied by it. Is that okay?

Excess skin is very common after massive weight loss either following gastric banding or bypass or for people who lose weight through changing their diet and exercise patterns. The problems described by this patient are very typical including the description of the excess skin as triggering 'disgust'. Patients often avoid looking at their bodies to avoid not only the emotion but the risk of being sick. Some patients physically retch during the treatment sessions when asked to contemplate or touch their own bodies. We have proposed that the role of disgust emotions has generally been overlooked in academic studies of body image and disfigurement, and we have reported some preliminary findings which suggest that disgust sensitivity predicts response to disfiguring conditions (Shanmugarajah et al., 2012) and also the self-management of wound care (Gaind et al., 2011). Given that disgust is an emotional response rather than a cognitive appraisal, we stress modifying behaviour at the outset of treatment with the aim of habituating the disgust response by repeat exposures.

Session 2

Review Data

Discussion of DAS Scores
These fall in a predictable pattern with high levels of social avoidance. These are pointed out to Deirdre and the role of social avoidance as a safety behaviour highlighted. DAS24 also highlighted the problems with intimacy. HADS scores show mild anxiety and mild depression. These are discussed in terms of anticipatory anxiety in social situations and depressed mood associated with feelings of loss.

Motivation, Readiness for Change and Self-Efficacy: Deirdre is interested in the model. She has found the scales very revealing but also very reassured that other people are reporting the same issues. She appears more engaged in therapy. *My daughter was not well last night and I was worried I might have to cancel this appointment.*

Introduction to Social Comparison Processes

Therapist discusses the way in which appearance is linked with success in media messages. Deirdre is asked to comment on her own appearance and the sources that she uses to think about how she believes her body should look, 'all-or-nothing thinking' (e.g. No one else looks like I do. 'Now I look like this, no one will ever want to have a relationship with me'). Examine counterarguments – use of alternative images of ordinary women to discuss how 'ordinary' women look: How do other people regard me? (fear of negative evaluation.) Pie charts are used to develop idea of different attributes by which others are valued (salience and valence of appearance). Compare self and best friend. Elicit strength of belief that appearance of body is the most important thing about her. Reduced from 80/100 to 30/100.

Exploration of Early Life Experiences: She has always been obese. Her mother was a single parent bringing up two daughters, 'Very busy: two jobs' and too easy to rely on take away food. Other children are cruel and called her names because of her size. She remembers being ashamed during games lessons – no one wanted to pick her for their team. She didn't tell anyone and used to bunk off school on games days. She engages in comfort eating. Her bad habits just built up. Her former partner worked shifts so she carried on with preparing food for children and then just picking at things for herself. She explains weight as the result of a lifetime of bad habits, junk food and comfort eating. These are added to formulation and discussed in terms of the long-term core beliefs around shame.

Restatement of Formulation

T: We have thought about the fact that you have finally taken steps to lose weight after a lifetime of being overweight and how you had an image of yourself all through weight loss. You had this goal that you could finally look like the 'me' you had always wanted to be. This 'ideal self' is partly built up from images in magazines and on TV and you had started thinking about a new way of dressing and looking for clothes in fashion shops rather than outsize shops. Then the excess skin started to appear and even though you tried exercise, you could not control it. You started to feel deeply disgusted when you looked at yourself and the feelings of shame about your own body were similar to the experiences you had when you were younger at school, and you have used the same approach of avoiding the problem. The overall feeling I am getting is of such disappointment – you finally tackled your weight and created another problem which makes you feel if anything, even worse.

So if we add these things to our diagram, can you see that all these things are linked together? If we look at this maintenance cycle, you can see that what you believe about your body links to how you feel about it and the behaviours you put in place to protect yourself as well as the physical sensations that you feel when you look at yourself. We need to start thinking how we can change this pathway so that you can think and feel differently and how this can help you to achieve your goals....

Elicit Patient Understanding

T: I want to do this by starting to think about the behaviour. Because you are avoiding touching yourself we don't have any real evidence about what might happen. You 'think' you know, but you are anticipating a response which might not happen or might not be as bad as you think. We also know that the more often you do something, the more likely it is that the fear and anxiety you experience will reduce and even disappear. This is the problem with avoidance: it prevents the opportunity to prove yourself wrong. I want you to see what happens if you can reduce the avoidance. I want you to try washing the skin on your tummy when you are in the shower. I want you to massage the skin slowly with some shower cream and to concentrate on caring for your body. What do you think will happen if you do that?

I don't think I can – it is making me feel sick already....

T: What is the worst thing that can happen?

I might be sick....

T: Then what would happen?

Well I am in the shower – I suppose there are worse places to be sick....

T: I think it would help if we practice it now. First of all I want to teach you some anxiety management exercises – just some simple breathing techniques. Then I will describe the situation to you and I want you to tell me how it makes you feel. Is that okay?

The session then continued by teaching breathing exercises. Deirdre was asked to talk through the process of having a shower and to describe touching and washing the skin. Disgust ratings were assessed on a 0–10 subjective unit of distress (SUDS) scales. Imagery continued until SUDs reduced and Deirdre used breathing exercises to help cope with the initial anxiety. Deirdre was encouraged to use neutral words to describe her skin: (soft, squidgy and spongy) rather than value judgements (repellant, disgusting and revolting).

From a theoretical perspective, what is happening here is rather interesting. Whilst it looks like a classical extinction paradigm, some psychologists would find habituation/exposure arguments persuasive, and yet others would emphasize cognitive change based on behavioural experimentation, even with visceral experiences such as repulsion. It is also important to remember that breathing exercises and other 'coping tactics' can sometimes take on the role of a safety signal, which a therapist would want to explore (maybe even when the tactic is offered and taught). There is a good review of this (Thwaites & Freeman, 2005).

Introduction to Compassionate Thinking

Homework

Behavioural exposure. Wash her tummy every day. Introduction to record-keeping.
Summary and Feedback

Session 3

Review of Homework and Reformulation

Deirdre appears more relaxed and smiles more. Review of homework; she has been massaging her tummy in the shower and recording the SUDS. She describes feeling very uncomfortable to start with – sick and could hardly touch herself for sustained time. SUDS have fallen from 8/10 to 3/10 then peaked back up to 6/10 before 2/10. She has found it helpful to think in terms of compassionate caring and to modify the words she is using.

'This is my body. This is my healthy body and I will look after it'.

She has gone one step further by looking at herself in the mirror. She does not like what she looks like, but she is trying not to avoid looking at herself. Physical symptoms of disgust and anxiety are less.

Rating of preoccupation with appearance is still 10/10.

Reformulation (Figure 7.10, Figure 7.11, and Figure 7.12).

Set Agenda

Review of behavioural monitoring using rating scales.

TTTT

Setting some further goals for the week. Troubleshooting using 'what if?' questions. Review of evidence in context of model.

Introduction to NATs

Homework

Continue with the shower routine. Introduce a second task of looking at herself in the mirror and rehearsing compassionate mind exercises. Recording of NATs is added to exposure task.
Summary and Feedback

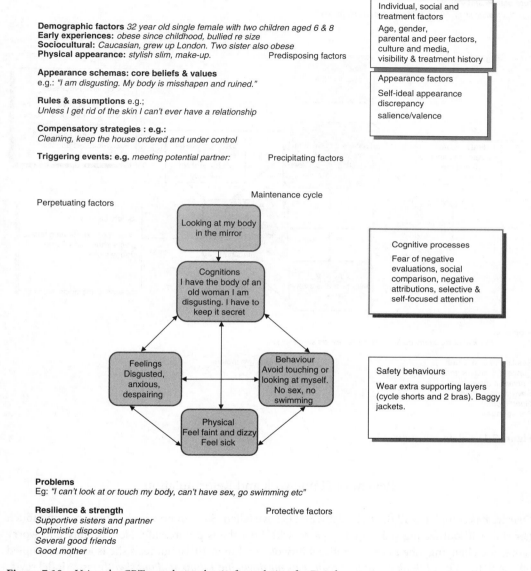

Demographic factors *32 year old single female with two children aged 6 & 8*
Early experiences: *obese since childhood, bullied re size*
Sociocultural: *Caucasian, grew up London. Two sister also obese*
Physical appearance: *stylish slim, make-up.*   Predisposing factors

Appearance schemas: core beliefs & values
e.g.: *"I am disgusting. My body is misshapen and ruined."*

Rules & assumptions e.g.;
Unless I get rid of the skin I can't ever have a relationship

Compensatory strategies : e.g.:
Cleaning, keep the house ordered and under control

Triggering events: e.g. *meeting potential partner:*   Precipitating factors

Individual, social and treatment factors

Age, gender, parental and peer factors, culture and media, visibility & treatment history

Appearance factors

Self-ideal appearance discrepancy
salience/valence

Perpetuating factors   Maintenance cycle

Looking at my body in the mirror

Cognitions
I have the body of an old woman I am disgusting. I have to keep it secret

Feelings
Disgusted, anxious, despairing

Behaviour
Avoid touching or looking at myself. No sex, no swimming

Physical
Feel faint and dizzy Feel sick

Cognitive processes

Fear of negative evaluations, social comparison, negative attributions, selective & self-focused attention

Safety behaviours

Wear extra supporting layers (cycle shorts and 2 bras). Baggy jackets.

Problems
Eg: *"I can't look at or touch my body, can't have sex, go swimming etc"*

Resilience & strength   Protective factors
Supportive sisters and partner
Optimistic disposition
Several good friends
Good mother

Figure 7.10   Using the CBT template to begin formulation for Deirdre.

Session 4

Emphasis on using data to support and revise formulation, explanation of the model and goal setting. Anxiety management, analysis of exposure task, analysis of NATs and cognitive biases and verbal and behavioural reattribution

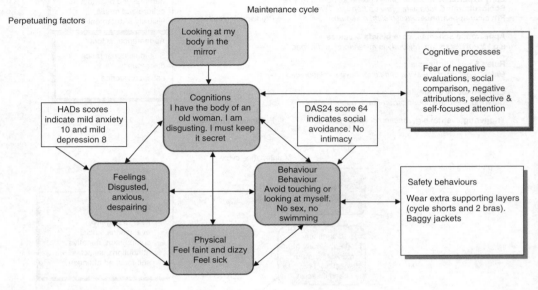

Core beliefs and values
e.g.: *"I am disgusting. My body is misshapen and ruined."*

Maintenance cycle

Perpetuating factors

Looking at my
body in the
mirror

HADs scores
indicate mild anxiety
10 and mild
depression 8

Cognitions
I have the body of an
old woman. I am
disgusting. I must keep
it secret

DAS24 score 64
indicates social
avoidance. No
intimacy

Cognitive processes

Fear of negative
evaluations, social
comparison, negative
attributions, selective &
self-focused attention

Feelings
Disgusted,
anxious,
despairing

Behaviour
Behaviour
Avoid touching or
looking at myself.
No sex, no
swimming

Safety behaviours

Wear extra supporting layers
(cycle shorts and 2 bras).
Baggy jackets

Physical
Feel faint and dizzy
Feel sick

Problems
Eg: *"I can't look at or touch my body, can't have sex, go swimming etc"*

Resilience & strength   Protective factors
Supportive sisters and partner
Optimistic disposition
Several good friends
Good mother
Set agenda

Figure 7.11   Reformulation.

Review of Homework and Reformulation

Deirdre has completed all the tasks daily. SUDS have fallen. She can now look at her body and touch her skin without feeling sick. She is pleased with how she is progressing. Noticeability and worry scores are changing. She rates the noticeability of her skin at 10/10 but feels she is less preoccupied by it at 8/10. *When I think about it, it really gets me down but I think it about slightly less.* Model revisited and connections between components explored.

Set Agenda

Revisiting NATs, Classifying Cognitive Processing Styles and Reattribution of Beliefs
Deirdre can make the connection between the behavioural exposure and the habituation of the disgust response. She also acknowledges that her tidiness and cleaning standards are related to high

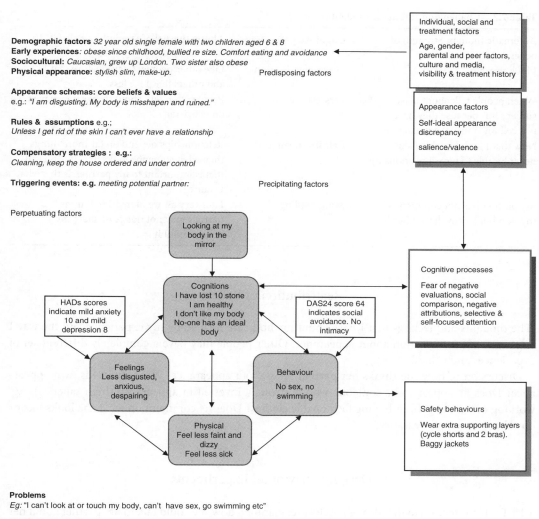

Demographic factors *32 year old single female with two children aged 6 & 8*
Early experiences*: obese since childhood, bullied re size. Comfort eating and avoidance*
Sociocultural: *Caucasian, grew up London. Two sister also obese*
Physical appearance: *stylish slim, make-up.*   Predisposing factors

Appearance schemas: core beliefs & values
e.g.: *"I am disgusting. My body is misshapen and ruined."*

Rules & assumptions e.g.;
Unless I get rid of the skin I can't ever have a relationship

Compensatory strategies : e.g.:
Cleaning, keep the house ordered and under control

Triggering events: e.g. *meeting potential partner:*   Precipitating factors

Perpetuating factors

Looking at my body in the mirror

Cognitions
I have lost 10 stone
I am healthy
I don't like my body
No-one has an ideal body

HADs scores indicate mild anxiety 10 and mild depression 8

DAS24 score 64 indicates social avoidance. No intimacy

Feelings
Less disgusted, anxious, despairing

Behaviour
No sex, no swimming

Physical
Feel less faint and dizzy
Feel less sick

Individual, social and treatment factors

Age, gender, parental and peer factors, culture and media, visibility & treatment history

Appearance factors

Self-ideal appearance discrepancy

salience/valence

Cognitive processes

Fear of negative evaluations, social comparison, negative attributions, selective & self-focused attention

Safety behaviours

Wear extra supporting layers (cycle shorts and 2 bras). Baggy jackets

Problems
Eg: "I can't look at or touch my body, can't have sex, go swimming etc"

Resilience & strength   Protective factors
Supportive sisters and partner
Optimistic disposition
Several good friends
Good mother

Figure 7.12   Reformulation following homework.

levels of disgust sensitivity and that other people have different standards – and can acknowledge that they may therefore also have different standards for what people should look like (reattribution of beliefs).

Safety Behaviours: Revisit the role of safety behaviours in maintaining avoidance and the role of avoidance in preventing disconfirmation of assumptions.

Table 7.2   Challenging automatic thought record.

Automatic thought Strength of belief 0–10	Cognitive processing	Alternative belief Strength of belief 0–10
I look terrible	Overgeneralization	Like other people, I have feature that I like and others that I lke less
When people talk about plastic surgery it is because they have noticed my unusual appearance	Personalisation	People often talk about things they have seen on television
Now that I look like this I shall never be able to have a relationship	Catastrophizing	Relationships depend on far more things than what someone looks like. If this is all that is important to my partner, is this what I want?
My partner has not commented on my skin but I know he loathes it.	Mind reading	I am very aware of my skin but my partner may not notice or share my beliefs about it

Reattribution of Beliefs

'The thoughts and feelings that I have about my body are formed by my experience and the way I select and use information about appearance. Other people may have a completely different set of experiences and values'.

Discussion of how she thinks her partner feels about appearance. What about his own appearance? Does he appear to be someone who is strongly invested in appearance (high salience), e.g. working out at the gym or buying fashionable clothes? Does he comment on what she looks like or on other women's appearance?

Design Behavioural Experiments

TTTT – Introduction to the Idea of Disclosure: Planning how she could talk to her partner about her skin and how she feels about it. What would it mean if the response was negative? What would she do? Introduction to triple column technique to identify the patterns of thinking that are making disclosure seem difficult (Table 7.2).[2]

Homework
Continue to shower and look at her skin as before.
Use triple column tool to monitor her thoughts about disclosure.
Summary and Feedback

---

[2]   Before the disclosure task goes ahead it is important to try to get more information about the partner. This could be by inviting them to the session – or as here by discussion with the patient. Whilst the results of disclosure are always uncertain, it is important to try to minimise the risk and prepare for an unhelpful response.

Session 5

Review of Homework and Reformulation

She is doing very well in touching her skin, able to walk around the bathroom without a towel and not avoiding her appearance in the mirror. Her daughter came in whilst she was getting ready, and they talked about the skin without her becoming upset. Her daughter suggested she could have some nicer underwear rather than the cycle shorts. She found herself explaining that she needed to wear the support garments and then questioning herself as to why. She tried without at home and felt a bit strange but okay.

T: Pointed out that she had designed and piloted her own behavioural experiment. Discussed in terms of self-efficacy beliefs and sense of mastery. What does this tell us about the connection between thoughts and behaviour? Reformulation and discussion of model.

Review cognitive thinking style in monitoring her thoughts about disclosure.

Set Agenda

Planning for disclosure to partner using TTTT.
Homework
Continue self-monitoring of activities with record of NATs and cognitive processing styles related to disclosure.
Go to buy some nice underwear.
Summary and Feedback

Session 6

Review of Homework and Reformulation

Washing and looking at her body is now a routine. She has bought some new underwear. She has talked to her partner about her skin and was planning to do this at the weekend, but he came up behind her to give her a cuddle and instead of backing away she took advantage of the moment to explain why she felt awkward. 'He was brilliant. It turned out he was relieved. He thought he'd done something wrong…we had a really good talk…He was honest with me. He did not pretend it wasn't there – he said he loved me for all the other things about me and it just wasn't important for him'.

She has also agreed to talk to the bariatric surgery support group as a successful example and feels good about this. She feels she is giving herself more credit for managing the weight loss. These were added to formulation in terms of positive evaluation from other people.

Set Agenda and Review Progress

Measure Noticeability and Worry

Worry is now down to 2/10 and noticeability down to 4/10. She is surprised that as she thinks about her skin less, she feels it is actually less noticeable to others.

Reattribution of Beliefs

Appearance is important to me, but it is not the way I am valued by other people. Review formulation and examine the evidence for her beliefs. She can see that she can re-evaluate her assumptions in the light of the new evidence about what other people really think. 'Feels more confident'.

Feedback from Behavioural Experiments (Disclosure)

Deirdre can identify cognitive processing styles. In particular she is aware of the tendency to 'mind read'.

Homework

Stop wearing the baggy jackets. Buy bathing costume.
Summary and Feedback

Sessions 7, 8 and 9

Consolidation and schema-focused reattribution. Review verbal disclosure in the context of core beliefs and assumptions and focus on self-efficacy and building intimacy and planning for long-term maintenance and ending

Review of Homework and Development of Final Reformulation (See Figure 7.13)

Deirdre has continued to talk to her partner and gradually move towards intimacy by allowing closer contact, hugs and cuddles. She has identified parts of her body which she is less self-conscious about (still dislikes her partner to focus on her tummy but happier with breasts), is wearing underwear rather than cycle shorts, and has established a sexual relationship by session 9. She still prefers to have the light off during sex, but she has a happy intimate relationship with her partner and feels good about herself. She has a swimming costume but decides to postpone swimming until she is on holiday next year. At this point the therapist checks back with her to ensure that this is not based on anxiety and avoidance and confirmed that this is a planned approach behaviour. There is no longer any disgust response to her own body, and she accepts that her body is nothing like what she had hoped and is far from her ideal body – but that is okay.

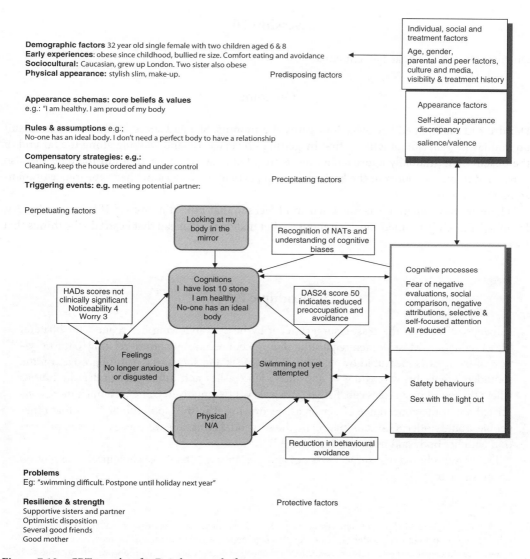

Figure 7.13 CBT template for Deirdre at end of treatment.

Set Agenda

Focus on Schema-Focused Reattribution

How important is her appearance in achieving what she wants to do? 'I would love to have lost the weight and not have all this skin. But I don't have to have an ideal appearance. The skin does not define me. I am a healthy fit woman with a partner who loves me and finds me attractive. I am not disgusting. I am not alone'.

Session 10

One more session is booked at 6 months.

Outcome

Deirdre had maintained her behaviour gains at 6 months. She had successfully worn a swimsuit on holiday in Tenerife, practising first by getting up very early and walking along the far end of the beach, then gradually approaching more crowded areas at busier times of the day. She also continued to offer support to the bariatric group particularly describing her appearance of managing excess skin.

'There are days when it gets me down and I feel sad that I did it to myself. If I won the lottery, I would definitely get something done about it – but that does not mean that I can't do the things that I want'.

Example 7.6

Esther is referred to the plastic surgery team by her GP following her request for bilateral breast reduction. Most women requesting this procedure have symptoms relating to the heaviness of the breasts measured by pain around the neck and shoulders, painful grooves on the shoulders where bra straps dig in and intertrigo (rashes and infections) under the breasts where the two skin surfaces rub. Esther gave a very different history. She was much more concerned about the appearance of her breasts, worrying that 'they look too big' and that other people would notice. On examination by the surgeon, her breasts were assessed as in proportion with her body and not excessively large.[2]

Esther was advised that surgery was not appropriate and offered psychological intervention which she accepted.

[2]   Note the problems of objective/subjective perception and bias in assessing appearance. A health professional is likely to be drawing from a wider range of more 'average' appearance rather than using media images of ideal appearance which patients often rely on. Nevertheless, although concepts such as 'in proportion' are not objective, they do influence the amount of tissue that the surgeon would be likely to remove. Bra cup size is another poor measure because it co-varies with back size and because cup size varies between brands.

Session 1

(After basic introductions)

T: Would you like to tell me something about your feelings about your breasts and the reasons that you thinking about a breast reduction?

The problem is that they are too big. I know that the doctor said that they are in proportion but that's just his opinion – they feel too big to me.

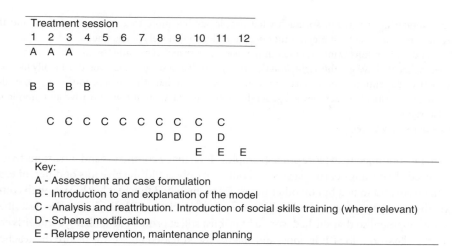

Key:
A - Assessment and case formulation
B - Introduction to and explanation of the model
C - Analysis and reattribution. Introduction of social skills training (where relevant)
D - Schema modification
E - Relapse prevention, maintenance planning

Figure 7.14   Treatment timeline.

T: Why do you think that having large breasts is a problem for you?
   It's embarrassing. I know loads of people think it is fantastic to have big breasts but I really hate it
T: I can see from your expression that you really don't like it but I am not really getting why…do you know what it is that worries you? What had you hoped might be different if your breasts were smaller?[3]
   I wouldn't have to worry about it….
T: It sounds as though you worry about it a lot of the time….
   (No response – patient looks down)
T: You mentioned other people and that they think it is good to have large breasts. What do you think about other women who have large breasts? Do you think it worries them?
   It depends – some people really like it and it makes them feel good about themselves.
T: But that isn't true for you….
   I hate them
T: Does having large breasts make you feel bad about yourself?
   Yes…I just don't want other people to notice
T: What would happen if they did notice?
   They would say something…
T: Have people said things to you?
   All the time….
T: Can you give me some examples?
   Well just yesterday…one of the other sales assistants was moaning about her small breasts then she looked at me and said 'I wouldn't mind some of yours….
T: How did that make you feel?
   Really awful. Everyone else looked at me.
T: It is an interesting example because she is actually sounding quite envious. It's not a negative comment, but you obviously find it really upsetting just telling me what she said
   It just happens all the time…

---

[3] It is important to observe the patient during assessment. People often disclose disgust emotions via facial expression or dropping eye contact when they feel high internal shame.

T: I am wondering if it is not so much what people say but more that they have noticed and then because they comment…it means other people look and you feel conspicuous
      Yes…and…I just don't want to stand out that way. It's not me…I'm quite shy…

T: So let me see if I have got this right. You describe yourself as a shy person – you don't really like being the centre of attention – and you feel that your breasts mean that other people notice you…they don't say anything critical, in fact they are generally complimentary, but it feels intrusive and unwelcome. Is that right?
      Yes – that's how it feels

This assessment continued to explore other examples of the many comments and intrusions that Esther had experienced. Two things particularly stood out. Not only could she give lots of different examples of things that were said to her, but on other occasions women had touched her breasts with comments such as 'Are those real?' She found this level of intrusion excruciatingly difficult. She also described very early chest development so that she had worn a bra whilst still at primary school. Boys and girls changed together in the classroom for P.E lessons, and she had been teased about this before the teachers had noticed and allowed her to change in the toilets. Unfortunately this once again singled her out as different. Her school uniform was designed for children not adolescents, and even though she wore the largest size of school blouse, this strained the buttons. She was able to describe in detail the experience of getting on the school bus when she was 10 and the bus driver looking at her breasts and saying to her, 'You're a big girl'. She recalled feeling embarrassed and ashamed and even though only 10, and not able to articulate or understand the sexual component of the comment, she knew it was inappropriate.

> It is often the case that even after many years people are often able to give a detailed account of an appearance-related experience using exactly the words that have been said to them. Sometimes they are clearly reliving the event with the same emotions. The experience has the same qualities as any other traumatic event. The point at which people get their medical diagnosis is often experienced this way, e.g. 'He said, "you've got a tubular breast deformity". He said I was deformed'. Trauma-focused therapy can therefore be the most appropriate first step in treatment for some people.

Esther was using clothes to support an elaborate repertoire of safety behaviours. Intrusions (staring at her chest when speaking to her) from both men (in particular) and other women were perceived to be an inevitable outcome unless she took steps to disguise her breasts. She always wore a bra and two Lycra vests. She admitted to owning about 200 tops, one of which she wore over the vests, and she always wore a cardigan over everything else. She had started being late for work because she could not select the appropriate top to wear and would try on many throwing the rejects into a big pile on her bed. She also dreaded summer because she was too hot and people would keep telling her to take off her jumper.

All this information was included within the formulation (see figure 7.15):

T: You have explained to me that you hate your breasts. You feel that they are too big and that this draws attention to you in a way that you dislike. It is not always negative attention but it can be very intrusive and sometimes inappropriate. You are a shy person and whilst you can see that a more extrovert individual does not have problems with having large breasts – so large breasts per se is not the prob-

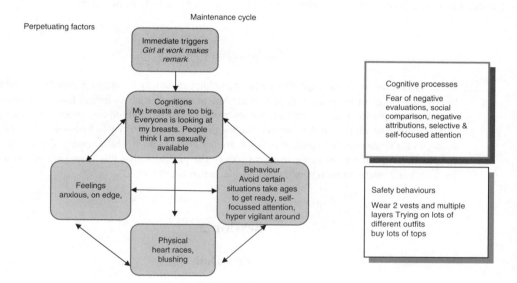

Demographic factors *30-year-old unmarried female*
Early experiences: *inappropriate sexual behaviour from adults*
Sociocultural: *Caucasian, grew up in surburbia, two brothers*
Physical appearance: *unremarkable*

Predisposing factors

Individual, social and
treatment factors

Age, gender,
parental and peer factors,
culture and media,
visibility & treatment history

Appearance schemas: core beliefs & values
e.g.: My large breasts make me appear a sexual object and sexually available

Rules & assumptions e.g.;
Unless I get my breasts made smaller I will be conspicuous & misperceived by others

Compensatory strategies: *e.g.: exercise partly to manage mood but also to reduce breast size*

Appearance factors

Self-ideal appearance
discrepancy

salience/valence

Triggering events: e.g. *social activities:*
Getting dressed in the morning

Precipitating factors

Perpetuating factors   Maintenance cycle

Immediate triggers
*Girl at work makes
remark*

Cognitions
My breasts are too big.
Everyone is looking at
my breasts. People
think I am sexually
available

Feelings
anxious, on edge,

Behaviour
Avoid certain
situations take ages
to get ready, self-
focussed attention,
hyper vigilant around

Physical
heart races,
blushing

Cognitive processes

Fear of negative
evaluations, social
comparison, negative
attributions, selective &
self-focused attention

Safety behaviours

Wear 2 vests and multiple
layers Trying on lots of
different outfits
buy lots of tops

Problems

Eg: *"I can't concentrate at work, started being late for work because of problems dressing, avoiding social situations"*

Resilience & strength   Protective factors
Good at job: hard worker

Figure 7.15   Using the CBT template to begin formulation for Esther.

lem – the difficulty is the mismatch between how you think other people see you and how you see yourself. Because of this you have considered having surgery to reduce your breasts and you have put in place some protective behaviours such as wearing vests and jumpers to flatten and cover your breasts. Unfortunately this in itself is becoming a problem because you are dependent on a small range of clothes and in the summer when it is hot, the extra layers are uncomfortable and draw attention to you – which is the key thing that you are trying to avoid. Is that right?
You must think I'm really stupid....

T: Does it sound stupid to you, when I summarise things like that?
No...it makes complete sense to me but other people must think I am mad

T: I don't think anyone who is concerned about their appearance is stupid or mad…think about all the information we are all bombarded with that is trying to convince us of how important our appearance is. But it is worth noting that for you, what other people think about you has become very important – in fact so important that it is interfering with your day to day life…so it is interesting how what I think is one of the first things that occurs to you…I think it is something that we should spend some time thinking about during these sessions….

Questionnaires and rating scales were then given for completion at home (DAS24, HADs and fear of negative evaluation) and appointments set up.

Esther was asked to complete a homework task by noting the size of the breasts of other women (of the same size and build as her) that she encountered during her working week. She was asked to note not only those who had smaller breasts (upward comparison) but those who had much bigger breasts than her (downward comparison) and to keep a simple tally in her diary.

Summary

T: So just to summarise, we have spent this session thinking about why having large breasts is a problem for you and some of the goals that you would like to achieve, such as feeling less self-conscious, reducing your preoccupation with your breasts, stopping worrying about how other people see you and wearing fewer clothes in the summer. We are going to meet regularly to help you develop some strategies for managing these problems. So we are not going to do anything about reducing the size of your breasts, but we are going to try to reduce the problems that this is causing you and the amount that it interferes with your day to day life. Is that okay?

Session 2

Review Data

Discussion of DAS Scores

These fall in a predictable pattern with high levels of social avoidance. Esther has identified a particular question about choice of clothing as being important for her. HADS scores show moderate anxiety and depression. These are discussed in terms of anticipatory anxiety in social situations and depressed mood associated with feelings of hopelessness and lack of control. FNE scores are consistent with the clinical interview, indicating high levels of preoccupation and worry about what other think about her.

The results of the homework task have surprised her. She has noticed more women who have breasts larger than her own than women who have smaller breasts. 'I thought it was going to be the other way around'. This was discussed with reference to Strenta and Kleck (1985) experiment and bias towards seeking confirming evidence for beliefs.

Esther was asked to comment on the proposition:

'In an average work situation where at least six women are present, I will have the largest breasts'.

Esther ranks her belief in this probability as 60%: 'I still think it is more likely than not, but it would probably have been higher than that before'.

Noticeability and Worry Graph

Noticeability is 8/10 and worry 8/10.
Discuss the new information in the light of the formulation (see Figure 7.16).

Set Agenda

Motivation, readiness for change and self-efficacy. Fear of negative evaluation and behavioural monitoring.

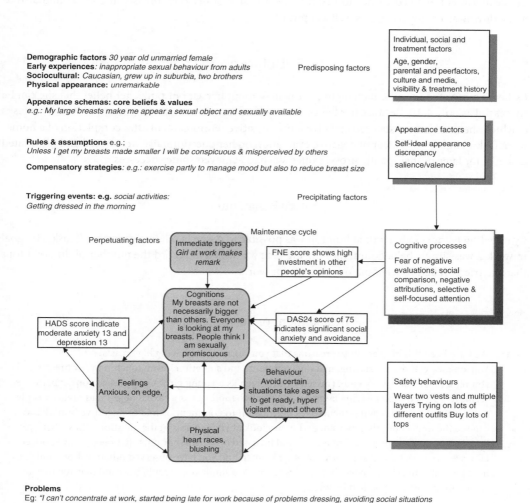

Figure 7.16 Reformulation for Esther.

Introduction to Social Comparison Processes

Therapist uses photographs of 'normal' breasts as comparison with media images, building on the previous homework task. Discussion of image manipulation and the information being used to develop ideals of appearance. Esther was asked to rank her own appearance in the context of the media images (4/10) and the 'normal' images (8/10). Esther is very surprised by the images:

> Do people really look like this? I think they look like pictures of women from the third world. They may be normal but I would hate to look like this.[4]

This experiment enabled Esther to begin to see the size of her own breasts in context and also to make downward comparisons as well as upward.

Self-Efficacy

Esther is motivated to work at changing her beliefs about herself but ranks her belief that she can be successful as only 4/10. Because her belief about self-efficacy is low, it is important to start with tasks at which she was likely to succeed and give lots of positive reinforcement after completion of a homework tasks. High levels of fear of negative evaluation on her questionnaire were noted and negotiated as a goal for later in therapeutic process once she had achieved some successes.

Safety Behaviours

By targeting Esther's behaviour at home, it was possible to design a relatively low threat task. Her goal in week 2 was simple behavioural monitoring. She was asked to record the number of different tops that she tried on before selecting one to wear for work.

Restatement of Formulation

T:　We have been thinking about the reasons that you worry about having big breasts.
　　You are aware of people staring, making comments and sometimes even touching your breasts and you remember being very embarrassed by this even as a young girl. A key part of your experience seems to be a sense that having large breasts marks people out as a sexual object and invites people to treat them as such, giving themselves permission to comment or make suggestive remarks. We can see the impact of this experience when we look at your scores on the questionnaires where you have become increasingly self-conscious and focussed on whether or not other people have noticed. However we have looked at pictures of other women and you have observed others at work and you have been able to acknowledge that other women have similar of larger breasts and that you may not stand out as much as you had believed.

---

[4]　Obtaining 'normal' images is not always easy. Most media images are influenced by cultural norms. Clinical photographs are sometimes accessible but ensuring that consent has been given for their educational use is essential.

So now I want to think about the behaviours that you have put in place to disguise your breasts – like only wearing tops that you believe look right – ones that conceal your breasts'. What I want you do this week is to keep a note of how many tops you try on each morning and how long it takes to get ready. That will help us to think about how we can help you to change. Is that okay?

Homework

Diary keeping. Esther was asked to log the number of tops she tried on and how long it took to get ready for each work day.
Summary and Feedback

Session 3

Review of Homework and Reformulation

Esther has completed the homework task, results as in Figure 7.17:
   'She is reluctant to show the therapist her notebook and expresses feelings of shame…"it's ridiculous – I had no idea it had got that bad"'.[5]

Set Agenda

Introduction to behavioural monitoring using rating scales. Esther has already kept simple record of clothing selection. Now this is extended to asking her to rate her anxiety as she completes this task.

TTTT

Setting some goals for the week. Troubleshooting using 'what if?' questions. Review of evidence in context of revised formulation.

Day	Number of tops	Time to get ready
Monday	22	2 h
Tuesday	16	1 h 40 min
Wednesday	9	1 h
Thursday	11	1 h
Friday	7	50 min

Figure 7.17 Monitoring time to get dressed and number of tops.

[5]   Collecting frequency data often reveals a strong component of obsessive compulsive disorder comorbid with body image anxiety and BDD. Similarly many patients acknowledge concerns about order and cleanliness. Some patients benefit from onward referral to mental health services.

Anxiety Management

Esther enjoys exercise. Identify gym session after work with her iPod as a means of promoting sense of well-being and self-efficacy. Breathing exercises and distraction. Review of risk of using these tactics as safety-seeking behaviours.

Introduction to NATs

Homework

Further discussion revealed that Esther had a huge number of tops – over 200. A homework task was designed to reduce that number down to 10 favourite tops to be hung on the back of her bedroom door. The others to be folded and stored elsewhere. These 10 tops were to be the sole source of tops to be worn at work in the following week.
Record using UBR form.
Summary and Feedback

Session 4

Review of Homework and Reformulation

Esther has completed the 'top selection' task (Figure 7.18).

She felt anxious initially but very pleased at reducing the time taken 'I was at work on time'. Breathing exercises are helpful during the task and at work. She comments that she is going to take some clothes to the charity shop so that she cannot slip back; her self-efficacy rating increased to 7/10.

Set Agenda

Focus on NATs, particularly on how she is thinking in the work place.

Day	Number of tops	Time to get ready	How anxious I felt 0–10
Monday	7	1 h	10
Tuesday	8	1 h	10
Wednesday	4	40 min	7
Thursday	2	1 h	6
Friday	2	50 min	6

Figure 7.18   Monitoring time to get ready and associated anxiety.

Design Behavioural Experiments

TTTT – first steps to answering comments or questions about her breasts, dealing with staring.

Homework

Increase social activity:
Monitor perceived staring and identify NATs.
Summary and Feedback

Session 5

Review of Homework

Esther has continued her rationing of available clothes. One day mid-week her discomfort peaked to 9/10 but has now fallen to 2/10. Exploring the 9/10 revealed that she spilt coffee on her top which she worried would draw people's attention to her chest. However, she resisted the impulse to put on a cardigan and noted that only two people commented on the coffee spill and no one went on to comment on her breasts. This was discussed with her in terms of a naturally occurring behavioural experiment in which she responded in an adaptive way (i.e. she did not automatically select an avoidance response such as putting on the cardigan and thus tested the belief that something that draws the eye to her chest will automatically result in an intrusive comment). She also reported that she 'panicked' at the end of the week when there were only two tops left clean to choose from, then she realized that this made life easier, 'relieved'. She took a big bag of clothes to the charity shop.
Recording NATs at work. Recognizing mind reading.
Practised response to staring – 'hard stare back'.

Set Agenda

Focus on using NATs to begin reattribution.
Practice and roll play of response to comments.

Homework

Continue self-monitoring of activities with record of NATs and cognitive processing styles. Begin to record counterarguments.
Summary and Feedback

Session 6

Review of Homework

Esther has used triple-column technique to record her thoughts at work. Weather is getting hotter and she is starting to get uncomfortable. Someone commented that she looked hot. She was able to make the connection herself about safety behaviour and being conspicuous (see figure 7.19).

She now feels she has control over what she is wearing and is no longer late for work.

Set Agenda

Measure Noticeability and Worry

Worry is now down to 5/10 and noticeability down to 6/10.

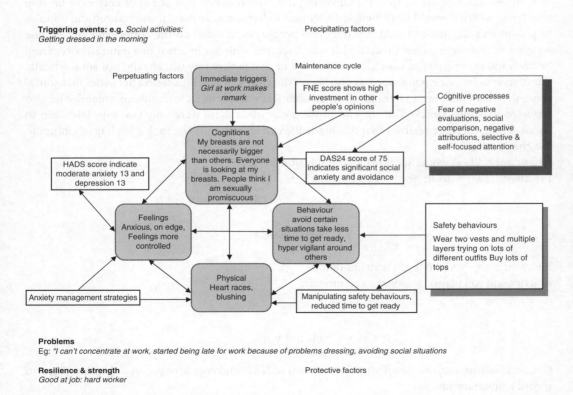

Figure 7.19   Building results from homework into reformulation for Esther.

Design of Behavioural Experiments

Building a hierarchy of clothes to remove – start with one of her vests, building up to removing her cardigan.

TTTT: Role Play Her Response If Her Breasts Are Mentioned

Esther has three different ways of answering questions and has taken some ideas from literature on a website for people buying large bras. 'The responses made me laugh…I can't imagine using them myself but it was interesting to see how the discomfort could be shifted to the one commenting rather than to the person who is the object….'

Homework

Begin hierarchy. Continue to monitor NATs.
Summary and Feedback

Session 7

Review of Homework

She has managed to leave off one vest all week. On her own in the office on Thursday, she took off her cardigan. She 'felt very odd' – but also felt that she was making real progress. She feels she can be more effective in self-management. Self-efficacy rating was 8/10.

Esther has dealt with her first comment since treatment began. She describes walking home and waiting at the crossing when a white van stopped and the driver stared at her and said, 'what a lovely pair!' Esther described feeling anxious and humiliated but then using the role play exercise to choose whether to accept the comment at face value. 'I looked at him – he was bald and overweight – I thought about saying something…I just thought…you aren't worth it. I just imagined the comment evaporating'.

Set Agenda

Review of evidence from behaviour change and the incident she reported. Introduce into formulation and focus on her feelings as a sexual object.

Focus on Reattribution

The white van episode has been a lucky behavioural experiment for Esther. She reflects on this as being the worst incident she could have imagined – but that in reality it was nothing like as bad as she had feared (discussed in terms of anticipatory and post hoc processing). It is also very useful because of the sexual comments – links back to her experience as a child. She is able to see that whilst some people make comments about her breasts, most people do not, and therefore, she is able to consider competing explanations (it was all about him not about me: he was just trying to show off to his mate). She has been able to build on her self-confidence to move up the hierarchy in terms of what she is wearing. She is now down to a vest and a top and can take off her cardigan 'when it is really hot. I prefer to have it on – but I can take it off if I need to'. No one has commented on her breasts at work. She is able to modify the belief that she has large breasts, 'they are probably larger than average but 50% of women have breasts that are average or above. I am within the normal range'.

Preparation for Ending

Plan for ending in four sessions.

Homework

Continue the work on dismantling safety behaviours.
Continue to record rationale counterarguments to NATs.
Summary and Feedback

Sessions 8, 9 and 10

Review of homework
Set agenda
Feedback from behavioural experiments
Schema-focused reattribution
Relapse prevention and planning
Preparation for ending
Homework
Summary and feedback

Session 11

Homework

Safety behaviours are dismantled completely. She is wearing just a bra and a top with a cardigan which she is able to remove. Someone commented on how nice her top was, and she was able to thank them rather than worry that this was really a reference to her breasts. She is sticking to the routine of choosing range of tops at the beginning of the week so that she does not have any decisions in the morning, 'works better that way'. She has thrown away the vests – 'I couldn't take them to the charity shop – too embarrassed. I thought about burning them….' She is very clear about the way in which her safety behaviours prevented her from evaluating the evidence about whether people noticed her breasts or not and that they had become a large part of the problem for her.

She recognizes that her breasts are normal – 'but I still wish they were smaller'. However, she is able to relate that to an ideal of appearance and that many women have things about their bodies that they would like to change.

She is able to deal with other people's intrusions: 'sometimes I use humour…more often I just say that I would rather they did not make personal remarks. Most people are alright with that and if they aren't – it too bad'.

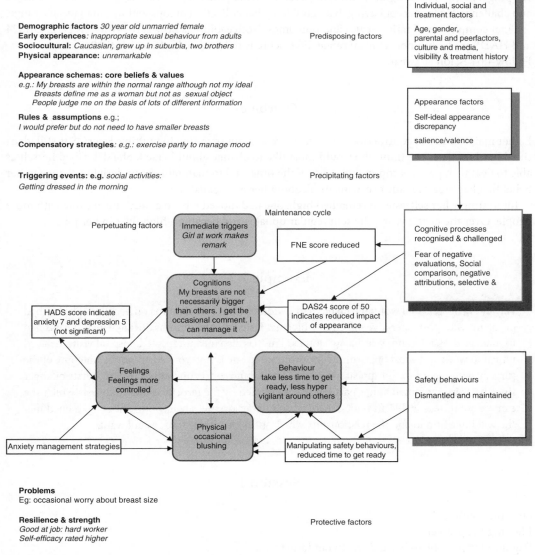

Figure 7.20 CBT template for Esther at completion of treatment.

She has been able to modify the underlying assumption that she 'needs to have smaller breasts' to one of preferring smaller breasts. The link to sexualization has been modified. Some people use my breasts to objectify me in a sexual way – but that is about them and their attitude to women and not about me. Most people use a range of different information to inform their impressions of me. Breasts are just part of being a woman (see figure 7.20).

Agenda

Keeping it going. Traffic lights: identifying a return to old patterns of thinking. Revisit her notebooks and challenge NATs. Accept having 'bad days'. Keep her collection of tops within a manageable range.

Final completion of rating scales and outcomes. Noticeability is now 2/10. Worry is 1/10. DAS24 and HADS are within non-clinical range. FNE score is reduced. Self-efficacy is 8/10.

Follow-up session at 1 year.

Outcome

Esther maintained her control over what she wore without reverting to multiple layers. She still identified her breasts as the thing she would most like to change about herself. She described herself as able to deal with people's comments 'most of the time' and to maintain the underlying change in her belief that her breasts made everyone think about her in a sexual way.

Interestingly her self-esteem remained high. She had moved jobs to a much busier role with more people. Over the next 2 years, she sent regular updates and became a high flyer in her job.

Example 7.7

Hayley is a 30-year-old woman who has had a wide excision of melanoma on her chest. She has had problems with post-operative infection which has lasted several months during which she has had to manage dressings and wear baggy clothes. This has also meant repeated hospital visits, delayed return to work and a lost opportunity for promotion. She is not worried about the outcome of the surgery with regard to the appearance of her chest, but reports uncontrollable outbursts of anger since her surgery, aimed at her partner. She is alarmed by the ferocity of her outbursts which she can see are unreasonable and not closely related to her partner's behaviour. She is frightened that she will force him to end the relationship, which she is clear that she does not want.

Session 1

Structure outline
Eliciting the problem
Begin to form problem list and treatment targets
Introduction to anger model
Early formulation

Outline of potential timeframe – need to attend
First homework assessment questionnaire completion, etc.

(After basic introductions)

T: Would you like to tell me something about your concerns about your recovery and what has triggered your request for this appointment now?

A year ago I found that I had skin cancer. I couldn't believe it. I am only 24. I went to the doctor with a mole and I never really expected that it was malignant so it was a huge shock when the biopsy was positive.

T: How did this make you feel? Can you remember what your reaction was to this shock?

I felt numb – as if I was in a terrible dream. My sister had been knocked off her bike and had just had a big operation and my parents had been really worried about her, and she had just started back at work, and then this happened to me….

T: So you were worried about your own health and your family just when they were recovering from one child being seriously ill, something happens to another.

That's just it. I just didn't think they would be able to handle it. My mum was just beginning to relax about my sister – and then it was my turn…I had to have chemotherapy – so then I had all my hair falling out…

T: Did you have anyone else to support you through this time?

I have some really good work friends who knew about it and then my partner – the unbelievable thing was that his Dad had cancer and had been going through the same thing.

T: Did you find this reassuring or upsetting?

I don't know…I think…I just felt guilty again. Why should he have to support me as well – it didn't seem fair.

T: Not fair for whom?

For him – well for me too I suppose.

T: So you felt that he did not deserve yet another person he cared about who was ill?

Yes, that's right. But I couldn't understand why he would want to be with me – I was bald, I felt tired all the time…

T: Did you ask him about it?

Yes, and he was wonderful. He just kept saying that we had been together for a long time, it did not make a difference and that he wanted to be with me whatever I looked like, and it would be okay.

T: Did you believe him?

Mostly…but then I would start thinking about it, and wondering why he did not just go and find someone else who looked normal…

T: Did you say that to him?

Yes…and then he would get really upset or angry and say that I did not trust him.

T: So if I summarise, you had to cope with the diagnosis of cancer and undergo an operation and chemotherapy, which made you lose your hair. Then just at this point you were very doubtful of his motives for being with you – and he then became very upset. So at a time when you really wanted his understanding and support – you have ended up with him upset and cross with you.

That's right…and it's all my fault, and I seem to keep doing it, making him more and more upset.

T: Let's just pause there. I think I am beginning to understand the background to what is happening. Can we now think about a specific example? Can you tell me about the last time that you felt you had upset your boyfriend?

It was last week. We were going to see some friends and we were late. He was trying to get me to hurry…

T: Why was he hurrying you?

It was…it sounds really stupid…it was, because I couldn't find anything to wear. I have only got a few things that fit me at the moment, and I had not done the washing so I was trying to wear something different – and then at the last moment I decided it was too tight so I wanted to change…

T: What did he say?

He told me I was making a fuss and I looked fine...T And what did you say?

I just flipped. I screamed at him that he didn't understand – why couldn't he just leave me alone – and lots of other horrible things...

T: What do you think about that now?

I think I was horrible to him. He was just trying to reassure me, I probably did look fine. It was just a really bad moment, and I just lost it...

T: So let's think about how you might like things to change. What would you say was the most important thing that you would want to be different?

I would like to stop screaming at him....

T: So if we are to think in terms of what we want to change here, or what the goal for treatment would be, the first thing would be to try to understand why you react like this and to establish some control, so that you could manage situations like this and did not just 'lose it' [write goal one on white board].

The first session then continued in the same way, to elicit more examples.

The formulation of her problem was then proposed.

T: You have described to me the way that you developed cancer suddenly and your appearance dramatically changed. You used the words 'not fair' about the effect of this on your relationship; at times you feel confident about it, but at other times you wonder why he wants to be with you.

The problem you describe is your outbursts and anger with him. The examples you have given me relate often – but not always – to your appearance – and result in a loss of control, shouting and abuse, and a real sense of regret afterwards. You are fine at work.

This is a helpful way of trying to understand anger [draws model] (Figure 7.21).

You can see that each angry outburst has a trigger. This is the event that immediately precedes it. However, the same trigger does not make different people angry or even the same person angry all of the time. What makes the difference is the way in which the trigger is appraised or understood. Lots of factors also contribute to this – you are more likely to be angry when you are tired for example

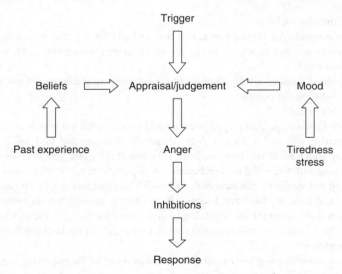

Figure 7.21 A model for analyzing irritability and anger from *Overcoming Anger and Irritability* by William Davies (Robinson, London, 2000) by permission of Constable & Robinson Ltd.

or if this is something that keeps on happening. We therefore need to collect more examples of this angry behaviour so that we can identify the triggers and the way in which you interpret them.

I can understand what you are saying, but I am really worried that I will say something I really regret…

T: I think that is very understandable at the moment; what I suggest is that you tell him about this appointment and let him know that you are trying to do something to change. You could also think about asking him to come to one of the sessions if you are happy about this. Is that okay?

Yes it is – I would really like him to know that I am trying to overcome this.

T: That's great. If you feel motivated to work at this, then I think your confidence in yourself to be able to do it will grow stronger as we get going…so you need to attend regularly at the times that we decide, for say 6 sessions to begin with. I will also be giving you tasks to do at home and record for me so that we can use the time between sessions to work on this too. Is that okay?

Anger questionnaires and appearance rating scales were then given for completion at home and appointments set up. Homework includes reading Davies (2008), Chapters 1–3.

Summary

T: So just to summarise, we have spent this session identifying some of the problems that you are having with anger and some of the goals that you would like to achieve such as reducing angry outbursts with your partner. We are going to meet regularly to help you develop some strategies for managing these problems.

Session 2

Review Data

Recording of Angry Outbursts: Hayley reported no examples of angry behaviour over the previous 2 weeks. She was pleased but puzzled by this. Therapist explained that frequency of target behaviour often reduces when behavioural recording starts and that she should continue monitoring in the same way.

DAS24: Scores fall at one standard deviation above the mean. These fall in a predictable pattern with high levels of irritability and self-consciousness. DAS24 also indicates some problems with attractiveness and femininity which are added to the formulation. HADS scores show moderate anxiety (11) and mild depression (8).

These are discussed in terms of anticipatory anxiety in social situations and depressed mood associated with feelings of loss.

Noticeability and Worry Graph: Hayley's assessment of herself on noticeability and worry was plotted onto the graph. Although she had had a melanoma, it was the bulky dressings, odour and discomfort which was the focus of her concern. Hayley rated the noticeability of her condition to others as 8/10 and the amount that she worried about it as 10/10.[6]

Set Agenda

Review Anger Model and Formulation

---

[6]   It is very important to understand the particular aspects of appearance that most concern the individual. These may not be the features that are most apparent to the observer. For example, it may be an area of pigmentation rather than the size or extent of a scar, the donor rather than recipient site or additional features of the wound (odour, texture, movement of excess skin, etc.).

Plan Homework

Restatement of Formulation

Reformulation to include issues about appearance. Hayley describes the cancer as 'unfair'. It occurred just after her sister had been injured. Her partner had already gone through worry about his father and now had to support her. Her wide local excision, which successfully removed the cancer, led to infection, a recognized complication, but one which meant that she worried about odour and felt unfeminine – an outcome which she again regarded as unfair. Her care in hospital, whilst largely positive, had resulted in extra appointments and time off college including having to drop a year in her studies – again regarded as unfair. Invited to think about how other people might respond to all these events, Hayley acknowledged that they might also feel a sense of unfairness and that they might feel both sad and angry and that both of these emotions would be rational.

Therapeutic Buddy

Discuss ways in which partner can help her with the programme. She decides to invite him to next session.

Homework

Continue with monitoring of anger and angry outbursts. Identify those clothes in which she feels comfortable and use the weekend for planning and to ensure that she has enough tops for the week ahead.

Summary and Feedback

Session 3

Hayley's partner Bert has come with her.

Review of Homework and Reformulation

Review of homework; Hayley and Bert have had two 'huge rows' since last session. Hayley has recorded the event and the trigger, together with how she appraised the situation (Table 7.3).

Session continued with Hayley generating alternative ways of appraising the triggers. She was then able to check these with Tom (Table 7.4).

Hayley was able to use this exercise to explain the anger model to Bert. It was helpful that one of the episodes involved an appraisal by him of Hayley's behaviour and both were able to reassure the other.

Table 7.3   Monitoring triggers and beliefs associated with angry outbursts.

What happened?	What was the trigger?	How was this appraised? What did you believe
Saturday evening Bert asked me if his blue shirt was ironed. I ended up screaming at him to do his own ironing, then I called him all kinds of names and screamed at him to get out of the house	Is my blue shirt ironed?	Why I am I responsible for his ironing? It is not fair that I am trying to manage all these other things including my illness and looking terrible and he expects me to do all this for him as well… He knows I haven't got much to wear and he is deliberately rubbing it in my face by dressing in his best things…
Wednesday evening Bert was trying to dig out a big plant in the garden and he pulled it and fell over backwards and I laughed… Bert was annoyed and then the whole thing got out of control again with me screaming at him to leave.	Bert threw the spade down and said I could do it myself if I could make a better job of it…	He is completely unreasonable; he knows I can't do that sort of thing at the moment. He isn't being fair - he doesn't understand how difficult it is for me.

Table 7.4   Generating alternative explanations for behaviour.

What was the trigger?	How was this appraised? What did you believe	Is there another way of looking at this?
Is my blue shirt clean? Bert threw the spade down and said I could do it myself if I could make a better job of it…	Why I am responsible for his ironing? It is not fair that I am trying to manage all these other things inlcuding my illness and looking terrible and he expects me to do all this for him as well… He knows I haven't got much to wear and he is deliberately rubbing it in my face by dressing in his best things… He is completely unreasonable; he knows I can't do that sort of thing at the moment. He isn't being fair – he doesn't understand how difficult it is for me (Bert's appraisal) I look really stupid-she has had all this to deal with and I can't even dig out a plant…	It is just a question. He had seen me doing the ironing and could see I had done one or two things of his as they were there – he was just checking out whether one of them was his shirt He had not made any connection about how what he wears impacts on how I feel about what I have to wear He was tired and felling humiliated. I know that when I am tired I am more likely to react badly. This was about him not about me… Actually- it was quite funny when it suddenly came out and I fell over…I would have laughed

Homework

Continue with monitoring of anger and angry outbursts. Describe the way the behaviour is appraised. Identify alternative explanations. Read chapters in Davies (2008). Maintain the habit of preparing clothes for the week at the weekend.

Summary and Feedback

Session 4

Review of Homework and Reformulation

Hayley has recorded four examples of events that have triggered an angry response. However, although the frequency has gone up, she has been able to evaluate her beliefs at the time and to manage her response more effectively by acknowledging that there might be another explanation. Bert has been helpful by walking away rather than by trying to argue with her. He also bought her a new jumper which is a bright colour, which she really likes, and she feels that she clearly got the message that she is worried about how she looks, even if he is not.

Set Agenda

Introduction to NATs and cognitive processing styles using triple column. Review noticeability and worry graph.
Plan alternative responses when she feels her anger being triggered.

Set Homework

Identification of cognitive processing styles.
Read further chapters in Davies.
Agree alternative management with Bert.
Summary and Feedback

Session 5

Bert has come to the session with Hayley.

Review of Homework

Triggers are identified and appraisal is modified. She and Bert have agreed to a time out period when one or other is annoyed. They have both read the self-help material and each feels that they understand Hayley's responses better.

Set Agenda

Review Hayley's perceptions of her appearance. Begin to consider a long-term maintenance plan. Plan for last session next time.

Homework

Continued monitoring of behaviour and complete reading.
Summary and Feedback

Session 6

Review of Homework and Reformulation

Hayley had no further angry episodes. Hayley's wound has healed and she is able to get into a more varied selection of clothes. She and Bert have booked a holiday together. Hayley formulates her angry outbursts as related to her sense of unfairness at all the things that happened to her and the perception that Bert had no understanding of how upset she was about her appearance-related problem. Had she known that this would take many weeks to resolve, she would have bought herself some clothes so that she did not feel so self-conscious and restricted.

Set Agenda

Keeping it going. Traffic lights: identifying a return to old patterns of thinking. Revisit her notebooks and challenge NATs. Accept having 'bad days'.

Completion of Rating Scales and Outcomes

Noticeability is now 2/10. Worry is 1/10. DAS24 and HADS are within non-clinical range. She is no longer as irritated, although she acknowledges that this varies according to how tired she is. She and Bert have a practised time out strategy for coping with rows. Hayley's rating of self-efficacy in managing her problem is increased.

Sessions 7 and 8

Review of Homework

Set Agenda

Monitoring of progress via continued behaviour recording and discussion in terms of the formulation and reattribution of beliefs from partner's behaviour as the cause of anger to the experience of the illness and the challenge to her beliefs about herself. Long-term planning for maintenance and preparation for ending.

Session 9

Completion of Rating Scales and Outcomes

Noticeability remains 2/10. Worry is 1/10. DAS24 and HADS are maintained within non-clinical range.

Summary and Feedback

Hayley feels that her anger is not an irrational response to the events of the last year, but that she now has it under control. She is less preoccupied with her appearance and feels that her partner has more insight into her concerns.

Outcome

Hayley and Bert were seen for a 6-month review. They reported lots of rows but described them in terms of any young couple. They were no longer worried that Hayley's response would be disproportionate and felt that they were able to discuss situations and each other's understanding of them in a calm way.

Long-Term Outcome and Maintenance of Change

Complete Maintenance

The ideal outcome for a CBT intervention is a change in beliefs and behaviour, which is maintained or even exceeded. For example, people attending a 2-day social interaction skills workshop at Changing Faces not only reported reduced social anxiety and avoidance immediately after treatment but maintained this at 6-week follow-up and at 6 months had made additional gains. The explanation is that they learned the principles of successful social interaction and were able to build on these successfully (Robinson et al., 1996).

However, some people will fail to maintain the target behaviour, and in practice, many people will achieve a partial long-term change.

Factors which contribute to successful maintenance include:

- Setting realistic goals
- Integrating the behaviour into lifestyle so that it becomes automatic
- Social reinforcement
- Continuing to perceive the behaviour as beneficial
- Distinguishing primary and secondary gains (e.g. many people have a long-term goal of finding a partner). To do this they need to become socially active, but whilst this increases the probability they will find a partner, it does not guarantee success. Working with this

group of people, it is important to help them to see the benefits of reducing social avoidance for its own sake.

Partial Maintenance

Some people may achieve the target and then slip back to a lower level of behavioural frequency. Factors which have a significant impact here are:

- *Seasonal variation.* The weather in the United Kingdom means that people become used to exposure of their arms and torso in the summer, only to cover up again after a few months. Explanation of this during treatment as part of relapse prevention, and building in a booster session at the start of the summer, either face-to-face or via e-mail/telephone is one strategy for overcoming this problem.
- *Negative comments from others.* One recurring theme in working with people who are visibly different is the impact of a single negative remark on social avoidance. Where social withdrawal and isolation occur, it is very common for people to describe word for word a remark made, sometimes years previously, by someone who might have been completely unaware of causing the behaviour change and distress which results. Rumination about this remark adds to its perceived importance and social withdrawal prevents disconfirming evidence from others.

Preparing people for the likelihood of negative attention and setting out a strategy for dealing with it are ways of anticipating distress and reducing impact on long-term outcome.
Other ways of countering slip-back include:

- Not viewing slip-back as failure. Everyone has 'bad days'. This is not predictive of future failure.
- Plan a specific response to slip-back (e.g. re-read Changing Faces literature).
- Recognize that behaviour change is challenging.

Slip-Back and Sub-maintenance

In this situation, behaviour change has been achieved at levels above the pre-treatment level but below the goal set. Different people may view this as success or failure. Helping people to accept that part of behaviour change is the reviewing of goals will help people to frame this as a success and encourage them to build on this.

Slip-Back and Failure

Factors contributing to this resumption of pre-treatment behaviour include attributions about low self-efficacy or personality type. (But because a CBT programme has built-in steps, this belief can be challenged with evidence of early successes, records from this stage and reminders of strategies employed in the successful part of the programme.)

Preparing people for the fact that behaviour change is not smooth, anticipating different rates of progress at different stages and encouraging goal setting which is not over ambitious are all ways of helping people to believe that slip-backs are not predictive of long-term failure.

Social Support and Therapeutic Partners

Given that social support is highlighted throughout the health psychology literature as predictive of good outcome in chronic conditions including disability, it is interesting that families and friends are not routinely involved in the delivery of therapeutic interventions.

Working within a CBT framework provides an opportunity to involve a therapeutic 'buddy' who can support people as they make significant changes. This can be via a prompt to complete homework, discussion of outcomes when behaviour change begins and practical support in the field. Partners can also be very helpful when slip-back occurs, reinforcing the progress made so far and reframing goals. An informed partner also works to support a programme rather than to sabotage it. When people are socially anxious, the 'kind' response is one of over-solicitous care which reduces motivation to overcome the problem. Frank discussion between therapist, patient and buddy about the potentially damaging effects of supposedly supportive but ineffectual responses is an integral part of enlisting the help of therapeutic buddies. Understanding the principles of behaviour change, particularly in an area where people are tempted to seek out new and novel surgical techniques, can be very helpful in avoiding problems halfway through treatment.

Summary

This chapter has presented session outlines with examples of very different clinical cases treated using a CBT approach. However, many people do not accept psychological intervention as an alternative to surgery, and it is important to avoid the impression that this is an approach that is acceptable to everyone. In practice, the number of sessions will vary, although CBT is a time-limited intervention, with evidence for change in up to 16 (maximum 20) sessions. Beyond this point the treatment gains are likely to be small. However, it is also possible to achieve significant gains in far fewer sessions especially where there is a real understanding of the CBT approach or where there are early successes associated with social skill development or rapid reattribution of beliefs. It is important to include the maintenance intervention and plan for relapse. A 6-month follow-up session is also useful. Finally, the current research found that adjustment may be affected over time. Life events, such as changing social groups (e.g. through a job change or moving house), weddings, special occasions and job interviews, can be particularly challenging, and it can be helpful to offer the opportunity for a 'top-up session' for times of difficulty such as these one-off events.

We do need to acknowledge that these are early days in treatment. We do not yet have good evidence for the benefits of CBT compared with surgical treatment nor do we have information about timing of treatment, how it works alongside surgical treatment and for whom it is most effective. At the same time, it should be recognized that the surgical treatments which people seek are, in fact, not always feasible, but may represent an idealized wish for an improvement which is not possible. Nevertheless, we would stress that the case examples provided here are demonstrations of the way in which treatment might be organized and are not intended to provide evidence of effectiveness of this approach.

Additional Resources

Other resources which are particularly useful for working with patients and which provide useful self-help reading and information are:

Cash, T.F. and Smolak, L. (eds) (2011) *Body Image: A Handbook of Science, Practice and Prevention*, Guilford press, New York.

Cash, T.F. (2008) *The body image workbook: an eight step program for learning to like your looks*, New harbinger, Oakland, CA.

Veale, D., Willson, R. and Clarke, A.(2008) *Overcoming Body Image Problems Including Body Dysmorphic Disorder*, Constable and Robinson, London, New York.

8

The Emerging Adult
Facilitating Transition from Child to Adult Service

Chapter Outline

CBT for Appearance Anxiety: Psychosocial Interventions for Anxiety Due to Visible Difference, First Edition.
Alex Clarke, Andrew Thompson, Elizabeth Jenkinson, Nichola Rumsey and Rob Newell.
© 2014 John Wiley & Sons, Ltd. Published 2014 by John Wiley & Sons, Ltd.

Introduction

This book does not address the particular challenges of appearance for children and young people, because this is a huge topic in its own right. However, we believe that the important transition from child to adult services should be considered here because many children will go on to be seen as part of adult services. The following section therefore introduces common problems surrounding the transition of young people from child to adult services, identifies strategies to improve transitional care and provides a brief summary of key issues to bear in mind when planning and engaging in therapy with young people during the transition period.

Introducing the Problem of Transition

Young people with complex health needs typically transfer from child to adult services between the ages of 16 and 18 (Royal College of Paediatrics and Child Health, 2003). Irrespective of their condition, the process of transition – referred to as 'transitional care' – is vital. For the young person, it is a significant life event (Por et al., 2004) at a developmental stage when they are already experiencing numerous challenges and insecurities associated with adolescence (e.g. see Holmbeck, 2002). If not managed carefully, this vulnerable period can result in disengagement with health services, increased non-compliance, poor health outcomes and premature death. Evidence detailing the risks associated with transition and the negative impact of poor transitional care is extensive (see Crowley et al., 2011). For example, Kipps et al. (2002) found that attendance for diabetes services – crucial for disease management – dropped from 94% before transition to 57% 2 years after transition. Oeffinger et al. (2004) implicated loss to follow-up as a factor in poor health outcome for survivors of paediatric cancer after moving to adult services. Somerville (1997) reported that following transition, one in five deaths from congenital heart disease were avoidable or premature, and Watson (2000) argued that non-compliance to drug regimens was a major factor contributing to unexpected transplant failure among patients within 36 months of transition.

The 'problem of transition' has been recognized as a health policy concern for over 20 years (Allen & Gregory, 2009). During this time, numerous condition-specific (see Crowley et al., 2011) and Department of Health (2006, 2008) recommendations for 'good' transition have been compiled – all of which acknowledge that the process must be carefully planned and attend to the psychosocial and educational as well as physical needs of the patient (see Blum et al., 1993). Despite this focused attention, a recent review of children's health services in the United Kingdom reported that transition remains a problem – the cause of 'complaint and unhappiness' among young people and their parents and of frustration and concern among health-care professionals (Kennedy 2010). The consensus is that transition is typically ignored or services are inconsistent (Baines 2009), and there is little empirical evidence to inform best practice regarding effective transitional care. Therefore, there is an urgent need for further research (Crowley et al., 2011; Watson et al., 2011). Kennedy (2010) recommends specific funding for this area and a cultural shift within the NHS towards identifying and meeting the needs of young people and movement away from 'bureaucratic barriers' between paediatric and adult care.

To date, the most useful evidence to guide best practice comes predominantly from qualitative psychosocial research of the combined experiences of those involved in the transition process. This identifies elements of transition that work well, psychosocial and organizational barriers that hamper successful transition and areas where care has failed to meet the needs of young people and in some cases their parents.

Transition from the Young Person's Perspective

Those who regard their transition as 'good', describe a positive, seamless and liberating experience marked by careful preparation, education and good communication between child and adult services (Department of Health, 2007; Crowley et al., 2011). However, the majority hold the opinion that the process is fraught, abrupt (unplanned) and a time of distress and anxiety (Maunder 2004; Department of Health, 2007).

One of the biggest challenges for the young person is adapting to the change in service culture within adult care (Olsen & Sutton, 1998). Whereas paediatric care is family centred and developmentally focused, the ethos of adult services emphasizes independence, self-management and direct communication with patients (McDonagh & Viner, 2006). Transition requires a change in self-perception which some may not be prepared to make (Viner, 1999) and young people can find it difficult to adjust. Many complain that staff treat them like adults and expect them to take responsibility for their own care without providing the necessary support (Anthony et al., 2009; Fleming et al., 2002; Visentin et al., 2006).

Loosing well-known carers is also an important event, adult clinics can feel alienating and unfamiliar (Viner, 1999), a place where young people either feel they know more about their condition and current treatment plan than staff or can struggle to get information about their care and the potential impact of their disease during adulthood (Department of Health, 2007). Many perceive a drop in care and lack of interest from adult health professionals and have reported feelings of being 'dumped, cut off and abandoned' (Shaw et al., 2004). These experiences heighten the risk of disengagement with health-care services.

Transition from the Parents' Perspective

Parents also perceive adult services as more formal and less focused on psychosocial care and can be emotionally attached to paediatric staff who have become an important component of their child's support and are often viewed as responsible for their child's survival (van Staa et al., 2011; Westwood et al., 1999). In addition, parents can be concerned that their expertise, which is generally respected within paediatric care, is less welcome within adult services (van Staa et al., 2011). As parents are important partners in transition, their anxieties around transition must be identified and addressed.

Transition from the Health Professionals' Perspective

One of the greatest challenges to health professionals during transition is that of organizational continuity. When standardized systems are not in place, it can be a time when neither paediatric nor adult services feel fully responsible for the young person (Royal College of Nursing, 2004). This can lead to patients receiving contradictory messages and conflicting advice.

Historically transition has not been part of health professional training programmes, and staff may not think of transition as part of their quality care, or lack motivation, expertise or confidence to adjust their care to meet the developmental and social needs of adolescents (Department of Health, 2007). As a result, risk factors associated with therapeutic non-compliance and poor clinic attendance among this age group may not be addressed. Risk factors include leaving home for further education or employment, greater independence and reduced parental involvement, increased social activity and engagement in risky health behaviours (see Weissberg-Benchell et al., 2007). Even among staff who are aware of these issues, if time and funds are not specifically allocated to allow them to attend to the particular needs of adolescents, the task of meeting the needs of large numbers of older adults takes precedence (Fleming et al., 2002).

In addition, as patients are now surviving into adult life with traditional childhood illnesses that would have been fatal 20 years ago (e.g. cystic fibrosis), adult specialists can be unfamiliar with or lack particular interest in managing such diseases (Department of Health, 2007; Viner & Keane, 1998). Paediatric staff are aware of this situation, and those who have established long-term relationships with patients and families may struggle to relinquish care. Anxiety about lack of expertise among adult services can delay transition, and inadvertent non-verbal cues expressing this anxiety to patients have been reported to undermine patient and parent confidence in adult care (Department of Health, 2006).

Guidance for Improving Transitional Care

Whilst acknowledging that the evidence is limited, in order to improve transitional care and develop best practice guidelines, there is an urgent need to pool the evidence on transition services. Current research (e.g. see McDonagh, 2006 and 2007) suggests health professionals should consider the following when planning transitional care:

- Timing: transition should be informed by the developmental needs of the individual patient; it should be flexible and individualized.
- Preparation for transition should start early, focusing on strengthening adolescents' independence.
- Transition should not take place during physical or psychological crises.
- Coordination and exchange of medical and psychosocial information between clinics (including GPs) is crucial.
- Support should be available to enable paediatric and adult staff to develop skills needed for working with young people.
- Transition pathways should be clear and well defined for all parties.
- Joint visits with paediatric and adult providers or 'transition clinics' may be particularly supportive.
- Families should feel involved and well informed.
- The young person should be seen alone for at least part of their consultation, thus supporting the young person's growing independence.
- It may be helpful to have clinics outside of school/college hours and use current communication methods.

Issues Pertinent to Caring for Young People with Appearance Concerns

There is little evidence available to suggest that young people's appearance concerns are considerably different to those of the older adult. What is unique is the potential intensity of these concerns and the extent to which they can impact on normal social and emotional development and quality of life during adolescence.

The Salience of Appearance to Young People

Physical appearance assumes enormous importance during adolescence. Appearance issues that did not concern the young person during childhood often become highly salient, and many believe that appearance contributes more than any other factor to levels of overall self-esteem (Coleman & Hendry, 1999; Harter, 1999; Levine & Smolak, 2002). Egocentrism evoked during this period leads to increased awareness and preoccupation with weight, shape, physical features and sexual attractiveness (Holmbeck, 2002; Jones et al. 2004). The emerging capacity for abstract thinking also leads to strong tendencies to engage in social comparison, which heightens sensitivity in relation to these characteristics (Pendley et al., 1997). The importance of appearance and attractiveness is further amplified by a youth culture that highly values appearance-related attributes (Ricciardelli et al., 2000) and promotes the 'supposed benefits of the body beautiful' (Rumsey & Harcourt 2007, p. 113). Fashion and physical appearance is often used to establish a social and sexual identity and as a statement that situates young people within their peer group (Grinyer, 2007). However, social pressures to conform to desirable and often unrealistic beauty ideals, particularly those perpetuated by messages from the media, create a high-risk environment for appearance concern among this already emotionally vulnerable group (Jones & Crawford, 2006; Kluck, 2010; Koo, 1995; Ricciardelli et al., 2000).

Cash's body image disturbance model (1996) suggests that the high value placed on appearance makes body image disturbance relatively commonplace within our society, and indeed, among the healthy adolescent population, evidence confirms that appearance anxiety and low body confidence are highly prevalent (Helfert & Warschburger, 2011; Rumsey & Harcourt, 2007). Some authors even refer to it as a 'normative' occurrence among adolescent girls (Smolak, 2004), and although generally not well represented within appearance and body image research (Smolak, 2004), an increasing number of studies have revealed that boys are similarly affected (e.g. see Jones and Crawford, 2005).

Adolescent girls generally wish to be thinner and express discontent with shape and individual body parts (Smolak, 2004) whereas boys tend to desire a thinner and more muscular body shape (Ata et al., 2007; McCabe & Ricciardelli, 2001). In a recent online survey of more than 800 young people from the United Kingdom, aged 11–18, 34% of boys and 49% of girls had been on a diet to change their body shape (Diedrichs et al., in submission), and more than 50% of 1200 adolescent girls reported that they would consider undergoing cosmetic surgery to change their appearance (Girlguiding UK, 2010).

With this backdrop, young people with a visible difference are likely to experience some degree of negative attention in the form of appearance-related teasing – the most common form of teasing among adolescents (Smolak, 2004) – staring, unsolicited hostile or intrusive questioning about their difference, bullying and social exclusion (Abrams et al., 2007; Adachi et al., 2003; Blakeney et al., 2005;

Carroll & Shute, 2005; Haavet et al., 2004; Kish & Lansdown, 2000). They are reported to be more likely to have fewer friends, academically underachieve and to have fewer vocational aspirations compared to their peers (e.g. see Kish & Lansdown, 2000).

Reluctance to Seek or Accept Support

Adolescents with an unusual appearance characteristically resent being identified on the basis of their difference, and adolescents in general are reluctant to explore an extremely sensitive and private issue, especially face to face with adults (Fox et al., 2007; Frost, 2003; Williamson, 2012). Many perceive a stigma attached to 'seeing a shrink' and are reluctant to seek and accept prescribed psychological therapy (Rickwood et al., 2007) or feel acutely self-conscious and embarrassed during sessions (Cartwright & Magee, 2006). This may be compounded during/after transition as the young person is required to build relationships with new and unfamiliar health professionals.

Health professionals also report practical difficulties with contacting young people (particularly those aged 16–18 years) who are likely to be at school/college during clinicians' work hours and can be hard to reach on the phone. Barke (2013) reports that young people often feel nervous returning phone calls or responding to letters of invitation for therapy. As such relationships between young people and health professionals are often still reliant on parent's practical support after transition. Utilizing current trends to contact and communicate with young people is again recommended (e.g. via text and online communication tools) and alternatives to face-to-face individual therapy, for example, online support (e.g. *YP Face It*, Williamson et al., 2012) or group sessions may be preferable for some (e.g. Maddern & Owen, 2004).

Factors that Can Promote Adjustment to a Visible Difference among Young People

As with the adult population, many young people with a visible difference are resilient, adjust well and can even thrive as a result. For example, the experience of living with appearance changes following a life-threatening event or from a congenital condition such as a cleft may result in personal growth and positive outcomes. These include a more positive attitude towards life, improved relationships, enhanced self-esteem and being more reflective, optimistic and empathic (Feragen, 2012: Wicks & Mitchell, 2010). Robust and rigorous evidence of the factors that might account for variation in psychosocial response is sparse among young people. However, among those who display resilience, the following have been reported as protective factors or useful coping strategies. Along with cognitive behavioural strategies (already identified for use with adults), these can be promoted and tailored to meet individual needs among young people who are struggling:

* **Social support and acceptance** of their altered appearance from their family and close friends (Enskar & Bertero, 2010; Larouche & Chin-Peukert, 2006; Sheng-Yu & Eiser, 2009; Williamson et al., 2010). Appearance-related teasing and criticism within the family is not helpful and is associated with a range of negative outcomes (see Bellew, 2012).

- For those who *acquire* a visible difference during adolescence, for example, following cancer treatment (e.g. scarring and alopecia) or burn injury, the role of the **peer shield** can be beneficial: a small group of close friends who adopt a strong caring attitude and spontaneously protect and shield the young person from distressing and negative reactions to their altered appearance by others (Larouche & Chin-Peukert, 2006; Williamson et al., 2010). Health professionals within oncology have reported the benefits of encouraging patients and counselling friends to engage this support mechanism (Williamson, 2012).

- While acknowledging that a dependence on camouflage as a sole coping strategy can be unhelpful (Coughlan & Clarke, 2002), some young people find it useful to employ practical and often innovative techniques to **conceal** an acquired visible difference or **enhance** overall appearance (with make-up, head gear, wigs, clothes, through the use of colour, make-up, clothing and jewellery). These strategies are reported as helpful to improve self-esteem and reduce self-consciousness during social activities – particularly if they are having a 'bad' day and feeling emotionally vulnerable (Williamson & Wallace, 2012).

- **Social skills** to help manage or limit negative reactions to sudden appearance change or when meeting new people are also essential as part of as toolbox of coping strategies. These include warning and preparing friends about an altered appearance using photos, texts and videos (thus avoiding awkward reactions to their 'new look'). Being proactive and confident in the provision of information to explain their difference, using pre-prepared responses or humour to deflect negative attention, manage teasing or to put others at ease can also be useful (Larouche & Chin-Peukert, 2006; Williamson et al., 2010).

- **Gradual social exposure**: 'testing' social responses to their appearance by revealing changes to close supportive family and friends first, those likely to reassure and offer support, and building a bank of positive experiences to draw upon before judging when it is 'safe' to reveal their altered appearance in public (Williamson et al., 2010).

- **Parental acknowledgement and understanding** of the pertinence of appearance change to the young person – rather than shying away from the topic or responding dismissively – has also been suggested as a factor that might contribute towards adolescent resilience. Williamson et al. (2010) found that parents of adolescents who appeared to be coping well engaged in 'parental shielding' when necessary (behaviours similar to those performed by peers), helped the young person to maintain and promote social integration and, most importantly, worked in partnership with their child to manage appearance change and any negative social reactions to it. Parents often request and appreciate advice on how to support their child's appearance concerns.

- **Support from school**, specifically interventions that promote self-esteem, coping and social skills training and to target appearance-related bullying have shown promise (Robinson et al., 1996), as have programmes that address issues pertaining to transition from primary to secondary school (Maddern & Owen, 2004). In addition to focusing on the individual, school-based interventions to promote acceptance of appearance diversity are essential. (See Diedrichs and Halliwell (2012) for a summary of effective content.)

- **Support from health professionals**: although empirical evidence is as yet sparse, qualitative reports suggest that young people highly value the health professional who takes the initiative to ask if they have appearance worries, takes their appearance concerns seriously and provides advice or refers them for specialist support (Williamson et al., 2012). At present access to specialist support is limited or ad hoc within the NHS and misperceptions concerning those most at risk of appearance anxiety can result in specific groups of patients with appearance distress being neglected. Some health professionals assume that boys cope better with an altered appearance than girls and that those whose appearance is minimally affected are less likely to experience distress. Evidence consistently shows this is not the case and it is safer to ask the patient if they have concerns rather than predict those at risk.

Romantic Issues

Developing romantic relationships are a normal and healthy part of growing up, and most adolescents have worries about dating. There are however particular issues that concern the young person with a visible difference. Research by Griffiths et al. (2012) has identified what some of these are and also factors that that can prevent or ameliorate them. Concerns and unhelpful behaviours – often underpinned by the belief that a conventionally attractive appearance is an essential attribute for romantic success – include:

- **Feeling unattractive** to others and worried that no one would want to date them. These young people often do not feel it is worth attempting to find a partner and give up on the dating scene before even trying.
- **Fear of negative evaluation**: worries about what current or potential partners think of their difference and a fear they may discuss 'it' with peers behind their back.
- **Avoidance behaviours**: some avoid social activities (e.g. swimming) or intimate behaviours that necessitate revealing normally concealed differences to their partners. They worry that revealing their difference will jeopardize the relationship.
- **Concealment can lead to feelings of guilt and anxiety**: guilt that they have not told their partner they have a 'difference' and anxiety about how and when they should broach the subject.
- **Difficulty talking to the opposite sex** (or potential same-sex partners): fear of negative evaluation and preoccupation with their difference can result in difficulties instigating conversations, thus reducing opportunities to meet partners and form relationships.

Among those with a positive attitude towards romantic issues, Griffiths et al. (2012) identified evidence of protective factors replicating those that promote overall healthy adjustments that are listed earlier: good social skills and the perception that they are well supported by friends and family. In addition to these, confident young people tend to hold the following beliefs and attitudes:

- **Feeling unattractive is normal for teens** (and therefore of no more a concern for them than their peers).
- **Attributes other than a physical appearance are important in attracting a partner**: a sense of humour, loyalty, friendliness, intelligence and so on. As such their self-worth was bolstered and they felt confident they had qualities that would be appealing. Following on from this belief was the view that potential partners that focused on their appearance difference in a negative manner were therefore 'shallow' and not worth their attention.
- **It's a part of who I am**: a unique part of their identity that sets them apart from the crowd and should be celebrated.
- **It could be worse**: some minimized their concerns by making downward comparisons with those worse off than themselves.

Young people with and without romantic concerns have collaborated to design a section within the YP Face It online support programme (Williamson et al. in submission) to address common concerns around romantic and intimate issues.

Transition as an Opportunity for Those with a Visible Difference

While there may be challenges for young people with appearance concerns during adolescence, it may be useful to view transition to adult care as an opportunity. Transition provides all parties with a reason to engage with one another and come together to discuss next steps. In practical terms this is an opportunity to ask young people about their appearance in a way that is both matter of fact and normalizing. The young person can see the reason they are having a conversation about their condition and their appearance as external (everyone does this when they are going through transition) rather than internal (I'm being asked about my appearance because I have a problem). These conversations may reveal concerns that can be addressed in sessions or may highlight the need for intervention and support for appearance anxiety.

Transition can be an opportunity to reset relationships and to set adult expectations of health care and engagement as well as a time to revisit information about conditions, thus ensuring young people have the knowledge and information they need to adjust positively. Particularly for young people with a genetic/congenital or early-onset condition, conversations about their condition and prognosis (including impact on appearance) may have taken place when they were very young, generally with parents. Transition is an excellent opportunity to ensure young people have the chance to ask questions and understand their condition holistically.

Research has identified that young people with a visible difference may want to meet others their own age with chronic health conditions and visible differences but want this to be for a specific and practical reason. Transition can be an opportunity to address this through group sessions as part of a transition programme giving young people an 'incidental' way to meet others with similar conditions and concerns. Sessions could be facilitated by both paediatric and adult care staff and could include input from older young people as well as clinicians. It is essential to remember that the young person is learning how to transition in all aspects of life; health care is just one. It is normal for some individuals to be resilient and sail through this stage, while others may struggle and need support. Young people with an altered appearance are not a homogenous group, their needs and development will be individual. In order to understand their experience and ensure concerns are picked up and addressed during transition, the following questions and issues discussed may be helpful:

1. Does the patient fully understand their condition; have they ever had a conversation with a clinician about it? This can be addressed by asking questions such as:
    *   Why do you think you come into hospital?
    *   If you were a doctor, how would you explain your condition?
        Both questions can indicate what aspects of their condition the young person is focused on and can highlight any misconceptions or gaps in knowledge. This may be a good time to go back over the young person's medical and psychosocial history with them and ask about their experience holistically in a conversational way, with no 'right' or 'wrong' answers.

2. As previously mentioned, a first step in adjusting to an altered appearance can be in acknowledging and legitimizing concerns (Clarke, 1999); see Chapter 5. In terms of discussing appearance, questions should normalize experience:
    - Some people with your condition/conditions similar to yours say they sometimes feel anxious about their appearance, have you ever felt this way?
3. Some young people may not talk directly about appearance concerns but may discuss concerns related to social anxiety, so asking the following questions may be a way to initiate a conversation:
    - Would you say you are quite confident in social situations/meeting new people? (If not, broaden discussion to ask if this is ever about appearance?)
    - Do people ever ask you about your appearance? (This can be used as a way to discuss how to manage questions/intrusive staring or comments.)
4. It is also useful to enquire about expectations of the future and treatment and establish if they realistic. For example, are patients' expectations of scars fading or of surgery realistic? Are they worrying about possible changes that might not happen or are highly unlikely? If so, discussing the future prognosis and putting risk factors into context may be beneficial.

Adaptation to an altered appearance is an evolving process that takes place throughout life (Prior, 2009). Ideally, many of these issues should be discussed throughout childhood as the young person develops, with knowledge deepening and becoming more detailed as the young person desires, and when they are developmentally ready.

Concluding Remarks

Transitional care should aim to encourage the patient's physical, psychological and social development rather than merely providing a physical transfer from paediatric to adult care: 'transition isn't about moving from department to department, it's about moving from your childhood to adulthood' (Department of Health, 2007). A successful transition therefore requires careful planning, management and a co-ordinated approach involving the young person, parent and health-care team (Crowley et al. 2011). In relation to those with a condition or injury that affects their appearance, transition can provide an opportunity for identifying appearance issues and co-ordinating access to appearance-specific support. Young people should be provided with the opportunity to discuss any appearance worries they may have in a supportive environment with health professionals who are cognizant of the common issues and concerns they may have and who are able to tailor and deliver care to meet individual needs.

9

Psychological Assessment for Cosmetic Surgery

Chapter Outline

Introduction

It is not surprising, given the growing popular consensus about the importance of appearance, that there has been a growth in the popularity of cosmetic surgery. Figures from the British Association of Aesthetic Plastic Surgeons (BAAPS) indicate a 6% increase in the number of people accessing cosmetic surgery (with BAAPS members) between 2010 and 2011, and this follows a tripling in numbers from 2003 to 2009. Ten per cent of requests are from men, and there are increasing requests for surgery at a younger age. However, this is an unusual area of medicine in that procedures with a range of risks and complications are undertaken in the absence of an underlying disease or medical condition. They are essentially procedures undertaken to enhance quality of life. Whilst anyone with the capacity to make an informed decision can make a decision to undergo surgery, there are major concerns about the evidence of effectiveness of cosmetic procedures in meeting patients' expectations. Marketing strategies which relate cosmetic procedures to well-being or psychosocial factors such as self-confidence encourage people to consider surgery to achieve what are primarily psychological goals. However, the evidence of improvements in well-being or on factors such as self-confidence is less well documented than purely physical outcomes such as the successful modification in size or shape of a feature. Satisfaction with outcome for one type of technique (e.g. breast reduction) tends to be higher than for other techniques (e.g. rhinoplasty), and there is a significant minority of patients whose preoccupation with a perceived abnormality of appearance is heightened rather than reduced by having surgery. This particular group, many of whom meet the diagnostic criteria for body dysmorphic disorder (BDD), often seek repeat procedures. It is essential that vulnerable patients such as these are counselled about the risks of surgery and are offered alternative treatment options.

Is Cosmetic Surgery Effective?

The fact that so many people not only access surgery but return for further procedures is often cited as evidence for their effectiveness. In the short term, many people report high levels of satisfaction with surgery or non-invasive procedures. However, there are other psychological explanations for why people might rate surgery highly, including cognitive dissonance. Psychologists would also point out that where preoccupation with appearance is the key problem, an effective solution is one that reduces it. Evidence that people are returning for further procedures aimed at modifying the same feature suggests that this fundamental goal has not been met.

Good, methodologically sound evidence is gradually being accrued, but several papers have discussed the fact that convincing evidence is not yet available for particularly for long-term outcomes (Moss & Harris, 2009; Sarwer et al., 2008, 2012a, b). Satisfactory research design including appropriate control groups would address many of the current gaps. Similarly, we need to include a wider variety of patient groups. Most research so far has been reported for women having breast surgery, mainly augmentation. It is also likely that certain procedures, notably rhinoplasty, include significant numbers of people who meet the diagnostic criteria for BDD and may therefore have very different outcomes. Similarly, the significant numbers of people who request surgery to remove excess skin after bariatric surgery include people with underlying eating disorders who despite the resulting health benefits of weight loss surgery may retain or develop a significant body image problem.

Many people requesting cosmetic procedures do so with the ultimate goal of achieving increased self-confidence. Cordeiro et al. (2010) and Clarke et al. (2012) have reported the typical presentation of those seeking surgery via a north London NHS clinic, suggesting that an underlying social anxiety underpins the expectation that appearance, if changed, will result in increased social skill and success. The evidence so far from clinics in the United Kingdom and United States supports post-operative satisfaction where the physical change meets the expectations set out pre-operatively (i.e. where the desired change in appearance has been achieved). Precise pre- and post-operative measurement can be helpful here. Reported gains in psychosocial expectations about increased self-confidence and self-esteem, improved quality of life and wider psychosocial goals are much more variable. Dissatisfaction is also commonly associated with unrealistic expectations or 'correction' of an anomaly that the patient was not worried by. The common factor here may be a failure to fully explore the problem from the patients' perspective; the aim of surgery is not to achieve the best aesthetic outcome, but the one that the patient is asking for which may not be the same. Failure to outline the limitations and complications of surgery in enough detail may also result in a dissatisfied patient. However, even when surgery has been very thoroughly discussed, patients may still attribute unrealistic potential benefits to surgery or seek to minimize the risk by distancing strategies, for example, 'because my surgeon is an international expert, my surgery will go well'.

A systematic rapid evidence review of cosmetic surgery outcomes is currently being undertaken jointly by the Centre for Appearance Research (CAR) and the Evidence for Policy Practice and Information (EPPI) Centre at the Institute of Education, sponsored by the UK Department of Health and should be available shortly (Brunton et al., 2012). This is likely to highlight the need for better quality research on patient outcomes.

Access to Surgery in the NHS

Access to cosmetic procedures via the NHS has been managed locally by Cosmetic Surgery guidelines issued by the relevant funding authority. This has led to a notorious variation in provision with some people accessing procedures relatively easily in certain areas of the country whilst others are unable to access treatment for procedures traditionally regarded as reconstructive (e.g. revision of burn scarring). The 'Low Priority Treatment Guidance' and the subsequent 'Procedures of Low Clinical Effectiveness (PoLCE)' guidance both try to introduce evidence-based decision making into assessment. In effect, both sets of guidance focus on the functional problems associated with appearance concerns, thus eliminating cosmetic procedures from the NHS almost completely. In particular, the provision for cosmetic surgery on grounds of extreme psychological distress has been removed from most guidelines, appropriately, given the lack of evidence that surgery has benefits for this group of patients. This does not stop people attempting to access surgery on these grounds, and PoLCE guidelines now suggest that surgery is only provided on the basis of psychological or psychiatric assessment and only after psychosocial approaches to treatment have been tried. However, referral to mental health services purely for assessment of suitability for cosmetic surgery is no longer sanctioned.

In the private sector, widespread publicity about the use of non-medical grade silicon in French Poly Implant Prosthesis (PIP) breast implants highlighted once again the problems with consumer protection and poor regulation of cosmetic procedures. The UK Department of Health set up a working party in 2012 under the leadership of Sir Bruce Keogh to make recommendations about higher standards of care in this sector. This working party report will be published in Spring 2013.

With all these changes in the United Kingdom, it is far more likely that psychological assessment will be regarded if not as routine, certainly as good practice in both the NHS and in the private sectors.

Psychological Screening by the Surgeon

Surgeons do not undergo comprehensive psychological training, but experienced surgeons are usually able to identify a patient where they have concerns. A typical referral notes that there is 'excessive' concern or 'concern is out of proportion to the size of the defect'. Other common comments are that the patient seems 'vague' about what they are trying to achieve or that their expectations of outcome seem excessive. Although a good screening tool will quantify some of these issues, a simple short tool has not yet been published, and surgeons are loath to administer (and then score) longer tools. Developing a short screen is the subject of a current research project at CAR, which if successful will fill this gap (Paraskeva, 2013).

NICE Guidelines

The NICE guidelines for OCD and BDD (NICE, 2005) recommend that all patients requesting cosmetic procedures have a simple screen as part of their initial surgical consultation. This is not a formalized questionnaire but a simple list of five questions which orientate the surgeon to an excessive preoccupation with appearance and the necessity of onward referral for psychological assessment.

Questions recommended by NICE for all patients requesting cosmetic treatments (www.NICE. org.uk):

- Do you worry about the way that you look and wish that you could think about it less?
- What specific concerns do you have about your appearance?
- On a typical day, how many hours is it on your mind? (consider > 1 hour excessive)
- What effect does it have on your life?
- Does it make it hard to do your work or be with friends?

Unfortunately, although a good start, the questions are basic and give little idea of what level of distress should be regarded as abnormal, hence the need for a standardized tool.

Onward Referral

Where an excessive concern with appearance is suspected, NICE guidelines recommend onward referral to a mental health professional with specific experience in treating BDD. There are two main problems with this recommendation. First, most patients attempting to access cosmetic treatments

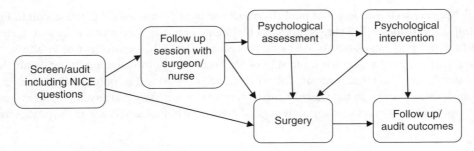

Figure 9.1 Suggested pathway for referral.

will have a high investment in their appearance and are likely to answer several of these questions affirmatively, whether there are underlying psychological difficulties or not. Second, a suitably qualified mental health professional is likely to be a psychologist with considerable experience of cognitive behaviour therapist (CBT), and waiting time for such a referral can be considerable. We would therefore suggest a stepped approach. A patient answering positively on any of the aforementioned five questions clearly needs a longer assessment and more detailed standardized assessment. This can be done by the surgeon or by an experienced practice nurse. It is often the case that the patient's motivation becomes clearer at this next stage. However, if there are still concerns, a specialist referral is helpful as mentioned later (Figure 9.1).

This pathway shows that patients who raise concerns have a second appointment with either the surgeon or cosmetic surgery practice nurse at which the psychological issues are explored more fully. They will then be either listed for surgery or referred for specialist psychological assessment and possible treatment. At this stage, patients may be screened out and offered alternative treatment, or they may be referred back to the surgeon for treatment, often having had further preparation in terms of goal setting, suggested reading or preparatory behaviour change, or following a longer psychological intervention. The final step in the pathway is the audit of outcome whether post surgically or following a psychological intervention. Patient-reported outcome measures for cosmetic procedures have recently been reviewed by Morley et al. (2012).

What Does the Surgeon Want from a Psychological Assessment?

A referral often fails to adequately describe the question that the surgeon is asking the psychologist. A referral may just ask for 'your opinion'. Psychiatrists usually interpret this as a request for a psychiatric assessment and answer the implicit underlying question about whether or not the patient has an underlying mental health problem. Although this information is an important part of assessment, it is a necessary rather than sufficient outcome. A surgeon is often asking for more. They usually want to know if surgery is likely to benefit the patient and the probability that they will be satisfied post-operatively. This is particularly likely if they are requesting a repeat procedure. In the NHS they also want to know whether this patient is 'exceptional' or whether there are grounds for treating them differently from the other patients who are referred for the same problem. We should therefore be providing an assessment that addresses these questions as far as we are able (however, it is important to note the difficulty with research evidence to guide these kinds of assessments). If in doubt about the purpose of assessment, it is always better to talk to the referrer first and clarify the issues that concern them.

What Does the Patient Want from a Psychological Assessment?

Patients are usually puzzled by the need for a psychological assessment and may assume that the surgeon is worried about their mental health. Sometimes they can assume that the psychological assessment is just a formality; they are there to tick a box. Conversely, the psychologist can be seen as standing between the patient and the surgery that they desire.

Clearly, it is important to acknowledge that assessment involves screening for factors that predict poor outcome, but assessment is equally about providing the opportunity to really understand the goals of surgery and setting out very clear objectives for what it is hoped that surgery is going to achieve. This is particularly important where surgery has not met expectations in the past. Many people are ambivalent about surgery, particular where they associate this with negative reactions from other people or where they associate it with vanity, and welcome the chance to talk this through more fully. Psychologists should also set out the evidence of effectiveness in terms of the procedure requested, which means having a good understanding of the relevant research literature, and should be able to advise about different approaches to managing appearance anxiety, where this is a feature. It is helpful to explain the function of the assessment at the outset, ideally in the appointment letter and again at the outset of the assessment, and to copy correspondence to the patient.

Ultimately the psychologist has a duty of care both to the patient and to the surgeon. It is therefore important to set out as far as possible why the particular recommendation from the psychologist is being made and on what basis. This should be summarized at the end of the consultation as well as the following correspondence. Ultimately it is up to the patient whether they ignore it by seeking a different surgical provider. However, it is certainly the case that patients can be very upset if they perceive that the psychologist has 'blocked' their surgery, even when there are very good reasons for doing so. Conversely, they can also be very grateful for a clear report that helps them to identify aspects of their decision that they had not thought of. It is also helpful to copy correspondence to the patient and to include some 'do's and don'ts' with respect to managing appearance anxiety. Additional reading is also useful, particularly self-help texts such as *Overcoming Body Image Problems* (which includes a chapter on cosmetic surgery) and *The Body Image Work Book* (see end of this chapter for details of both these texts).

A Framework for Psychological Assessment

Clarke et al. (2005) developed a framework which provides a standardized structure for cosmetic assessments and a basis for collecting outcomes (see Table 9.1). Since publication, we have updated it in line with evidence and better measures. The focus of the assessment using this framework is to help the patient to describe the feature they dislike in very clear objective terms (larger, smaller) rather than value judgements (nicer, more attractive) so that the surgeon can objectively discuss the surgical goals. The assessment also aims to set out the goals for change in terms of behaviour change and the wider impact that they are hoping the surgery will have on their lives. This helps to identify

Table 9.1 A framework for psychological assessment following requests for cosmetic surgery (adapted from Clarke 2005). Reproduced with permission from Elsevier.

Psychological indications for surgery	Evidence	Post-operative goals and expectations	Outcome measures
Appearance-related distress in excess of normative discontent	Clinical history, scores on standardized measures, e.g. BDDQ, DAS24, HADs, FNE, COPS, VAS 0–10	Significant reduction in appearance-related distress	Self-reported improvement Reduction in test scores Reduction in medication use
High perceived noticeability and worry related to a specific feature	Patient can provide a clear description of defect No hierarchy of concerns Early experience including bullying, abuse Current psychiatric morbidity assessed including eating disorders, BDD, self-harm Recent life events Internal/external motivation for change Core values and attitudes to surgery	Specific concern reduced No new concerns Consistent with core values	Reduced score on noticeability (0–10) and worry (0–10)
Direct impact of appearance concerns on behavioural function	Social avoidance Sexual avoidance or inhibition Excessive use of camouflage, clothing as safety behaviours Impact on social, employment and sexual role	Positive behaviour and lifestyle changes	Reduced social avoidance (DAS24 and self-report) Improved sexual functioning Reduced safety behaviour Positive changes in social, employment of sexual roles
Realistic understanding of procedure and expectations of outcome	Patient able to describe procedure Patient able to describe risks Patient able to describe objective change, e.g. make my nose smaller rather than 'nicer' or 'like it was before' goal of improvement rather than correction or perfection	Patient satisfaction with process and outcome	Outcome meets expectations (above 70%) No request for revision No complaints
Active participation in shared decision making and treatment	Patient proactive in information gathering, managing behavioural goals such as smoking cessation, weight management Regular attendance at appointment Planning post-surgical goals	Implementation of post-surgical goals and lifestyle change	Adherence to post-surgical instructions, e.g. scar management, dressing clinical appointments, wear supportive bra, long-term outcomes

unrealistic expectations and those patients who have essentially psychosocial goals which may be amenable to another approach including a combined psychological and surgical intervention. Routine measures are included to provide baseline data and to compare the level of appearance concern with a normative and clinical population.

A major component of a useful psychological assessment is the separation of the physical goals for surgery from the psychosocial goals (e.g. make my nose smaller vs. make me feel more confident). This then allows a discussion of how exactly those goals are going to be measured and whether there are any alternative means of achieving self-confidence and overcoming social anxiety. It is also the opportunity to talk about normative behaviour. Many people talk about hating having their photo taken as part of the reasons that they are considering surgery, but many ordinary people dislike or avoid having their photos taken. Similarly, many people avoid nakedness even in front of a partner and breasts come in all shapes and sizes. People are often surprised to find that their behaviour is not as unusual as they thought it was.

Case Examples

The following examples are all for patients requesting rhinoplasty, but all present in a very different way:

Example 1

Ayesha was referred with a request for surgery to her nose. The trigger for this request was her future graduation and the photographs that she knew her family would want to display.

Ayesha explained that she had become aware that she disliked her nose during adolescence. She could recall no significant triggers or remarks from others and had never experienced bullying in relation to her appearance. She reported no previous psychiatric history, no significant appearance concerns other than her nose. She was vague about how she thought it should change although she felt it was 'too big for my face'. Her psychometric measures were all unremarkable. She had successfully completed her university degree and was looking for a job, and her motivation for surgery was focused on feeling more confident in social and work situations.

In addition to the vagueness about how she wanted her nose to change and the important landmark of starting a new job, the main concern identified during assessment was her reluctance to tell anyone about surgery. When asked how she would feel if others commented on her altered appearance, she was appalled and felt that this would be deeply shaming. It was evident as we discussed this that her cultural and personal values were strongly against cosmetic surgery which she associated with vanity. Making a decision which is not consistent with core values can lead to difficulties particularly when the procedure does not meet expectations, and following this discussion she chose not to go ahead. It is interesting that it was only during the psychological assessment that this patient herself became aware of the mismatch between her planned behaviour and her underlying beliefs. This is a very common outcome during assessment and it often becomes evident when people recognize that a procedure which substantially alters appearance cannot necessarily be kept secret from other people. Ayesha's report is illustrated in the following:

Dear X

Thank you for referring Ayesha who is aged 22, and who I saw for assessment on October 5, 2012.

History and Current Appearance-Related Concerns

Ayesha is considering surgery to reduce the size of her nose. The trigger for this request is her graduation and the associated photographs next year.

Objectively, Ayesha's nose is unremarkable, but she feels that it is too large. She was vague about the physical changes which she hoped would be made via surgery. She is particularly self-conscious about her appearance in profile and has been concerned since adolescence. Her focus on her nose fluctuates, and she recognizes that on a good day she is completely unconcerned. She gives no history of bullying or comments from others about her nose throughout her school years. There are no other appearance-related concerns, no psychiatric history including eating disorders nor self-harm.

Ayesha is seeking a job in human resources. Although she knows from feedback at university that she is perceived by others to be positive and confident, she does identify some concerns about how others see her in meetings and whether they are wondering about her nose, but recognizes that there is no evidence of this scrutiny from other people. Apart from this mild social anxiety, there is no evidence of social avoidance associated with her nose; however, she identifies increased social confidence and self-esteem as the main goals for surgery.

Psychometric Measures

On a series of psychometric measures, her scores are as follows:

On Derriford Appearance Scales (DAS24), Ayesha obtained a score of 34 which falls at the mean for a **non-clinical** female population. In other words, her concern about her appearance is not excessive and can be described in terms of normative discontent; she is very similar to other women of her age in the premium she places on what she looks like.

On the Hospital Anxiety and Depression Scale, her scores for anxiety and depression are as follows:

Anxiety: 13, moderate clinical range
Depression: 4 not significant

On the fear of negative evaluation scale, it is evident that she is highly attuned to what other people think about her and keen that people will judge her in a positive light.

Finally, she reports looking at her nose in the mirror (up to seven times a day) and for about 30 minutes in total.

Psychological Opinion

The scores are consistent with someone who is keen to be viewed in a positive way, who dislikes taking risks and who is rather 'a worrier' particularly about doing well at a new job and being approved of. Her colleagues' regard is very important to her, and although she is no more invested in her appearance than other women of her age, her graduation and associated photographs has highlighted a long-term dislike of her nose.

My main concern about Ayesha is that she has very clear views about plastic surgery, believing that it indicates vanity or self-preoccupation. She tells me that she would think less of other people if she knew that they had had surgery. When I put it to her that others might well observe that she had had surgery, she was concerned about this. We discussed the way in which she might take the initiative and tell people at the outset, but she thinks this would be quite difficult to do, and she clearly acknowledges the paradox in having surgery to avoid the scrutiny of others but undergoing a procedure that has a good chance of attracting it. As a general principle, I advise people to avoid actions that are inconsistent with their core values and beliefs. In situations where surgery fails to meet expectations or where there is a recognized complication leading to a suboptimal outcome, people often struggle with self-blame for acting in a way that they had doubts about. We also discussed the fact that finishing university and beginning a new job is a significant life event and that the anxiety and lack of confidence she is experiencing is a natural response to this change and wanting to be seen to do well. I suggested to her that she postpone any decisions about surgery until she has had a chance to settle into her job.

We then spent the rest of the session discussing the things that are helpful and less helpful in managing her concerns about appearance.

It will help to **avoid** the following

- Excessive self-scrutiny in the mirror
- Asking other people's opinion about appearance
- TV programmes such as 'Embarrassing Bodies' or articles promoting cosmetic surgery as a means of modifying psychological outcomes including online forums.

Summary and Recommendations

Ayesha is considering surgery at a point when she is facing a significant life change. Her anxiety about self-confidence can be viewed as a normal response to the stress of beginning a new job, and her fluctuating body image anxiety is likely to increase at times of stress. I think that there are risks for her in undergoing surgery, partly because it is hard to identify clear physical goals, but most of all because of the discord between her intended behaviour and her core values. I note that surgery had been booked to take place quite soon, and I have advised Ayesha to postpone this for now and to consider her decision very carefully in 6–12 months' time and to discuss it with close friends or family. In the meantime I have recommended that she read about body image concerns, and I have recommended 'Overcoming body image concerns' particularly the chapter on cosmetic surgery. I would be very happy to see her again if she would like to talk this through further or to develop further psychological strategies to manage her appearance anxiety.

Cc: patient

Example 2

Psychological assessment is often requested for a patient who is asking for a repeat procedure. The following is an example report for a patient who had been very unhappy following his original surgery and who had a significant degree of nasal asymmetry following this surgery.

Very commonly the assessment reveals BDD or a patient who feels they were rushed into a procedure without proper time to think about it. This patient assumed that because the surgeon was well known that there would be no complications from surgery. He felt that this appointment was rushed and he did not have a chance to ask questions; the surgeon told him that he could clearly see what the problem was and that he could 'leave surgery to him'. On the day of surgery, the surgeon he had spoken to was not there, and he was asked permission for someone else to do it. Although he was not happy about this, he felt that he would face a long wait if he declined. He subsequently very much regretted this decision. The following is his report; despite the previous problems, he was recommended for surgery and did well.

Thank you for referring Mr Baker who is aged 38 and for your summary of the details of his nasal asymmetry. I saw him for assessment on September 27, 2012.

History and Appearance-Related Concerns

He is considering further surgery to his nose in an attempt to overcome the difficulties that you have summarized, following an earlier rhinoplasty. As you know, Mr Baker was injured in an assault when he was 14 and his nose broken. He tolerated the change in appearance for many years despite comments and questions from other people, but he became worried about the deterioration in his nose over time and therefore had surgery at the age of 21, 6 years ago.

Mr Baker works for the inland revenue. He has a long-term partner and is not concerned that his appearance is an issue in relationships. He has no other appearance concerns and no history of psychiatric disorder or eating problems. He does recognize that his self-consciousness about his nose makes him irritable and quick tempered at times. In the past he has been very preoccupied by his nose, studying his appearance for long periods in the mirror. He stopped this himself when he realized it increased his anxiety. Similarly, he recognizes that he tends to modify how he stands and to scan other people to see if they have noticed his nose. This has been very much more marked in the past, and whilst he might have met the criteria for a diagnosis of BDD in the past, I would not include him within this category at this point.

With the benefit of hindsight, Mr Baker realizes that he should have done more research about the surgery. In retrospect, he recognizes that he was not given enough time to make a decision, and he feels that the surgeon did not really listen to him. This resulted in overcorrection of a detail which did not worry him. This is in sharp contrast to the present situation where he feels that you have taken trouble to listen to him, to clarify his objectives, give him time to think things through and to refer him to me.

Goals and Understanding of the Procedure

In terms of his expectation of outcome, he told me that he understands a second rhinoplasty to be a complicated operation. He understands that there are significant limits to what is possible and he described these competently to me. He understands that he may see far less change than he hopes for. In addition to the asymmetric appearance, he dislikes the 'feeling' or hardness of the tissue at the tip but understands that this may not change. I asked him if he could live with his nose as it is now and he said that he thought he could but that it would be easier for him if he felt that he had done all that was possible – however minimal the benefit. He defined this in terms of asking a surgeon who listens to him and whom he therefore trusts to do his best to achieve those procedures which have been discussed and agreed upon.

Psychometric Assessment

On a series of psychometric measures, he scored as follows:

Derriford Appearance Scale: 46. This score places him at the mean for a population of men of his age concerned about his nasal appearance. Individual items reveal only mild appearance anxiety, and there is no evidence of social avoidance.

On the **Hospital Anxiety and Depression Scale**, his scores of 8 on depression and 8 for anxiety are just at the margin of the clinical range, consistent with the mild appearance anxiety. Other scale scores are favourable with little evidence of fear of negative evaluation or impact on day to day life. He rates the noticeability of his nose to others as 3/10 and worry about his nose as 6/10. He spends 15–20 minutes per day looking at nose in the mirror over four occasions.

Psychological Opinion

These data support my impression of a man who has largely overcome the intense preoccupation with his nose that characterized his behaviour in the past.

I discussed some relevant research findings with Mr Baker including the fact that excessive scrutiny of an individual feature appears to alter the internal representation of that feature (body image) including the associated emotional response, in the same way as anorexia affects perceived body size, and any abnormality identified with his own appearance is likely to appear far less evident or important to an observer.

In terms of management of this concern, it will help to **avoid** the following:

- Excessive self-scrutiny in the mirror
- Asking other people's opinion about appearance
- TV programmes such as 'Embarrassing Bodies' or articles promoting cosmetic surgery as a means of modifying psychological outcomes including online forums
- Repeated surgical procedures.

Conversely, it is important that social activities or opportunities to do presentations at work are not avoided because of self-consciousness of appearance.

Summary and Recommendations

In summary then, I found Mr Baker to be thoughtful and insightful. He recognizes that the options are limited and that he is likely to achieve less than his ideal. He feels that he could manage without surgery if he had to but would prefer to achieve any gains possible. He feels he has a good relationship with you, has had time to think and plan. Above all he is clear that this is a final procedure and any residual concerns about his nose are things that he will manage himself or with my help. On this basis I think he is a good candidate for the surgery you plan.

Example 3

The following example is given for comparison. Again this is a patient who reports an unsatisfactory experience with a previous surgeon but where the evidence of significant body image problems is much more marked and where surgery is unlikely to be helpful.

Many thanks for referring this 42-year-old woman who attended the appointment for psychological assessment on September 15, 2011. She is requesting repeat rhinoplasty.

History and Current Appearance-Related Concerns

Pippa had a rhinoplasty paid for by her parents when she was 18, as a result of her appearance distress. Objectively, on the basis of photographs, her nasal appearance was unremarkable, and her preoccupation was associated with generalized anxiety about her appearance, bullying at school, social phobia and psychological problems throughout her teenage years which became focused on her nose. She left school at 15, has no qualifications and has not had any significant employment since then. With the benefit of hindsight, I think that she fitted the picture of BDD and that first surgery should have been avoided, and she has never managed to get established with living independently. She has not had any contact with mental health services although she has in the past, taken anti-depressive medication prescribed by her GP.

The next step in this journey (as she reported it, and I have not investigated this with any other parties) is that she attended a private cosmetic surgery clinic with a friend who was investigating a different procedure, and whilst she was waiting in the waiting room, she was approached by a clinician who pointed out to her that her original rhinoplasty had not been done correctly and that she needed further revision. He recommended that she be referred to his NHS clinic and she followed through on this advice. In the event, he was not available and the surgery was carried out by someone else. Unfortunately, this surgery has not had a good technical outcome.

Pippa presents now with a series of problems affecting her nose which you have documented. In terms of her current situation, it is clear that she is depressed and totally preoccupied about the appearance of her nose. She does not have any employment or social life and is socially avoidant, and the original dysmorphic symptoms are now exacerbated by a surgical complication.

Psychometric Assessment

On a series of psychometric measures, she scores as follows:

Derriford Appearance Scale: The score of 65 on this scale falls over one standard deviation above the mean for a population of women concerned about nasal shape. This represents extreme social anxiety and avoidance and is consistent with a history of a disengagement from the kind of everyday life that would be normal for a woman of her age and which she would like to enjoy.

Hospital Anxiety and Depression Scale: Her scores of 15 for anxiety and 14 for depression fall within the moderate clinical range consistent with preoccupation with her appearance.

Other psychometric measures reveal a fear of negative evaluation and problems with contemplating relationships because of a belief that others will judge her on the basis of the appearance of her nose as she judges herself.

Psychological Opinion
The data are consistent with the clinical impression of someone who has a pronounced body image concern and a preoccupation with accessing surgery to correct the current deficit. She anticipates a very significant change in her feelings and her ability to live a normal life following surgery. Rather than surgery, the focus for intervention is psychological and geared towards reducing her level of preoccupation.

Summary and Recommendations
This lady has significant appearance concerns of longstanding and meets the diagnostic criteria for BDD. She has been treated for depression in the past. Surgery has failed to meet expectations and is unlikely to do so in the future given her current level of preoccupation with her appearance. I was very pleased that Pippa accepts that at this point, we have to consider a psychological approach to her difficulties. She has a lot of ground to make up in terms of the social and employment opportunities that she has not yet started. She would benefit from referral to mental health services with a recommendation that she be assessed by someone with a specialist interest in BDD. Cc: patient and GP

Common Problems in Referral

Liaising with the GP

Many patients seek surgery without the knowledge of their GP and are reluctant for them to be informed. Surgeons vary in how they approach this. Many insist that the GP is included in correspondence since legally, if not, the surgeon becomes responsible for all aspects of their medical care whether or not related to cosmetic surgery. Professional bodies recommend that GPs are informed, and we would recommend that this advice is followed.

Health Professionals' Knowledge of Cosmetic Procedures

Plastic surgery is a highly specialist field with a very misleading press. Other doctors may assume that procedures are easily 'fixed' or may fail to appreciate the difficulty of meeting expectations. One of the most difficult situations to negotiate is one is where a colleague, for example, a psychiatrist has recommended surgery on mental health grounds, but the psychological assessment suggests that the procedure is very unlikely to achieve the result the patient is hoping for. When this happens, it is helpful to discuss with your colleague and work out a plan that both can support, so that the surgeon is offered helpful advice rather than trying to make a judgement between the differing views of two colleagues.

Summary

As regulation of the cosmetic surgery industry becomes more robust, it is likely that requests for psychological assessment will become more common. The framework mentioned earlier provides that basis for structuring assessment with the goal of providing a useful report for both the surgeon and the patient making their decision. Psychologists who undertake these assessments should have a good basic knowledge of the evidence for the effectiveness of different cosmetic procedures and the psychometric measures available. Above all, good liaison with the referrer and a clear understanding that surgery can have variable outcomes is essential.

Additional Resources

Cash, T.F. (2007) *The Body Image Workbook: An Eight Step Program for Learning to Like Your Looks*, New Harbinger, Oakland, CA.

Veale, D., Willson, R. and Clark, A. (2009) *Overcoming Body Image Problems (Including Body Dysmorphic Disorder)*, Constable Robinson, London.

10

Models of Service Delivery

Chapter Outline

CBT for Appearance Anxiety: Psychosocial Interventions for Anxiety Due to Visible Difference, First Edition.
Alex Clarke, Andrew Thompson, Elizabeth Jenkinson, Nichola Rumsey and Rob Newell.
© 2014 John Wiley & Sons, Ltd. Published 2014 by John Wiley & Sons, Ltd.

Alongside development of treatment approaches, different models of delivery should also be considered. The following are currently available within the United Kingdom.

Lay-Led Support

Changing Faces and Let's Face It are the best known of these organizations. They both provide direct access to support and information. However, it is more difficult for these organizations to offer a multidisciplinary approach, for example, supporting people through surgery, compared with a service embedded within the hospital setting.

Specialist Services

Outlook

The Outlook unit at Frenchay Hospital in Bristol employs psychologists with a specialism in altered appearance and is funded by the NHS. The disadvantage of this service is the need for referral from an NHS practitioner and the potential for misperception and non-attendance by patients.

Embedded Services

Royal Free Hospital, London

The Royal Free Service is an example of an embedded service with psychologists working alongside medical and surgical colleagues. This is a model that exists in many plastic surgery, dermatology and burn units. This is probably the gold standard in that psychological and physiological aspects of a condition can be considered in the same setting, and training and consultancy with other health professionals is very easily accessed. It also facilitates joint approaches to research.

Access to Psychology Services

In some NHS settings referral for psychological input is accessed via generic health psychology services (as is the case at The Rotherham NHS Foundation Trust). In other NHS settings specialist clinical psychology services often exist attached to burn centres, head and neck cancer centres and other medical services. For example, there is a particularly large clinical psychology service within the Sheffield Teaching Hospitals NHS Foundation Trust where a large number of medical specialisms have access to clinical psychology services. Where this is the model, it is helpful for practitioners to be able to access specialist supervision from people working primarily within body image and altered appearance.

Access to Mental Health Services

Physical health clinicians may refer to mental health services, and at the time of writing there are a number of pilot schemes involving providing psychological well-being training to physical health-care clinicians. Liaison psychiatry services may also offer a service for people with body image concerns, particularly BDD, and may occasionally be set up as an embedded service, for example, within orthographic or dermatology services.

Mapping Service Models onto Stepped Care

All the services listed earlier provide valuable input for patients. The immediate support offered by the charitable sector has the advantage of offering input when concerns about appearance may be most salient and offers the social support identified as a key predictor of good outcome by the ARC research programme. Changing Faces also provides training and resources to health professionals, for example, mandatory training in psychosocial care for health professionals working on burns units. Attendance at these training days allows nurses, prosthetists, allied health professionals and doctors to develop an expertise in psychosocial intervention at levels 1–3.

The remaining services mentioned earlier all provide input at level 4 and also provide teaching, training and research. Whilst access to services is easier close to bigger specialized centres, the development of the online programmes and increasing interest in this specialized area of work means that patients should no longer be hearing the message that a visible difference in appearance is something they 'just have to get used to' without help and support.

Appendix

This appendix comprises a modified version of the full report of a research programme funded by The Healing Foundation. The research programme was undertaken by The Appearance Research Collaboration (ARC)

Nichola Rumsey (Principle Investigator), James Byron-Daniel, Alex Clarke, Sally-Ann Clarke, Diana Harcourt, Elizabeth Jenkinson, Antje Lindenmeyer, Hayley McBain, Tim Moss, Stanton Newman, Rob Newell, Krysia Saul, Emma Thomas, Andrew Thompson and Paul White.

Acknowledgment: The ARC would like to make members of the Advisory Panel, Olivia Giles, Pam Warren, Luke Wiseman, Brendan Eley and Terry Paterson for their input throughout the research programme.

Factors and Processes Associated with Psychological Adjustment to Disfiguring Conditions

One of the clear findings to emerge from research examining the challenges faced by people with disfigurement is that not all people are equally affected. Over the past two decades it has become clear that a proportion of those affected adapt positively to the demands upon them, in some cases perceiving their visible difference as a positive advantage. At the beginning of the research project described follow, the research community was only in the foothills of the journey to understand the psychological factors and processes underpinning these differences.

Previous research has been characterized by small sample sizes, and by a focus in individual studies on the impacts of one particular condition resulting in disfigurement. It was clear that in order to improve understanding of the many factors and processes implicated in adjustment, research involving a large sample of people with a variety of disfigurements resulting from a broad range of

CBT for Appearance Anxiety: Psychosocial Interventions for Anxiety Due to Visible Difference, First Edition.
Alex Clarke, Andrew Thompson, Elizabeth Jenkinson, Nichola Rumsey and Rob Newell.
© 2014 John Wiley & Sons, Ltd. Published 2014 by John Wiley & Sons, Ltd.

conditions was needed. Accordingly, a consortium of the leading UK researchers in the field was convened. Through discussion and debate, this consortium designed a series of studies with the aim of identifying and investigating the psychosocial factors and processes contributing to successful adjustment to disfiguring conditions, with particular emphasis on those aspects which are amenable to change. An advisory panel of people with personal experience of disfigurement and clinicians involved in their care contributed to the project throughout, including the design, reporting and dissemination stages. The project was carried out over a period of 3 years. This work would not have been possible without the generous funding awarded by The Healing Foundation and support of the Worshipful Company of Tin Plate Workers.

The project aims were, first, to clarify the psychosocial factors and processes which contribute to variation in adjustment in people with visible disfigurement and, second, to use the results to inform the development of packages of support and intervention. A series of studies was designed to address these aims. In order to address the bias in published research on samples recruited from hospital settings (and, therefore, the recruitment of only those people currently in treatment), participants were recruited from community as well as health care settings. The biggest study comprised a large sample cross-sectional survey of 1265 participants with visible differences resulting from a variety of causes. A battery of validated measures relevant to the cognitions, emotions and behaviours of people with disfigurement were used (Study 1) together with free text questions which were analyzed using qualitative methods (Study 2). Two longitudinal studies were conducted – first, a re-administration of the validated measures after a 9 month interval with 360 participants (Study 3) and, second, a qualitative interview study of stability and change in adjustment with a subsection ($n = 26$) of participants from the third study (Study 4). Eight follow-on studies employing a range of methodologies focused in more depth on specific topics, including positive adjustment (Study 5), black and minority ethnic community views of disfigurement (Study 6), the perspective of South Asians with vitiligo (Study 7), appearance concerns and hostility in social situations (Study 8), the development of a scale to assess appearance distress in intimate situations (Study 9), the experiences of women with limb prostheses (Study 10), the role of appearance concerns in rheumatoid arthritis (Study 11) and the beliefs, experiences and training needs of general practitioners (GPs) (Study 12).

Background and Rationale for the Research Programme

A literature review completed by the consortium confirmed that the factors identified in the literature as potential contributors to adjustment to disfigurement prior to this programme of research included the following:

Physical and Treatment-Related Factors

These include the aetiology, extent, type and severity of the disfiguring condition and the treatment history of each individual. Contrary to the expectations of the lay public, many health care providers and the pioneer researchers in this field, the bulk of research, clinical experience and personal accounts written by those affected demonstrate that the extent, type and severity of a disfigurement are not consistent predictors of adjustment, although the visibility of the condition to others can exacerbate distress (Rumsey & Harcourt, 2004; Thompson & Kent, 2001).

Socio-Cultural Factors

These factors provide the context for adjustment and include age and developmental stage, gender, race, social class and cultural milieu. Also included in this category are parental and peer group influences. In addition, many writers have pointed to the role played by the media in creating and exacerbating the pressures on those distressed by their appearance – although the impact of media and other socio-cultural factors has been shown to vary between individuals (Tiggemann, 2004).

Psychological Factors and Processes

Factors included in this category include the structure of a person's self-esteem and self-image (e.g. the weight given to the opinions of others and to broader societal standards), a person's person-ality/disposition, coping repertoire, perceptions of social support, levels of psychological well-being (e.g. anxiety, depression) and social anxiety, feelings of shame and the perceived noticeability of the visible difference to others. These factors can be broadly categorized as affective (relating to feelings), cognitive (relating to thoughts) or behavioural (relating to behaviour) and are on the whole more amenable to change than physical, treatment-related or socio-cultural factors (Rumsey & Harcourt, 2005; Thompson & Kent, 2001). Fajervik-Morton's systematic review (2008) of the literature relating to adults with visible differences (which initially included 1191 potentially relevant articles and the final inclusion of 12 studies) concluded that the evidence was not sufficiently strong to draw firm conclusions about which factors exacerbate distress or promote adjustment and whether variation is related to the structure and organization of appearance-related information. This review confirmed the existing conviction of this research collaboration that an elucidation of these factors and processes should be a priority in this programme.

Previous research has focused on the problems and difficulties associated with visible difference. In addition, the large majority of participants in previous research have been recruited from the population seeking treatment for their condition. In order to understand the breadth of adjustment, it was also considered crucial to gather information from those who were not seeking treatment and/or perceived treatment to be irrelevant in addressing their needs. Accordingly this research also focused its recruitment efforts on a sample drawn from the community.

For the researchers and clinicians in this collaboration, the key priorities were, first, to clarify those factors and processes that exacerbate distress and/or promote successful psychological adjust-ment in people with visible differences and, second, by focusing on those factors which are amenable to change, to use this knowledge to inform the development and refinement of a comprehensive range of methods of support and intervention designed to promote positive adjustment.

Theoretical Underpinning

The challenge of developing comprehensive models and theories to guide and underpin research relating to appearance have been discussed by Thompson and Kent (2001) and Rumsey and Harcourt (2005). Early cognition models of body image disturbance focused on the discrepancy between an individual's perceived actual and ideal selves and described the process by which an individual's thinking can become more and more dominated by negative thoughts about their appearance (Thompson et al., 1999). Cash's (1997) cognitive–behavioural model recognizes that past, cultural and interpersonal experiences, physical characteristics and personality attributes influence the development of body image attitudes and schema.

In relation specifically to disfigurement, perspectives on stigma (Goffman, 1963), shame (Kent & Thompson, 2002) and social exclusion (Leary, 1990) have informed the development of a number of models (including those by members of this collaboration, see Chapter 3). Whilst models may help to organize collective thinking, at their current level of sophistication, they cannot yet provide a comprehensive representation of the complexities of factors, the relationships between them and the dynamic nature of adjustment. At the time of this research, no single model stood out as offering a comprehensive framework to guide research and clinical intervention. The available models were either limited in scope, falling short of providing a comprehensive understanding of individual experiences of appearance or incorporated measures that could not easily be used in clinical practice. None of the existing models had been tested on a large and diverse population of people with visible differences. The research team consequently considered it timely to marshal the plethora of variables implicated in adjustment in previous research in a format suitable for the purpose of guiding this research programme.

Mindful of the need to achieve a consensus within the group and of the imperative for the outputs of this research to inform interventions, the members of this collaboration adopted a pragmatic approach in developing a framework to guide the current programme. This approach involved integrating the main findings and trends in this area of research, encompassing aspects of previous models developed by members of the team and other leading commentators in the field (see Figure A1). The framework was designed to facilitate the identification and clarification of those factors which have the potential to be amenable to change through psychosocial support and intervention – either as an adjunct or, where appropriate, as an alternative to surgical and medical interventions. In addition, and in contrast to previous research in this area, which has focused mainly on the problems and difficulties associated with disfigurement, this programme also aimed to identify and clarify factors contributing to 'resilience' and positive adjustment. The result was a descriptive, working framework of inputs, mediating processes and outputs designed to be broad enough to capture the range of experiences of those affected, but specific enough to allow for predictions about the susceptibility to distress or positive adjustment of those affected by a visible difference. The initial framework was used to consider the emerging findings of the project and was further refined following the analysis and synthesis of the results.

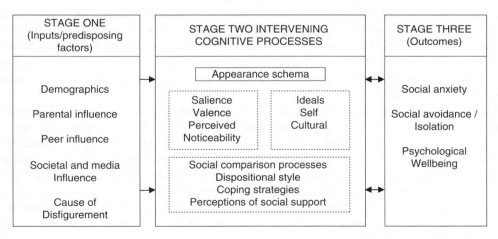

Figure A1 Working framework of adjustment to disfiguring conditions. From Rumsey and Harcourt, 2012. Reproduced with permission from Oxford University Press.

Within this framework, the process of adjustment to visible differences is conceptualized as having three facets. The first is the social and psychological context, comprised of predisposing factors such as demographic characteristics, socio-cultural setting, and family environment. While all of these factors play a part in adjustment and an understanding of their influence is important, their relative impermeability may make them less amenable to intervention. The current programme of research therefore acknowledged the presence and influence of these factors, but maintained a predominant focus on cognitive processes, which are more amenable to change through interventions.

The second facet of the model comprised intervening cognitive processes, which contribute to the differentiation between good and poor adjusters. We took the view that these are best understood from a social cognition perspective, with particular reference to the functioning of the self-concept. From this viewpoint, an individual can be conceptualized as having a cognitive representation of him or herself, which includes a representation of appearance. The appearance aspect of the self-representation can be more or less salient at any time and thus play a greater or lesser part in the working self-concept (Higgins & Brendl, 1995). As a result of this, there will be variation in the extent to which a person's perception of his or her own appearance is involved in attending to and appraising activity in the social environment and in subsequent memories of past experiences (Moss & Carr, 2004, Bargh et al., 1988). In addition to the salience of appearance within the self-concept, there can also be a variation in the evaluative valence of the appearance – that is, the way a person looks can be seen by that person in a positive or negative light (Sarwer & Crerand, 2004). Appearance can also be judged by individuals as being closer to or further from their internalized cultural ideals (Altabe & Thompson, 1996). When appearance is generally more salient, negatively valenced and further from ideals, adjustment will be poorer. Some of the important ways in which appearance can be made more salient and prone to negative evaluation include social comparison processes (Green & Sedikides, 2001) and positive or negative experiences of social encounters, as well as subjective perceptions of the perceived severity and the perceived noticeability of the disfiguration to others (Rumsey et al., 2004). Other more stable variables, such as attributional style (Crocker et al., 1991), some coping processes (Fauerbach et al., 2002) and perceptions of social support (Robinson, 1997), may also serve to exacerbate or ameliorate distress (see also Moss, 1997b). As members of this collaboration recognized the need to provide knowledge that would inform effective interventions, particular attention was paid to those cognitive processes which are amenable to change, including salience, valence, perceived noticeability and severity, to the relation of the appearance evaluation to subjective individual and perceived cultural ideals and norms, and to the way in which social comparison relates to these. The research programme also provided the opportunity to assess the value and utility of conceptualizing adjustment in this way.

The third facet of the model focused on the observable and experienced effects of appearance concerns. Existing work has already demonstrated the importance of social anxiety and avoidance (for reviews, see Thompson & Kent, 2001; Rumsey & Harcourt, 2004) and, to a lesser extent, shame and hostility (Kent & Thompson, 2002). Although for the purpose of modelling these are conceptualized in this framework as outcomes, it is acknowledged that these constructs also serve a function in setting the psychological context for the cognitive processes described earlier. There is an ongoing debate amongst researchers in the area (including those in this collaboration) and most are of the view that they are not simply the last links in a chain, but part of a dynamic process in which experience informs cognition.

Design Considerations in the Research Process

The Use of Mixed Methodologies

This research collaboration adopted a mixed methods approach. Debate concerning the relative merits of quantitative and qualitative methods has ranged for some time and has been termed by some 'the paradigm wars' (Dures, 2009). In the recent past, quantitative and qualitative approaches were viewed by many as incompatible as the two approaches are underpinned by different sets of assumptions about what knowledge can be acquired and the methods of acquisition. However, there is now widespread recognition that adherence solely to one or other set of assumptions can impose an unnecessary rigidity on research. Research in 'real world' settings, particularly research which is orientated to client needs rather than driven primarily by academic concerns, requires a flexible approach that can cope with complex, multi-factorial issues and takes practicalities into account (Dures, 2009). The current consensus is that both methodological approaches have merits, particularly in research in which pragmatism and critical realism have a place (Denscombe, 2008). Proponents of mixed methods argue that understanding can be enhanced to a greater extent through the use of both approaches rather than by one in isolation, but also believe that their use should be justified in relation to the research question and that the rationale should be clearly specified. Johnson et al., (2007) have defined mixed methods as 'a third methodological or research paradigm ... that will often provide the most informative, complete, balanced and useful research results' (p. 129). The different studies should talk to each other, much like a conversation (Bryman, 2007).

In order to address the first aim of this research programme (to identify psychosocial factors and processes contributing to adjustment), and in view of the small sample sizes used in previous research and the tentative nature of previous conclusions, a strong driver for the research collaboration was to generate a large sample size. In addition, we wished to generate sufficient participant numbers to assess the utility of our conceptual framework. Having made the decision to undertake a large-scale, quantitative study with only a limited qualitative element, a series of follow-on studies was designed using a variety of predominantly qualitative methodologies. These were intended to generate a more in-depth understanding of particular topics and to illuminate the detail of individual experience. The studies were developed in order to expand understanding of elements of the framework, including a qualitative study of those identifying themselves as positive adjusters (Study 4), the particular issues relating to ethnicity (Studies 5 and 6) and an examination of appearance concerns and aggression (Study 7). In response to the Advisory Committee (see The Role of the Advisory Panel in the Research Process), work was initiated to develop a measure of the role of appearance concerns in intimate relationships (Study 8), to study the appearance concerns of people with prosthetic limbs (Study 11) and to better understand the beliefs, decision-making processes and training needs of GPs (Study 10). In addition, the role of appearance concerns in the adjustment for those with rheumatoid arthritis was examined as a particular example of the potential interplay of functional and appearance concerns (Study 9).

Amongst others, Thompson and Kent (2001) and Rumsey and Harcourt (2005) have noted the pressing need for longitudinal research to explore the dynamic, fluctuating nature of adjustment in relation to disfigurement. Accordingly, it was also a priority for the collaboration to include such an element in the programme of research. Study 3 explores the issue of stability and change in adjustment over time.

For a diagrammatic representation of the studies included in the research programme, see Figure A2.

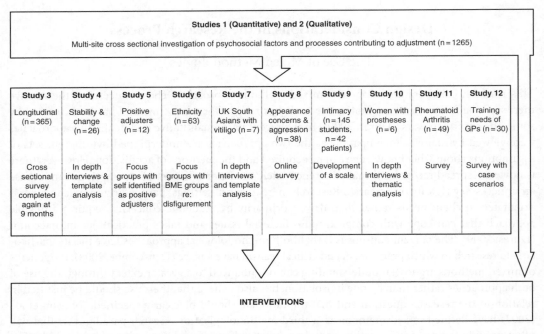

Figure A2   Studies included in the ARC research programme.

The Role of the Advisory Panel in the Research Process:

The Advisory Panel included three representatives with experiences of living with different types of disfigurement (Olivia Giles, Luke Wiseman and Pam Warren). Additional members included a general (family) practitioner (GP, Dr Terry Paterson) and the Chief Executive (Mr Brendan Eley) of The Healing Foundation (funders of the research). Two plastic surgeons showed initial interest in joining the Advisory Panel, however, despite repeated invitations to engage with the project in the first 12 months, they were unable to contribute. Accordingly, a third consultant plastic surgeon (Mr Nigel Mercer) who was a member of the Steering Committee for the Centre for Appearance Research (CAR) was kept abreast of developments within the project and offered comments as appropriate. At the first meeting of the panel, the project team presented their plans for Study 1, including the draft of the questionnaire pack and the letter, information and consent sheets to be given to potential participants. Panel members offered constructive comments on the letters and questionnaires, and, where feasible, appropriate changes were incorporated into the final versions. It was also suggested that the community sample be expanded to include more user groups, as the experience of panel members was that the possibility of participating in research was perceived as a welcome opportunity to increase understanding of the lived experience of people with disfiguring conditions. In the second round of meetings, the project lead met with panel members individually to summarize the results of the preliminary analyses from the cross-sectional study (Study 1) and to discuss plans for the follow-up studies and for the intervention strand of the project. At this point, two members suggested the inclusion of a study on the effects of appearance concerns on intimate relationships, and one was especially supportive of the idea that a study of people using prosthetic devices would be useful. The lack of knowledge and understanding about the impact of visible disfigurements amongst GPs was also highlighted. These ideas were all incorporated into follow-on studies within the programme (see Figure A2). Panel members were consulted on an individual basis in a third round of meetings in which the results, plans for outputs and dissemination and plans for further research were discussed and finalized.

In summary, the following actions were taken in response to advice from the Advisory Panel:

- Changes to recruitment letter to the community sample
- An enlarged base for the recruitment of the community sample to include more user groups
- The initiation of a study on the role of appearance and intimacy
- An exploration of the knowledge of GPs in relation to disfigurement
- Inclusion of a study on experiences of people with prosthetic devices
- Inclusion of prosthetists, psychiatrists and primary care workers in plans for dissemination.

Study 1: Psychological Factors and Processes Associated with Adjustment to Disfiguring Conditions

The largest part of the research programme comprised a cross-sectional multi-centre study. As discussed earlier, previous work (Carr et al., 2000; Carr et al., 2005; Fajervik-Morton, 2008; Rumsey et al., 2004; Thompson & Kent, 2001) had provided data on the prevalence and consequences of appearance concerns in people with a range of disfiguring conditions; however, many questions had also been raised about the psychological factors and processes underpinning the considerable variation in adjustment. These questions could only be answered through the medium of a large data set. In addition, a large sample size was needed to allow an investigation of condition-specific effects and a more detailed examination than hitherto of the impact of non-clinical and non-psychological variables (e.g. age, gender and social class) on adjustment.

The key research aims in this major study were, first, to establish the prevalence of adjustment and distress in participants recruited from the community and from outpatient settings and, second, to establish what psychosocial factors and processes are associated with positive adjustment and distress in people with visibly disfiguring conditions.

The large-scale nature of the study dictated a predominantly quantitative approach; however, mindful of the need to capture the large range of individual differences in experience and the potential richness of qualitative data, we also included an open-ended response box qualitative element in the data collection (see Study 2).

Methods

Sample and Recruitment
Visible differences result from a wide variety of congenital anomalies (e.g. a cleft of the lip; neurofibromatosis), illnesses (e.g. arthritis), chronic conditions (e.g. vitiligo, acne), injuries (e.g. burns) or surgical interventions (e.g. following surgery to remove malignant tumours). In order to sample as widely as possible, the project was organized around four geographical regions: Bristol (lead site),

London (site 2), Bradford/Sheffield (site 3) and Warwick (site 4), with researchers at each site working to promote participation by a broad spread of respondents at various stages of the treatment journey.

As the opportunities for recruitment through clinics and the community varied between hospitals and geographical regions, and as the organizational and logistical constraints affecting recruitment were different in every site, the regional principal investigators negotiated the practical details of sampling and recruitment on a local basis, within the framework agreed for the whole study (i.e. target numbers for each condition, inclusion and exclusion criteria and ethical guidelines for the research. For details, see the following).

Inclusion Criteria
Participants were men and women aged 18 years or over, with fluency in written and spoken English, who perceived themselves as having a visible difference. (The resources necessary to study children and adolescents are considerable, and data collection is complicated by the need for specialist interviewers and age appropriate assessments. Subsequent studies focusing specifically on adjustment in children and adolescents will be informed by this research programme).

Exclusion Criteria
Participants with identifiable psychosis or dementia were excluded. In this study, participants unable to read and write in English were excluded, as there were no measures available in non-English languages which were equivalent to those selected for the study. Adequate representation of members of ethnic minority communities was promoted by actively seeking those who were able to read and speak English, as the research collaboration recognized that an understanding of cultural differences is an important gap in the existing body of knowledge about adjustment to problems of appearance. Further efforts were made to address this in Studies 5 and 6 of the programme.

Sampling through Outpatient Clinics
As in previous studies, outpatient clinics were targeted as a cost-effective means of accessing patients seeking medical intervention. A wide range of clinics were approached as potential sites for recruitment and each site organized recruitment in local clinics, overseen by the regional principal investigator. Outpatient clinics taking part were as follows:

- Sheffield/Bradford: head and neck cancer, prosthetics, dermatology, ophthalmology and general plastics (including burns), cleft lip and palate clinics (trauma/ENT)
- London: general plastics, ocular plastics, ocular prosthetics and rheumatology clinics
- Bristol: laser, general plastics, skin cancer and ophthalmology clinics.

In total, 650 participants were recruited via outpatient clinics, from London, Sheffield/Bradford and Bristol sites.

Sampling through Non-Medical Sources (the 'Community' Sample)
Despite the associated challenges, it was considered a priority in this research programme to learn more about the broader constituency of people with visible differences and, in view of the commitment of the collaboration to focus on positive adjustment, to also sample those who were not actively

seeking treatment or intervention at the time of participation. This type of recruitment is more challenging, and several strategies were considered by the consortium, including the distribution of study materials on a house-to-house basis and recruitment via relevant self-help groups, through advertisements on the internet and through local media. In the end, participants were recruited via city centre and rural GP practices in the South West (via the Bristol site) and through practices in the Midlands (via the Warwick site). As recruitment (particularly in the Midlands) was slow to pick up, additional recruitment was achieved via advertisements on the websites of self-help groups and through press releases in local press.

In total, 615 participants were recruited via the community, from the Warwick and Bristol sites. Two large GP surgeries (one rural and one urban) were involved from the Bristol region and 10 surgeries across the Midlands.

Sample Size
Estimates of the number of people affected by various forms of visible difference vary, as do methods of categorizing them on the basis of the type of disfigurement (e.g. people with a specific condition such as vitiligo or those with the broader categorization of 'skin conditions'). As a result, notions about the most appropriate sample size needed to achieve a representative population of those affected and of the numbers needed to demonstrate similarities and differences between types of disfigurement are fluid. As there is now a broad consensus in the literature that condition-specific effects play a much more minor role in adjustment and distress than psychological and socio-cultural factors, the benefits (compared to the costs) of exhaustive sampling by types and subtypes of condition are questionable. It was therefore agreed that a spread of conditions would be sampled, with differing outpatient clinics targeted by each site.

Sample size calculations relied on the previous experience of the group and on the assumption that within the largest study (Study 1), for the clinic sample, a minimum of 12 'conditions' would be sampled. An a priori power analysis for multiple regression (assuming standard levels of significance and a power of 0.95) indicated that in the presence of small effects (e.g. $R^2 = -0.04$) a minimum sample size of 851 cases would be needed to assess the significance of up to 25 variables in a global hypothesis test. This allowed a range of superficially different types of disfigurement to be examined and meaningful comparisons of subgroups to be made, together with a purposive sampling of subgroups of participants for the qualitative and longitudinal studies. A process of quota sampling for rarer conditions was adopted in order to facilitate statistical analysis, with a minimum target of 30.

Materials

Written Information
A standardized pack of written information and questionnaires was distributed to all participants. This included an information sheet clearly stating principles relating to identity protection, the right to withdraw from studies at any time and procedures for the storage and destruction of records. There were minor differences in this information between sites (i.e. university contact information, names of consultants collaborating, etc). A consent form and a form to consent to be contacted about further studies were also included.

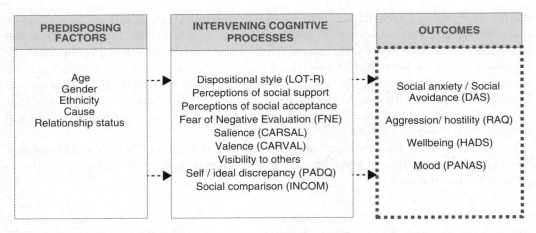

PREDISPOSING FACTORS	INTERVENING COGNITIVE PROCESSES	OUTCOMES
Age Gender Ethnicity Cause Relationship status	Dispositional style (LOT-R) Perceptions of social support Perceptions of social acceptance Fear of Negative Evaluation (FNE) Salience (CARSAL) Valence (CARVAL) Visibility to others Self / ideal discrepancy (PADQ) Social comparison (INCOM)	Social anxiety / Social Avoidance (DAS) Aggression/ hostility (RAQ) Wellbeing (HADS) Mood (PANAS)

Figure A3   Operationalizing the framework – choosing appropriate measures.

Measures

In order to adapt the conceptual framework (Figure A1) adopted by the research team for data collection and analysis purposes, it was necessary to consider how best to operationalize the variables.

The decisions relating to the choice of measure and the designation of variables as 'process' or 'outcome' generated considerable debate within the collaboration and among the Advisory Panel. Guiding principles for the final choice of measures included a primary focus on variables which were considered modifiable through intervention and on questionnaires which had face validity for participants and which were straightforward to complete. 'Generic' questionnaires (e.g. the HADS) enabling comparisons with previous research and with reports of adjustment to a range of other conditions were also included. The inclusion of measures which offered the possibility of capturing profiles indicative of positive adjustment was also a priority. This was particularly challenging as many of the questionnaires used in previous research have an exclusively negative focus in the wording of questions. In the case of variables for which suitable measures did not exist (e.g. perceived levels of social acceptance of a disfiguring aspect of appearance), questions derived from findings from the previous literature and on the clinical experience of the group were constructed to capture participants' responses. Other considerations included the overall number of questionnaires that should be included in the participant packs and the burden on participants. A summary of the chosen measures is given in Figure A3.

Predisposing Factors

Demographics
Participants were asked to indicate their postcode, age, gender, family status/living arrangements, nationality and ethnicity.

Participants were also presented with two open-ended questions at the close of the questionnaire. The first asked for feedback about the questionnaire pack and the second asked if the respondent had any general comments about the way their appearance does or does not affect their lives and whether impacts were positive or negative (see Study 2).

Cause
Participants were asked to select a cause of the main difference in appearance from a list of 11 options (including 'other' with room to specify).

Treatment Information
Participants were asked to state whether they had received treatment to change their appearance and, if so, the earliest and latest dates these treatments were received. They were also asked to state if they were awaiting any treatments.

Area of Appearance Concern
Participants indicated their area of concern by ticking on a checklist of the parts of their body about which they were most sensitive. These were later classified into the broad headings of visible to others/difficult to disguise (face, hands, neck, head) and non-visible (easier to disguise).

Intervening Cognitive Processes

Dispositional Style
Optimism
To assess levels of optimism, a shortened four-item version of the Life Orientation Test-Revised (*LOT-R*; Scheier et al. 1994) was utilized. Responses took the form of a five-point Likert scale, ranging from 1 (strongly agree) to 4 (strongly disagree). Total scale scores ranged from 4 to 20, with higher scores indicating a more optimistic outlook. The scale was designed to be viewed as measuring a continuum, with no 'cut-offs' for optimism or pessimism. Scheier et al. (1994) have demonstrated adequate internal consistency (alpha = 0.78) and test–retest reliability that indicates stability over time ($r = 0.68$ at 4 months, $r = 0.60$ at 12 months, $r = 0.56$ at 24 months, $r = 0.79$ at 28 months).

Socio-Cognitive Factors

Social Support
The scale utilized is a shortened four-item version of the Short-Form Social Support Questionnaire (Sarason et al. 1983). The responses relating to the quantity of support were considered primers and were not included in the analysis. Quality ratings ranged from 1 (very satisfied) to 6 (very dissatisfied), and scores ranged from 4 to 24, with higher scores representing greater satisfaction with their social network. The authors have reported good psychometric properties for the scale.

Perceptions of Social Acceptance
To assess feelings of social acceptance, two items with a seven-point Likert scale ranging from 1 (not at all) to 7 (completely) assessed the extent to which the respondent felt accepted by their social group and society in general. Total scores ranged from 2 to 14, with higher scores indicating higher levels of acceptance.

Fear of Negative Evaluation

The Brief Fear of Negative Evaluation (FNE) scale (Leary, 1983) examines whether concern about other people's opinions regarding themselves is a characteristic of the individual. Twelve items were presented and participants asked to score each statement from 1 (not at all characteristic of me) to 5 (extremely characteristic of me). Scores ranged from 12 to 60, with high scores indicating a greater fear of negative evaluation. The authors have cited adequate psychometric properties, with high levels of internal consistency (alpha = 0.90), a 4-week test–retest reliability with a student population yielding a 0.75 reliability coefficient and acceptable levels of construct validity.

Appearance-Related Processing

Valence of Appearance

The CARVAL (Moss & Rosser, 2012b) is a six-item valence questionnaire that measures how positively or negatively a participant evaluates their own appearance. Responses ranged from 1 (strongly disagree) to 7 (strongly agree), with higher total scores indicating a more positive self-evaluation of their own appearance. Potential scale scores ranged from 6 to 36. The scale demonstrates good internal consistency (alpha = 0.89) and very good test–retest reliability with a student population at 3 months ($r = 0.95$).

Salience of Appearance

The CARSAL (Moss & Rosser, 2012b) measures the extent to which appearance is part of a person's working self-concept or how important it is to a person (salience). Response ranged from 1 (strongly disagree) to 7 (strongly agree), with higher total scores indicating appearance forming a greater part of the self-concept. Potential scale scores ranged from 6 to 36. The scale demonstrates good internal consistency (alpha = 0.86) and good test–retest reliability with a student population at 3 months ($r = 0.89$).

Visibility to Others

By rating on a seven-point Likert scale ranging from 1 (extremely easy) to 7 (impossible), participants were asked how difficult they felt it was to hide or disguise the aspects of their appearance about which they were most concerned.

Physical Appearance Discrepancy

The PADQ (Altabe, 1996; Altabe & Thompson, 1996) distinguishes the discrepancy between how a person perceives they look and how they or their significant others would ideally like them to look ('ideal' discrepancy) or how they ought or should look in relation to duty, responsibility or obligation ('should' discrepancy). A large 'ideal' discrepancy is associated with feelings of disappointment, dissatisfaction, shame and embarrassment due to unfulfilled desires and a belief they have lost esteem in the opinion of others. A high 'should' discrepancy is associated with fear, feeling threatened, resentment and guilt due to the belief that they have transgressed the moral standard of either themselves or the significant others. The two subscales of 'ideal' and 'should' discrepancy consist of four items each, with responses ranging from not at all different to extremely different yielding a total score for each subscale ranging from 4 to 28, with higher scores indicating greater discrepancy.

Social Comparison

The social comparison scale is a brief version of the Gibbons and Buunk (1999) Iowa-Netherlands Comparison Orientation Measure (INCOM). The scale measures frequency of social comparisons. Participants were asked to complete the scale in reference to their appearance and responses ranged from 1 (strongly disagree) to 5 (strongly agree), with higher total scores indicating a higher frequency of engagement in social comparison. Potential scale scores ranged from 11 to 55. The scale demonstrated good internal consistency (alpha = 0.83) and concurrent validity ($r = 0.88$). The authors also cited adequate test–retest reliability for up to 4 weeks and 1 year as yielding correlation coefficients of 0.71 and 0.60, respectively.

Outcomes

Social Anxiety and Social Avoidance

Derriford Appearance Scale Short Form (DAS24; Moss et al., 2004). The DAS24 is a 24-item version of the DAS59 (Carr et al., 2000) and is a measure of social anxiety and social avoidance in relation to appearance. It has been widely used in research related to disfigurement in the recent past. Norms derived from UK populations exist. Total scores range from 11 to 96, with lower scores representing low levels of social anxiety and social avoidance. It has adequate internal consistency (alpha = 0.92), test–retest reliability ($r = 0.82$), concurrent validity with the DAS59 ($r = 0.88$) and convergent validity with measures of anxiety, depression, social avoidance, social distress, fear of negative evaluation, negative affect and shame ($r < 0.45$).

Positive and Negative Affect

The Positive and Negative Affect Schedule (PANAS; Watson et al., 1988) assesses how respondents rate how they have felt over the past week in relation to a number of positive and negative emotions. Two subscales of negative affect (NA) and positive affect (PA) are a summed score of 10 questions. Scores for each subscale range from 10 to 50, with higher scores indicating greater identification with those feelings. The authors report convergent validity with several measures of affective disorders (Beck et al., 1961; Derogatis et al., 1974; Spielberger et al., 1970). The measure demonstrates adequate internal consistency (alpha = 0.80 for PA; 0.85 for NA).

Anxiety and Depression

The Hospital Anxiety and Depression Scale (HADS; Zigmond & Snaith, 1983) is a valid and reliable 14-item self-screening questionnaire for depression and anxiety in patients with physical health problems. For measures of mood, the scale scores range from 0 to 21, with higher scores indicating greater levels of anxious or depressed mood. A score of 0–7 for either subscale is regarded as being in the 'normal' range, a score of 8–10 is suggestive of the presence of moderate levels of anxiety or depression and a score of >11 indicates 'caseness', a high likelihood that a person would be diagnosed to be suffering from clinical anxiety or clinical depression.

Literature reviews of the HADS (e.g. Bjelland et al., 2002) have found the HADS to show adequate internal consistency over a range of studies, including those translated into languages other than English and good concurrent validity when compared to a range of other anxiety and depression scales ($r = 0.60$–0.80). The HADS has also been used to good effect in previous studies with patients with facial disfigurements (Martin & Newell, 2004).

Anger/hostility

The Refined Aggression Questionnaire (RAQ) (Bryant & Smith, 2001) is a brief version of Buss and Perry's (1992) Aggression Questionnaire and has been found to have similar psychometric properties (Bryant & Smith, 2001). This aggression scale uses 12 items to assess whether aggressive behaviour is characteristic of the respondent, with responses ranging from strongly disagree to strongly agree. Divided into four factors, physical aggression, hostility, verbal aggression and anger, each factor has an individual score with lower scores representing lower levels of that particular type of aggression. The scale score ranged from 3 to 15 after appropriate item score reversals.

Procedure

Research Governance

Ethical approval for the study was given by NRES.

As the research programme developed, the lead site (UWE) was also required to apply for substantial and minor amendments to NRES to undertake the follow-on studies (six amendments in total). All additions and minor changes to the original protocol (e.g. the reduction of the longitudinal data point for the cross-sectional questionnaire to 9 months from 12 months) were agreed by NRES and local university ethics committees.

Protocols Relating to Recruitment

Outpatient Clinics

Patients attending the participating outpatient clinics were sent invitations to take part along with an information sheet 2 weeks prior to their appointment. The researcher approached potential participants on the day of their appointment explaining the nature of the study and answering any potential questions. Once informed consent was obtained, participants were given a questionnaire booklet to complete either in clinic or to be taken away and sent back via freepost envelope.

Community Recruitment

In the South West (coordinated by the Bristol site), READ codes (used by some GPs to classify patients by condition) were used to identify possible participants with conditions that were potentially disfiguring. In the Midlands, participants were recruited through face-to-face approaches in practice waiting rooms and via leaflets and posters displayed in surgeries and community centres. Some participants also responded to adverts placed in the press, online or in local areas (such as community notice boards).

In the South West, all patients identified via READ codes were sent the standardized pack including invitation letter, information sheet, consent form, further studies form and freepost envelope. Participants were asked in the letter to consider taking part, and if they were willing, to complete all forms and measures and to return these in the freepost envelope.

In the Midlands (coordinated by the Warwick site), researchers were present in GP surgeries and all attendees during a given time period were given an information sheet and asked to consider taking part. If they were interested and eligible, the researcher explained the nature of the study and answered any questions. Once informed consent was obtained, participants were given a question-naire booklet to complete either in the surgery or to be taken away and sent back via freepost envelope.

Those participants who volunteered as a result of advertising were sent packs by post and were given the opportunity to speak to a researcher via email or telephone. Those recruited from adverts or websites and those who had no named health professional contact received the same pack as all other participants, with the addition of a section on the consent form to provide us with a GP con-tact. This contact was informed of these participants' engagement in the project.

In all cases, participants took part on a voluntary basis and were not remunerated for their par-ticipation. Once received, data were stored securely (see following text), receipts were logged and thank you letters were sent to each participant.

Results

Participants

A total of 1265 participants took part in the study, 615 of whom were recruited from the community and 650 from outpatient clinics.

In the whole sample, 867 were female (68.5%) and 354 were male (28.0%). In the community sample, 474 were female (77.2%) and 120 were male (19.5%). Similarly, 393 of those in the clinic sample were female (60.4%) and 234 were male (35.9%).

The mean age of the whole sample was 47.3 years (range 18–91, SD 16.7 years), with the mean age in the community sample being 44.9 years (range 18–91; SD 16.2 years), which was marginally lower than the clinic mean age of 49.7 years (range 18–89; SD 16.9 years).

In the whole sample, 783 (61.9%) people reported being married or living with a partner, 183 (14.6%) living with friends or relatives and 287 (22.9%) living alone.

In the whole sample, 81% were white, with the other 12% either Pakistani, Indian, Black Caribbean, Black African or other. The percentages are similar in both the clinic and community sample.

Sample means and standard deviations for the outcome measures are presented according to the method of recruitment (Table A1) and geographical area of recruitment (Table A2), and the distribu-tions for social anxiety (DAS24), anxiety (HADS) and depression (HADS) by geographical area of recruitment are illustrated in Figures A4a–c.

Table A1 Sample means and standard deviations for outcome measures according to the method of recruitment.

	Clinic M(SD)	Community M(SD)
Social anxiety	41.26(16.38)	43.44(15.97)
Anxiety	7.96(4.74)	8.46(4.50)
Depression	5.00(3.76)	5.21(3.77)
Aggression	25.15(9.35)	25.59(9.37)
Negative affect	31.88(8.99)	31.27(8.70)
Positive affect	19.71(8.61)	20.55(8.60)

Table A2 Sample means and standard deviations for outcome measures according to the geographical area of recruitment.

	N	DAS M(SD)	Anxiety M(SD)	Depression M(SD)	Aggression M(SD)	Positive affect M(SD)	Negative affect M(SD)
London (UCL)	228	44.25(17.09)	8.41(4.63)	5.19(3.86)	25.36(8.96)	31.76(8.81)	20.99(8.64)
Warwick	357	43.93(16.35)	8.93(4.61)	5.64(3.83)	26.38(9.43)	30.53(8.76)	21.52(9.01)
Bristol	396	41.27(15.71)	7.91(4.48)	4.58(3.53)	24.07(9.06)	32.29(8.72)	19.08(8.09)
Sheffield/ Bradford	280	40.16(15.68)	7.52(4.75)	5.08(3.86)	25.89(9.85)	31.79(9.08)	19.05(8.46)

There were no statistically significant main effects for method of recruitment or geographical location on any of the outcome measures ($p > 0.001$). As a consequence, the decision was taken to consider the data set to be a single group in subsequent analyses. Data are presented for each outcome variable separately.

Internal Consistency

The values for Cronbach's alpha for all outcome variables across the sample and subsets of the sample according to gender and recruitment are all high, demonstrating good internal consistency on all measures ranging from 0.778 to 0.935.

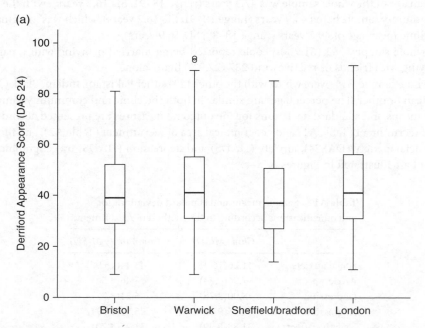

Figure A4 Comparative box-and-whisker plots for (a) DAS24, (b) HAD anxiety and (c) HAD depression by geographical location.

(b)

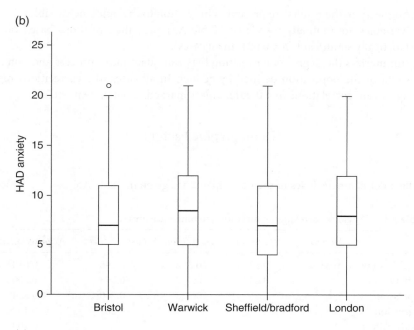

(c)

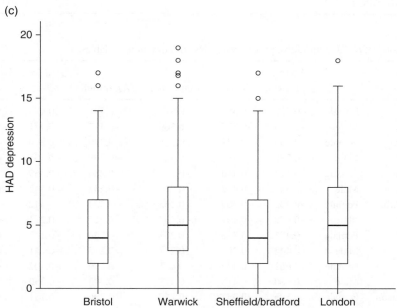

Figure A4 (*Continued*)

The Relationships between Variables

In the following section, the results are presented in relation to the outcome variables.

Outcome variables are mutually correlated (Table A3) and all correlations based on the entire sample are statistically significant ($p < 0.001$, in all cases).

Table A4 summarizes the degree of correlation between quantitative process and outcome variables for all strata of the population defined by gender. In all cases, the correlations reported are statistically significant correlations ($p < 0.001$), unless marked † to denote $p > 0.05$.

Demographic Factors

Gender
The age and gender characteristics of the participants are given in Table A5.

Table A3   Pearson's correlation matrix for outcome measures.

	Anxiety	Depression	Aggression	Positive affect	Negative affect
Social anxiety	0.637	0.571	0.382	−0.398	0.610
Anxiety		0.637	0.437	−0.394	0.700
Depression			0.380	−0.560	0.554
Aggression				−0.267	0.459
Positive affect					−0.408

Table A4   Correlation of quantitative process variables with outcome variables.

		Social anxiety	Anxiety	Depression	Aggression	Positive affect	Negative affect	N
Optimism	Female	−0.537	−0.588	−0.578	−0.497	0.473	−0.531	832
	Male	−0.543	−0.597	−0.569	−0.417	0.471	−0.504	331
Fear of negative evaluation	Female	0.535	0.521	0.338	0.380	−0.340	0.541	838
	Male	0.587	0.581	0.448	0.309	−0.351	0.611	346
Social acceptance	Female	−0.613	−0.460	−0.510	−0.280	0.359	−0.461	859
	Male	−0.543	−0.452	−0.512	−0.232	0.342	−0.453	350
Satisfaction with social support	Female	−0.432	−0.369	−0.455	−0.324	0.342	−0.389	853
	Male	−0.472	−0.407	−0.484	−0.212	0.271	−0.361	349
Salience	Female	0.473	0.386	0.207	0.264	−0.142	0.336	857
	Male	0.444	0.287	0.227	0.217	−0.141	0.275	333
Valence	Female	0.661	0.422	0.461	0.290	−0.402	0.408	861
	Male	0.580	0.416	0.472	0.205	−0.350	0.426	335
Social comparison	Female	0.305	0.331	0.160	0.286	0.151	0.347	859
	Male	0.268	0.255	0.074[a]	0.184	0.007[a]	0.236	350
Appearance discrepancy	Female	0.584	0.334	0.391	0.203	−0.265	0.338	856
	Male	0.488	0.336	0.373	0.122	−0.241	0.315	352

[a] $p > 0.05$.

Table A5 Age and gender frequencies for whole sample[a].

Age group	Male	Female	Total N (%)
18–25	35	97	137(11)
26–35	42	169	216(18)
36–45	60	170	235(19)
46–55	61	158	226(18)
56–65	79	138	225(18)
> 65	71	125	199(16)
Total N(%)	354(28)	867(68.5)	1221

[a]44 cases (3.5%). Missing data

Mean values and standard deviations for each outcome variable by gender are given in Table A6.

Graphical displays of the distribution of social anxiety (DAS24), anxiety (HADS), depression (HADS) and aggression (RAQ) by gender are given in Figure A5.

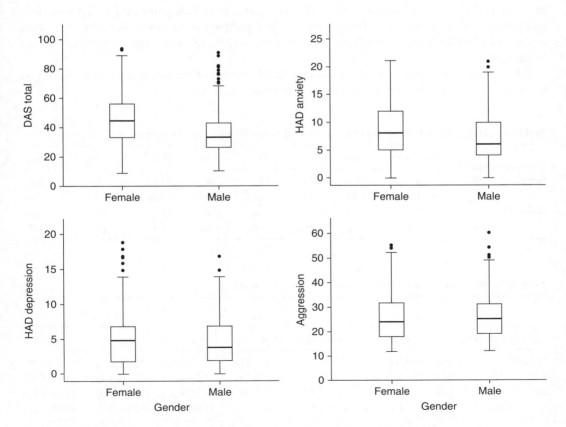

Figure A5 Distributions of social anxiety, anxiety, depression and aggression by gender.

Table A6   Mean values for outcome variables by gender.

Variable	Female	Male	N
Social anxiety	44.95(16.18)	35.87(14.56)	
Anxiety	8.67(4.64)	6.97(4.37)	
Depression	5.16(3.78)	4.97(3.75)	
Aggression	25.07(9.42)	26.07(9.06)	
Positive affect	31.02(8.92)	33.10(8.55)	
Negative affect	20.70(8.82)	18.35(7.72)	

ANOVAs reveal that the scores for women are significantly higher (indicating more distress) on the DAS24, $F(1, 1213) = 71.51$, $MSE = 247.64$, $p < 0.001$, $\eta_p^2 = 0.056$, and higher on anxiety, $F(1, 1212) = 26.44$, $MSE = 20.79$, $p < 0.001$, $\eta_p^2 = 0.021$, and negative affect, $F(1, 1171) = 13.52$, $MSE = 72.53$, $p = 0.165$, $\eta_p^2 = 0.011$. Conversely, males scored higher than females on positive affect, $F(1, 1172) = 10.63$, $MSE = 77.80$, $p = 0.001$, $\eta_p^2 = 0.009$. However, the effect sizes for all significant differences are judged to be small, ranging from 0.011 to 0.056).

In relation to the number of areas reported as sensitive, the application of the chi-square test of association indicates that there are statistically significant differences in the profiles between male and female ($\chi^2 = 51.21$, $df = 6$, $p < 0.001$), with females reporting considerably more areas of concern and with a statistically significant linear component ($\chi^2 = 33.99$, $df = 1$, $p < 0.001$). See Table A7 for frequencies.

Table A8 illustrates the mean values and standard deviations of the outcome variables according to whether or not the disfigurement was normally visible to others.

Table A7   Frequency of the number of areas reported as sensitive according to gender.

		None marked	One	Two	Three	Four	Five	Six or more	Total
Female	N	95	201	153	134	90	73	121	867
	%	11.0	23.2	17.6	15.5	10.4	8.4	14.0	100
Male	N	77	113	58	33	24	11	38	354
	%	21.8	31.9	16.4	9.3	6.8	3.1	10.7	100

Table A8   Mean values for outcome measures by visibility to others.

	Visible/ non-visible	N	DAS24	Anxiety	Depression	Aggression	Positive affect	Negative affect
Female	Yes	404	46.67(15.45)	9.26(4.70)	5.55(3.82)	26.03(9.42)	30.52(8.82)	21.73(9.05)
	No	460	43.44(16.67)	8.15(4.52)	4.81(3.73)	24.21(9.35)	31.46(8.99)	19.80(8.52)
Male	Yes	165	38.32(15.03)	7.62(4.35)	5.43(3.93)	26.52(9.32)	31.92(9.06)	19.66(8.02)
	No	188	33.72(13.82)	6.40(4.33)	4.56(3.54)	25.68(8.82)	34.16(7.93)	17.18(7.26)

*44 = gender not stated, 4 = missing data

Table A9   Correlation of outcome variables with age.

	Social anxiety	Anxiety	Depression	Aggression	Positive affect	Negative affect	N
Female	−0.325	−0.209	−0.068	−0.321	0.121	−0.272	865
Male	−0.393	−0.210	−0.124	−0.277	0.000	−0.292	351

Two-way ANOVAs show that females report significantly poorer mean values than males on social anxiety (DAS24), anxiety, positive affect and negative affect ($p < 0.001$, in all cases) and those with a visible concern report significantly poorer mean values on social anxiety, anxiety, depression, positive affect and negative affect ($p < 0.001$, all cases) and on aggression ($p = 0.024$)

Age
Table A9 summarizes the extent of the correlation between age and each outcome measure according to gender. In all cases, the correlations reported are statistically significant correlations ($p < 0.001$).

Significant negative correlations were found between age and social anxiety, (see Figure A7) anxiety, depression, aggression and negative affect for all sample subgroups.

Visibility and Areas of Concern

Area of Concern
Participants were asked to indicate all areas of the body about which they had concern. Some participants reported only one area and others recorded multiple areas of concern. The frequency with which participants 'checked' each area and percentages of participants 'checking' each area are presented in Table A10. Sixty-five per cent had concerns about an area normally visible to others (including forehead, ears, eyes, nose, mouth, hands or cheeks). Some participants indicated more than one area of the body and accordingly the frequency does not equal the overall sample size.

Visibility of Main Area of Concern
Using the one area participants indicated as being their main concern only, 590 of the participants were classed for subsequent analyses as having an area of concern normally visible to others and the remaining 671 classed as having concerns less often visible to others. The means and standard deviations for scores on the outcome measures are presented for those with 'visible' and 'non-visible' areas of concern in Table A11.

Mean levels of social anxiety and social avoidance are significantly higher on average amongst those with a visible concern ($F(1, 1209) = 20.598, p < 0.001$), but the effect is small (partial beta^2 = 0.017).

The mean levels for anxiety is significantly higher amongst those with a visible concern than those without ($p < 0.001$), as is mean depression ($p < 0.001$), mean aggression ($p = 0.014$) and mean negative affect ($p < 0.001$). Mean positive affect is significantly lower amongst those with a visible concern ($p = 0.013$) (Table A11).

Numbers of Area of Concern
Table A12 reports the percentage of participants reporting one or multiple areas of concern, by outcome variable.

Table A10 Frequency and percentage of participants reporting area of concern.

Visible area	N	%	Non-visible area	N	%
Eyes	193	15.3	Abdomen	341	27.0
Nose	172	13.6	Thighs	281	22.2
Cheeks	138	10.9	Breasts	247	19.5
Mouth	133	10.5	Lower legs	236	18.7
Hands	156	12.3	Upper arms	213	16.8
Forehead	105	8.3	Buttocks	176	13.9
Ears	81	6.4	Feet	175	13.8
			Neck	143	11.3
			Knees	139	11.0
			Hips	125	9.9
			Scalp	115	9.1
			Back	114	9.0
			Forearms	112	8.9
			Chest	110	8.7
			Shoulder	72	5.7
			Genitalia	60	4.7

Table A11 Means and standard deviations for visible and non-visible areas on outcome measures.

Visible	N	Social anxiety	Anxiety	Depression	Aggression	Positive affect	Negative affect
Yes	590	44.24(15.66)	8.79(4.66)	5.48(3.83)	26.20(9.42)	30.91(8.91)	21.14(8.78)
No	671	40.63(16.51)	7.68(4.55)	4.76(3.68)	24.62(9.25)	32.17(8.75)	19.22(8.36)

Table A12 Mean and standard deviations for the number of areas of concern by outcome variable.

	Social anxiety	Anxiety	Depression	Aggression	Positive affect	Negative affect
None	32.71 (14.44)	6.42 (4.58)	4.09 (3.60)	23.08 (8.84)	33.64 (8.58)	16.88 (7.10)
One	37.24 (13.94)	7.24 (4.60)	4.29 (3.38)	23.38 (8.65)	32.84 (8.00)	18.59 (7.96)
Two	39.71 (14.32)	7.80 (4.36)	4.89 (3.42)	25.32 (9.31)	31.53 (9.39)	19.66 (8.13)
Three	43.64 (14.19)	8.71 (4.24)	5.42 (3.83)	26.25 (9.22)	31.74 (8.53)	20.10 (8.49)
Four	47.62 (15.48)	8.84 (4.30)	5.21 (3.51)	26.93 (9.99)	31.34 (9.21)	20.12 (8.16)
Five	51.95 (14.77)	9.76 (4.06)	6.44 (4.24)	26.86 (9.57)	29.75 (9.55)	23.48 (8.95)
Six or more	56.21 (14.95)	10.82 (4.55)	7.01 (4.08)	28.99 (9.47)	27.95 (8.52)	25.43 (9.38)
Total	42.32 (16.21)	8.20 (4.63)	5.10 (3.77)	25.36 (9.36)	31.58 (8.85)	20.12 (8.61)

For all measures, a one-way ANOVA for trends shows that there is a statistically significant trend with increasing levels of poor adjustment occurring on average with increasing number of sensitive areas endorsed. Mean scores for social anxiety and avoidance are plotted by the number of areas of concern reported, as shown in Figure A6.

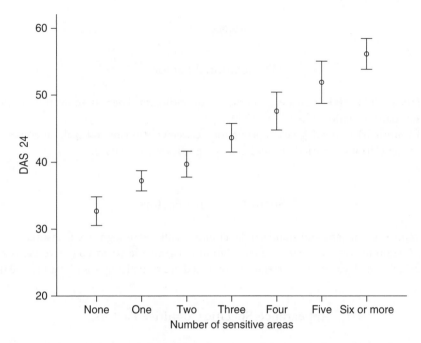

Figure A6 95% confidence interval for mean social anxiety according to the number of areas of concern reported.

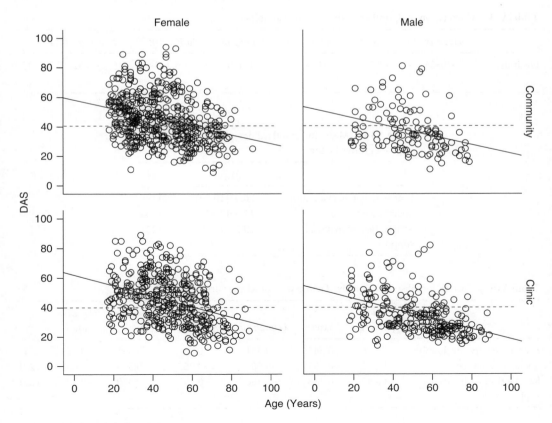

Figure A7 Social anxiety against age.

Dispositional Factors

Higher scores on the LOT-R indicate greater levels of optimism. There is an overall sample mean of 13.69 and standard deviation of 3.37 ($n = 1250$).

Table A13 summarizes the degree of correlation between optimism and each outcome variable. In all cases, the correlations reported are statistically significant ($p < 0.001$).

Socio-Cognitive Factors

Table A14 reports the means and standard deviations on all socio-cognitive measures.

Table A15 summarizes the degree of correlation between the socio-cognitive factors and each outcome variable. In all cases, the correlations reported are statistically significant ($p < 0.001$).

Appearance-Specific Cognitive Factors

Table A16 reports means and standard deviations for all appearance-related cognitive measures.

Table A13 Correlation of optimism with outcome variables.

	Social anxiety	Anxiety	Depression	Aggression	Positive affect	Negative affect	N
Optimism	−0.535	−0.592	−0.568	−0.459	0.475	−0.529	1205

Table A14 Mean and standard deviations for all socio-cognitive factors.

	M(SD)	N
Fear of negative evaluation	36.63(10.59)	1199
Social acceptance	11.35(2.83)	1254
Satisfaction with social support	19.75(4.61)	1251

Table A15 Correlation of socio-cognitive factors with outcome variables.

	Social anxiety	Anxiety	Depression	Aggression	Positive affect	Negative affect	N
Fear of negative evaluation	0.576	0.545	0.351	0.337	−0.351	0.563	1241
Social acceptance	−0.585	−0.453	−0.500	−0.257	0.353	−0.461	1251
Satisfaction with social support	−0.442	−0.386	−0.460	−0.291	0.330	−0.390	1251

Table A16 Mean and standard deviations for all appearance cognitions.

	M(SD)	N
Salience	31.44(8.08)	1252
Valance	21.45(8.06)	1261
Social comparison	35.73(7.27)	1255
Appearance discrepancy	29.96(11.41)	1254

Table A17 Correlation of the appearance cognitions and the outcome variables.

	Social anxiety	Anxiety	Depression	Aggression	Positive affect	Negative affect	N
Salience	0.495	0.370	0.197	0.233	−0.158	0.331	1251
Valence	0.648	0.428	0.448	0.245	−0.394	0.422	1258
Social comparison	0.322	0.322	0.130	0.249	0.122	0.330	1253
Appearance discrepancy	0.580	0.349	0.372	0.166	−0.268	0.351	1251

Table A18 Mean and standard deviations for each outcome variable according to level of disguisability.

	Social anxiety	Anxiety	Depression	Aggression	Positive affect	Negative affect	N
Extremely easy	30.58(12.38)	5.78(4.40)	3.59(3.09)	23.57(8.87)	34.61(9.14)	17.06(7.44)	83
Very easy	32.18(11.79)	6.32(4.23)	3.84(2.99)	22.99(8.84)	34.22(7.21)	16.82(6.09)	77
Quite easy	36.74(12.22)	7.30(4.23)	4.13(3.22)	23.35(8.22)	32.40(7.68)	18.05(7.40)	219
Moderate	41.68(13.59)	8.54(4.15)	4.84(3.35)	25.83(9.44)	30.97(8.61)	20.18(8.11)	247
Quite difficult	48.32(15.57)	9.10(4.59)	5.78(3.81)	26.90(9.41)	30.23(9.06)	22.14(9.17)	230
Very difficult	52.21(16.49)	9.67(4.73)	6.43(4.06)	26.83(9.98)	30.13(9.68)	22.78(9.66)	171
Impossible	47.93(16.92)	9.07(5.03)	6.36(4.35)	27.05(9.86)	30.68(9.42)	21.72(9.47)	152

Table A17 summarizes the degree of correlation between the appearance cognitions and the outcome variables. In all cases, the correlation reported are statistically significant ($p < 0.001$, in all cases).

Subjective perceptions of disguisability and visibility when clothed have been treated as categorical variables as they are single-item measures. As expected, the degree of disguisability differs on average between those that have a focus for concern that is normally visible to others and those who do not ($\chi^2 = 103.64$, $df = 6$, $p < .001$) with greater difficulty amongst those with a visible concern ($\chi^2 = 95.480$, $df = 1$, $p < 0.001$).

Table A18 summarizes means and standard deviations of the outcome variables according to the levels of disguisability. A one-way ANOVA for trend indicates that there are statistically significant trends with poorer adjustment being associated with an increasing difficulty to disguise ($p < 0.001$, in all cases).

This is illustrated for scores for levels of social anxiety and avoidance (DAS24) in Figure A8.

Mean levels of each outcome according to reported level of visibility to others when clothed are given in Table A19. Analysis, using an analysis of variance for a one-way, between-subjects design, indicates that there are statistically significant differences on all outcome measures for reported levels of visible concern ($p < 0.01$, in all cases).

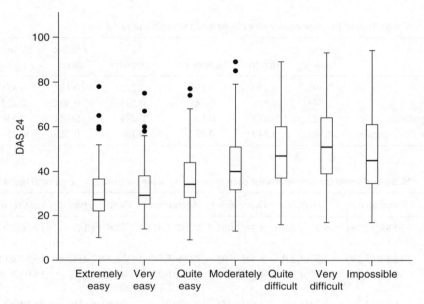

Figure A8   Social anxiety and ratings of disguisability.

Table A19   Mean outcome variables according to reported level of visibility when clothed.

	Social anxiety	Anxiety	Depression	Aggression	Positive affect	Negative affect	N
1 Not at all visible to others	36.81(14.24)	7.52(4.71)	4.36(3.58)	24.84(9.25)	33.58(8.03)	18.56(8.01)	270
2	38.48(13.11)	7.22(3.95)	4.35(3.48)	24.02(9.13)	32.55(9.13)	18.93(7.26)	122
3	43.22(16.40)	8.28(4.60)	4.93(3.75)	24.41(8.60)	31.46(8.60)	19.45(8.49)	69
4 Moderately	44.11(16.64)	8.71(4.30)	5.22(3.53)	25.28(9.39)	30.64(8.33)	19.64(8.14)	196
5	48.61(14.83)	9.23(4.44)	6.01(3.74)	28.62(9.76)	30.10(9.26)	22.13(9.12)	97
6	45.90(16.41)	8.59(4.32)	5.82(3.66)	25.96(9.00)	29.69(8.40)	21.11(8.59)	109
Very visible	45.54(16.50)	8.62(4.94)	5.65(4.03)	25.67(9.51)	31.27(9.42)	21.57(9.31)	353

Regressions by Outcome Variable

Hierarchical stepwise multiple regression was used to assess the ability of the measured demographic, visibility, dispositional, socio-cognitive and appearance-related socio-cognitive factors to predict levels of social anxiety (DAS24), psychological well-being (PANAS and HADS) and aggression (RAQ). In the following, each outcome variable is modelled using hierarchical linear regression. The predictors in block 1 are the biographic and demographic variables of age, gender, recruitment method and living arrangements. Objective visibility forms block 2. The variable optimism forms block 3. The socio-cognitive factors, fear of negative evaluation, social acceptance and satisfaction with social support, form block 4. The appearance cognitions of salience, valence, social comparison, appearance discrepancy and subjective visibility (disguisability and visibility when clothed) form block 5. All variables are included in the regression as the operational model has several outcomes (see Figure A9).

In the model, gender, method of recruitment, living arrangements (with 'living alone' and 'living with friends' collapsed together and 'living with partner' as another), subjective visibility, disguisability (coded 0 if easy to disguise and 1 if an expression of difficulty has been made) and visibility when clothed (coded 0 if not visible or mild and 1 if moderate through to extreme) are used as dummy variables.

Appearance-Related Social Anxiety and Avoidance

When entering the variables as described earlier, 66.2% of the observed sample variation in the DAS24 was accounted for by the regression model given in Table A2 and this effect was statistically significant, $R^2 = 0.662$, $F(16, 1038) = 127.191$, $MSE = 85.91$, $p < 0.001$.

In the fitted model for social anxiety and avoidance (DAS24), there are no significant effects attributable to living arrangements, recruitment or social comparison. There are relatively small but statistically significant gender effects with females scoring 2.2 points higher on DAS24 than males ($p = 0.002$).

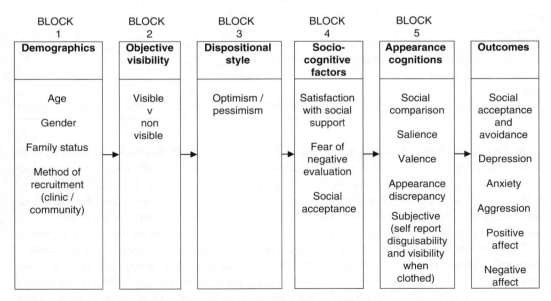

Figure A9 Further development of the model for the purpose of multiple regression.

Table A20   Regression model for social anxiety and avoidance (DAS24).

Variable	Coef	Std error	Beta	T	p	VIF	Incremental R²	P
Constant	43.25	3.471		12.46	<0.001			
Age	−0.139	0.020	−0.144	−6.82	<0.001	1.369		
Gender								
Male	—	—	—	—	—			
Female	2.178	0.688	0.062	3.17	0.002	1.159		
Recruitment								
Community	—	—	—	—	—			
Clinic	0.840	0.611	0.062	1.375	0.170	1.145		
Family								
Alone	—	—	—	—	—			
With friends	−1.106	1.012	−0.025	−1.09	0.275	1.610		
With partner	0.527	0.728	0.016	0.72	0.469	1.525	0.157	<0.001
Visible								
No	—	—	—	—	—			
Yes	−1.680	0.619	−0.053	−2.71	0.007	1.176	0.004	0.023
Optimism	−0.560	0.110	−0.119	−5.11	<0.001	1.663	0.216	<0.001
Fear of negative Evaluation	0.199	0.038	0.131	5.22	<0.001	1.923		
Social acceptance	−1.259	0.134	−0.223	−9.39	<0.001	1.731		
Satisfaction with social support	−0.263	0.075	−0.076	−3.53	<0.001	1.419	0.174	<0.001
Salience	0.246	0.045	0.123	5.47	<0.001	1.545		
Valence	0.483	0.055	0.240	8.86	<0.001	2.262		
Discrepancy	0.166	0.037	0.116	4.52	<0.001	2.019		
Social comparison	0.016	0.048	0.007	0.34	0.737	1.416		
Disguisability								
Less difficult	—	—	—	—	—			
Reported difficult	3.904	0.681	0.123	5.73	<0.001	1.418		
Visibility when clothed								
Not/mild	—	—	—	—	—			
Moderate/severe	−2.680	0.680	−0.085	−3.94	<0.001	1.415	0.111	<0.001

In the regression model, there were relatively strong and statistically significant negative relationships between age (beta = −0.144, $p < 0.001$), optimism (beta = −0.199, $p < 0.001$) and social acceptance (beta = −0.233, $p < 0.001$) with scores for social anxiety and social avoidance (DAS24). Likewise, there were relatively strong and statistically significant positive relationships between scores for fear of negative evaluation (FNE) (beta = 0.131, $p < 0.001$), salience (beta = 0.123, $p < 0.001$), valence (beta = 0.240, $p < 0.001$), appearance discrepancy (beta = 0.116, $p < 0.001$) and disguisability (beta = 0.123, $p < 0.001$).

There are smaller but statistically significant effects attributable to the visibility of the main area of concern to others; however, the direction of the effects is in the opposite direction to the direction indicated by the bivariate analyses. After allowing for all of the aforementioned effects, those who perceived their area of concern to be visible scored lower on average on the DAS24 than those without a visible concern by 2.7 points (beta = −0.053, $p = 0.007$) and those reporting high levels of visibility when clothed scored lower than those with relatively lower levels of self-reported visibility (beta = −0.085, $p < 0.001$).

Anxiety

When entering the variables as described previously, 46.4% of the observed sample variation in anxiety was accounted for by the regression model given in Table A20 and this effect was statistically significant, $R^2 = 0.464$, $F(16, 1037) = 56.157$, $MSE = 11.263$, $p < 0.001$.

In the fitted model for anxiety, there were no statistically significant effects attributable to age, gender, living arrangements, method of recruitment, visibility of the main area of concern, valence, appearance discrepancy or disguisability. In the model, both optimism (beta = −0.341, $p < 0.001$) and acceptance (beta = −0.132, $p < 0.001$) were negatively related to anxiety, and fear of negative evaluation (beta = 0.086, $p = 0.002$) and salience (beta = 0.086, $p = 0.002$) were positively related to HAD anxiety. The relative magnitude of beta identifies these four variables as being the dominant effects.

Table A21 Regression model for anxiety (HADS).

Variable	Coef	Std error	Beta	T	p	VIF	Incremental R^2	P
Constant	10.900	1.255		8.69	<0.001			
Age	−0.003	0.007	−0.012	−0.44	0.659	1.373		
Gender								
Male	—	—	—	—	—			
Female	0.286	0.249	0.028	1.15	0.251	1.159		
Recruitment								
Community	—	—	—	—	—			
Clinic	0.352	0.222	0.039	1.59	0.112	1.147		
Family								
Alone	—	—	—	—	—			
With friends	−0.483	0.367	−0.038	−1.32	0.188	1.611		
With partner	0.045	0.264	0.005	0.17	0.865	1.529	0.066	<0.001
Visible								
No	—	—	—	—	—			
Yes	0.361	0.224	−0.040	1.61	0.108	1.178	0.012	<0.001
Optimism	−0.462	0.040	−0.341	−11.64	<0.001	1.663	0.284	<0.001
Fear of negative evaluation	0.095	0.014	0.218	6.91	<0.001	1.925		
Social acceptance	−0.213	0.048	−0.132	−4.41	<0.001	1.723		
Satisfaction with social support	−0.061	0.027	−0.061	−2.25	0.025	1.419	0.088	<0.001
Salience	0.049	0.016	0.086	3.03	0.002	1.547		
Valence	0.007	0.020	0.012	0.36	0.719	2.263		
Discrepancy	0.016	0.013	0.039	1.20	0.229	2.022		
Social comparison	0.040	0.017	0.063	2.31	0.021	1.416		
Disguisability								
Less difficult	—	—	—	—	—			
Reported difficult	0.068	0.247	0.007	0.28	0.783	1.418		
Visibility when clothed								
Not/mild	—	—	—	—	—			
Moderate/severe	−0.630	0.246	−0.069	−2.56	0.011	1.415	0.015	<0.001

There are relatively small but statistically significant effects in the anxiety model for satisfaction with social support (beta = −0.061, $p = 0.025$), social comparison (beta = 0.063, $p = 0.021$) and visibility when clothed (beta = −0.069, $p = 0.011$) with the effect in the direction contrary to the direction indicated by the bivariate analyses.

Depression

When entering the variables as described previously, 45.9% of the observed sample variation in depression was accounted for by the regression model given in Table A22 and this effect was statistically significant, $R^2 = 0.459$, $F(16, 1037) = 54.929$, $MSE = 7.805$, $p < .001$.

Table A22 Regression model for depression (HADS).

Variable	Coef	Std error	Beta	T	p	VIF	Incremental R²	P
Constant	14.773	1.044		14.15	<0.001			
Age	0.014	0.006	0.060	2.24	0.025	1.373		
Gender								
Male	—	—	—	—	—			
Female	−0.569	0.207	−0.067	2.74	0.006	1.159		
Recruitment								
Community	—	—	—	—	—			
Clinic	0.062	0.184	0.008	0.33	0.738	1.147		
Family								
Alone	—	—	—	—	—			
With friends	−0.300	0.305	−0.029	−0.98	0.326	1.611		
With partner	0.112	0.220	0.014	0.51	0.610	1.529	0.018	0.002
Visible								
No	—	—	—	—	—			
Yes	0.119	0.187	0.016	0.64	0.524	1.178	0.007	0.007
Optimism	−0.387	0.033	−0.345	−11.71	<0.001	1.663	0.320	<0.001
Fear of negative evaluation	0.024	0.011	0.066	2.08	0.038	1.925		
Social acceptance								
Satisfaction with social	−0.254	0.040	−0.190	−6.32	<0.001	1.723		
support	−0.151	0.022	−0.183	−6.71	0.001	1.419	0.098	<0.001
Salience	−0.015	0.014	−0.032	−1.12	0.262	1.547		
Valence	0.050	0.016	0.104	3.03	0.003	2.263		
Discrepancy	0.015	0.011	0.043	1.33	0.184	2.022		
Social comparison	−0.022	0.014	−0.042	−1.53	0.126	1.416		
Disguisability								
Less difficult	—	—	—	—	—			
Reported difficult	0.397	0.205	0.053	1.93	0.053	1.418		
Visibility when clothed								
Not/mild	—	—	—	—	—			
Moderate/severe	−0.293	0.205	−0.039	−1.43	0.154	1.415	0.016	<0.001

In this model, the variables method of recruitment, living arrangements, visibility of main area of concern, salience, appearance discrepancy, social comparison, disguisability and visibility when clothed were not statistically significant predictors of depression. The variables optimism (beta $= -0.345$, $p < 0.001$), social acceptance (beta $= -0.245$, $p < 0.001$) and satisfaction with social support (beta $= -0.183$, $p < 0.001$) were all negatively associated with depression and valence (beta $= 0.104$, $p = 0.003$) was positively associated with depression.

To a lesser extent, there was a statistically significant positive relationship between age and HAD depression in the sample (beta $= 0.060$, $p = 0.025$) and FNE and HAD depression (beta $= 0.066$, $p = 0.038$). There was a small gender effect (beta $= -0.067$, $p = 0.006$) with males scoring 0.57 points higher, on average, than females on depression after adjusting for all other variables in the model.

Aggression

When entering the variables as described previously, 30.7% of the observed sample variation in aggression scores was accounted for by the regression model given in Table A23 and this effect was statistically significant, $R^2 = 0.307$, $F(16, 1038) = 28.691$, $MSE = 61.794$, $p < 0.001$.

Table A23 gives the fitted model for aggression. In this model, the variables method of recruitment, living arrangements, visibility of main area of concern, scores for fear of negative evaluation, social acceptance, salience, valence, appearance discrepancy, disguisability and visibility when clothed were not statistically significant predictors of aggression. The regression model captures strong and statistically significant negative effects between aggression and optimism (beta $= -0.358$, $p < 0.001$) and age (beta $= -0.218$, $p < 0.001$). There was an appreciable gender effect with males, on average, scoring 3.3 points higher than females on the aggression scale and this effect was statistically significant (beta $= -0.158$, $p < 0.001$).

To a lesser extent, there was a statistically significant negative relationship between satisfaction with social support and aggression (beta $= -0.073$, $p = 0.018$) and between social comparison and aggression (beta $= 0.064$, $p = 0.038$).

Positive Affect

When entering the variables as described previously, 29.2% of the observed sample variation in positive affect scores was accounted for by the regression model given in Table A24 and this effect was statistically significant, $R^2 = 0.307$, $F(16, 1026) = 26.495$, $MSE = 56.513$, $p < 0.001$.

Table A24 gives the fitted model for positive affect. In this model, the effects for age, gender, method of recruitment, living arrangements, visibility of main area of concern, social acceptance, appearance discrepancy, disguisability and visibility when clothed are not statistically significant effects. The regression model captures strong and statistically significant positive associations between positive affect and each of optimism (beta $= 0.280$, $p < 0.001$) and satisfaction with social support (beta $= 0.108$, $p < 0.001$) and strong negative associations between positive affect and each of fear of negative evaluation (beta $= -0.186$, $p < 0.001$) and valence (beta $= -0.183$, $p < 0.001$). There was a relatively small but statistically significant positive association between positive affect and salience (beta $= 0.080$, $p = 0.014$) and between positive affect and social comparison (beta $= 0.076$, $p = 0.015$).

Negative Affect

When entering the variables as described previously, 44.3% of the observed sample variation in negative affect scores was accounted for by the regression model given in Table A25 and this effect was statistically significant, $R^2 = 0.443$, $F(16, 1025) = 51.035$, $MSE = 42.248$, $p < 0.001$.

Table A23　Regression model for aggression.

Variable	Coef	Std error	Beta	T	p	VIF	Incremental R²	P
Constant	43.656	2.946		14.82	<0.001			
Age	−0.125	0.017	−0.218	−7.22	<0.001	1.370		
Gender								
Male	—	—	—	—	—			
Female	−3.318	0.583	−0.158	−5.69	<0.001	1.157		
Recruitment								
Community	—	—	—	—	—			
Clinic	0.535	0.518	0.029	1.03	0.302	1.145		
Family								
Alone	—	—	—	—	—			
With friends	−1.547	0.859	−0.059	−1.80	0.072	1.614		
With partner	0.368	0.617	0.019	0.60	0.551	1.526	0.011	<0.001
Visible								
No	—	—	—	—	—			
Yes	0.234	0.525	0.012	0.45	0.66	1.176	0.004	0.024
Optimism	−0.999	0.093	−0.358	−10.75	<0.001	1.662	0.173	<0.001
Fear of negative evaluation	0.047	0.032	0.052	1.45	0.148	1.921		
Social acceptance	0.010	0.113	0.003	0.092	0.092	1.726		
Satisfaction with social support	−0.149	0.063	−0.073	−2.36	0.018	1.419	0.012	<0.001
Salience	0.056	0.038	0.047	1.47	0.143	1.544		
Valence	0.012	0.046	0.010	0.260	0.795	2.259		
Discrepancy	−0.032	0.031	−0.037	1.02	0.308	2.016		
Social comparison	0.084	0.040	0.064	2.07	0.038	1.416		
Disguisability								
Less difficult	—	—	—	—	—			
Reported difficult	0.606	0.577	0.032	1.05	0.294	1.418		
Visibility when clothed								
Not/mild	—	—	—	—	—			
Moderate/severe	0.177	0.577	0.009	0.31	0.758	1.414	0.007	0.105

Table A25 gives the fitted model for negative affect. In this model, the effects for gender, method of recruitment, living arrangements, visibility of main area of concern, salience, valence, appearance discrepancy, disguisability and visibility when clothed are not statistically significant effects. The regression model captures a strong and statistically significant positive association between negative affect and scores on fear of negative evaluation (beta = 0.297, $p < 0.001$) and strong and statistically significant negative associations between negative affect and optimism (beta = −0.222, $p < 0.001$) and social acceptance (beta = −0.138, $p < 0.001$). There were weaker, but statistically significant, negative associations between negative affect and age (beta = −0.068, $p = 0.013$) and satisfaction with social support (beta = −0.078, $p = 0.005$) and a positive association between negative affect and social comparison (beta = 0.067, $p = 0.016$).

Table A24 Regression model for positive affect.

Variable	Coef	Std error	Beta	T	p	VIF	Incremental R²	P
Constant	19.778	2.826		7.00	<0.001			
Age	−0.018	0.017	−0.034	−1.10	0.272	1.373		
Gender								
Male	—	—	—	—	—			
Female	−0.722	0.562	−0.036	−1.29	0.199	1.156		
Recruitment								
Community	—	—	—	—	—			
Clinic	−0.662	0.499	−0.037	−1.33	0.185	1.148		
Family								
Alone	—	—	—	—	—			
With friends	−0.134	0.825	−0.005	−0.16	0.871	1.615		
With partner	0.210	0.595	0.011	0.35	0.725	1.535	0.020	<0.001
Visible								
No	—	—	—	—	—			
Yes	−0.008	0.504	0.000	−0.16	0.987	1.173	0.003	0.089
Optimism	0.737	0.089	0.280	8.24	<0.001	1.669	0.201	<0.001
Fear of negative evaluation	−0.159	0.031	−0.186	−5.09	<0.001	1.936		
Social acceptance	0.211	0.110	0.067	1.92	0.055	1.743		
Satisfaction with social support	0.210	0.061	0.108	3.45	0.001	1.421	0.042	<0.001
Salience	0.090	0.037	0.080	2.46	0.014	1.543		
Valence	−0.207	0.045	−0.183	−4.64	<0.001	2.264		
Discrepancy	0.012	0.030	0.015	0.41	0.683	2.024		
Social comparison	0.095	0.039	0.076	2.44	0.015	1.417		
Disguisability								
Less difficult	—	—	—	—	—			
Reported difficult	1.078	0.556	0.061	1.94	0.053	1.421		
Visibility when clothed								
Not/mild	—	—	—	—	—			
Moderate/severe	0.058	0.554	0.003	0.11	0.916	1.413	0.028	<0.001

Clinic-Specific Data

In order to explore the potential impact of the aetiology of the disfiguring condition on adjustment, the data derived from outpatient clinics were examined. A summary of the outcome variables by clinic is given in Table A26. Box and whisker plots in Figure A10a–c show the extent of individual variation within each outpatient clinic.

Table A27 shows the percentages of participants scoring low, mild or moderate to high on HADS for anxiety and depression in the overall sample ($n = 1259$).

Table A25 Regression model for negative affect.

Variable	Coef	Std error	Beta	T	p	VIF	Incremental R²	P
Constant	23.921	2.444		9.79	<0.001			
Age	−0.036	0.014	−0.068	−2.50	0.013	1.372		
Gender								
Male	—	—	—	—	—			
Female	−0.293	0.486	−0.015	−0.60	0.546	1.156		
Recruitment								
Community	—	—	—	—	—			
Clinic	0.612	0.432	0.035	1.42	0.157	1.148		
Family								
Alone	—	—	—	—	—			
With friends	−0.580	0.714	−0.024	−0.81	0.417	1.616		
With partner	−1.034	0.516	−0.058	−2.00	0.045	1.538	0.094	<0.001
Visible								
No	—	—	—	—	—			
Yes	0.086	0.436	0.005	0.20	0.843	1.172	0.010	0.001
Optimism	−0.569	0.077	−0.222	−7.35	<0.001	1.672	0.208	<0.001
Fear of negative evaluation	0.246	0.027	0.297	9.15	<0.001	1.932		
Social acceptance	−0.427	0.095	−0.138	−4.49	<0.001	1.743		
Satisfaction with social support	−0.147	0.053	−0.078	−2.80	0.005	1.420	0.125	<0.001
Salience	0.003	0.032	0.003	0.09	0.925	1.542		
Valence	0.037	0.039	0.034	0.96	0.338	2.270		
Discrepancy	0.034	0.026	0.043	1.29	0.196	2.035		
Social comparison	0.081	0.034	0.067	2.41	0.016	1.416		
Disguisability								
Less difficult	—	—	—	—	—			
Reported difficult	−0.029	0.481	−0.002	−0.060	0.952	1.420		
Visibility when clothed								
Not/mild	—	—	—	—	—			
Moderate/severe	0.191	0.479	0.011	0.40	0.691	1.412	0.007	0.005

Table A28 shows the percentages of participants scoring low, mild or moderate to high on HADS for anxiety and depression split by clinic ($n = 1259$).

Discussion

One of the most notable achievements in Study 1 of this research programme was to achieve a large sample size, delivering a substantial body of data relating to adjustment to appearance concerns from a sample of 1265 participants. To our knowledge, this was and remains the largest scale study in the

Table A26   Mean and standard deviations for each outcome variable by clinic.

	N	Social anxiety M(SD)	Anxiety M(SD)	Depression M(SD)	Aggression M(SD)	Positive affect M(SD)	Negative affect M(SD)
Plastics	225	46.03(17.23)	8.88(4.65)	5.28(3.77)	26.59(8.88)	31.77(8.50)	21.26(8.84)
Dermatology	89	43.80(14.31)	8.55(4.29)	5.64(4.16)	26.59(10.61)	30.52(8.91)	20.08(9.10)
Laser	38	43.03(16.39)	8.39(4.82)	3.74(3.03)	24.63(9.48)	34.26(7.98)	20.76(8.36)
Cleft lip and palate	11	42.64(14.03)	10.36(6.05)	3.64(2.34)	32.09(11.32)	31.73(6.77)	25.09(8.69)
Burns	18	42.22(17.66)	7.39(4.39)	5.39(4.73)	27.83(10.38)	31.06(8.79)	20.24(7.21)
Ophthalmology	39	39.23(13.33)	7.89(4.89)	4.98(3.24)	22.52(8.55)	32.40(9.67)	19.26(9.11)
Head and neck cancer	34	38.09(14.96)	7.24(4.95)	5.76(3.91)	23.97(9.55)	30.18(10.11)	18.64(9.45)
Prosthetics	54	36.28(17.00)	6.19(5.08)	4.74(4.01)	25.70(10.00)	34.56(9.94)	17.37(7.70)
Ocular Prosthetics	30	35.00(12.53)	5.97(4.13)	3.37(3.51)	21.80(7.25)	34.69(8.81)	18.10(6.75)
Rheumatoid arthritis	36	34.31(12.65)	6.94(3.77)	4.81(3.63)	22.94(8.31)	30.00(8.88)	17.88(6.94)
ENT	17	33.06(17.08)	5.35(3.76)	5.88(3.52)	20.47(6.60)	31.56(8.88)	14.63(6.17)
Melanoma	36	32.33(16.15)	7.25(5.22)	4.08(3.41)	21.64(7.99)	30.00(9.55)	16.81(7.80)

(a)

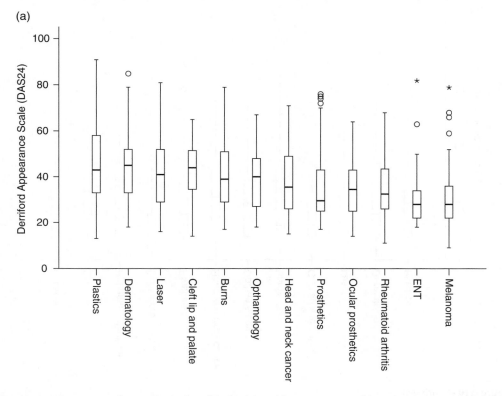

Figure A10   Comparative box-and-whisker plots for (a) social anxiety scores, (b) anxiety scores and (c) depression scores by condition.

(b)

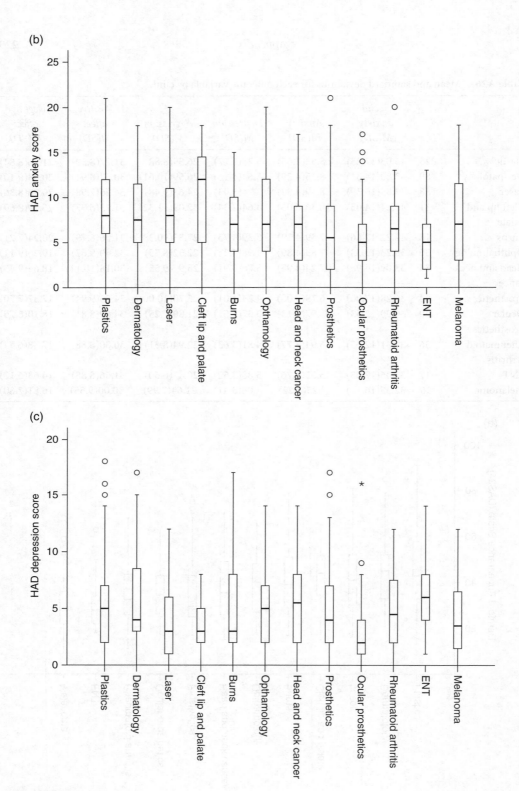

(c)

Figure A10 (*Continued*)

Table A27   Percentage of participants with low (0–7), mild (8–11) and moderate/high (12–21) levels of anxiety and depression.

Category	N	Anxiety score 0–7	8–11	12–21	Depression score 0–7	8–11	12–21
All participants	1259	48.2	27.2	24.5	76.4	16.7	6.9

Table A28   Percentage of participants with low (0–7), mild (8–11) and moderate/high (12–21) levels of anxiety and depression by clinic category.

Clinic category	N	Anxiety score 0–7	8–11	12–21	Depression score 0–7	8–11	12–21
Plastics	226	42.0	30.5	27.4	75.2	18.1	6.6
Dermatology	88	50.0	25.0	25.0	71.6	15.9	12.5
Laser	38	36.8	39.5	23.7	92.1	5.3	2.6
Cleft lip and palate	11	36.4	9.1	54.5	90.9	9.1	0.0
Burns	18	50.0	33.3	16.7	72.2	16.7	11.1
Ophthalmology	61	54.1	19.7	26.2	78.7	18.0	3.3
Head and neck cancer	34	50.0	26.5	23.5	67.6	20.6	11.8
Prosthetics	54	64.8	18.5	16.7	79.6	11.1	9.3
Ocular prosthetics	30	80.0	6.7	13.3	86.7	10.0	3.3
Rheumatoid arthritis	36	63.9	27.8	8.3	75.0	22.2	2.8
ENT	17	82.4	5.9	11.8	70.6	23.5	5.9
Melanoma	36	63.9	11.1	25.0	83.3	13.9	2.8

field to date. A particularly noteworthy addition to previous understanding is the data derived from the community sample. Levels of distress in this population were considerable and comparable to participants recruited from hospital settings. The homogeneity of the two data sets resulted in the majority of these initial analyses being performed on the complete data set, in contrast to our initial assumption when embarking on this research that we would be comparing and contrasting the data from the community- and hospital-based samples. Clearly, previous research, which focused on the problems and difficulties of those actively seeking treatment, has revealed only the tip of the iceberg of appearance-related distress amongst those with disfiguring conditions.

Mean levels of depression were low in the sample compared to general population norms, echoing previous research (Moss & Carr, 2004; Rumsey & Harcourt, 2005). The mean level of anxiety was in the low to mild range. The level for positive affect was quite high and negative affect quite low compared with normative values. The mean level for aggression fell in the low to moderate range. However, the variance in the sample was high, and substantial numbers of participants showed significant levels of distress.

The data from clinic attendees were examined for any notable patterns in scores for adjustment or distress. There are many difficulties inherent in classifying the various conditions which result in disfigurement (e.g. patients attending a dermatology or plastics clinic will have disfigurements resulting from a large number of different aetiologies). Our analyses were limited to differences in the type of clinic attended. The overall impression was one of similarities rather than differences in profiles from the various clinics – once again adding to the impression that individual psychological factors and processes were a bigger determinant of adjustment. Taken on its own, however, the lack of differences between clinics in this data set should be treated with caution. Despite minimum recruitment targets for every clinic, the relative challenges associated with recruitment varied considerably with resulting differences in final sample sizes. The profile for participants with a cleft of the lip and/or palate is one of greater distress as reflected in scores for negative affect, aggression and anxiety than for participants from other clinics; however, the sample is also the smallest ($n = 11$), reflecting the low preponderance of patients of 18 years and over attending this particular outpatient clinic. In addition, adjustment profiles may vary as a result of the age profiles of attendees (e.g. the relatively high numbers of older adults attending melanoma and rheumatoid arthritis clinics).

Demographic variables:
The mean age of participants was 47 years, with a range of 18–91 years. The respondents in this study represent a sample with an older profile than in the majority of previous research, offering a useful insight into appearance concerns in middle and older adulthood. There were negative correlations between increasing age and scores for social anxiety and social avoidance, aggression, negative affect, depression and anxiety. So, bearing in mind the limitations of a cross-sectional sample, the picture in this study is one of positive adjustment increasing with age. However, the relationships are not dramatic and many older participants were also concerned and distressed about their appearance. These results are consistent with previous research and should not be taken as indicating that appearance concerns are the preserve only of the young.

The importance of appearance in late adolescence and early adulthood has been highlighted by many (Harris & Carr, 2001; Liossi, 2003; Lovegrove & Rumsey, 2005), and Cash et al.'s (1986) survey of 15–74-year-olds found that body image concerns diminished with age. However, Rosser (2008) has also pointed out that the role of age in appearance adjustment is not straightforward, and Lansdown et al. (1991) pointed to the crucial role of appearance concerns throughout the lifespan. Rumsey and Harcourt (2005) reported data from older people (over 60 years) with skin conditions which indicated that although fewer people in this age group expressed significant concerns, a sizable proportion were distressed about aspects of their appearance. Rather than a reduction in levels of concern compared with younger people, the focus and nature of the appearance concerns appeared to be different. The stereotypes of appearance considered desirable earlier in life were less important, but aspects of self- presentation, such as appearing smart and fit, remained important.

Several commentators have noted the bias in previous research towards female participants and have highlighted the need to explore the concerns of men in more detail (Rumsey & Harcourt, 2005). Although 68.5% of the participants in this study were female, we still managed to recruit a sizeable sample of men ($n = 354$). A higher proportion of women were recruited from outpatient clinics than from community settings. It may be that women are more helpful and more interested in sharing their experiences or perhaps that the GP practices used as a basis for large segments of the community recruitment had more women attending surgeries and/or who have attended in the past (leading to their inclusion in the READ code classifications used as the basis for mailshots).

Whilst noting the lack of research with males, previous studies (including people with and without visible disfigurement) have in the main suggested that women are more prone to having significant levels of appearance concerns and body dissatisfaction than men (e.g. Cash et al., 2004; Harris & Carr, 2001). This has been attributed to the impact of societal norms which infer that the importance of appearance is more specific to women than to men (Rosser, 2008) and greater familial concern with the appearance of daughters than sons (Schwartz & Sprangers, 1999). However, in relation to body image concerns in the general population, Cash and Pruzinsky (2002) have commented that both genders experience distress and White (2008) reported that teenage boys are more distressed about their appearance than girls. In the current study, levels of social anxiety and social avoidance, anxiety and negative affect were higher for women, but perhaps the most notable finding is that the effect sizes were small. Women were also more likely to have multiple areas of concern than men. There were no significant differences in relation to depression; however, men had a higher mean score on aggression. Levels of positive effect were higher for women. Newell (2000) concluded that research findings examining the role of gender in adjustment to visible differences are contradictory. Our findings endorse the suggestion that both males and females should be included in further research on appearance-related adjustment and distress and in efforts to meet the needs of those adversely affected.

Eighty-one per cent of the sample classified themselves as white, with similar profiles from both the clinic and community recruitment settings. Although the sample includes participants from a greater mix of ethnic backgrounds than much of the research hitherto, numbers are proportionately low, and the collaboration felt it appropriate to study the effects of cultural background in more detail in two of the subsequent studies (Studies 5 and 6).

Visibility and areas of concern:
The findings relating to the impacts of the perceived visibility or otherwise of a disfigurement to others are mixed. Approximately, 65% indicated that their main concern related to the appearance of their face, head or neck, and 12.3% indicated their hands. Levels of distress were higher in this grouping, mirroring earlier research about the greater impact of visible disfigurements, compared with those which are more easily camouflaged or covered up (see e.g. Kent & Keohane, 2001). In addition, increasing levels of distress were associated with perceptions of increasing difficulty in being able to disguise the aspect of appearance in question. However, in the regression analyses, a lack of visibility to others in everyday situations was associated with greater distress (higher levels of depression, anxiety, aggression and negative affect, lower positive affect and higher levels of fear of negative evaluation by others). It should be noted, however, that the effect sizes were small, and other appearance-related cognitions had a much greater impact on adjustment. This mixed picture of the effects of visibility to others may have resulted from shortcomings in our measures; however, Moss and Rosser (2008) have also highlighted the complex nature of the relationship between visibility and adjustment. Rosser et al. (2008) noted the likelihood of an effect of ease of concealment and also that the personal salience and valence attached to a particular body part may further complicate matters. Major and Granzow (1999) and Smart and Wegner (1999) raised the possibility of the 'Preoccupational Model of Secrecy' which discusses the possible negative impact of concealment associated with the threat of the stigma being discovered and/or fear of revealing the stigma. Those with a difference which is routinely visible to others may be forced to develop strategies to deal with the reactions of others (e.g. using camouflage or developing 'stock' answers to common questions) and may perceive this to be effective. Avoidance of the need to develop these strategies may increase fears of negative evaluation by others and may feed insecurity in more intimate situations when the disfigurement will become visible. Further research is warranted in this area.

Previous research has consistently shown the lack of a linear relationship between severity and concern/distress. In the light of these findings, and as the focus of this research related to subjective psychological factors and processes, there was no objective assessment of the severity of the participants' disfigurement in this study. Various explanations for the lack of relationship between severity and adjustment/distress have been put forward. Lansdown et al. (1997) suggested that those with 'minor' differences have to face a variability in responses from others that limits the ability to predict these responses with any certainty, and this can act as a deterrent to developing self-efficacy in responding effectively. For those with more severe (and visible to others) disfigurements, there is a more consistent reaction, thus prediction of responses is relatively easy. Moss (2004) illustrated the complexities of the severity and the disguisability of disfigurement and adjustment in reporting a U-shaped parabola in a sample of 400 people with a variety of disfigurements for visible disfigurements, with no such relationship for those able to routinely conceal their difference. Moss refined Lansdown's explanation in speculating that both minor and severe disfigurements produce consistent and more easily predictable responses from others, with those in the mid-range provoking more variety.

Several studies have highlighted the importance of subjective assessments of severity. Moss (2004) and Rumsey et al. (2004) found a linear relationship between subjectively assessed severity of appearance and adjustment, highlighting the importance of personal evaluation of a problem. Our results showed a striking relationship between increasing numbers of areas of concern and growing levels of distress, particularly in relation to social anxiety and social avoidance around appearance (DAS24). Participants in the community sample were more likely to report multiple areas of concern than those recruited in hospital settings, and women had greater numbers of areas of concern than men.

A relatively small percentage (25.7%) of the sample reported being concerned about only one area. It is important for clinicians and researchers to note that people with a disfiguring condition affecting one body part may also have significant concerns about other aspects of appearance. Twenty-seven per cent reported concerns about their abdomens, 22% in relation to the appearance of their thighs and 14% were unhappy with the appearance of their buttocks. These results may reflect concerns about weight, and it is possible that these worries may override their issues about a disfiguring condition. Weight-related concerns were greater in the community sample. The prevalence of weight concerns in the general population comes as no surprise in the current context of rising levels of obesity; however, more research is needed to unpick the similarities and differences in different types of concern.

The Multivariate Nature of Adjustment

The measures chosen as the outcomes in our conceptual framework were significantly correlated, supporting the view that adjustment is multi-factorial (see e.g. Rumsey et al. 2004). The psychological characteristics of those who were positively adjusted included higher levels of optimism, greater feelings of social acceptance and satisfaction with social support, a lack of concern about negative evaluations by others and a self-system with lower levels of salience and valence afforded to appearance-related information. Levels of social anxiety and social avoidance were low, as were levels of negative affect, general anxiety and depression. These people felt their disfigurements were reasonably easy to disguise, and they tended to be older than people with higher levels of distress.

An identical regression model was used to interrogate the data for each outcome variable. In relation to social anxiety and social avoidance, an impressive 66.2% of the variance was explained by the model. The higher percentage explained in this equation was to some extent expected as the measure in question (the DAS24) was designed specifically to assess levels of distress in people with disfigurements; however, the figure is unusually high for research in this field. In this regression model, there were no effects of living status, method of recruitment or of appearance-related social comparisons. There was a small gender effect, with women more distressed than men, and strong negative effects of age (older people were less distressed), optimism and social acceptance. As levels of fear of negative evaluation, salience and valence increased, so did distress.

Similar pictures emerged when applying the regression model to the other outcome measures. The model predicted approximately 30% of the variance for positive affect, 45% for negative affect and 46% for both anxiety and depression. Rather than comment on the results of each regression in detail (which would be an enormous task), in the discussion which follows, the primary focus is on the regression for social anxiety and social avoidance, as the DAS24 is the outcome measure most specifically relevant to disfigurement, and as other research have identified predictors of the more general measures of anxiety and depression.

Dispositional style:
In this study, dispositional style (specifically optimism/pessimism) had a strong effect on many of the outcome variables, including depression, anxiety, aggression, negative effect and to a lesser extent appearance-related social anxiety and avoidance, and increased the goodness of fit of several of the regression models to an appreciable extent. In the health psychology literature, there has been a consensus for some time that optimism is adaptive in the face of adversity. Research specifically examining optimism in the context of appearance has been lacking, and this study would suggest that this may be a key factor in adjustment. This is particularly relevant in the context of intervention, as some researchers believe optimism can be taught – Seligman (1998), for example, developed programmes to help adults and children change from a pessimistic to an optimistic view of life.

Socio-cognitive processes:
Levels of fear of negative evaluation from others, social acceptance and satisfaction with social support correlated significantly with all the outcome measures in this study. These results are consistent with the previous literature in this area. Confidence in social situations has been highlighted as key to adjustment by many commentators in this field (see e.g. Partridge, 1990). Fear of negative evaluations by others and avoidance of social situations have been thought to play central roles in social difficulties relating to threats to body image, regardless of the actual behaviour of others (Newell, 2000).

The benefits of social support as a positive resource in a variety of situations are widely accepted, and good quality social support is commonly regarded as an asset which can be mobilized to act as a buffer to stress in people with disfigurements (Blakeney et al., 1990). Liossi (2003) found that people with appearance concerns who reported higher levels of social support had lower levels of social anxiety and social avoidance (also measured by the DAS24). Her data suggested that social support may protect people from distress even when they have dysfunctional appearance schemata. She proposed that good social support may promote effective coping strategies, for example, by facilitating exposure to feared situations (see also Baker, 1992). Personal accounts testify to the benefits of feeling at ease with familiar others, who are perceived as seeing beyond superficial appearances to the 'real person beneath' (Rumsey & Harcourt, 2005).

The role of appearance-related cognitions:

In addition to confirming the role of these socio-cognitive processes in adjustment, this study has highlighted the considerable contribution of cognitive processes relating more specifically to appearance-related issues. The salience of appearance concerns, the value attached to appearance, appearance-related self-ideal discrepancies and appearance-related social comparison processes correlated significantly with all outcome measures. Their effects were particularly apparent in scores relating to social anxiety and social avoidance (DAS24), but their role also impacted on levels of anxiety, depression, aggression, positive affect and negative affect.

The results indicate that appearance concerns are complex and can be debilitating; however, the good news is that they involve factors which are amenable to intervention, offering a strong endorsement of the potential of cognitive–behavioural approaches to address the needs of those affected. The results of this study supported the tentative conclusion drawn from previous research that the appearance concerns of people both with and without disfigurements contribute to a range of processes including beliefs about the impressions formed by others on the basis of appearance, and perceptions of the self (Moss, 2004; Rumsey & Harcourt, 2005; Thompson & Kent, 2001). The current results further indicated that the way people process appearance-related information contributes to their level of adjustment. These mechanisms are not new in the psychological literature, but until now have not been demonstrated so clearly in people with disfiguring conditions. Associations between processing styles and psychological distress including anxiety (Bar-Haim et al., 2007) and depression (Mogg & Bradley, 2005; Strunk & Adler, 2009) have been demonstrated in general population samples, and there has been some evidence of appearance-related cognitive biases resulting in increased recall of appearance-related information (Altabe & Thompson, 1996) in people with high levels of body image concern. An increased likelihood of interpreting ambiguous situations as appearance related and negative has been shown in people who are obese (Jansen et al., 2007) and in those with eating disorders (Cooper, 1997) compared to those without. Rosser et al. (2010) found in a sample of people without disfigurements that appearance concerns appear to include a propensity to interpret ambiguous stimuli as appearance related and negative (without any priming) and that those with high levels of concern have a tendency to attend preferentially to stimuli they believe to be appearance related when given a choice.

Taken with the results of the current study, a picture is emerging of people (with or without disfigurements) in whom higher levels of appearance concern result in attentional biases. These are people who perceive the world in a way that reinforces and exacerbates their distress. Their processing biases (e.g. preferential attention and interpretation of ambiguous information as negative) may lead to a perception of the world that is dominated by the appearance issue(s) of concern, perhaps resulting in hyper-vigilance towards threatening stimuli and self-reinforcing perceptions regardless of the actual environment (Mathews, 1990; Rosser, 2008).

Social comparison processes help us to contextualize and understand ourselves in relation to others. Rosser (2008), for example, highlighted that people placing a higher value on appearance in their self-definition are more vulnerable to making negative (upward) comparisons with others. The more frequently people engage in social comparisons the more likely they are to have difficulties relating to body image, eating behaviours and self-esteem (Thompson et al., 1991). This is likely to be the result of the tendency to use unrealistic standards of comparison (e.g. from the media) resulting in unhelpful upward comparisons associated with more negative affect. (Patrick et al., 2004). Despite the enthusiasm of several researchers for the potential of social comparison processes to extrapolate from the body image literature and to expect a significant contribution from these processes to adjustment in the context of disfigurement, these effects are not evident in the quantitative data of this study. This may be an artefact of the measure used. In the light of other socio-cognitive processes being specific to appearance-related information (see below), it may be that the chosen scale was too general in its orientation. Social psychologists have highlighted the complexity of social comparison processes. In addition, as there was evidence of social comparison processes at work in the qualitative data derived from the studies (reported in subsequent sections), we feel this variable should remain under consideration in future research.

The cognitive processes of valence (the value attributed to appearance) and the salience of appearance issues in processing information, and the perception of the discrepancy between the self and social norms were also shown to play significant parts in the regression models. The concept of valence relates to the positive or negative emotional charge associated with aspects of the self-system. The valence of a self-attribute such as appearance mediates our feelings about ourselves in relation to that attribute. The emotional content of self-attributes also has implications for one's global self-esteem as it plays a part in the way self-relevant information is evaluated and affects the positioning of an attribute within a self-system. The analysis showed that valence contributed to a significant extent to levels of positive affect, depression and appearance-related distress.

Increased salience in cognitive processing is associated with increased accessibility of information and processing strategies (Markus & Nurius, 1986). As the result of increased accessibility, more salient information is not only considered more important to the individual, but is also more likely to be frequently employed in the perception and experience of the world. Highly salient self-information and processing strategies may become chronically accessible. As salient information is more frequently accessed, it becomes yet further defined and reinforced and also becomes more established and has a greater resistance to modification. New information is more likely to be manipulated to fit prior knowledge, rather than a process of modifying previous knowledge to incorporate the new. In the analyses of data from this study, the salience of appearance-related information was shown to contribute to levels of social anxiety and social avoidance and general anxiety.

Rosser (2008) and others have explained how the self-concept can be conceptualized as being organized hierarchically into mental representations or self-schemas which direct the processing of self-relevant information. Poorer adjustment is likely when appearance is a more central aspect of the self-concept and when this is dominated by appearance-related (rather than non-appearance-related) issues. He has offered a useful overview of how appearance-related schema may influence levels of adjustment and distress in people without disfigurements which may be helpful in interpreting the results of this study. Rosser cites Baldwin's (1992) description of how the self-system is important in constructing templates (schemata) which influence our interactions with other people. If new information fits within a schema's parameters, specific assumptions, expectations and predictions will be implemented by the schema to make sense of information and of how best to process it. For more established schemata, the information they contain is more central, accessible and frequently involved in cognitive processing and interpretation than non-schematic information. In this way, schemata aid processing and also bias it towards what is expected. Once activated the schema allocates how attention is distributed and how information is processed. The potential for bias is considerable as the result of preferential attention to schematic information. Established schemata are more heavily defined and less susceptible to integrating novel information. They affect how we attend to, store, retrieve and ultimately perceive our environment. Problems arise when biases cause dysfunctional preferential attention and misevaluation of information, and as an emotional element is also associated, this can have significant emotional implications (Greenberg & Safran, 1987). Self-schemata are theorized by their proponents as central, most salient, highly elaborated and strongly defined within the self-system and are referred to as 'affect laden' due to their emotional as well as informational content (Altabe & Thompson, 1996). Should a schema with a prevalent negative content gain dominance in the processing system, information processing on all levels could be influenced and manipulated to reinforce negative expectations. Building on the work of Moss (2004), Rosser (2008) has described that for people with significant appearance-related concerns, a maladjusted self-schema would become highly central with negative generic appearance information and processing biases chronically accessible – leading to a self-reinforcing cycle where appearance information is more frequently acknowledged, processed and employed in processing and interpreting the world.

Limitations of this study

There are a number of limitations to this study which should be considered when interpreting the results. Prior to the commencement of the study, the assumption was that those actively seeking treatment for their condition would have greater levels of appearance-related distress and perhaps that previous research, which focused on populations such as these, was inherently biased in this respect. Accordingly, considerable efforts were made to recruit from community sources. In the event, differences between the adjustment profiles for the two groups were minimal. The extent to which clinic and community samples are truly different populations was a source of debate amongst the collaboration during the research process. Although the large majority of the community sample (those recruited through general practices) were not accessing treatment at the time of the study, many will have experienced treatment in the past. Nevertheless, an important message from these results is that substantial numbers of people who are not seeking treatment will be experiencing appearance-related distress, which could be amenable to intervention.

Although all participants believed themselves to have a disfigurement of some sort, in relation to the community sample (a substantial proportion of whom were not seen face to face by a member of the research team), this issue is impossible to police. The research team attempted to minimize this possibility by using READ codes as a basis for recruitment in all participating practices which used them. This enabled targeted recruitment to those classified by their GP as having a condition which was potentially disfiguring.

The response rates to approaches to participate in the study varied from clinic to clinic, method of approach (e.g. in person, by poster, by post or online) and, within this, from week to week. A meaningful overall figure is impossible to calculate; thus, we are not able to assess the representativeness of our sample through conventional means. All the researchers involved in the recruitment process were aware of the need to sample broadly, and all made considerable efforts to ensure this was achieved. Nevertheless, as acknowledged earlier, there is an under-representation of participants from ethnic minority groups in the current study, and more women agreed to take part than men.

It could also be argued that the lack of an objective rating of disfigurement is a limitation of the study, as is the broad (type of clinic attended), rather than a very specific, aetiology of the disfigurement for each participant. In addition to the lack of a relationship between severity and distress in the previous literature (outlined earlier), an accurate 'objective' rating for every participant would have been logistically very difficult to achieve. Our results offer support to the value of assessing subjective assessments of severity, as these are likely to be more revealing as indicators of adjustment for clinicians, therapists and researchers.

Appealing as the explanations of cognitive processes offered earlier are in attempting to interpret a large and complex data set, it should be noted that cognitive architecture can only be inferred as it cannot be directly observed. Concepts such as 'schemata' are to some extent notional, and the various processes and biases in attentional processes such as salience, valence, self-discrepancy and social comparison are inevitably somewhat contrived. In reality, they are interconnected, mutually dependent and overlapping. With these health warnings in mind, however, the results of the study have led us to revisit and recast the conceptual framework of adjustment presented in the introductory section earlier. In this revised model, the important role of appearance-specific cognitions is acknowledged and highlighted. Although the model is presented in a linear format, the dynamic nature of the self-system is also very evident in this and subsequent studies.

Variables other than the ones measured in this study are also certain to play some part in adjustment. Three main factors are usually presented as promoting resilience or vulnerability in the psychological literature (Luthar et al., 2000). These comprise the characteristics of the individual (cognitive functioning, personality variables, self-efficacy and self-perception), characteristics of the individual's family and the individual's social context. Resilience is a product of a mutual influence between these three factors, which may function as potential mediators or moderators of the relation between stressors, risks and outcomes. The collaboration chose to focus on those factors which are most amenable to intervention, and thus variables relating to family functioning and the influence of social context are not prominent in this work. In addition, in order to keep the burden of assessment at an acceptable level and to include measures which could offer a profile of positive as well as negative adjustment, difficult decisions were made and additional 'individual' factors which have featured in previous research, such as shame, were omitted from Study 1. Where these factors are apparent in the later follow-on studies, this is highlighted in later discussion.

Despite these omissions, the percentages of the variance explained by the variables that were included in the study are impressive, especially when viewed in relation to other comparable research.

Implications of the results

Advances in knowledge about the process and the consequences of cognitive mechanisms are of relevance to understanding the development and maintenance of appearance concerns in people with disfiguring conditions and are particularly useful in informing the development of interventions designed to meet the needs of those affected. The results of this study also emphasize the importance of understanding the subjective worlds of people with appearance concerns and the place of their subjective perceptions in their cognitive architecture. Taken with findings from previous research discussed earlier, it is clear that these are likely to be better indicators of the need for intervention than the aetiology and physical characteristics of the disfigurement.

As Rosser has recently noted (2008) in relation to the appearance concerns of people without disfigurements, more work is needed to examine in detail the influence and role of self-referent appearance-related information within the self-system and the influence of appearance-related information processing at all stages from attention to retrieval. However, the results of this study leave no doubt that appearance-specific cognitions play a significant role in the relative levels of adjustment and distress experienced by people with disfiguring conditions.

The conceptual framework used to guide this study (see Figure A1) was revisited in the light of these findings and in the light of the results from the additional studies outlined in the following. The revised framework is presented in the synthesis of results in Section 'Overall Synthesis of the Results of the Research Programme'.

Study 2: Qualitative Analysis of Free Text Responses to the Question 'Do You Have Any General Comments about the Way in Which Your Appearance Affects Your Life, whether Positively or Negatively?'

Study Lead: Antje Lindenmeyer.

Rationale and Findings

In an attempt to offer participants in Study 1 the opportunity to expand on their individual experiences and in order to supplement responses to standardized measures employed in Study 1 with qualitative data, an open-ended response question was included in the participant packs.

Thematic analysis was employed to analyze these open-ended responses (Braun & Clarke 2006). Two major themes were identified.

Theme 1: 'Falling Short of the Ideal'
Most participants described themselves as explicitly or implicitly falling short of an appearance ideal, in relation to their disfiguring condition, size (too big or too small) or shape. Some went beyond this, describing themselves as *'ugly', 'not looking right', 'deformed', 'unsightly', 'freakish', 'ruined', 'horrid'* or *'misshapen'* and using strong metaphors such as 'to describe their appearance. Many discussed the pressure of trying to match up to appearance ideals.

Theme 2: 'Personal Meanings of Appearance'
Sub-themes in this category included the following:

1. **Self and Appearance**. This encompassed expressions of disruption to the sense of self, resulting from negative emotions about appearance, and a sense that the person's true purpose in life had been thwarted or disrupted by their appearance, for example, in relation to a career or relationships.

> If I wasn't feeling so bad about my appearance, I could do anything I wanted;

> My appearance has meant I have never had a sexual relationship or a boyfriend.

These accounts included clear expressions of negative emotions such as self-hate and shame

> I hate the way my skin rules my life

> I hate the way I look; I hate myself

> I am ashamed of my appearance and it holds me back

and a sense that their real selves were 'hidden' behind their difference. Some spoke of resolving earlier difficulties positively.

> I do not feel I have let it stop me from living a full life

> It turned out OK with me getting a good job

2. The sub-theme *Other People's Responses* included reports of actual or anticipated comments, staring and bullying from others

    > I have spent my life being laughed at, pointed at and called names

    in addition to the importance of both positive and hurtful responses from partners, families and friends.

    > slight comments from [partner] really hurt, even if he says he's joking.

    The sense of being misjudged and/or misunderstood by others and of these misjudgements being attributed to the appearance of the participant was strong.

    > My appearance is the defining key to how others react and respond to me
    >
    > I know that others will judge me by my appearance and I resent this
    >
    > It only takes one event to knock my confidence

3. A variety of strategies for *Coping with Appearance* were evident in responses, including acceptance

    > This is who I am,

    attributing little importance to appearance, pragmatism

    > no use in feeling sorry for myself,

    covering up the perceived 'difference' from others and avoidance

    > I keep myself to myself. I now prefer solitary activities.

Discussion

Respondents wrote of a mix of appearance-related concerns, including those relating to disfigurement, weight/shape and also the effects of ageing. This is an important point. Professionals working in the area of disfigurement should note that appearance concerns may not be limited to the consequences of the disfiguring condition and these should not be addressed in isolation.

The pressure exerted by socio-cultural standards and the resulting 'self-ought' discrepancy are widely evident in the responses. These are particularly salient in the responses to Theme 1, focusing on the sense of falling short of societal ideals. The second theme illustrates the influence of appearance concerns on attributions for many aspects of the life course including disruption to employment and relationships. Change was seen to exacerbate distress, including the impact of life events, such as divorce and children leaving home, changes to social groupings and also changes in the status of their condition, for example, fluctuations in chronic conditions. For some, there was a sense that significant proportions of their lives had been dominated or given over to their appearance issue.

The impact of other people's reactions and judgements was also highlighted, and several respondents mentioned their concern about possible as well as actual responses. There is also a reminder within this theme that partners, families and friends can offer positive support but can also be unhelpful.

A wide range of coping strategies were mentioned. Effective techniques were reported to include acceptance, relegating the appearance concern to a low level of importance in the overall life experience and a sense of pragmatism. Others talked of coping less well and of hiding the feature(s) which were the focus of their appearance concern to the best of their ability.

Practical issues, such as the need for particular shoes or clothes, or the need to use makeup are mentioned, and many resented the time, effort and money required to deal with or disguise aspects of their appearance. Associated functional issues and pain relating to the underlying condition were also apparent, particularly in those with arthritis and for those with skin conditions.

These responses illuminate the quantitative data obtained in Study 1. They are also a reminder of the multi-factorial nature both of appearance dissatisfaction – which is often an amalgam of several issues, and to factors determining levels of adjustment to these issues. The responses were also illustrative of the dynamic nature of adjustment.

Study 3: Adjustment to Disfiguring Conditions over Time

Rationale and Results

Thompson and Kent (2001), Rumsey and Harcourt (2005) and Bessell and Moss (2007) and other commentators have noted the pressing need for longitudinal research to explore the extent of stability and change in adjustment to disfigurement over time. Study 3 reports a longitudinal study in which responses to standardized measures were repeated over a 9 month period. Study 4 comprises qualitative data derived from in-depth interviews of a subsection of respondents who identified themselves as stable in their adjustment and those who perceived their adjustment levels to have changed.

All participants who opted to take part in further studies were sent a follow-up questionnaire pack at 9 months (see Section Methods of Study 1). A total of 349 completed questionnaires were returned. There was no statistically significant difference between those who responded at time 2 compared to the total sample in relation to gender ($\chi^2 = 2.707$, $df = 1$, $p = 0.100$), method of recruitment ($\chi^2 = 0.691$, $df = 1$, $p = 0.406$) or objective visibility ($\chi^2 = 0.347$, $df = 1$, $p = 0.556$). Independent-samples t-test reveals that those who responded at follow-up had a significantly higher mean level of appearance discrepancy ($p < 0.001$) and valence ($p = 0.002$) than those who did not respond, although the effects sizes were small ($d = 0.24$).

Longitudinal Changes
Table B1 summarizes the correlations between scores on measures at time 1 (baseline) and time 2 (follow-up) and the mean differences between scores on measures at time 1 (baseline) and time 2 (follow-up). All correlations (Pearson's r) given in Table B1 were statistically significant $p < 0.001$.

Also given is the test–retest intraclass correlation coefficient (ICC) for scores at the first and second time points. In this case, the ICC1 is numerically equivalent to Cronbach's alpha and all

Table B1 Descriptive and inferential statistics for responders at follow-up (*p*-value for paired samples *t*-test).

	Correlation		Differences		
	r	*ICC1*	*Mean*	*SD*	*P*
Discrepancy	0.688	0.816	−0.36	9.00	0.469
Optimism	0.776	0.873	0.11	2.31	0.374
Support satisfaction	0.596	0.747	0.25	4.69	0.323
Social comparison	0.675	0.806	0.06	5.88	0.861
Valence	0.738	0.849	−0.33	5.71	0.281
Salience	0.719	0.835	0.18	6.00	0.579
Fear of negative evaluation	0.757	0.861	0.60	7.54	0.143
Social anxiety and avoidance	0.841	0.913	1.18	9.21	0.017
Anxiety	0.768	0.869	0.20	3.16	0.245
Depression	0.746	0.853	0.17	2.82	0.256
Aggression	0.798	0.888	−0.06	5.98	0.858
Positive affect	0.633	0.775	0.64	7.48	0.113
Negative affect	0.729	0.843	0.30	6.73	0.416

values for ICC1 given in Table B1 are statistically significant, $p < 0.001$. There were no statistically significant changes in key outcomes other than on the DAS24 for which a small but statistically significant increase in mean scores was observed ($p = 0.017$, $d = 0.12$).

Predictors of Adjustment at Follow-Up

Social Anxiety and Social Avoidance (DAS24)
At the 9-month follow-up point, 70.7% of the variance in DAS24 scores was accounted for by the regression model given in Table B2 and this effect was statistically significant, $R^2 = 0.707$, $F(16, 262) = 39.599$, $MSE = 80.24$, $p < 0.001$.

In comparison to the model for the baseline data, there remain statistically significant effects for gender, optimism, fear of negative evaluation, social acceptance, valence and appearance discrepancy, with the direction of the effects remaining the same. For the baseline data, age, objective visibility, satisfaction with social support and salience were all statistically significant predictors of scores on the DAS24; however, these effects were no longer significant for the longitudinal data. No additional variables were significant longitudinally compared to the baseline model.

Anxiety (HADS)
For the longitudinal sample, 54.5% of the variance in anxiety was accounted for by the regression model given in Table B3 and this effect was statistically significant, $R^2 = 0.545$, $F(16, 279) = 19.674$, $MSE = 10.10$, $p < 0.001$.

When comparing the model for the baseline data with the model given in the following, there remain statistically significant effects for optimism, fear of negative evaluation, social acceptance and salience, with the direction of the effects remaining the same. At baseline, satisfaction with social support, social comparison and visibility when clothed were all significant predictors but this was

Table B2 Regression model for DAS24.

Variable	Coef	Std error	Beta	T	P	VIF	ΔR^2	P
Constant	41.04	7.421		5.53	<0.001			
Age	−0.070	0.044	0.065	−1.57	0.118	1.521		
Gender								
Male	—	—	—	—	—			
Female	3.623	1.390	0.094	2.61	0.010	1.161		
Recruitment								
Community	—	—	—	—	—			
Clinic	1.286	1.136	0.040	1.13	0.258	1.120		
Living Status								
Alone	—	—	—	—	—			
With friends	2.779	2.072	0.056	1.34	0.181	1.557		
With partner	2.690	1.387	0.079	1.94	0.053	1.494	0.192	<0.001
Objective Visibility								
No	—	—	—	—	—			
Yes	−1.320	1.192	−0.041	−1.11	0.269	1.232	0.193	0.665
Optimism	−0.651	0.219	0.145	−2.97	0.003	2.125	0.265	<0.001
Fear of negative evaluation	0.292	0.078	0.187	3.76	<0.001	2.224		
Social acceptance	−1.565	0.255	−0.283	−6.13	<0.001	1.904		
Satisfaction with social support	−0.183	0.120	−0.060	−1.52	0.129	1.388	0.169	<0.001
Salience	0.141	0.091	0.065	1.56	0.120	1.572		
Valence	0.421	0.108	0.204	3.89	<0.001	2.469		
Discrepancy	0.173	0.071	0.119	2.45	0.015	2.106		
Social comparison	−0.022	0.095	−0.010	−0.235	0.814	1.598		
Disguisability								
Less difficult	—	—	—	—	—			
Reported difficult	3.552	1.333	0.111	2.66	0.008	1.545		
Visibility when clothed								
Not/mild	—	—	—	—	—			
Moderate/severe	−2.483	−1.360	0.077	−1.83	0.69	1.607	0.081	<0.001

not the case in the longitudinal data. There was a small statistically significant effect due to age which did not feature in the baseline model but otherwise no additional variables were significant longitudinally compared to the model based on scores at baseline.

Depression (HADS)

For depression, 51.5% of the variance was accounted for by the regression model given in Table B4 and this effect was statistically significant, $R^2 = 0.515$, $F(16, 263) = 17.460$, $MSE = 8.19$, $p < 0.001$.

When comparing the model for the baseline data with the model given earlier, statistically significant effects remained for age, optimism and social acceptance with the direction of the effects remaining the same. At baseline, gender, fear of negative evaluation, satisfaction with social support

Table B3   Regression model for anxiety.

Variable	Coef	Std error	Beta	T	p	VIF	ΔR²	P
Constant	7.887	2.633		3.00	0.003			
Age	0.033	0.016	0.108	2.12	0.035	1.501		
Gender								
Male	—	—	—	—	—			
Female	0.209	0.492	0.019	0.42	0.672	1.156		
Recruitment								
Community	—	—	—	—	—			
Clinic	−0.335	0.402	−0.037	−0.83	0.406	1.121		
Living status								
Alone	—	—	—	—	—			
With friends	0.685	0.724	0.049	0.95	0.345	1.548		
With partner	0.750	0.492	0.078	1.53	0.128	1.503	0.067	0.002
Objective visibility								
No	—	—	—	—	—			
Yes	−0.138	0.421	−0.015	−0.33	0.744	1.224	0.002	0.489
Optimism	−0.470	0.078	−0.367	−6.05	<0.001	2.133	0.366	<0.001
Fear of negative evaluation	0.072	0.028	0.161	2.60	0.010	2.23		
Social acceptance	−0.278	0.090	−0.178	−3.09	0.002	1.917		
Satisfaction with social support	−0.041	0.043	−0.047	−0.95	0.341	1.397	0.078	<0.001
Salience	0.114	0.032	0.185	3.54	<0.001	1.574		
Valence	0.024	0.038	0.041	0.63	0.528	2.462		
Appearance Discrepancy	−0.019	0.025	−0.045	−0.744	0.458	2.087		
Social comparison	0.052	0.034	0.082	1.56	0.121	1.599		
Disguisability								
Less difficult	—	—	—	—	—			
Reported difficult	−0.153	0.473	−0.017	−0.32	0.747	1.550		
Visibility when clothed								
Not/mild	—	—	—	—	—			
Moderate/severe	0.156	0.481	0.017	0.32	0.747	1.605	0.032	0.006

and valence were all significant predictors but this was not the case for the longitudinal data. No additional variables were significant longitudinally compared to the baseline model.

Aggression

For aggression, 32.9% of the variance at time 2 was accounted for by the regression model given in Table B5 and the effect was statistically significant, $R^2 = 0.329$, $F(6, 263) = 8.062$, $MSE = 65.987$, $p < 0.001$.

When comparing this model to the model for the baseline data, only optimism remained statistically significant with the direction of the effect remaining the same. At baseline age, gender, satisfaction with social support and social comparison were all significant predictors but this was not the case for the longitudinal data. No additional variables were significant longitudinally compared to the baseline model.

Table B4 Regression model for depression.

Variable	Coef	Std error	Beta	T	p	VIF	ΔR²	P
Constant	13.828	2.371		5.83	<0.001			
Age	0.028	0.014	0.104	1.99	0.048	1.501		
Gender								
Male	—	—	—	—	—			
Female	0.519	0.443	0.054	1.17	0.242	1.156		
Recruitment								
Community	—	—	—	—	—			
Clinic	0.380	0.362	0.048	1.05	0.296	1.121		
Living status								
Alone	—	—	—	—	—			
With friends	0.497	0.652	0.041	0.76	0.446	1.548		
With partner	0.737	0.443	0.088	1.66	0.097	1.503	0.042	0.035
Objective visibility								
No	—	—	—	—	—			
Yes	0.154	0.379	0.019	0.41	0.685	1.224	0.002	0.418
Optimism	−0.533	0.070	−0.478	−7.62	<0.001	2.133	0.389	<0.001
Fear of negative evaluation	0.026	0.025	0.067	1.05	0.296	2.227		
Social acceptance	−0.397	0.081	−0.290	−4.89	<0.001	1.917		
Satisfaction with social support	−0.008	0.038	−0.011	−0.22	0.826	1.397	0.069	<0.001
Salience	−0.015	0.029	−0.027	−0.50	0.615	1.574		
Valence	0.032	0.034	0.062	0.92	0.259	2.462		
Appearance Discrepancy	0.016	0.022	0.044	0.72	0.475	2.087		
Social comparison	−0.027	0.030	−0.047	−0.87	0.383	1.599		
Disguisability								
Less difficult	—	—	—	—	—			
Reported difficult	0.366	0.426	0.046	0.86	0.391	1.550		
Visibility when clothed								
Not/mild	—	—	—	—	—			
Moderate/severe	−0.628	0.434	−0.079	−1.45	0.148	1.605	0.013	0.325

Positive Affect

For positive affect, 36.8% of the variance was accounted for by the regression model given in Table B6 and this effect was statistically significant, $R^2 = 0.368$, $F(16, 260) = 9.465$, $MSE = 47.506$, $p < 0.001$.

When comparing this model to the one for the baseline data, optimism, fear of negative evaluation and social comparison remain statistically significant at time 2 with the direction of the effect remaining the same. At baseline, salience and valence were significant predictors but this was not the case for the longitudinal data. No additional variables were significant longitudinally compared to the baseline model. In this fitted model, those living with friends or partner scored significantly lower than those living alone and this effect was not detected in the original baseline model.

Table B5   Regression model for aggression.

Variable	Coef	Std error	Beta	T	p	VIF	ΔR²	P
Constant	38.79	6.729		5.76	<0.001			
Age	−073	0.040	−0.113	−1.83	0.068	1.501		
Gender								
Male	—	—	—	—	—			
Female	0.188	1.257	0.008	0.15	0.881	1.156		
Recruitment								
Community	—	—	—	—	—			
Clinic	0.163	1.028	0.008	0.16	0.874	1.121		
Living status								
Alone	—	—	—	—	—			
With friends	0.124	1.849	0.004	0.07	0.946	1.548		
With partner	2.053	1.257	0.101	1.63	0.104	1.503	0.095	<0.001
Objective visibility								
No	—	—	—	—	—			
Yes	0.002	1.076	0.000	0.00	0.999	1.224	0.001	0.631
Optimism	−1.189	0.199	−0.441	−5.98	<0.001	2.133	0.210	<0.001
Fear of negative evaluation	0.086	0.070	0.092	1.22	0.223	2.227		
Social acceptance	0.233	0.230	0.071	1.01	0.312	1.917		
Satisfaction with social support	−0.155	0.109	−0.085	−1.43	0.155	1.397	0.017	0.080
Salience	0.017	0.082	0.013	0.21	0.835	1.574		
Valence	0.041	0.098	0.033	0.42	0.674	2.462		
Appearance Discrepancy	−0.075	0.064	−0.086	−1.17	0.242	2.087		
Social comparison	0.064	0.086	0.048	0.75	0.456	1.599		
Disguisability								
Less difficult	—	—	—	—	—			
Reported difficult	−0.157	1.209	−0.008	−0.130	0.896	1.550		
Visibility when clothed								
Not/mild	—	—	—	—	—			
Moderate/severe	0.350	1.20	0.018	0.284	0.776	1.605	0.006	0.891

Negative Affect

In negative affect, 55.8% of the variance was accounted for by the regression model given in Table B7 and this effect was statistically significant, $R^2 = 0.558$, $F(16, 260) = 20.533$, $MSE = 40.045$, $p < 0.001$.

In comparison to the model for the baseline data, there remained statistically significant effects for optimism, fear of negative evaluation and social acceptance with the direction of the effects also the same. At baseline, age, satisfaction with social support and social comparison were all significant predictors but this was not the case for the longitudinal data. This second model detected a small but statistically significant positive effect of negative affect which was not detected in the original baseline model. No additional variables were significant longitudinally compared to the baseline model.

Table B6   Regression model for positive affect.

Variable	Coef	Std error	Beta	T	p	VIF	ΔR²	P
Constant	18.348	5.753		3.19	0.002			
Age	−0.059	0.034	−0.104	−1.73	0.086	1.495		
Gender								
Male	—	—	—	—	—			
Female	−1.443	1.069	−0.072	−1.35	0.178	1.158		
Recruitment								
Community	—	—	—	—	—			
Clinic	−0.652	0.881	−0.039	−0.74	0.460	1.130		
Living status								
Alone	—	—	—	—	—			
With friends	−3.015	1.570	−0.118	−1.92	0.056	1.547		
With partner	−2.278	1.067	−0.129	−2.13	0.034	1.496	0.095	<0.001
Objective visibility								
No	—	—	—	—	—			
Yes	−1.514	0.917	−0.090	−1.65	0.100	1.223	0.001	0.631
Optimism	0.768	0.169	0.325	4.55	<0.001	2.094	0.210	<0.001
Fear of negative evaluation	−0.275	0.060	−0.336	−4.59	<0.001	2.202		
Social acceptance	0.586	0.196	0.203	2.99	0.003	1.907		
Satisfaction with social support	0.121	0.092	0.076	1.31	0.193	1.389	0.017	<0.001
Salience	0.088	0.070	0.077	1.25	0.214	1.584		
Valence	0.018	0.083	0.017	0.22	0.827	2.410		
Appearance Discrepancy	−0.010	0.054	−0.014	−0.19	0.847	2.050		
Social comparison	0.207	0.073	0.176	2.81	0.005	1.603		
Disguisability								
Less difficult	—	—	—	—	—			
Reported difficult	0.068	1.030	0.004	0.066	0.948	1.544		
Visibility when clothed								
Not/mild	—	—	—	—	—			
Moderate/severe	1.080	1.050	0.064	1.029	0.305	1.607	0.006	<0.001

Changes in Adjustment

Changes in outcome measures from baseline to 9 month follow-up were calculated and then related to demographics, dispositional style, socio-cognitive factors and appearance cognitions. In the following, absolute changes in outcome measures are considered; the greater the absolute change the greater the variation on that measure. Relative changes in the absolute change are related to factors recorded at baseline.

Social Anxiety and Social Avoidance (DAS24)

Changes from baseline to follow-up in scores on the DAS24 were found to be negatively correlated with age ($r = −0.158$, $n = 342$, $p = 0.003$, two-sided), social acceptance ($r = −0.241$, $n = 345$, $p = 0.016$) and optimism ($r = −0.183$, $n = 344$, $p = 0.001$). Scores were positively correlated

Table B7 Regression model for negative affect.

Variable	Coef	Std error	Beta	T	p	VIF	ΔR^2	P
Constant	23.481	5.282		4.44	<0.001			
Age	0.012	0.031	0.019	0.38	0.702	1.495		
Gender								
Male	—	—	—	—	—			
Female	0.695	0.982	0.031	0.71	0.480	1.158		
Recruitment								
Community	—	—	—	—	—			
Clinic	0.620	0.809	0.034	0.77	0.44	1.130		
Family								
Alone	—	—	—	—	—			
With friends	−0.817	1.441	−0.029	−0.57	0.571	1.547		
With partner	−0.686	0.980	−0.035	−0.70	0.484	1.496	0.094	<0.001
Objective visibility								
No	—	—	—	—	—			
Yes	0.330	0.842	0.018	0.39	0.696	1.223	0.010	0.001
Optimism	−0.991	0.155	−0.381	−6.39	<0.001	2.094	0.208	<0.001
Fear of negative evaluation	0.249	0.055	0.277	4.52	<0.001	2.202		
Social acceptance	−0.368	0.180	−0.116	−3.04	0.042	1.907		
Satisfaction with social support	−0.081	0.085	−0.046	−0.95	0.341	1.389	0.125	<0.001
Salience	0.141	0.065	0.113	2.18	0.030	1.584		
Valence	−0.055	0.076	−0.046	−0.72	0.472	2.410		
Appearance discrepancy	0.041	0.050	0.049	0.83	0.410	2.050		
Social comparison	0.043	0.067	0.033	0.64	0.522	1.603		
Disguisability								
Less difficult	—	—	—	—	—			
Reported difficult	−1.637	0.945	−0.089	−1.73	0.084	1.544		
Visibility when clothed								
Not/mild	—	—	—	—	—			
Moderate/severe	0.858	0.964	0.046	0.89	0.374	1.607	0.007	0.005

with appearance discrepancy ($r = 0.129$, $n = 345$, $p = 0.016$), valence ($r = 0.211$, $n = 349$, $p < 0.001$), salience ($r = 0.153$, $n = 346$, $p = 0.004$) and fear of negative evaluation ($r = 0.136$, $n = 346$, $p = 0.012$).

These results suggest that younger, pessimistic people, who do not feel socially accepted, who self-report a large discrepancy from the norm and who worry about what others think and place a high value on appearance, are more likely to change on the DAS24. However, in a multiple regression analysis, only perceived social acceptance was a significant predictor of absolute changes in DAS24 (i.e. after accounting for the effect of social acceptance, no other variable provides an additional contribution to the absolute changes in scores on the DAS 24).

Anxiety

Changes in scores relating to anxiety between baseline and follow-up were found to be negatively correlated with age ($r = -0.179$, $n = 345$, $p = 0.001$, two-sided) and optimism ($r = -0.117$, $n = 347$, $p = 0.001$) and positively associated with social comparisons ($r = 0.134$, $n = 349$, $p = 0.012$, two-sided).

These results suggest that younger, pessimistic people, who compare themselves to others, are more likely to experience change in anxiety. However, age is the dominant factor and is the only variable predictive of absolute changes in anxiety in a multiple regression analysis.

Depression

Changes in scores relating to depression between baseline and follow-up were found to be negatively correlated with age ($r = -0.174$, $n = 345$, $p = 0.001$, two-sided), social acceptance ($r = -0.143$, $n = 348$, $p = 0.007$), optimism ($r = -0.203$, $n = 347$, $p < 0.001$) and satisfaction with social support ($r = -0.115$, $n = 346$, $p = 0.033$) and positively associated with appearance discrepancy ($r = 0.150$, $n = 348$, $p = 0.005$), valence ($r = 0.186$, $n = 352$, $p < 0.001$) and fear of negative evaluation ($r = 0.113$, $n = 349$, $p = 0.035$, two-sided).

These results suggest that younger, pessimistic people, who do not feel socially accepted, who are less satisfied with their social support, who self-report a large discrepancy from the norm and who evaluate their appearance negatively and fear negative evaluations from others, are more likely to experience a change in depression. Optimism was the best predictor. In the multiple regression model, no variable made a significant additional contribution to the prediction of the absolute change in scores on depression after the inclusion of optimism.

Aggression

Changes from baseline to follow-up in aggression were found to be negatively associated with optimism ($r = -0.232$, $n = 344$, $p < 0.001$) and positively associated with social comparison ($r = 0.187$, $n = 346$, $p < 0.001$, two-sided) and salience ($r = 0.134$, $n = 347$, $p = 0.013$, two-sided).

These results suggest that more pessimistic people, who compare themselves to others and place a high value on appearance, experience a change in aggression. Optimism was the best predictor, and in a multiple regression model, both optimism and social comparison were statistically significant predictors of absolute changes in aggression ($R^2 = 0.266$, $F(2,316) = 12.042$, $MSE = 16.801$, $p < 0.001$).

Positive Affect

None of the variables were significantly correlated with absolute changes in positive affect.

Negative Affect

Changes from baseline to follow-up in negative affect were found to be negatively associated with age ($r = -0.169$, $n = 334$, $p = 0.002$), social acceptance ($r = -0.213$, $n = 336$, $p < 0.001$), optimism ($r = -0.257$, $n = 336$, $p < 0.001$) and satisfaction with social support ($r = -0.123$, $n = 335$, $p = 0.025$, two-sided) and positively associated with appearance discrepancy ($r = 0.227$, $n = 336$, $p < 0.001$, two-sided), valence ($r = 0.212$, $n = 340$, $p < 0.001$), social comparison ($r = 0.163$, $n = 338$, $p = 0.003$), salience ($r = 0.182$, $n = 337$, $p = 0.001$, two-sided) and fear of negative evaluation ($r = 0.261$, $n = 340$, $p < 0.001$).

These results suggest that younger, pessimistic people, who do not feel socially accepted and are less satisfied with their social support and self-report a large appearance discrepancy from the norm, negatively evaluate their own appearance, place a high value on appearance and fear negative evaluations from others, are more likely to experience change in negative affect. Optimism and appearance discrepancy were the best two predictors and both were jointly predictive of absolute change in negative affect in the multiple regression ($R^2 = 0.098$, $F(2, 313) = 16.935$, $MSE = 20.779$, $p < 0.001$).

Discussion

The findings of this longitudinal study offer further strong support for the consensus framework developed to guide this research programme. Indeed, the regression model accounted for a very impressive 70.7% of variation in the DAS24 at 9 month follow-up – a figure that is even greater than the (already very sizeable) variance accounted for at baseline. Furthermore, the majority of the components that predicted appearance-related anxiety at baseline continued to do so at follow-up and there was also a high degree of consistency in the predictors of anxiety and depression, aggression, positive affect and negative affect at both baseline and follow-up.

Overall, the results of this study indicated a picture of stability rather than change over the 9 month follow-up period; mean scores on most outcome measures changed relatively little over time (although there was a small, significant increase in mean DAS scores between baseline and follow-up). However, focusing on the relatively consistent mean scores detracts from the fact that many participants did record a change in self-reported outcomes over time. Participants who reported a change tended to be younger, have a more pessimistic outlook and be more affected by appearance cognitions (salience and discrepancy) and the views of others (feeling socially excluded and more bothered by others' judgements of them). This follow-up data therefore supports the findings of the initial cross-sectional study in identifying socio-cognitive factors as appropriate targets for change in supportive interventions. However, as with the cross-sectional study, it would be an error to assume from these findings that appearance-related distress and concerns are not an issue for older people.

This sample represented 27.5% of the total sample of Study 1. Analyses indicated that in the main the respondents were representative of the original sample. The degree of importance placed on appearance was greater at baseline amongst those choosing to participate in the follow-up study than amongst non-respondents. They also had a greater discrepancy between self and ideal self. These differences may indicate that those with a heavier emphasis on appearance in their self-definitions and view of the world may be more engaged with research in this area than those who are resilient to appearance-related distress (Rumsey & Harcourt, 2005).

This sample of 349 constitutes the largest longitudinal sample to date; however, more longitudinal research is needed. Study 4 addresses the need for an investigation into people's subjective experiences of change over time.

Study 4: Experiences and Adjustment in People with Visible Difference over Time – A Qualitative Study

Study Leads: Andrew Thompson, Sally-Ann Clarke, Elizabeth Jenkinson & Hayley McBain.

Small-scale longitudinal qualitative studies have followed-up people with visible difference over time. Most notably the early work of MacGregor (1990) involved interviews over a 16 year period.

However, this work has not focused on adaptation over the course of time and the relationship of adjustment to events in the person's life. Little is known about the course of psychological adjustment to appearance over time and factors which facilitate positive coping. In particular, research exploring the subjective aspects of this experience is lacking. Accordingly, this study adopted a specific focus on the qualitative accounts of participants' perceptions of the factors associated with better or worse adaptation to their appearance over time.

Twenty-six participants were purposively selected from those who had previously completed the ARC battery of psychometric measures at baseline and follow-up at 9 months (Studies 1 and 3), on the basis of their self-categorization into one of four groups of adjustment ('well-adjusted stable', 'distressed stable', 'improvement in adjustment' or 'deterioration in adjustment'). Semi-structured interviews were conducted based on a schedule developed on the basis of a priori themes emerging from previous studies of visible difference. Template analysis (King 1998), was used to explore and refine themes derived from the aims of the research programme and the conceptual model used in Study 1, namely, predisposing factors to different levels of adjustment, intervening cognitive processes associated with different levels of adjustment and outcomes associated with different levels of adjustment.

In relation to 'predisposing factors', participants in all groups reported a range of life stressors, including financial (unemployment, time away from work due to poor health), social difficulties (relationship and family) and health concerns (pain, disability). Participants in all groups also reported appearance-related stressors, including perceptions of negative reactions to their appearance from others. Daily hassles were common across all groups. Negative life events appeared to be associated with greater appearance salience, larger perceived differences in appearance compared with the norm, a greater sense of identity loss and a stronger sense of disruption to the self-concept to a greater extent in those who defined themselves as having a deterioration in adjustment than in other self-selected adjustment groups; however, there were no notable differences in the frequency or type of stressors experienced between the groups, suggesting that adjustment over time is better explained by intervening psychological factors.

When examining responses in relation to 'intervening cognitive processes' those in the 'well-adjusted, stable' group reported greater cognitive flexibility in relation to their core views of themselves and of their appearance. They also reported making external attributions in the appraisal of the reactions of others

> They think your burns are disgusting … they think somehow they are contagious …. they are just generally bigots mate, but some are a bit slow, they live in a boring little town.

and to have developed coping skills that boosted self-efficacy. Their 'difference' was only peripheral to their definitions of self. This contrasted with the distressed (stable) group or deteriorated group.

> I feel ugly … really really ugly. Just other people looking at me, how I feel in myself, it's sort of like a self-conscious thing.

Those in the well-adjusted (stable) group reported a high level of engagement in social behaviour and a low level of engagement in avoidance strategies, whereas the other groups reported low levels of engagement and use of avoidance in coping. These positive copers made downward social comparisons.

There's always someone worse off than yourself, you see it all of the time and you thank your lucky stars you're not them.

Those who classified themselves as distressed (over time, or more recently) had an idealized view of others.

I think I've let it get on top of me and I think I'm weak for letting that happen … you see other people on the telly … or hear stories about what other people have gone through … and I get angry with myself thinking you're an idiot …. silly for letting it get on top of you.

Maintaining stability of positive adjustment was described as exerting an ongoing demand on resources, but the stable well-adjusted group considered the demands to be within their control. They actively sought to overcome challenges and recognized that positive adjustment required investment. The concept of self-efficacy distinguishes this group from the stable distressed group.

I'm in charge …. I think that's the way I've lived my life. Get on with it and do the best you can … sod em and get on with it.

The latter group reported a more passive approach to the challenges posed by difference.

I think because my skin has been bad for so long …. I think I've just come to accept that it's bad … and that's why I've let it get on top of me …. so because it's bad, I shouldn't go out, or mix much.

In relation to responses relevant to the outcomes element of the framework, social interaction skills appeared to be crucial in relation to outcomes in all groups. The ability to interact with others, to confront issues of differences in appearance and to enlist support when necessary distinguished between those who self-identified as well adjusted

The benefits of wearing a short sleeved shirt in the summer out-weigh any other sort of concern.

or distressed.

I don't seem to have the confidence to let other people see it.

Improvement was associated with good aesthetic outcomes following treatment, greater awareness of cognitive coping strategies and effective social and professional support. Deterioration in adjustment was associated with the occurrence of negative life events, and an increase in appearance salience due to a range of factors (i.e. the reactions of others, functional disability, the need for further treatment). Those coping well were more likely to be engaged socially and to report behaviours and attitudes inconsistent with cognitive and behavioural avoidance relating to the disfigurement.

Questionnaire data (from Study 3) were examined for participants within each group. There were discrepancies between the participants' self-reported perceptions of adjustment and their scores on psychometric measures, particularly for the stable well-adjusted and improvement groups. For example, despite having self-selected as 'coping well', three participants scored within the clinical range for anxiety and depression at both data collection points. There was also a wide range of scores on social anxiety and avoidance and in relation to fear of negative evaluation for participants in this group.

The study reinforces and exemplifies findings in the related quantitative cross-sectional and longitudinal surveys and has implications for our understanding of adaptation to visible difference over time and how to shape appropriate support and intervention. There were also striking variations in the pictures of adjustment over time offered by scores derived from standardized measures and respondents' self-reported adjustment status, offering support for the value of mixed methods studies and the imperative of assessing subjective perceptions of adjustment. The findings added support for an approach to intervention which includes addressing core beliefs relating to the role of appearance and its contribution to the self-system, the importance of behavioural experimentation in mediating and changing such beliefs and the role of social perception and interaction in successful adaption.

Follow-On Studies (5–12)

The follow-on studies were developed in order to expand understanding in relation to key aspects of the overall research framework (**Study 5: A Qualitative Study of the Experiences of People who Identify Themselves as Having Adjusted Positively to a Visible Difference**) or particular elements of the framework that have been under-researched in the past, such as the impact of ethnic group membership (**Study 6: Focus Groups to Examine the Views of People from Ethnic Minority Communities Concerning Facial Disfigurements and Other Forms of Visible Differences; Study 7: A Qualitative Study Exploring the Experiences of UK South Asians Living with Vitiligo**) and appearance concerns and aggression (**Study 8: Appearance Concern, Hostility and Social Situations**).

Condition-specific population groups about whom little research exists were also targeted as being worthy of exploratory study. Patients seeking treatment for arthritis have commented to several of the authors that their appearance concerns are rarely addressed in the health care system (**Study 11: In the Context of Rheumatoid Arthritis, Does Appearance Matter?**). The role of the combination of functional needs and appearance concerns in people with a prosthesis has been alluded to by researchers in the past, yet remains under-researched (**Study 12: Women with Limb Prostheses: Experiences and Adjustment**). The Advisory Panel encouraged the collaboration to consider the impact of appearance concerns on intimate situations (**Study 9: Developing a Scale to Measure the Impact of Appearance Concerns on Intimate Behaviours**) and also highlighted the lack of knowledge and understanding about the psychosocial consequences of disfigurement and appearance concerns amongst GPs – the primary gatekeepers to services (**Study 12: Working with Patients with Visible Differences: General Practitioners' Beliefs, Decision-Making Processes and Training Needs**). The follow-on studies also reflected the personal research interests of the members of the collaboration.

Study 5: A Qualitative Study of the Experiences of People Who Identify Themselves as Having Adjusted Positively to a Visible Difference

Study lead: Diana Harcourt

Acknowledgement: The focus groups and data analysis were conducted by Katie Egan.
An article based on this work has been published (Egan et al., 2011).

To date, the majority of research in the field of visible difference has focused on the experiences of people who report having problems such as difficulties in social situations and on negative outcomes, such as anxiety and depression. However, many people living with a visible difference do not report such problems. For example, whilst 30–50% of participants in a study of 650 people with a visible difference reported significant levels of distress (Rumsey et al., 2004), the majority (50–70%) did not. Furthermore, more than 70% of respondents to a survey by the Cleft Lip and Palate Association reported positive consequences of having their cleft. Further, Thompson et al. (2002) reported that some people with vitiligo spontaneously developed coping strategies not unlike those used within treatment. More, recently, Saradijian et al. (2007) reported that some people using a prosthesis were using a variety of strategies to minimize their distress. Thompson & Broom (2009) purposively selected people who identified themselves as coping well with a disfigurement and found a range of adaptive coping strategies being used.

Clearly, many people do deal positively with the challenges they face and succeed in minimizing the impact of their visible difference (Rumsey, 2002). Yet, prior to this research programme, the factors contributing to positive adjustment have been poorly understood. It has also been suggested by Eiserman (2001) that it is unethical to focus on pathology and not to consider positive aspects and outcomes of the experience of living with a visible difference. Whilst some research has examined positive aspects of chronic illness including benefit finding and adversarial growth (e.g. Petrie et al., 1999; Sodergren & Hyland, 2000; Sodergren et al., 2004), there is currently very limited research focusing on visible difference. The little research which has been conducted has shown that humour, a good sense of self, family support and faith all contributed to resilience and success amongst individuals with Moebius syndrome (Meyerson, 2001) and inner strength and a valued social circle were identified in those with a craniofacial difference (Eiserman, 2001). These studies and others (e.g. Fortune et al., 2005) have focused on specific conditions as opposed to visible difference more generally.

This study aimed to explore the experiences of people reporting positive consequences of having a visible difference and identifying themselves as having positively adjusted to living with an appearance that differs from 'the norm'.

Focus groups and interviews were conducted with 12 participants recruited from the original sample who had identified as having adjusted. The participants were aged 31–80 years and had a variety of visible differences. The transcripts were analyzed using inductive thematic analysis (Braun & Clarke, 2006).

Four main themes emerged from the data: attaching little significance to appearance *(being yourself with it…not hiding away or being embarrassed by it)*, personal growth, relationships with others being unaffected by appearance and adopting a range of coping strategies including acceptance, positivity, a good sense of humour, determination, and tackling things on a daily basis. *(I've just learned to accept that you know, I can't change it … don't hide it, just get out there and enjoy your life and basically be positive; It would be easy to hang every bad day on your disfigurement …. whereas actually it could be a multitude of other things causing it; To my recollection, I've never said 'why me?' … why not me is more the case).* Resilience, determination, positivity, downward comparisons, social support, spirituality, humour, taking things day-by-day, taking responsibility, distraction, and helping others were seen as paramount to positive adjustment.

The findings provide insight into the behaviours, personal outlooks and broad range of cognitive strategies that may contribute to adaptive coping and the themes could usefully be explained in more depth. They also reinforced the need for intervention strategies focusing on cognitive processing, including strategies to encourage individuals to identify positive consequences of the disfigurement and to avoid attributing problems to their appearance.

Study 6: Focus Group Studies of the Views of People from Ethnic Minority Community about Disfigurement

Study leads: Rodger Charlton, Krysia Saul & Nichola Rumsey.
A paper based on this study has been published (Hughes et al., 2009).

Acknowledgement: The data collection an analyses were conducted by Jennifer Hughes, Heidi Williamson, Emma Thomas and was facilitated by Mark Johnson.

There is a paucity of research exploring the views of different cultural and ethnic groups concerning individuals with visible difference. As few standardized appearance measures have been translated, most appearance-related research has been conducted in English speaking cultures (predominantly the United States and the United Kingdom) and with individuals who have a good command of the English language.

People of South Asian descent, that is, those ethnic groups originating from the Indian subcontinent, constitute one of the largest ethnic minority groups in the United Kingdom, encompassing 4% of the total population. It is important to be aware that this group is diverse, as it includes people who speak different languages, possess varying literacy rates, have different religious beliefs and who are from different cultural heritages. The heterogeneity of this group cannot be overemphasized.

Exploring the views of the South Asian populations regarding visible differences is a priority given that issues of disfigurement, stigma and shame may be particularly bound to membership of specific cultural and ethnic groupings (Papadopoulos et al., 1999). This study was therefore designed to examine the views of UK South Asian communities towards individuals with visible differences.

Nine focus groups were conducted with 63 participants representing 4 South Asian communities (Indian Hindu, Indian Sikh, Bangladeshi Muslim, Pakistani Muslim) on the topic of facial disfigurement and visible difference. The discussion was conducted in the native language of the groups. Following translation and transcription, the data were analyzed using template analysis (Kent 2000).

Eight key themes were identified including **definitions of disfigurement** (which commonly associate visible differences with intellectual and physical disability or a 'poor' character), **beliefs about the cause of the visible difference** (*This is God's way of punishing you*), **the consequences of disfigurement** (*Parents would be worried about their child's marriage; they will lack confidence. They might be isolated by others but they will also isolate themselves*), **reactions from others** (*People would stare; You'll never get someone with a disfigurement on a stage*), **social exposure of people with disfigurement** (*We feel conscious about taking them into the public and being ridiculed, so for that reason we would not take them out much; They hide them away because they see it as kind of a shameful and embarrassing thing*), **cultural and generational differences** (*We [the young] understand how things work, how society thinks, whereas they [older people] are stuck in their own times*) and **attitudes towards medical interventions** (*It is right to do surgical reconstruction but wrong to do cosmetic surgery. It is a great sin to try to change the way of looks. Allah will punish them*).

The focus group interviews offered a unique insight into views regarding visible differences held by South Asian communities in the United Kingdom. A number of themes were identified, some of

Table C1	Interventions suggested by Bengali older females.

- The myths about the foetal disorders should be dispelled.
- Posters can help.
- Bengali health sessions should be arranged more to raise awareness.
- City council can arrange different 'talks' and trainings to encourage people to bring light to these matters.
- Social workers play a very important role. Children in schools can be made more aware of these issues. Social circles can be arranged by the city council.
- Women, both daughters-in-law and mothers-in-law, should attend these types of social groups.
- 'Mohila Shomity' type of women's groups can be very helpful.
- Bengali people should have more volunteering mentality to help raise awareness.

which have been highlighted in previous literature, in particular the impact of disfigurement upon social acceptability and the prospect of marriage (Rozario, 2007).

Religious beliefs and cultural views/practices appear to be deep-rooted within the South Asian population and therefore it is of no surprise to find both these entities cutting across the majority of themes that emerged. They are applied to both the cause and origin of the visible difference as well as to the consequences of that difference.

A number of areas were identified that could inform interventions to eradicate the negative consequences of visible difference. These included raising levels of knowledge and understanding of the difference amongst the general population as well as improving the lived experience of those with the difference and their family. Participants suggested that education was needed to dispel myths and to raise awareness of sources of support for people with visible differences. Members of the Bengali Older Female focus group were particularly keen to express their suggestions for interventions to improve the experiences of those with visible differences and parents of children with visible differences. See Table C1.

Study 7: A Qualitative Study Exploring the Experiences of British South Asians Living with the Disfiguring Skin Condition Vitiligo

Study leads: Andrew Thompson, Sally Clarke & Robert Newell

A paper based on this study has been published (Thompson et al., 2010).

Vitiligo is a visible condition which affects the appearance of the skin through the loss of pigmentation and is consequently more noticeable in darker skinned individuals. It has been associated with a range of psychosocial difficulties such as depression, impaired quality of life, low self-esteem and negative thoughts about appearance, difficulties in sexual relationships and poor body image (Ongenae et al., 2006).

Beliefs about the cause and nature of illness are linked to adjustment and there is some evidence that such beliefs may vary according to culture and ethnicity (Firooz et al., 2004). However, the majority of psychosocial research in psychodermatology and in disfigurement has been with white

Western populations (Thompson & Kent, 2001). One study involving Black Americans with vitiligo suggested that the loss of pigment has been characterized as a punishment for engaging in sexual activity with White Americans (Porter & Beuf, 1991). Research involving Nigerians with vitiligo revealed high levels of stigmatization associated with the condition and beliefs that it is in some way connected with leprosy (Onunu & Kubeyinje, 2003). Previous research investigating the psychosocial impact of vitiligo in Asian populations is suggestive of significant impairments in quality of life, particularly in the areas of personal and social relationships in this population. The condition has been associated with comparatively higher levels of psychological morbidity than in comparative groups (Matto et al., 2002).

A detailed understanding of the role played by ethnicity and culture is limited by the small number of studies and by a heavy reliance in these studies on quantitative assessment, using generic measures that lack sensitivity to cultural issues. The present study is guided by a previous qualitative investigation of vitiligo in a non-Asian population (Thompson et al., 2002). The aim here is to explore the ways in which Asian individuals manage and adjust to vitiligo, with a particular focus on the role of ethnicity and culture.

Seven in-depth interviews were conducted with British adults of South Asian descent or family of origin living with vitiligo. The participants were recruited via NHS clinics and through the Vitiligo Society. The qualitative method of template analysis (Kent, 2000) was used to analyze the transcripts.

Participants described feeling visibly different and all had experienced stigmatization to some extent. A range of distress was apparent in participants. Five key themes were identified. These comprised the **culturally specific impact of vitiligo**.

> Asian society is a lot based on looks and status and to have vitiligo obviously puts you down…it's a stigma

> My Mum just said, well who's going to marry you with your skin like that, because a lot of arranged marriages are pretty much based on looks and like status

The comments included those alluding to a loss of ethnic identity as the result of depigmentation and the consequent lightening of skin. The second theme encompassed a **range of impacts on the individual**, including shame, disgust and difficulties with intimacy.

> I think it's horrible and disgusting

> I couldn't let someone get close, or be close to someone enough to do that [get married]

> I didn't let my husband see me when I was naked

The third theme encompassed the range of **coping strategies** reported by participants, including social avoidance and concealment,

> I can't answer my door without make-up on because I just, I would just have a panic attack,

confrontation and explaining, overcompensation and denial. **Social support** came in a variety of guises, including from family, friends, clinicians and support groups (via the internet). Living with vitiligo was seen as an **ongoing burden**.

> Oh, it, it's horrible, how do I sum it up? It's a burden on me because it's there all the time.

The findings of this study broadly support the consensus model developed to guide this research but highlight the need to carefully assess cultural associations of disfigurement. Further, they suggest that in addition to individual therapeutic interventions there is a need for community interventions designed to dispel myths and to raise awareness of appropriate sources of support and treatment.

Study 8: Appearance Concern, Hostility and Social Situations

Study leads: Tim Moss, James Byron-Daniel

Previous work in the field of visible differences has alluded to the importance of hostility as an aspect of psychosocial adjustment (Moss, 1997b) and led to the inclusion of the hostility measure in the pack of measures used in Studies 1 and 3. Initial analysis of data from the cross-sectional study confirmed potentially important relationships between adjustment to visible difference/disfigurement and feelings of hostility. It was therefore considered appropriate to attempt to investigate this relationship further.

Aggression is a likely outcome in people who have high levels of narcissism when they are faced with threatening or challenging feedback in social situations (Kernis et al., 1989). Narcissism is often related to (although not identical to) high self-esteem; however, for hostility to occur it is also necessary to have a 'poor other' esteem (i.e. a sense of superiority and a low opinion of others (Baumeister et al., 1996).

It may also be the case that narcissism and superiority are defence mechanisms functioning to protect a more hidden, core view of the self as weak, vulnerable or damaged. Aggression and hostility are the manifestation of these defences in the face of threat to the self through challenges from others. Aggression and hostility may serve to protect a person's perceived position in a social ranking system when this is under threat (Gilbert et al., 2007). It is not difficult to see how these processes might occur in people with appearance concerns when in a situation in which appearance becomes highly salient. In order to investigate these possibilities, the following study investigated reactions to certain, hypothetical situations in people with differences in appearance, measuring concepts such as self-esteem, adjustment to disfigurement and hostility.

Thirty-eight participants took part in an online survey comprising six social situation vignettes involving judgements about the consequences of anti-social behaviour. Participants also completed standardized measures of appearance concerns, self-esteem, perceived social ranking, aggression and narcissism.

Those who were more poorly adjusted to their appearance were more sensitive to verbal and behavioural attacks from others when these were associated with appearance. This relationship between appearance-related adjustment and hostility was found to be mediated by perceived social ranking and narcissism.

The results confirmed that hostility and aggression should be included in outcome studies when researching the impacts of visible difference. Interventions should be designed to focus on personally sensitive social situations (e.g. how to deal with appearance-specific threats) rather than generic social skills when seeking to reduce hostility in people with appearance concerns.

Study 9: Developing a Scale to Measure the Impact of Appearance Concerns on Intimate Behaviours

Study leads: Elizabeth Jenkinson, Alex Clarke and Tim Moss

Anecdotal reports from clinicians and from people with visible differences suggest that a substantial number of those affected experience problems in the initial stages of physical closeness such as touching, hugging or kissing. Surgical intervention and ongoing treatment can also mean that patients' personal lives and relationships with partners are negatively impacted and research into the psychosocial impact of visible differences has reported high levels of social anxiety experienced by many (Rumsey & Harcourt, 2005).

During the course of this research programme, members of the advisory panel queried why questions concerning intimate behaviours and sexual relationships were not included in the questionnaire pack, as they all agreed that this was an important component of adjustment to visible difference. The little research that has been previously conducted in this area confirms that sexual relationships and intimacy can be affected by appearance concerns. Gamba et al. (1992) found that in patients with head and neck cancer, 74% reported difficulties with their sexual relationship after surgery. Porter et al. (1990) also found that in patients with vitiligo, the majority reported problems with sexual relationships but also with behaviours that may lead to intimacy, such as dating or revealing their body to others. Ramsey and O'Reagan (1988) found that patients with psoriasis reported similar anxieties.

Following a review of scales, none were deemed suitable for inclusion in the cross-sectional questionnaire study (Study 1). Although scales for the measurement of sexual satisfaction and sexual behaviour exist (for an overview see Popovic, 2005), they tended to neglect the types of more subtle social behaviours that may be a prelude to sex (e.g. touching behaviours) often reported as difficult by those with appearance concerns. The research team decided to address this problem by developing a scale during the course of the programme that could be used in future research with this population.

This scale, comprising items generated through qualitative responses from people with visible differences and examples from clinical experience was administered to 145 adults without visible differences aged 18–75 years and was piloted on 41 attendees at a plastic surgery outpatient clinic sample along with the other standardized scales included in Study 1.

The scoring profiles were very different for the two populations. Few effects linking appearance and distress in intimate behaviours were found in the non-disfigured sample; however, the intimacy scale was found to have high face validity in the clinic setting, with the clinic sample reporting that their intimate behaviour was greatly affected by their appearance. Their responses to the scale were illustrative of pronounced, and sometimes debilitating, appearance concerns in the context of intimate situations and when socializing with potential partners, highlighting that the role of appearance concerns in intimacy and sexual relationships is an under-researched but important issue to understand and to address in the context of interventions. The scale is currently undergoing further refinement.

Study 10: Women with Limb Prostheses – Experiences and Adjustment

Study leads: Rob Newell, Andrew Thompson, Sally Clarke

People with a limb absent from birth or through trauma or disease are subject to significant challenges as a result, independent of the direct consequences of the original source of their absent limb.

Amongst these are phantom pains and other phantom phenomena (Katz & Melzack, 1990), as well as poorer quality of life and other psychosocial indicators (Demet et al., 2003).

Use of prostheses where a limb is absent or lost is an aspect commonly involved in the development or rehabilitation of physical function. However, surprisingly, little is known about patterns of prosthetic use (Murray & Fox, 2002) or psychological adaptation to the loss or absence of a limb, as research is generally limited to anecdotal reports and small surveys (Rybarczyk et al., 1995). In particular, there is little examination of the attitudes of the person using the prosthesis or their experiences of prosthesis use, focusing instead on functional characteristics of the prosthesis and their putative effects on use (e.g. Millstein et al., 1986; Balance et al., 1989).

In a relatively recent study, Saradjian et al. (2007) focused on the experiences of 11 male amputees. Using interviews, the authors found that participants reported that prosthesis use reduced their sense of difference. However, there is some suggestion that the experiences of men and women of limb absence and prosthesis use may be different. Accordingly, this study aimed to complement the work of Saradjian et al. by interviewing women about their experiences.

Semi-structured interviews were conducted with six women aged 29–67 with limb prostheses. Four had lower limb prostheses and two had upper limb prostheses. The interviews were transcribed and analyzed using thematic analysis and following the pragmatic approach of Burnard (1991) to organize the data. Participants had previously taken part in Study 1 and at that time had indicated their interest in taking part in further studies.

Seven themes (some with sub-themes) were derived from the interview data. These themes comprised psychological adaptation, physical adaptation, independence, the role of others, emotional impact and support, social impact, body image and self-image.

In the main, respondents offered a picture of positive adaptation to the loss or absence of a limb, with few signs of significant distress. Participants did however acknowledge the extent of the task involved in successful adaptation. There was an emphasis on the need for a positive mental attitude, involving confronting and resolving difficulties and asserting independence.

> Whether I'm in a wheelchair or whether I'm walking I'll be fairly independent because I'm quite an independent minded person, so I shall be able to get on one way or another.

A variety of styles of psychological adaptation to limb absence were evident in the accounts. For some, limb absence was a challenge, which, although not welcome, had to be faced. The majority of responses were characteristic of a positive outlook.

> It doesn't bother me that much that I can't wear it, [a necklace] I don't weep every night thinking oh I want to wear a diamond.

> Like I say the barriers are up in your head.

Despite a general picture of positive adaptation, there were also expressions of loss, regret and frustration.

> There's no other way of describing it, people say 'oh you get used to it', no you don't, I don't know who tells them that nonsense that you get used to it, it's having a great big plastic thing shoved on your leg, and it's a great big heavy plastic thing and you're shuntering it along like Long John Sliver, it's rubbish, it's rubbish, that's what it's like.

The attitudes and behaviours of members of the public and social acquaintances were a source of discomfort to participants. It was also clear that participants spent considerable time predicting, observing, preparing for and responding to the actual or assumed reactions of others.

> When I go to the Juniors I've got to walk through some classrooms to get to my base so there will be so many of them either looking or pointing or saying something.

Participants suggested that members of the public appeared to regard it as acceptable to interact with respondents in ways which would normally be regarded as impolite, intrusive and harassing. One respondent inferred from this that it was because having a missing limb meant that they were less of a person.

> Like you're less of a human being than they are.

> I always wear the artificial limb because I don't want people to look at me and think there's the lady with one arm.

The imperative of appearing 'normal' to others was mentioned by several respondents and was often linked to concealment of the limb absence

> For a good while I didn't go out, not until I felt that, I wanted to be able to be as normal as I possibly could

Several respondents appeared to view the prosthetic limb as something functional and as a useful aid to passing as 'normal', rather than as something to be incorporated into the person's sense of self.

> I can never accept it as me although it's something I have got, otherwise I don't walk, I've got to use it every day otherwise I don't walk and I don't want not to be able to walk. But it's still not me.

Although there was a range of responses, respondents mostly reported that limb absence had made little or no difference to their social lives. All reported having dates and boyfriends, and all either were or had been married. Respondents were also asked about their experiences of intimate relationships. All respondents reported having dates and boyfriends, and all were married at the time of the study or had been married in the past.

> He touches me there, it's not like it's out of bounds or anything, it's no more out of bounds than any other part of my body.

The accounts by women with prostheses in the current study add to the weight of evidence regarding the role of active coping strategies in mediating adjustment to visible difference, particularly in the face of often negative behaviours by members of the public. This in turn reinforces the importance of promoting both such active coping in people with visible difference and education and attitude change in the general public.

The frequently reported finding in visible difference research that the responses of others can be experienced very negatively was repeated here, as was the description of inferences made about the attitudes of others from their behaviours. Confronting obstacles and regarding them as challenges were identified as important in adaptation.

This is a small sample, and so the picture of successful adaptation, whilst encouraging, is not necessarily representative of this population as a whole. A more complete understanding of psychological adjustment in this group is needed.

Study 11: In the Context of Rheumatoid Arthritis Does Appearance Matter?

Study leads: Hayley McBain, Stanton Newman
This study has been published (McBain et al., 2012).

Rheumatoid arthritis (RA) is the single greatest cause of disability in the United Kingdom (Goff & Barasi 1999). At present, there is no treatment to either cure or prevent the disease; therefore, the main aim is to reduce its impact on peoples' lives by limiting symptoms, reducing disability and improving quality of life (Pollard et al., 2005). Disfigurement of the hands is a common and significant complication of RA and once these changes occur, they are not reversible medically and may require surgery.

Despite a large amount of research looking at psychological impact of RA during the course of the disease, very little research has focused on the psychological effects of body image and disfigurement. Early research on body image and attractiveness in RA has produced somewhat mixed results with some suggesting no difference to the normal population (Cornwell & Schmidt, 1990) and others suggesting diminished body image (Skevington et al., 1987). Rumsey et al. (2002) report higher levels of anxiety and depression in patients with rheumatic conditions including RA, compared to both normative levels as well as in comparison to people with burns, head and neck cancer and eye conditions. Those patients with rheumatic conditions experiencing higher levels of distress spoke of embarrassment, self-consciousness and distress in relation to their appearance, with specific mention of the appearance of their joints. Concerns regarding the noticeability of the condition were also reported along with the use of avoidant and concealment behaviours. In a study on patients with RA and lupus, Monaghan et al. (2007) found that perceived appearance and physical disability were predictive of depression but not anxiety in RA patients.

Very few studies have focused on the physical and psychological issues surrounding observable hand disfigurement in RA, despite this being the most overtly exposed area and the identification that hands are one of the areas most affected by the illness (Cornwell & Schmidt, 1990). Due to the lack of consistency in the results of previous research into appearance concerns, this study investigated whether hand disfigurement due to RA has an independent impact on psychological well-being.

Forty-nine patients with and 32 with no visible hand disfigurement recruited from outpatient rheumatology clinics in London completed a booklet of psychosocial questionnaires. In addition to the scales included in Study 1, participants completed measures relating to levels of functional disability and feelings of stigmatization. The mean age of the patients was 59 years, with a range from 23–78 years.

In line with the results of the main study, optimism had the strongest predictive effect of all the psychological variables. Those with an observable hand disfigurement scored higher on measures of functional disability and feelings of stigmatization. They also rated their appearance more negatively than those with no hand disfigurement. When controlling for functional disability, all significant differences between the groups disappeared, highlighting the additional impact of this factor.

Participants with an observable hand disfigurement were 2.62 times more likely to be clinically depressed than those with no observable hand disfigurement. Conversely, those with no observable hand disfigurement were 1.68 times more likely to be clinically anxious. Appearance-related social anxiety and avoidance were predicted by age and living status, as well as objective hand disfigurement and the psychological variables of valence, salience, functional disability, satisfaction with social support and social acceptance. Younger participants were more likely to avoid and to be anxious about social situations – suggesting that concerns about the appearance of their hands may be impacting on their social functioning to a greater extent than for older participants. Regression analysis revealed that high ideal appearance discrepancy, low optimism and low satisfaction with social support predict higher levels of anxiety. Higher ratings of functional disability and low optimism predicted the majority of the variance in depression. The visibility of the hand disfigurement did not independently affect mood, but may contribute to feelings of appearance-related social anxiety and avoidance.

The findings suggest that it is not simply the observable nature of the hand disfigurement but the visible disability when moving which may have an effect on feelings of stigmatization and the participants' evaluation of their own appearance – that is, in movement, the disfigurement may be felt to be particularly salient. The results highlight the additional (and interactive) effect of functional disability and the need to address these aspects in the context of treatment.

Study 12: Working with Patients with Visible Differences – General Practitioners' Beliefs, Decision-Making Processes and Training Needs

Study leads: Elizabeth Jenkinson and Tim Moss

GPs have been identified as 'gatekeepers' to existing psychological support services by psychologists working in the field of appearance (Rumsey & Harcourt, 2005, p. 146). Despite their pivotal role, GPs are not routinely trained in dealing with the psychosocial needs of those with appearance concerns and may find it hard to identify appearance-related distress from other health concerns or mental illness. When appearance issues are acknowledged, Hopwood and Maguire (1988) suggest that professionals working with these patients often underestimate the problems of adjusting to their appearance. This may be due to an over reliance on the biomedical approach to the assessment of patient adjustment. A growing evidence base of psychological research suggests biomedical factors such as visibility, severity and type of condition are, in fact, not reliable predictors of psychological adjustment (Robinson, 1997; Rumsey et al., 2003) and advocates adopting a more bio-psychosocial approach (Engel, 1980), considering psychological factors alongside physical assessment.

Charlton et al. (2003) suggested that efforts should be made to enable GPs to appropriately identify and advise patients with concerns about their appearance and noted that more support and training is needed in this area. The authors considered that consultations with patients presenting with appearance issues present a quandary for GPs. The decision to refer for surgical intervention may not always be appropriate. Furthermore, the expectations of patients that their visible difference would be aesthetically improved through surgery may be raised and lead patients to believe feelings of self-consciousness about their appearance may be cured. However, referral for surgical or medical treatment may be the only option as the alternative of offering psychological support may not be feasible if no services are available in the locality or in cases in which patients are not willing to engage with psychological input. Charlton and colleagues argued that more research is needed at primary care level to gauge current levels of GP knowledge and to inform education for practitioners.

Therefore, the focus of this research was to explore the existing perceptions, beliefs and referral patterns of primary care practitioners in the context of working with patients with disfigurements. A better understanding in this field was considered essential in future efforts to design appropriate training packages.

This study recruited UK-based fully qualified ($n = 17$) and trainee ($n = 8$) GPs, in addition to 25 medical students ($n = 25$). Participants responded to 12 vignettes about hypothetical patients with disfigurements, either online or via email. The vignettes were systematically varied in relation to the severity and visibility to others of the disfiguring condition, and the levels of distress of the 'patients' were systematically varied. The vignettes were designed by the research team and contained details describing hypothetical patients and scenarios. These vignettes (all of which were approximately 100 words in length) included information about the age, gender, condition, severity and visibility of the patients' conditions as well as painting a picture of their current levels of psychological distress. A number of variables were also kept constant across vignettes, including socioeconomic status, sex, age (30–50), relationship status and living arrangements.

Example Vignette

Sarah, 32, lives locally in a flat with her husband, Nick. She works at a local university as an HR manager. A recent stroke has left the left side of her face in paralysis. Over the last few months, she has been tired every day and more on edge than usual. She feels 'jumpy' when on her own and has been feeling anxious even thinking about going to work. She has been staying at home whenever possible and trying to wear her hair so it covers the affected side of her face in order to conceal it from others.

Participants were asked to identify the patients' problems and to rate the likelihood of recommending referral to a range of services in primary, secondary or tertiary settings. They also provided qualitative responses to open-ended questions.

All groups of participants offered bio-psychosocial explanations and consequences of having the disfigurement. Thematic analysis of qualitative data suggested an acknowledgement of the need for psychosocial support for patients, but also barriers to provision within the National Health Service. Participants were most likely to refer patients who were described as experiencing high levels of distress to psychological services, either in community or hospital settings. Participants also responded to the level of severity and the degree of visibility to others of the condition in their referral patterns. This does not reflect the consistent finding of a lack of a relationship between the severity and visibility of a disfigurement and the associated levels of psychosocial distress in published research. Many participants reported that they felt ill-equipped to offer psychosocial support themselves and expressed the need for training in this respect.

The findings indicated that further training for primary care practitioners would be advantageous, and support in treatment decision-making when working with patients with disfigurement would be helpful in promoting appropriate referrals for support and intervention.

Overall Synthesis of the Results of the Research Programme

As outlined in the Introduction to the Appendix, Studies 5–12 were designed to be exploratory in nature. In view of this, the findings from these studies should be taken as suggestive rather than indicative. Nevertheless, many of the findings resonate with the results of the larger-scale Studies 1–4. In particular, they highlight the range and complexity of individual experiences and are helpful in formulating recommendations relating both to interventions and future research agendas. The findings from Studies 5–12 are integrated where appropriate, with the results of Studies 1–4 in the section that follows.

Profiles of Adjustment and Distress

The participants in this programme of research demonstrated very variable profiles of adjustment and distress. In line with previous research, significant numbers of participants reported high levels of distress, with 51.7% participants scoring above the clinical cut-off for anxiety and 23.6% for depression (Study 1). Difficulties and distress, which were often considerable, were experienced by those sampled through outpatient clinics and from the community. It is clear that the populations of both those actively seeking treatment and those who are not contain within them significant proportions of those with often debilitating levels of unmet psychosocial need.

The results also provided a profile of the psychological characteristics of those with disfiguring conditions who can be considered to be well adjusted (Studies 1, 4 and 5). Adjustment is multi-factorial (all studies). Some of the components contributing to positive adjustment or distress and identified or suggested in previous research were confirmed and clarified, including dispositional style (optimism/pessimism) (Studies 1 and 4) and cognitive processes such as levels of satisfaction with social support (Studies 1, 3–5 and 10), fear of negative evaluation (Studies 1 and 4) and perceived social acceptance (Studies 1 and 4). The interpretation of the responses of others has been highlighted as a crucial factor in adjustment in previous research and was also a recurring feature of the results of this programme (Studies 2 and 10).

One of the most striking finding of this research is the role in adjustment played by appearance-specific cognitions, including salience, valence and appearance-related self-discrepancies (Studies 1, 3 and 4). These appearance-specific issues may cause distress in the absence of other more general signs of psychological need (e.g. anxiety or depression) (Studies 1, 4, 9 and 10) but nevertheless impact negatively on many aspects of the lives of those affected. In those without obvious signs of general psychopathology, the existence of appearance-related distress may be less obvious to clinicians and others involved in their care. However, unhelpful appearance-specific cognitions and behaviours are likely to be amenable to intervention, and this is urgently needed to improve the quality of life of people with significant levels of distress.

Other factors and processes produced contradictory findings within this programme and are in need of further research, including the issue of the visibility of a disfigurement to others. The results (Studies 1, 3 and 10) suggest that in the same way that social interaction can be difficult because of the fear of others' reactions to a visible disfigurement (e.g. on the face), similar problems arise when conditions are not normally visible, because of the fear of disclosure during intimate situations. Both responses are connected to the concern people have to avoid negative evaluation, with the fear of negative evaluation acting to reinforce the negative appraisal of appearance in those for whom appearance has a high premium. Once this view of the world is established, it is self-reinforcing through the selective attention to and negative appraisal of the information that sustains it.

The contributions of some other factors, hitherto neglected in research, were also highlighted, including aggression in response to appearance-related threats (Studies 1 and 8), the role of social comparison processes (Studies 1, 4 and 10) and the compounding negative impacts of functional disability (Studies 10 and 11).

Positive Adjustment and Resilience

The impact of cognitive processes such as dispositional style and appearance-related cognitions was particularly apparent in those who self-reported as positive adjusters. These people talked of the experience of disfigurement as one of personal growth (Studies 5 and 10) and reported a number of strategies that appeared to work well including pragmatism and 'getting on with it' in the face of challenges (Studies 5 and 10), acceptance and determination (Study 2) and engaging with problems and difficulties rather than avoiding them (Studies 3, 5 and 7).

In the longitudinal study (Study 4), there was a striking lack of concordance between the self-classification as a positive adjuster (stable or improved over time) and the scores on standardized measures, which did not necessarily paint the same picture of positive adjustment. Once more, the crucial importance of taking into account each person's subjective beliefs and assessment about their level of adjustment is highlighted. It is not sufficient, and may even be misleading, to rely solely on standardized measures in this regard.

The Impact of Appearance-Related Distress

The impact of appearance-related distress on a wide range of daily activities was striking. These include negative effects on cognitions about the self, social functioning and intimate relationships (Studies 1–4, 6, 7 and 9). The limiting effects of appearance-related distress should be systematically assessed and addressed in the context of interventions.

The Multiple Nature of Appearance Concerns

Distress relating to appearance can relate to many different aspects of the body (Studies 1 and 2). Some participants focused their concerns clearly and exclusively on their disfigurement. Others expressed dissatisfaction with additional issues including weight, shape and the effects of ageing on appearance. In some cases, these latter concerns caused more distress than the disfigurement. Interestingly, the consequences for the individual of concerns about aspects of appearance which are not normally considered to be disfigurements (such as body shape and size and the effects of ageing) appeared to be strikingly similar to the consequences associated with disfigurement (Studies 1 and 2). The findings stress the need for a comprehensive assessment of each of the sources of appearance-related distress in those affected and a need to tailor intervention appropriately. There would be little point in focusing a surgical or psychological intervention on the aspect of appearance affected by a disfiguring condition, when, in fact, the person is equally or more stressed by other aspects of their looks.

More research is needed to unpick further the similarities and differences in the impact of concerns about weight, shape and ageing in comparison with the consequences of disfigurement. However, the findings add credence to the legitimacy of considering the appearance concerns of those with and without disfigurements as comprising one continuum. In efforts to increase public education and understanding of the consequences of disfigurement, this may be a fruitful way of 'normalizing' the distress experienced by those affected.

The Dynamic Nature of Adjustment

In contrast to the rather static picture of adjustment and distress painted by previous, predominantly cross-sectional research, and the widely held assumption that time is a greater healer in relation to adjustment to disfigurement, this programme of research has also brought into sharp relief the dynamic nature of adjustment over time. We understand more as the result of this programme about the day to day 'work' of having an appearance concern. Lansdown et al. (1997) describe this as an 'Achilles heel' and it is clear that in meeting the challenges and demands of everyday life as we all do, excess stress often manifests itself as renewed preoccupation with appearance for those who perceive themselves to be disfigured. This finding fits with the clinical observation that people often seek surgery or physical solutions at times when they feel most vulnerable and are at risk of making poor decisions.

Fluctuations in the salience and impact of appearance concerns are triggered by a variety of events and changes, including life events, developmental milestones, signs of ageing and the cumulative impact of daily hassles such as the reactions of others (Studies 2 and 4). Even when adjustment is positive over long periods of time, coping with a visible difference can be an ongoing strain on resources (Studies 2 and 10), and, at times, particular stress and change may become the focus of distress.

These findings are a strong endorsement of the need for regular screening and easy access to appropriate intervention at all life stages for those with congenital disfigurements and at all stages of rehabilitation following later onset.

The Impact of Age, Gender and Ethnicity

The focus on this research programme has been on those psychological factors and processes which are amenable to change. However, the data from the cross-sectional and longitudinal studies offer findings which challenge some widely held assumptions about the impact of some demographic factors, including age and gender.

The span of ages of the participants was large (18–91 years) (Studies 1–12). There were overall decreases in levels of distress with age, but individual variation was considerable, and large numbers of older people were distressed about their appearance.

In line with previous research, levels of appearance-related distress were higher in women, but in this research programme differences between men and women were small, and many men had significant and, in some cases, debilitating concerns about their appearance (Studies 1–4). Study 9 illustrated that men and women may respond differently to appearance-specific threats in social situations, with men more prone to responses underpinned by aggression and hostility. The widely held assumptions that younger people are affected to a greater extent than older people and that women are more prone to appearance-related distress than men should be avoided by health care professionals and by those developing and providing methods of support and intervention.

Although someone's ethnic origin is to all intents and purposes 'fixed' and therefore not amenable to change, the influence of cultural and religious beliefs was a focus within this research programme, as this is an area which has been under-researched in the past. The under-representation of people from black minority ethnic groups (BMEs) in treatment settings has been remarked upon by researchers from this collaboration in the past, and there has been concern that treatment has been perceived as either irrelevant or inappropriate for their needs. Within the ethnic groupings included in Studies 6 and 7, there was evidence of the strong influence on the beliefs, attitudes and personal experience of people with disfigurement resulting from cultural and religious beliefs. These results indicate a need for support for members of ethnic groups who have disfigurements (Studies 6 and 7) and also for educational initiatives to dispel myths and promote positive adjustment in those affected within ethnic communities (Studies 6 and 7).

A Framework of Adjustment to Disfigurement

The advantages and drawbacks of diagrammatic representations of adjustment and distress in relation to disfigurement have been discussed earlier in this appendix (including e.g. the acknowledged difficulty of designating psychological variables as 'process' or 'outcome') and were a source of considerable debate within this collaboration. Having used diagrams earlier in this report to illustrate aspects of the methodology and the analyses, it was considered prudent to further modify these in the light of the results of the overall programme. Consumers of research findings have a penchant for reproducing diagrams of complex processes such as these, often without the associated health warnings about the illusion of simplicity implied by boxes and lines. Figure A11 is an attempt to highlight the iterative process of adjustment with an emphasis on factors amenable to intervention and the need to represent the dynamic and fluctuating nature of well-being and distress. This diagram is not intended to be definitive, but hopefully goes some way to capturing the complexities of the processes involved and may be more useful as a heuristic for those unfamiliar with the field.

The high levels of individual variation that are evident in this research programme (Studies 1–4, 5, 8, 10–12) indicate the need to develop a range of interventions and packages of support. Based on these results, and on the findings of previous research, members of this collaboration have advocated the stepped approach to intervention illustrated through the main text. Thus, we have developed a framework which allows us to choose from a range of interventions according to the level of need of the client (Figure 2.1). Whilst one person may benefit from a detailed psychological input, many others will respond positively to less intensive measures.

This book is part of the ongoing effort to provide appropriate packages of support and intervention for all levels of need. Training packages for health professionals (Study 12), which should emphasize the need for routine screening for signs of distress in people with disfiguring conditions and the need to develop appropriate referral pathways for clients according to need, are also being developed.

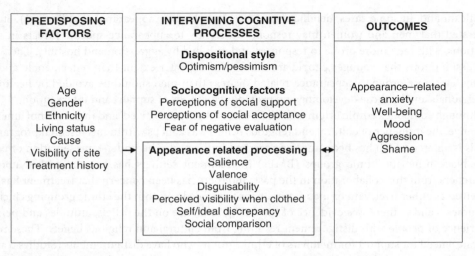

Figure A.11 Working framework of adjustment to disfiguring conditions adapted to include results of the ARC research programme. Reproduced from Thompson, A. 2012 Researching appearance: models, theories and frameworks, in Oxford Handbook of the Psychology of Appearance (eds N. Rumsey and D. Harcourt), p102. © Oxford University Press, 2012, with kind permission.

Conclusions and the Way Forward

This series of studies represents the largest programme of research in this area to date. The quantitative and qualitative results have confirmed the considerable distress experienced by many people with disfiguring conditions. The research has also provided a much greater understanding of the factors and processes involved in positive adjustment. The ongoing effort of coping with a disfiguring condition and the multi-factorial nature of adjustment and distress are clear as is the huge range of individual variation in the experiences of those affected.

Socio-cognitive and appearance-specific cognitions are key in adjustment and are amenable to intervention. In addition, the results indicate that adjustment is labile and can be influenced by a myriad of factors. These fluctuations indicate the need for routine screening together with referral pathways for specialist assessment and appropriate support and intervention.

Although this research has shown that the cognitive architecture of each individual and the personal interpretation of appearance-related information are key in adjustment, it is also evident that the person's social and cultural context are of considerable importance. For the most vulnerable, messages from the media and from society are relentless and even the most resilient can be affected by the barrage of appearance information omnipresent in their societal context. Efforts should also be directed at developing methods of public education designed to reduce the pressure on those who are vulnerable to appearance concerns, and interventions should be adapted to suit the cultural context. Examples of such initiatives can be found on the website of the Centre for Appearance Research (CAR) (www1.uwe.ac.uk/research/appearanceresearch/car).

As is usually the case in research, the findings of this research programme offer clear pointers for the research agenda of the future. This agenda includes further examination of specific issues such as the impact on adjustment of the visibility and disguisability of a difference. The effects of functional disability in the context of disfigurement also warrant a more detailed exploration. Gender differences in the manifestation of distress, a better understanding of the similarities and differences in body image and appearance concerns in those with and without disfigurements and the development of culturally sensitive measures specifically relating to the appearance concerns of those with visible differences are also research priorities. This research programme focused on the adjustment of adults, and there is a pressing need to examine these issues in young people. This research will be a considerable undertaking, not least because it will require the development of measures appropriate to each developmental stage.

Resources

Rating Scales

Intervening Cognitive Processes

Optimism
Life Orientation Test-Revised (LOT-R) (Scheier and Carver 1987). http://www.psy.miami.edu/faculty/ccarver/sclLOT-R.html

Social Networks
Short Form Social Support Questionnaire (Sarason et al. 1983). http://web.psych.washington.edu/research/sarason/files/SocialSupportQuestionnaireShort.pdf

Fear of Negative Evaluation
The Brief Fear of Negative Evaluation (FNE) scale (Leary 1983).

Social Comparison
Iowa-Netherlands Social Comparison measure (INCOMM) (Gibbons & Buunk 1999). http://www.sonoma.edu/users/s/smithh/psy445/materials/sco.pdf

Valence of Appearance
The CARVAL (Moss & Rosser 2012a, 2012b). Contact: Dr. Tim Moss, tim.moss@uwe.ac.uk

Salience of Appearance
The CARSAL (Rosser & Moss 2012). Contact: Dr. Tim Moss, tim.moss@uwe.ac.uk

CBT for Appearance Anxiety: Psychosocial Interventions for Anxiety Due to Visible Difference, First Edition.
Alex Clarke, Andrew Thompson, Elizabeth Jenkinson, Nichola Rumsey and Rob Newell.
© 2014 John Wiley & Sons, Ltd. Published 2014 by John Wiley & Sons, Ltd.

Physical Appearance Discrepancy
The PADQ (Altabe & Thompson 1995). Available in Thompson et al. (1999).

Outcomes

Social anxiety and social avoidance
Derriford Appearance Scale Short Form (DAS24; Carr et al. 2005).
DAS59 (Carr et al. 2000). http://www.derriford.info/

Psychological Well-being

Anxiety and depression
The Hospital Anxiety & Depression Scale (HADS; Zigmond & Snaith 1983). http://shop.gl-assessment.co.uk/home.php?cat=417

Anger/hostility
The Refined Aggression Questionnaire (RAQ) (Bryant & Smith 2001)

Body Image assessment manuals and questionnaires

www.body-images.com

Noticeability and Worry Graph (see Chapter 4)

How noticeable is your condition to other people? 0–10
How much do you worry about it? 0–10

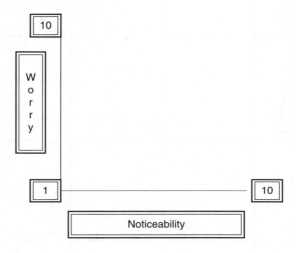

Unhelpful Beliefs Record (UBR) Form (see Figure 6.4)

Date	Situation Describe the situation leading to unpleasant emotion	Emotion Type of emotion (e.g. sad, angry ashamed, disgusted, anxious)	Automatic thought Description of the thought or image in your mind (e.g. Everyone is looking; I won't be able to speak to him/her etc.)	Alternative thought Is there another way of looking at it? (e.g. what would I say to a friend; am I jumping to conclusion etc.)	Outcome Replace the unhelpful thought/image with the alternative balanced thought. Now re-rate the intensity of emotion	What else could I do? List other positive coping strategies that could be used to challenge the unhelpful thought or increase confidence
		Intensity 0–10	Intensity of thought 0–10	Intensity of alternative 0–10	Intensity 0–10	

Triple Column Technique (Burns 1989) (see Chapter 7)

Automatic thought Strength of belief 0–10	Cognitive processing style (e.g. personalization, jumping to conclusions etc.)	Alternative belief Strength of belief 0–10

Beliefs Framework (see Chapter 7)

Date	Situation	Belief and strength 0–10	What really happened	Strength of original belief 0–10

SOURCES OF SUPPORT

Changing Faces is a UK charity that supports and represents people who have disfigurements of the face or body from any cause. Address: Changing Faces, 33–37 University Street, London WC1E 6JN. Tel: 0845 4500 275
Website: http://www.changingfaces.org.uk

Other Sources of Help

Achondroplasia.co.uk, Tel: 01761 471 257, Website: www.achondroplasia.co.uk
Provides support and information for people with short limb dwarfism and their families and carers.

Alopecia Patient's Society – Hairline International, Website: www.hairlineinternational.com
Offers help, support and advice to people with alopecia and all hair loss conditions.

Arthritis Care, Helpline: 0808 800 4050, Website: www.arthritiscare.org.uk
Provides support and information for people with all forms of arthritis.

The Arthrogryposis Group (TAG), Tel: 01299 825781, Website: www.tagonline.org.uk
Offers support and advice to those with arthrogryposis.

The Bell's Palsy Network, Website: www.bellspalsy.net
Offers online information, support and advice for those with Bell's palsy and other related conditions.

The Birthmark Support Group, Tel: 0845 045 4700, Website: www.birthmarksupportgroup.org.uk
Support group for people with birthmarks.

Breast Cancer Care, Helpline: 0808 800 6000, Website: www.breastcancercare.org.uk
Offers support, information and advice to those with or recovering from breast cancer.

British Acoustic Neuroma Association, Tel: 01623 632143, Website: www.bana-uk.com
Offers information and advice to people with acoustic neuroma and offers local support groups.

British Allergy Foundation, Helpline: 020 8303 8583 (Monday to Friday 9.00–17.00), Website: http://www.allergyuk.org
Patient information service for people with all types of allergies including skin allergies.

British Association of Dermatologists, Tel: 020 7383 0266, Website: www.bad.org.uk
Fact sheets on general dermatological conditions.

British Association of Skin Camouflage, Tel: 01226 790744, Website: www.skin-camouflage.net
Offers training, advice and assistance.

British Red Cross Skin Camouflage Service, Helpline 0300 012 0276, Website: http://www.redcross.org.uk/What-we-do/Health-and-social-care/Health-and-social-care-in-the-UK/Skin-camouflage, Email: skincam@changingfaces.org.uk

Burn Centre Care, Website: http://www.burncentrecare.co.uk/support.html

Children's Burns Trust (CBT), Website: www.cbtrust.org.uk
Provides information, advice and financial support for burned and scald injured children and their families as well as prevention and awareness campaigns.

Cleft Lip & Palate Association (CLAPA), Website: www.clapa.com
Provide information, advice and practical support to people with and affected by cleft lip and/or palate in the UK.

DebRA, Helpline: 01344 771961 (Monday to Friday 9.00–17.00), Website: www.debra.org.uk
Helps people with epidermolysis bullosa (EB), by providing travelling specialist nurses, financial support, respite and more. DebRA also funds research into EB.

Ehlers-Danlos Support Group, Website: www.ehlers-danlos.org
Provides information, support and advice.

Herpes Viruses Association (SPHERE) and Shingles Support Society, Helpline: 020 7609 9061 (24-hour message service), Website: www.herpes.org.uk
Treatment information and self-help tips for those suffering from shingles, cold sores and herpes-related viruses.

Ichthyosis Support Group, Website: http://www.ichthyosis.org.uk/
Provides an information network and support system for children and adults affected by ichthyosis.

Let's Face it, Tel: 01843 833724, Website: www.lets-face-it.org.uk.
Information, advice and support for people with facial differences and their families.

Limbless Association, Helpline: 01277 725 182, Website: www.limbless-association.org
Provides information, advice and support to the limbless community.

Lupus UK, Helpline: 01708 731251 (Monday to Friday 09.00–17.00), Website: www.lupusuk.org.uk
Advice, help and support to people affected by lupus, including discoid lupus.

Lymphoedema Support Network, Website: www.lymphoedema.org/Index.asp
Provide information and support to patients with Lymphoedema.

Macmillan, Website: www.macmillan.org.uk, Tel: 0808 808 00 00 (Monday–Friday 9.00–20.00)
Provide practical, medical and financial support for those affected by cancer.

National Ankylosing Spondylitis Society, Tel: 01435 873527, Website: www.nass.co.uk
Provides information and advice to those with AS. Also offers a forum for patients.

National Eczema Society, Helpline: 0870 271 3604 (Monday to Friday 13.00–16.00), Website: www.eczema.org
Support and advice to people with eczema.

National Lichen Sclerosus Support Group (UK), Website: www.lichensclerosus.org
Information and support about lichen sclerosis.

Neurofibromatosis Association, Helpline: 020 8439 1234 (Monday to Friday 9.00–17.00), Website: www.nfauk.org
Supports, advises and help people affected by neurofibromatosis.

Nevus Outreach, Website: www.nevus.org
Offers support and information.

Psoriasis Association, Helpline: 01604 711129 (Monday to Friday 9.00–17.00), Website: www.timewarp.demon.co.uk/psoriasis.html
Advice, help and support to people suffering from psoriasis.

Psoriasis Forum, Website: www.psoriasis-help.org.uk
Interactive forum offering support groups to people suffering from psoriasis.

Psoriasis and Psoriatic Arthritis Alliance (PAPAA), Website: www.papaa.org
UK registered charity dedicated to helping people affected by psoriasis and psoriatic arthritis.

Raynaud's Scleroderma Association, Tel: 01270 872776 (Monday to Friday 9.00–17.00), Freephone Message Service: 0800 917 2494, Website: www.raynauds.org.uk
Information and support to people affected by Raynaud's and scleroderma.

The Thyroid Eye Disease Charitable Trust (TED), Tel: 0844 800 8133, Website: www.stuartchad-wick.me.uk/TED/index.html, Email: ted@tedct.co.uk
Provides information, care and support to people with thyroid eye disease and offers a network of support groups.

UK Craniofacial Support Group, Tel: 01454 850557, Website: www.headlines.org.uk
Support and advice for people with any form of craniofacial condition or syndrome.

Vitiligo Society, Helpline: 020 7840 0855 (Monday to Friday 10.00–17.00), Website: www.vitiligosociety.org.uk
Information, help and support for people with vitiligo.

Xeroderma Pigmentosum (XP) Support Group, Helpline: 01494 890981 (Monday to Friday 9.00–21.00), Website: www.xpsupportgroup.org.uk
Support, help and information to those affected by xeroderma pigmentosum and other photosensitive conditions.

References

Abrams, A.N., Hayes, E.P. and Penson, R.T. (2007) Psychosocial issues in adolescents with cancer. *Cancer Treatment Reviews*, 33, 622–630.

Adachi, T., Kochi, S. and Yamaguchi, T. (2003) Characteristics of non-verbal behaviour in patients with cleft lip and palate during interpersonal communication. *Cleft Palate-Craniofacial Journal*, 40, 310–316.

Allen, D. and Gregory, J. (2009) The transition from children's to adult diabetes services: understanding the 'problem'. *Diabetic Medicine*, 26 (2), 162–166.

Altabe, M. (1996) Issues in the assessment and treatment of body image disturbance in culturally diverse populations, in *Eating Disorders, Obesity, and Body Image: A Practical Guide to Assessment and Treatment* (ed J.K. Thompson), American Psychological Association Books, Washington, DC.

Altabe, M. and Thompson, J.K. (1995) Body image disturbance: advances in assessment and treatment, in *Innovations in Clinical Practice: A Source Book* (eds L. Vandecreek S. Knapp and T.L. Jackson), pp. 89–110, Professional Resource Press, Sarasota, FL.

Altabe, M.N. and Thompson, J.K. (1996) Body image: a cognitive self-schema? *Cognitive Therapy and Research*, 20, 171–193.

Annon, J. (1974) *The Behavioural Treatment of Sexual Problems*, vol. 1. Enabling Systems Inc, Honolulu.

Anthony, S.J., Kaufman M., Drabble A., Seifert-Hansen M., Dipchand A.I. and Martin K. (2009) Perceptions of transitional care needs and experiences in paediatric heart transplant recipients. *American Journal of Transplant*, 9 (3), 614–619.

Ata, R.N., Ludden, A.B. and Lally, M.M. (2007) The effect of gender and family, friend, and media influences on eating behaviours and body image during adolescence. *Journal of Youth and Adolescence*, 36, 1024–1037.

Baines J.M. (2009) Promoting better care: transition from child to adult services. *Nursing Standard*, 23 (19), 35–40.

Baker, C. (1992) Factors associated with rehabilitation in head and neck cancer. *Cancer Nursing*, 15, 395–400.

Balance, R., Wilson, B. and Harder, J.A. (1989) Factors affecting myoelectric prosthetic use and wearing patterns in the juvenile unilateral below elbow amputee. *Canadian Journal of Occupational Therapy*, 56, 132–137.

CBT for Appearance Anxiety: Psychosocial Interventions for Anxiety Due to Visible Difference, First Edition.
Alex Clarke, Andrew Thompson, Elizabeth Jenkinson, Nichola Rumsey and Rob Newell.
© 2014 John Wiley & Sons, Ltd. Published 2014 by John Wiley & Sons, Ltd.

Baldwin, M.W. (1992) Relational schemas and the processing of social information. *Psychological Bulletin*, 112, 461–484.

Bandura, A. (1997) *Self-Efficacy: The Exercise of Control*. Freeman, New York.

Bar-Haim, Y., Lamy, D., Pergamin, L., Bakermans-Kranenburg, M.J. and van Ijzendoorn, M.H. (2007) Threat-related attentional bias in anxious and non- anxious individuals: a meta-analytic study. *Psychological Bulletin*, 133, 1–24.

Bargh, J.A., Lombardi, W.J. and Higgins, T.E. (1988) Automaticity of chronically accessible constructs in person X situation effects on person perception: it's just a matter of time. *Journal of Personality and Social Psychology*, 55, 599–605.

Barke, J. (2013) Young peoples' experiences of Neurofibromatosis type 1. Unpublished thesis dissertation. University of the West of England.

Baumeister, R.F., Smart, L. and Boden, J.M. (1996) Relation of threatened egotism to violence and aggression: the dark side of high self-esteem. *Psychological Review*, 103, 5–33.

Beck, A.T., Ward, C.H., Mendelson, M., Mock, J. and Erbaugh, J. (1961) An inventory for measuring depression. *Archives of General Psychiatry*, 4, 561–571.

Bellew, R. (2012) The role of the family, in *The Oxford Handbook of the Psychology of Appearance* (eds N. Rumsey and D. Harcourt), pp. 239–252, Oxford University Press, London.

Bessell, A. and Moss, T.P. (2007) Evaluating the effectiveness of psychosocial interventions for individuals with visible differences: a systematic review of the empirical literature. *Body Image: An International Journal of Research*, 4 (2), 227–238.

Bessell, A., Clarke, A., Harcourt, D., Moss, T. and Rumsey, N. (2010) Incorporating user perspectives in the design of an online intervention tool for people with visible differences: face IT. *Behavioural & Cognitive Psychotherapy*, 38, 577–596.

Bessell, A., Brough, V., Clarke, A., Harcourt, D., Moss, T. and Rumsey, N. (2012) Evaluation of FACE IT, a computerised psychosocial intervention for disfigurement related distress. *Psychology, Health & Medicine*, 17 (5), 565–577.

Bjelland, I., Dahl, A.A., Haug, T.T. and Neckelmann D. (2002) The validity of the Hospital Anxiety and Depression Scale. An updated literature review. *Journal of Psychosomatic Research*, 52, 69–77.

Blakeney, P., Portman, S. and Rutan, R. (1990) Familial values as factors influencing long-term psychological adjustment of children after severe burn injury. *Journal of Burn Care and Rehabilitation*, 11, 472–475.

Blakeney, P., Thomas, C., Holzer, C., Rose, M., Berniger, F. and Meyer, W.J. (2005) Efficacy of a short-term, intensive social skills training programme for burned adolescence. *Journal of Burn Care and Rehabilitation*, 26, 546–555.

Blum R.W., Garell D., Hodgman C.H., Slap G.B. (1993) Transition from child-centred to adult health-care systems for adolescents with chronic conditions. A position paper of the Society for Adolescent Medicine. *Journal of Adolescent Health*, 14, 570–576.

Bradbury, E. (1996) *Counselling People with Disfigurement*. BPS Books, Leicester.

Braun, V. and Clarke, V. (2006) Using thematic analysis in psychology. *Qualitative Research in Psychology*, 3, 77–101.

Brunton, G., Paraskeva, N., Caird, J., et al. (2012) Psychosocial Predictors, Assessment and Outcomes of Cosmetic Interventions: A Systematic Rapid Evidence Review (Part 11). EPPI Centre, Social Science Research Unit, Institute of Education, University of London, London.

Bryant, F.B. and Smith, B.D. (2001) Refining the architecture of aggression: a measurement model for the Buss-Perry Aggression Questionnaire. *Journal of Research in Personality*, 35, 138–167.

Bryman, A. (2007) Barriers to integrating quantitative and qualitative research. *Journal of Mixed Methods Research*, 1, 1–18.

Bull, R. and Rumsey, N. (1988) *The Social Psychology of Facial Appearance*. Springer Verlag, New York.

Burnard, P. (1991) A method of analysing interview transcripts in qualitative research. *Nurse Education Today*, 11, 461–466.

Burns, D.D. (1989) *The Feel Good Handbook: Using the New Mood Therapy in Everyday Life*. Morrow, New York.

Buss, A.H. and Perry, M. (1992) The Aggression Questionnaire. *Journal of Personality and Social Psychology*, 63, 452–459.

Carr, A., Harris, D. and James, C. (2000) The Derriford Appearance Scale (DAS59): a new scale to measure individual responses to living with problems of appearance. *British Journal of Health Psychology*, 5, 201–215.

Carr, A., Moss, T. and Harris, D. (2005) The DAS24: a short form of the Derriford Appearance Scale (DAS59) to measure individual responses to living with problems of appearance. *British Journal of Health Psychology*, 10, 285–298.

Carroll, P. and Shute, R. (2005) School peer victimisation of young people with craniofacial conditions: a comparative study. *Psychology, Health & Medicine*, 10 (3), 291–304.

Cartwright, J. and Magee, H. (2006) The Views and Experiences of Patients Living with Disfiguring Conditions and Health Professionals Involved in Their Care. Report of a qualitative study. Healing Foundation: London.

Cash, T.F. (1996) The treatment of body image disturbances, in *Body Image, Eating Disorders, and Obesity: An Integrative Guide for Assessment and Treatment* (ed J.K. Thompson), pp. 83–107, APA, Washington, DC.

Cash, T.F. (1997) *The Body Image Workbook: An 8-step Program for Learning to Like Your Looks*. New Harbinger, Oakland, CA.

Cash, T. F. (2007) *The Body Image Workbook: An Eight Step Program for Learning to Like Your Looks*. New Harbinger, Oakland, CA.

Cash, T.F. and Fleming, E.C. (2002) The impact of body-image experiences: development of the body image quality of life inventory. *International Journal of Eating Disorders*, 31, 455–460.

Cash, T.F. and Pruzinsky, T. (2002) *Body Image: A Handbook of Theory, Research and Clinical Practice*. Guilford Press, New York.

Cash, T.F. and Smolak, L. (eds) (2011) *Body Image: a Handbook of Science, Practice and Prevention*. Guilford Press, New York.

Cash, T.F., Winstead, B.A. and Janda, L.H. (1986) The great American shape-up. *Psychology Today*, 20, 30–37.

Cash, T., Melnyk S. and Hrabosky, J.I. (2004) The assessment of body image investment: an extensive revision of the appearance schemas inventory. *International Journal of Eating Disorders*, 25, 305–316.

Charlton, R., Rumsey, N., Partridge, J., Barlow, J. and Saul, K. (2003) Editorial: disfigurement – neglected in primary care? *British Journal of Primary Care*, 53, 6–8.

Chren, M.M., Lasek, R.J., Sahay, A.P. and Sands, L.P. (2001) Measurement properties of Skindex-16: a brief quality of life measure for patients with skin diseases. *Journal of Cutaneous Medicine and Surgery*, 5, 105–110.

Clarke, A. (1999) Psychosocial aspects of facial disfigurement: problems, management and the role of a lay-led organisation. *Psychology, Health & Medicine*, 2, 128–141.

Clarke, A. (2001) Social rehabilitation in head and neck cancer. Unpublished DPsych thesis, City University, London.

Clarke, A. and Cooper, C. (2001) Psychological rehabilitation after disfiguring injury or disease: investigating the training needs of specialist nurses. *Journal of Advanced Nursing*, 34 (1), 18–26.

Clarke, A., Lester, K.J., Withey, S.J. and Butler, P.E.M (2005) A funding model for a psychological service to plastic and reconstructive surgery in UK practice. *British Journal of Plastic Surgery*, 58 (5), 708–713.

Clarke, A., Hansen, E., White, P. and Butler, P. E. M. (2012) Low priority? A consecutive study of appearance anxiety in 500 patients referred for cosmetic surgery. *Psychology, Health & Medicine*, 17 (4), 440–446.

Clark, D. and Wells, A. (1995) A cognitive model of social phobia, in *Social Phobia: Diagnosis, Assessment and Treatment* (eds R.G. Heimberg, M.R. Liebowitz, D.A. Hope and F.R. Scheier), pp. 69–93, Guilford, New York, London.

Coleman, J. and Hendry, L. (1999) *The Nature of Adolescence*. Routledge, London.

Cooper, M. (1997) Cognitive theory in anorexia nervosa and bulimia nervosa: a review. *Behavioural and Cognitive Psychotherapy*, 25, 113–145.

Crowley, R., Wolfe, I., Lock, K. and Mckee, M. (2011) Improving the transition between paediatric and adult healthcare: a systematic review. *Archives of Disease in Childhood*, 96, 548–553.

Cordeiro, C.N., Clarke, A., White, P., Sivakumar, B., Ong, J. and Butler, P.E. (2010) A quantitative comparison of psychological and emotional health measures in 360 plastic surgery candidates: is there a difference between aesthetic and reconstructive patients? *Annals of Plastic Surgery*, 65, 349–353.

Cornwell, C.J. and Schmitt, M.H. (1990) Perceived health status, self-esteem and body image in women with rheumatoid arthritis or systemic lupus erythematosus. *Research in Nursing & Health*, 13, 99–107.

Cororve, M.B. and Gleaves, D.H. (2001) Body dysmorphic disorder: a review of conceptualisations, assessment and treatment strategies. *Clinical Psychology Review*, 21, 949–970.

Coughlan, G. and Clarke, A. (2002) Shame and burns, in *Body Shame: Conceptualisation, Research and Treatment* (eds P. Gilbert and J. Miles). Brunner-Routledge, pp. 155–170. Hove.

Crocker, J., Voelkl, K., Testa, M. and Major, B. (1991) Social stigma: the affective consequences of attributional ambiguity. *Journal of Personality and Social Psychology*, 60, 218–228.

Davies, W. (2008) *Overcoming Anger and Irritability*. Constable and Robinson, London.

Demet, K., Martinet, N., Francis, G., Paysant, J. and Andre, J. (2003) Health related quality of life and related factors in 539 persons with amputation of upper and lower limb. *Disability Rehabilitation*, 25, 480–486.

Denscombe, M. (2008) Communities of practice: a research paradigm for the mixed methods approach. *Journal of Mixed Methods Research*, 22, 351–372.

Department of Health (2006) *Transition: Getting it Right for Young People. Improving the Transition of Young People with Long Term Conditions from Children's to Adult Health Services*. The Stationery Office, DH, London.

Department of Health (2007a) Considering Cosmetic Surgery? http://webarchive.nationalarchives.gov.uk/+/www.dh.gov.uk/en/Publichealth/CosmeticSurgery/DH_4123795 (accessed on August 12, 2013).

Department of Health (2007b) Transition: getting it right a film by Greg, Toyah, Craig, AJ and Chris (DVD). A centre screen production for the department of Health. Available from the Department for Education and Skills.

Department of Health (2008) *Transition: Moving On Well*. The Stationery Office, DH, London.

Derogatis, L.R., Lipman, R.S., Rickels, K., Uhlenhuth, E.H. and Covi, L. (1974) The Hopkins Symptom Checklist (HSCL): a self-report symptom inventory. *Behavioral Science*, 19, 1–15.

Diedrichs, P.C. and Halliwell, E. (2012) School-based interventions to promote positive body image and the acceptance of diversity of appearance, in.*The Oxford Handbook of the Psychology of Appearance* (eds N. Rumsey and D. Harcourt), London, pp. 531–550, Oxford University Press.

Diedrichs, P.C., Paraskeva, N. and New, A. (in submission) Quick fixes and appearance concerns.

Durani, P., McGrouther, D.A. and Ferguson, M.W. (2009) The patient Scar Assessment questionnaire: a reliable and valid patient-reported outcomes measure for linear scars. *Plastic & Reconstructive Surgery*, 123, 1481–1489.

Dures, E. (2009) An exploration of the psychosocial impact of epidermolysis bullosa on the daily lives of affected adults and identification of associated support needs. Unpublished PhD Thesis, University of the West of England.

Egan, K., Harcourt, D., Rumsey, N. and The Appearance Research Collaboration (2011) A qualitative study of the experiences of people who identify themselves as having adjusted positively to a visible difference. *Journal of Health Psychology*, 16 (5), 739–749.

Eiserman, W. (2001) Unique outcomes and positive contributions associated with facial difference: expanding research and practice. *Cleft Palate Craniofacial Journal*, 38 (3), 236–244.

Elkadry, E.A., Kenton, K.S., Fitzgerald, M.P., Shott, S. and Brubaker, L. (2003) Patient-selected goals: a new perspective on surgical outcomes. *American Journal of Obstetrics & Gynaecology*, 189 (6), 551–558.

Endriga, M. and Kapp-Simon, K. (1999) Psychological issues in craniofacial care: state of the art. *Cleft Palate Craniofacial Journal*, 36 (1), 3–11.

Engel, G.L. (1980) The clinical application of the biopsychosocial model. *American Journal of Psychiatry*, 137, 535–544.

Enskar, K. and Bertero, C. (2010) Young adult survivors of childhood cancer; experiences affecting self-image, relationships, and present life. *Cancer Nursing*, 33 (1), E18–E24.

Falvey, H. (2012) Cross-cultural differences, in *The Oxford Handbook of the Psychology of Appearance* (eds N. Rumsey and D. Harcourt), pp. 36–46, Oxford University Press, London.

Fauerbach, J.A., Heinberg, L.J., Lawrence, J.W., Bryant, A.G., Richter, L. and Spence, R.J. (2002) Coping with body image changes following a disfiguring burn injury. *Health Psychology*, 21, 115–121.

Feragen, K.B. (2012) Congenital conditions, in *The Oxford Handbook of the Psychology of Appearance* (eds N. Rumsey and D. Harcourt). pp. 353–371, Oxford University Press, London.

Finlay, G.K. and Khan A.L. (1994) The dermatology quality of life index – a simple practical measure for routine clinical use. *Clinical and Experimental Dermatology*, 19, 210–216.

Firooz, A., Bouzari, N., Fallah, N., Ghazisaidi, B., Firoozabadi, M. R. and Dowlati, Y. (2004) What patients with vitiligo believe about their condition. *International Journal of Dermatology*, 43, 811–814.

Fleming, E., Carter, B. and Gillibrand, W. (2002) The transition of adolescents with diabetes from the children's health care service into the adult health care service: a review of the literature. *Journal of Clinical Nursing*, 11 (5), 560–567.

Fortune, D.G., Richards, H.L., Kirby, B., Bowcock, S., Main, C.J. and Griffiths, C.E.M. (2002) A cognitive behavioural symptom management programme as an adjunct in psoriasis therapy. *British Journal of Dermatology*, 146, 458–465.

Fortune, D.G., Richards, H.L., Griffiths, C.E.M and Main, C.J. (2004) Targeting cognitive behaviour therapy to patients' implicit model of psoriasis; results from a patients preference controlled trial. *British Journal of Clinical Psychology*, 43, 65–82.

Fortune, D., Richards, H., Griffiths, C. and Main, C. (2005) Adversarial growth in patients undergoing treatment for psoriasis: a prospective study of the ability of patients to construe benefits from negative events. *Psychology, Health & Medicine*, 10, 44–56.

Fox, F.E., Rumsey, N. and Morris, M. (2007) 'Ur skin is the thing that everyone sees you can't change it!': exploring the appearance-related concerns of young people with psoriasis. *Developmental Neurorehabilitation*, 10 (2), 133–141.

Frost, E. (2003) *Getting Close to Girl's Bodies: Some Research Dilemmas*. Issues in Qualitative Research Methods Seminar Series. University of the West of England, Bristol.

Gaind, S., Clarke, A. and Butler, P.E.M. (2011) The role of disgust emotions in the self-management of wound care. *Journal of Wound Care*, 20 (7), 346–350.

Gamba, A., Romano, M., Grosso, I.M., et al. (1992) Psychosocial adjustment of patients surgically treated for the head and neck cancer. *Head and Neck*, 14, 218–223.

Gibbons, F. and Buunk, B. (1999) Individual differences in social comparison: development of a scale of social comparison. *Journal of Personality and Social Psychology*, 76, 129–142.

Gilbert, P. (2009) *The Compassionate Mind*. London: Constable and Robinson, London.

Gilbert, P. (2010) *Compassion Focused Therapy: Distinctive Features*. Routledge, London.

Gilbert, P. and Miles, J. (eds) (2002) *Body Shame: Conceptualisation, Research and Treatment*. Brunner Routledge: East Sussex.

Gilbert, P., Broomhead, C., Irons, C., et al. (2007) Development of a striving to avoid inferiority scale. *British Journal of Social Psychology*, 46, 633–648.

Girlguiding UK (2010) www.girlguiding.org.uk/girlattitudes (accessed on June 3, 2011).

Goff, L.M. and Barasi, M. (1999) An assessment of the diets of people with rheumatoid arthritis. *Journal of Human Nutrition and Dietetics*, 12, 93–101.

Goffman, E. (1963) *Stigma: Notes on the Management of Spoilt Identity*. Englewood Cliffs, NJ, Prentice Hall.

Grandfield, T., Thompson, A. R. and Turpin, G. (2005) An attitudinal study of responses to dermatitis using the implicit association test. *Journal of Health Psychology*, 10, 821–829.

Green, J.D. and Sedikides, C. (2001) When do self-schemas shape social perception? The role of descriptive ambiguity. *Motivation and Emotion*, 25, 67–83.

Greenberg, L.S. and Safran, J.D. (1987) *Emotion in Psychotherapy*. New York, Guilford Press.

Griffiths, G., Williamson, H. and Rumsey, N. (2012) The romantic experiences of adolescents with a visible difference: exploring concerns, protective factors and support needs. *Journal of Health Psychology*, 17 (7), 1053–1064.

Grinyer, A. (2007) *Young People Living with Cancer: Implications for Policy and Practice*. Open University Press, Maidenhead.

Haavet, O.R., Straand, J., Saugstad, O.D. and Grunfeld, B. (2004) Illness and exposure to negative life experiences in adolescence: two sides of the same coin? A study of 15-year-olds in Oslo, Norway. *Acta Paediatrica*, 93, 405–411.

Habib, N. and Saul, K. (2012) Culture and Ethnicity, in *The Oxford Handbook of the Psychology of Appearance* (eds N. Rumsey and D. Harcourt). pp. 203–216, Oxford University Press, London.

Halliwell, E and Diedrichs, P. (2012) Influence of the media, in *The Oxford Handbook of the Psychology of Appearance* (eds N. Rumsey and D. Harcourt), pp. 217–238, Oxford University Press, London.

Harris, D.L. and Carr, A.T. (2001) Prevalence of concern about physical appearance in the general population. *British Journal of Plastic Surgery*, 54, 223–226.

Harter, S. (1999) *The Construction of the Self: A Developmental Perspective*. Guilford Press, New York.

Helfert, S. and Warschburger, P. (2011) A prospective study on the impact of peer and parental pressure on body dissatisfaction in adolescent girls and boys. *Body Image*, 8, 101–109.

Higgins, E.T. and Brendle, C.M. (1995) Accessibility and applicability: some 'activation rules' influencing judgment. *Journal of Experimental Social Psychology*, 31, 218–243.

Holmbeck, G.N. (2002) A developmental perspective on adolescent health and illness: an introduction to the special issues. *Journal of Pediatric Psychology*, 27, 409–415.

Hopwood, P. and Maguire, G.P. (1988) Body image problems in cancer patients. *British Journal of Psychiatry*, 153, 47–50.

Hughes, J., Naqvi, H., Saul, K., et al. (2009) South Asian community views about individuals with a disfigurement. *Diversity in Health and Social Care*, 6, 241–253.

Jones, D.C. and Crawford, J.K. (2005) Adolescent boys and body image: weight and muscularity concerns as dual pathways for body dissatisfaction. *Journal of Youth and Adolescence*, 34, 629–636.

Jansen, A., Smeets, T., Boon, B., Nederkoorn, C., Roefs, A. and Mulkens, S. (2007) Vulnerability to interpretation bias in overweight children. *Psychology & Health*, 22, 561–574.

Johnson, R.B., Onwuegbuzie, A.J. and Turner, L.A. (2007) Toward a definition of mixed methods research. *Journal of Mixed Methods Research*, 1, 112–133.

Jones, D.C. and Crawford, J.K. (2006) The peer appearance culture during adolescence: gender, and body mass variations. *Journal of Youth and Adolescence*, 32 (2), 257–269.

Jones, D.C., Vigfusdottir, T.H. and Lee, Y. (2004) Body image and the appearance culture among adolescent girls and boys: an examination of friend conversations, peer criticism, appearance, magazines, and the internalisation of appearance ideals. *Journal of Adolescent Research*, 19, 323–339.

Katz, J. and Melzack, R. (1990) Pain 'memories' in phantom limbs: review and clinical observations. *Pain*, 43, 319–336.

Kent, G. (2000) Understanding the experiences of people with disfigurements: an integration of four models of social and psychological functioning. *Psychology, Health & Medicine*, 5, 117–129.

Kent, G. and Keohane, S. (2001) Social anxiety and disfigurement: the moderating effects of fear of negative evaluation and past experience. *British Journal of Clinical Psychology*, 40, 23–34.

Kent, G. and Thompson, A. (2002) The development & maintenance of shame in disfigurement: Implications for treatment, in *Body Shame: Conceptualisation, Research and Treatment* (eds P. Gilbert and J. Miles), pp. 106–116, Brunner-Routledge, Hove.

Kennedy, I. (2010) Getting it right for children and young people: overcoming cultural barriers in the NHS so as to meet their needs. Department of Health, London.

Kernis, M. H., Grannemann, B. D. and Barclay, L. C. (1989) Stability and level of self-esteem as predictors of anger arousal and hostility. *Journal of Personality & Social Psychology*, 56 (6), 1013–1022.

King, N. (1998) Template analysis, in *Qualitative Methods and Analysis in Organizational Research* (eds G.Symon and C.Cassell), pp. 11–22. Sage, London.

Kipps, S., Bahu, T., Ong, K., et al. (2002), Current methods of transfer of young people with Type 1 diabetes to adult services. *Diabetic Medicine*, 19, 649–654.

Kish, V. and Lansdown, R. (2000) Meeting the psychosocial impact of facial disfigurement: developing a clinical service for children and families. *Clinical Child Psychology and Psychiatry*, 5 (4), 497–512.

Kleve, L., Rumsey, N., Wyn-Williams, M. and White, P. (2002) The effectiveness of cognitive-behavioural interventions provided at outlook: a disfigurement support unit. *Journal of Evaluation in Clinical Practice*, 8, 387–395.

Kluck, A.S. (2010) Family influence on disordered eating: the role of body image dissatisfaction. *Body Image*, 7, 8–14.

Koo, J. (1995) The psychosocial impact of acne: patients' perceptions stop. *Journal of the American Academy of Dermatology*, 32, 26–30.

Kuyken, W., Padesky, C.A. and Dudley, R. (2009) *Collaborative Case Conceptualization: Working Effectively with Clients in Cognitive-Behavioural Therapy*. The Guildford Press, New York.

Lansdown, R., Lloyd, J. and Hunter, J. (1991) Facial deformity in childhood: severity and psychological adjustment. *Child: Care, Health and Development*, 17, 165–171.

Lansdown. R., Rumsey, N., Bradbury, E., Carr, A. and Partridge, J. (1997) *Visibly Different: Coping with Disfigurement*. Butterworth Heinemann, London.

Larouche, S.S. and Chin-Peukert L. (2006) Changes in body image experienced by adolescents with cancer. *Journal of Paediatric Oncology Nursing*, 23, 200–209.

Leary, M. R. (1983) A brief version of the fear of negative evaluation scale. *Personality and Social Psychology Bulletin*, 9, 371–375.

Leary, M.R. (1990) Responses to social exclusion: social anxiety, jealousy, loneliness, depression and low self-esteem. *Journal of Social and Clinical Psychology*, 9, 221–229.

Levine, M.P. and Smolak, L. (2002) Body image development during adolescence, in *Body Image. A Handbook of Theory, Research, and Clinical Practice* (eds T.F. Cash and T. Pruzinsky), pp.74–82, Guilford Press, New York.

Liossi, C. (2003) Appearance related concerns across the general and clinical populations. Unpublished PhD Thesis, City University London.

Lovegrove, E. (2002) Adolescence, appearance & anti-bullying strategies.Unpublished PhD Thesis, University of the West of England, Bristol.

Lovegrove, E. and Rumsey, N. (2005) Ignoring it doesn't make it stop: adolescents, appearance and anti-bullying strategies. *Cleft Palate-Craniofacial Journal*, 42, 33–44.

Luthar SS, Cicchetti D & Becker B (2000) The construct of resilience: A critical evaluation and guidelines for future work. *Child Development*, 71, 3, 543–562.

MacGregor, F.C. (1990) Facial disfigurement: problems and management of social interaction and implications for mental health. *Aesthetic Plastic Surgery*, 14, 249–257.

Madera, J.M. & Hebl, M.R. (2012). Discrimination against facially stigmatized applicants in interviews: An eye-tracking and face-to-face investigation. *Journal of Applied Psychology*, 97, 317–330.

Maddern, L. and Owen, T. (2004) The outlook summer group: a social skills workshop for children with a different appearance who are transferring to secondary school. *Clinical Psychology*, 33, 25–29.

Major, B. and Granzow, R. H. (1999) Abortion as stigma; cognitive and emotional implications of concealment. *Journal of Personality and Social Psychology*, 77, 735–745.

Markus, H. and Nurius, P. (1986) Possible selves. *American Psychologist*, 41, 954–969.

Martin C.R. and Newell R.J. (2004) Factor structure of the hospital anxiety and depression scale in individuals with facial disfigurement. *Psychology, Health & Medicine*, 9, 327–336.

Mathews, A. (1990) Why worry? The cognitive function of anxiety. *Behaviour Research and Therapy*, 28, 455–468.

Matto, S.K., Handa, S., Kaur, I., Gupta, N. and Malhotra, R. (2002) Psychiatric morbidity in vitiligo: prevalence and correlates in India. *Journal of European Academy of Dermatology & Venereology*, 16, 573–578.

Maunder, E.Z. (2004) The challenge of transitional care for young people with life-limiting illness. *British Journal of Nursing*, 13 (10), 594–596.

McBain, H., Newman, S., Shipley, M. and Members of the ARC Collaboration (2012) The impact of appearance concerns on anxiety and depression in rheumatoid arthritis. *Musculoskeletal Care*, 11 (1) 19–30.

McCabe, M.P. and Ricciardelli, L.A. (2001) Body image and body change techniques among young adolescent boys. *European Eating Disorders Review*, 9 (5), 335–347.

McDonagh, J.E. (2006) *Growing Up Ready for Emerging Adulthood: An Evidence Base for Professionals Involved in Transitional Care for Young People with Chronic Illness and/or Disabilities*. www.erpho.org.uk/Download/Public/15195/1/emerging%20adulthood.pdf (accessed on December 4, 2008).

McDonagh, J.E. (2007) Transition of care: how should we do it? *Paediatrics & Child Health*, 17 (12), 480–484.

McDonagh, J.E. and Viner, R.M. (2006) Lost in transition? Between paediatric and adult services. *British Medical Journal*, 332, 435–436.

Meyerson, M.D. (2001) Resiliency and success in adults with Moebius Syndrome. *Cleft Palate Craniofacial Journal*, 38, 231–235.

Millstein, S.G., Heger, H. and Hunter, G.A. (1986) Prosthetic use in adult and upper limb amputees: a comparison of the body powered and electrically powered prostheses. *Prosthetics and Orthotics International*, 10, 27–34.

Mogg, K. and Bradley, B.P. (2005) Attentional bias in generalized anxiety disorder versus depressive disorder. *Cognitive Therapy and Research*, 29 (1), 29–45.

Monaghan, S.M., Sharpe, L., Denton, F., Levy, J., Schrieber, L. and Sensky, T. (2007) Relationship between appearance and psychological distress in rheumatic diseases. *Arthritis & Rheumatism*, 57, 303–309.

Morley, D., Jenkinsson, C. and Fitzpatrick R. (2012) A Structured Review of Patient Reported Outcomes Measures used in Cosmetic Surgical Procedures. Report to the Department of Health. Health Services Research Unit, Department of Public health, University of Oxford, UK.

Moss, T. (1997a) Individual variation in adjusting to visible differences, in *Visibly Different: Coping with Disfigurement* (eds R. Lansdown, N. Rumsey, E. Bradbury, A. Carr and J. Partridge). pp. 121–130. Butterworth Heinemann, Oxford.

Moss, T.P. (1997b) Individual differences in adjustment to perceived abnormalities of appearance. Unpublished PhD thesis, University of Plymouth.

Moss, T.P. (2005) The relationship between subjective and objective ratings of disfigurement severity and psychological adjustment. *Body Image: An International Journal of Research*, 2, 151–159.

Moss, T. and Carr, A. (2004) Understanding adjustment to disfigurement: the role of the self-concept. *Psychology & Health*, 19, 737–748.

Moss, T.P. and Harris, DL. (2009) Psychological change following plastic surgery: a prospective controlled outcome study psychology. *Health & Medicine*, 14 (5), 567 –572.

Moss, T. and Rosser, B. (2008) Psychosocial adjustment to visible difference. *The Psychologist*, 21 (6), 492–495.

Moss T. and Rosser, B. (2012a) Adult psychosocial adjustment to visible differences: physical and psychological predictors of variation, in *The Oxford Handbook of the Psychology of Appearance* (eds N. Rumsey and D. Harcourt), pp. 273–294, Oxford University Press, London.

Moss, T.P. and Rosser, B.A (2012b) The moderated relationship of appearance valence on appearance self consciousness: development and testing of new measures of appearance schema components. *PLoS ONE*, 7 (11), e50605.

Muftin, Z. (2013) A randomised controlled feasibility trial of online compassion-focused self-help for psoriasis. *Body Image: An International Journal of Research*, 10, 13 (Dissertation abstracts and summaries).

Murray, C.D. and Fox, J. (2002) Body image and prosthesis satisfaction in the lower limb amputee. *Disability and Rehabilitation*, 24, 925–931.

Newell, R (1999) Altered body image: a fear-avoidance model of psychosocial difficulties following disfigurement. *Journal of Advanced Nursing* 30, 5, 1230–1238.

Newell, R.J. (2000) *Body Image and Disfigurement Care*. Routledge, London.

Newell, R. and Clarke, M. (2000) Evaluation of self-help leaflet in treatment of social difficulties following facial disfigurement. *International Journal of Nursing Studies*, 37, 381–388.

Newman, S., Steed, E. and Mulligan, K. (2008) *Chronic Physical Illness: Self-Management and Behavioural Interventions*. Oxford University Press, London.

NICE (2005) Brief Guidelines for the Treatment of PTSD. http://www.nice.org.uk/nicemedia/live/10966/29771/29771.pdf CG26 (accessed on November 6, 2012).

Oeffinger, K.C., Mertens A.C., Hudson M.M., et al. (2004) Health care of young adult survivors of childhood cancer: a report from the childhood cancer survivor study. *Annals of Family Medicine*, 2 (1), 61–70.

Olsen, R. and Sutton, J. (1998) More hassle, more alone: adolescents with diabetes and the role of formal and informal support. *Child: Care, Health and Development*, 24, 1, 31–39.

Ong, J.L., Clarke, A., Johnson, M., White, P., Withey, S. and Butler, P.E. (2007) Does severity predict distress? The relationship between subjective and objective measures of severity in patients treated for facial lipoatrophy. *Body Image: An International Journal of Research*, 4, 239–248.

Ongenae, K., Beelaert, L., van Geel, N. and Naeyaert, J. M. (2006) Psychosocial effects of vitiligo. *European Academy of Dermatology & Venereology*, 20, 1–8.

Onunu, A. N. and Kubeyinje, E. P. (2003) Vitiligo in Nigerian Africa: a study of 351 patients in Benin City. *International Journal of Dermatology*, 42, 800–802.

Papadopoulos, L., Bor, R., Payne, C.M. and Legg, C. (1999) Coping with the disfiguring effects of vitiligo: a preliminary investigation into the effects of cognitive behaviour therapy. *British Journal of Meical Psychology*, 72, 385–396.

Paraskeva, N. (2013) Psychological assessment prior to cosmetic procedures: brief report on a pilot study. *Journal of Aesthetic Nursing*, 2 (2) 89.

Partridge, J. (1990) *Changing Faces: the Challenge of Facial Disfigurement*. Penguin, London.

Patrick, D.L., Bushnell, D.M. and Rothman M. (2004) Performance of two self-report measures for evaluating obesity and weight loss. *Obesity Research*, 12, 48–57.

Pendley, J.S., Dahlquist, L.M. and Dreyer, Z. (1997) Body image and psychosocial adjustment in adolescent cancer survivors. *Journal of Pediatric Psychology*, 22 (1), 29–43.

Petrie, K.J., Buick, D.L., Weinman, J. and Booth, R. J. (1999) Positive effects of illness reported by myocardial infarction and breast cancer patients. *Journal of Psychosomatic Research*, 47, 537–543.

Phillips, K.A. (1996) *The Broken Mirror*. Oxford University Press, New York.

Pollard, L., Choy, E.H. and Scott, D.L. (2005) The consequences of rheumatoid arthritis: quality of life measures in the individual patient. *Clinical and Experimental Rheumatology*, 23, S.43–S.52.

Popovic, M. (2005) Intimacy and its relevance in human functioning. *Sexual and Relationship Therapy*, 2, 31–49.

Por, J., Goldberg, B., Lennox, V., Burr, P., Barrow, J. and Dennard, L. (2004) Transition of care: health care professionals' view. *Journal of Nursing Management*, 12, 354–361.

Porter, J. R. and Beuf, A. H. (1991) Racial variation in reaction to physical stigma: a study of degree of disturbance by vitiligo among black and white patients. *Journal of Health and Social Behavior*, 32, 192–204.

Porter, J.R., Beuf, A.H., Lerner, A. and Nordlund, J. (1990). The effects of vitiligo on sexual relationships. *Journal of American Academy of Dermatology*, 22, 221–222.

Prior, J. (2009) 'Coping quite well with a few difficult bits': living with disfigurement in early adolescence. *Journal of Health Psychology*, 14 (6), 731–740.

Price, R. (1990) A model for body image care. *Journal of Advance Nursing*, 15, 585–593.

Prichard, I.J. and Tiggemann, M. (2012) The effect of simultaneous exercise and exposure to thin-ideal music videos on women's state self-objectification, mood and body satisfaction. *Sex Roles*, 67, 201–210.

Proschaska, J.O. and Diclemente, C.C. (1984) *The Transtheoretical Approach; Crossing the Traditional Boundaries of Therapy*. Krieger, Malabar, FL.

Pusic, A., Liu, J.C., Chen, C.M., et al. (2007) A systematic review of patient-reported outcome measures in head and neck surgery. *Otolaryngology Head and Neck Surgery*, 136, 525–535.

Pusic, A.L., Klassen, A.F., Scott, A.M., Klok, J., Cordeiro, P.G.M., Cano, S.J. (2009) Development of a new patient-reported outcome measure for breast surgery: the BREAST-Q. *Plastic & Reconstructive Surgery*, 124, 345–353.

Ramsey, B. and O' Reagan, M. (1988) A survey of the social and psychological effects of psoriasis. *British Journal of Dermatology*, 118, 195–201.

Reich, J. W., Zautra, A.J. and Hall, J. S. (eds) 2010 *Handbook of Adult Resilience*. Guilford press: New York.

Ricciardelli, L.A., McCabe, M.P. and Banfield, S. (2000) Body image and body change methods in adolescent boys: role of parents, friends, and the media. *Journal of Psychosomatic Research*, 49 (3), 189–197.

Rickwood, D.J., Deane, F.P and Wilson, C.J. (2007) When and how do young people seek professional help for mental health problems? *Medical Journal of Australia*, 187, S35–S39.

Robinson, E. (1997) Psychological research on visible differences in adults. In: R. Lansdown, N. Rumsey, E. Bradbury, A. Carr and J. Partridge (Eds), pp. 102–111. *Visibly Different: Coping with Disfigurement*. Oxford: Butterworth Heinemann.

Robinson, E., Rumsey, N. and Partridge, J. (1996) An evaluation of the social skills interaction skills workshops for people with disfiguring conditions. *British Journal of Plastic Surgery*, 49, 281–289.

Rollnick, S., Allison, J., Ballsiotes S., et al. (2002) Motivational interviewing and its adaptations, in *Motivational Interviewing: Preparing People for Change* (eds W.R. Miller, W.R. and S. Rollnick) pp. 270–283. Guilford, New York.

Rosser, B. (2008) Cognitive information processing biases and appearance adjustment: the role of the appearance self-schema. Unpublished PhD Thesis. University of the West of England.

Rosser, B., Moss, T. and Rumsey, N. (2010) Attentional and interpretative biases in appearance concern: an investigation of biases in appearance-related information processing. *Body Image: An International Journal of Research*, 7 (3), 251–254.

Royal College of Nursing (2004) *Adolescent Transition Care: Guidance for Nursing Staff*. RCN, London.

Royal College of Paediatrics and Child Health (2003) *Bridging the Gaps: Health Care for Adolescents*. RCPCH, London.

Rozario, S. (2007) Growing up and living with neurofibromatosis1 (NF1): a British Bangladeshi case-study. *Journal of Genetic Counselling*, 16, 551–559.

Rumsey, N. (2002) Body image & congenital conditions with visible differences, in *Body Image: A Handbook of Theory, Research & Practice* (eds T. Cash and T. Pruzinsky). pp. 226–233. Guilford, New York.

Rumsey, N. and Harcourt, D. (2004) Body image & disfigurement: issues & interventions. *Body Image: An International Journal of Research*, 1, 83–97.

Rumsey, N. and Harcourt, D. (2005) *The Psychology of Appearance*. Oxford University Press, London.

Rumsey, N. and Harcourt, D. (2007) Visible difference amongst children and adolescents: issues and interventions. *Developmental Neurorehabilitation*, 10 (2), 113–123.

Rumsey, N., Clarke, A. and Musa, M. (2002) Altered body image: the psychosocial needs of patients. *British Journal of Community Nursing*, 7, 563–566.

Rumsey, N., Clarke, A., White, P. and Hooper, E. (2003) Exploring the psychosocial concerns of outpatients with disfiguring conditions. *Journal of Wound Care*, 12, 247–252.

Rumsey, N., Clarke, A., White, P., Wyn-Williams, M. and Garlick, W. (2004) Altered body image: auditing the appearance-related concerns of people with visible disfigurement. *Journal of Advanced Nursing*, 48, 443–453.

Rybarczyk, B.D., Nyenhuis, D.L., Nicholas, J.J., Cash, S.M. and Kaiser, J. (1995) Body image, perceived social stigma, and the prediction of psychosocial adjustment to leg amputation. *Rehabilitation Psychology*, 40, 95–110.

Saradjian, A., Thompson, A.R. and Datta, D. (2007) The experience of men using an upper limb prosthesis following amputation: positive coping and minimizing feeling different. *Disability and Rehabilitation*, 30, 871–883.

Sarason, I.G., Levine, H.M., Basham, R.B. and Sarason, B.R. (1983) Assessing social support: the Social Support Questionnaire. *Journal of Personality and Social Psychology*, 44, 127–139.

Sarwer, D. and Crerand, C. (2004) Cosmetic medical treatments. *Body Image: An International Journal of Research*, 1, 88–99.

Sarwer, D. and Spitzer, J.C. (2012a) Body image dysmorphic disorder in persons who undergo aesthetic medical treatments. *Aesthetic Surgery Journal*, 32 (8), 999–1009.

Sarwer, D.B. and Spitzer, J.C. (2012b) Cosmetic surgical procedures for the body, in *Encyclopaedia of Body Image and Human Appearance* (ed T. Cash). Elsevier, New York.

Sarwer, D., Pruzinsky, T., Cash, T.F., Goldwyn, R.M., Persing, J.A. and Whitaker, L.A. (2006) *Psychological Aspects of Reconstructive and Cosmetic Plastic Surgery*. LWW, New York.

Sarwer, D.B., Infield, A.L., Baker, J.L., et al. (2008) Two year results of a prospective multi-site investigation of patient satisfaction and psychological status following cosmetic surgery. *Aesthetic Surgery Journal*, 28 (3), 245–250.

Scheier, M. F. and Carver, C. S. (1987) Dispositional optimism and physical well-being: the influence of generalized outcome expectancies on health. *Journal of Personality*, 55 (2), 169–210.

Scheier, M.F., Carver, C.S. and Bridges, M.W. (1994) Distinguishing optimism from neuroticism (and trait anxiety, self-mastery, and self-esteem): a re-evaluation of the Life Orientation Test. *Journal of Personality and Social Psychology*, 67, 1063–1078.

Schwartz, C.E. and Sprangers, M.A.G. (1999) Methodological approaches for assessing response shift in longitudinal quality of life research. *Social Science & Medicine*, 48, 1531–1548.

Seligman, M.E.P. (1998) *Learned Optimism*, 2nd edn. Pocket Books, New York.

Shanmugarajah, K., Gaind, S., Clarke, A. and Butler, P.E.M. (2012) The role of disgust emotions in the observer response to facial disfigurement. *Body Image: An International Journal of Research*, 9 (4), 455–461.

Shaw, K. L., Southwood, T. R. and McDonagh, J. E. (2004) User perspectives of transitional care for adolescents with juvenile idiopathic arthritis. *Rheumatology*, 43 (6) 770–778.

Sheng-Yu, F. and Eiser, C. (2009) Body image of children and adolescents with cancer: a systematic review. *Body Image*, 6 (4), 247–256.

Skevington, S.M., Blackwell, F. and Britton, N.F. (1987) Self-esteem and perception of attractiveness: an investigation of early rheumatoid arthritis. *British Journal of Medical Psychology*, 60, 45–52.

Smart, L. and Wegner, D.M. (1999) Covering up what can't be seen: concealable stigma and mental control. *Journal of Personality and Social Psychology*, 77, 474–486.

Smolak, L. (2004) Body image in children and adolescents: where do we go from here? *Body Image*, 1, 15–28.

Sodergren, S.C. and Hyland, M.E. (2000) What are the positive consequences of illness? *Psychology and Health*, 15, 85–97.

Sodergren, S.C., Hyland, M.E., Crawford, A. and Partridge, M.R. (2004) Positivitiy in illness: self-delusion or existential growth? *British Journal of Health Psychology*, 9, 163–174.

Somerville, J. (1997) Management of adults with congenital heart disease: an increasing problem. *Annual Review of Medicine*, 48, 283–293.

Spielberger, C.D., Gorsuch, R.L. and Lushene, R.E. (1970) *Manual for the State-Trait Anxiety Inventory*. Consulting Psychologists Press, Palo Alto, CA.

Storry J (1997) John Storry, in *Visibly Different: Coping with Disfigurement* (eds R. Lansdown, N. Rumsey, E. Bradbury, T. Carr and J. Partridge), pp. 31–38, Butterworth Heineman, London.

Strenta, F. and Kleck, R. (1985) Physical disability and the attribution dilemma: perceiving the causes of social behaviour. *Journal of Social and Clinical Psychology*, 3, 129–142.

Strunk, D.R. and Adler, A.D. (2009) Cognitive biases in three prediction tasks: a test of the cognitive model of depression. *Behaviour Research and Therapy*, 37, 34–40.

Thompson, A.R. (2011) Adaptation in long-term conditions: the role of stigma particularly in conditions that affect appearance, in *The Textbook of Long-term Conditions* (eds S. Randall and H. Ford), pp. 121–136, Wiley, London.

Thompson, A.R. (2012) Researching appearance: models theories and frameworks, in *Oxford Handbook of Appearance* (eds N. Rumsey and D. Harcourt), pp. 91–109, Oxford University Press, Oxford.

Thompson, A.R. and Broom, L. (2009) Positively managing intrusive reactions to disfigurement: an interpretative phenomenological analysis of naturalistic coping. *Diversity in Health & Care*, 6, 171–180.

Thompson, A. and Kent, G. (2001) Adjusting to disfigurement: processes involved in dealing with being visibly different. *Clinical Psychology Review*, 21, 663–682.

Thompson, J.K., Heinberg, L.J., Altabe, M. and Tantleff-Dunn, S. (1999) *Exacting Beauty: Theory, Assessment and Treatment of Body Image Disturbance*. APA, Washington, DC.

Thompson, A.R., Kent, G., and Smith, J.A. (2002) Living with vitiligo: dealing with difference. *British Journal of Health Psychology*, 7, 213–225.

Thompson, A.R., Clarke, S.A., Newell, R., Gawkrodger, G. and The Appearance Research Collaboration (2010) Vitiligo linked to stigmatisation in British South Asian women: a qualitative study of the experiences of living with vitiligo. *The British Journal of Dermatology*, 163, 481–486.

Thwaites, R and Freeston, M.H. (2005) Safety-seeking behaviours: fact or function? How can we clinically differentiate between safety behaviours and adaptive coping strategies across anxiety disorders? *Behavioural and Cognitive Psychotherapy*, 33 (2), 177–188.

Tiggemann, M. (2004) Body image across the adult lifespan: stability and change. *Body Image*, 1, 29–41.

Turner, S., Thomas, P., Dowell, T., Rumsey, N. and Sandy, J. (1997) Psychological outcomes amongst cleft patients and their families. *British Journal of Plastic Surgery*, 50, 1–9.

Van Staa, A.L., Jedeloo, S., van Meeteren, J. and Latour, J.M. (2011) Crossing the transition chasm: experiences and recommendations for improving transitional care of young adults, parents and providers. *Child, Care, Health and Development*, 37 (6), 821–832.

Veale, D., Willson, R. and Clark, A. (2009) Overcoming body image problems (including body dysmorphic disorder). Constable Robinson: London.

Veale, D., Ellison, N., Werner, T., Dodhia, R., Serfaty, M. and Clarke, A. (2012) Development of a cosmetic screening questionnaire (COPS) for screening body dysmorphic disorder. *Journal of Plastic, Reconstructive & Aesthetic Surgery*, 65 (4), 530–532.

Viner, R. (1999) Transition from paediatric to adult care. Bridging the gaps or passing the buck? *Archives of Disease in Childhood*, 81, 271–275.

Viner, R. and Keane, M. (1998) *Youth Matters: Evidence-Based Best Practice for the Care of Young People in Hospital*. Action for Sick Children, London.

Visentin, K., Koch, T., Kralik, D. (2006) Adolescents with type 1 diabetes: transition between diabetes services. *Journal of Clinical Nursing*, 15 (6), 761–769.

Watson, A.R. (2000) Non-compliance and transfer from paediatric to adult transplant unit. *Pediatric Nephrology*, 14, 469–472.

Watson, D., Clark, L. A. and Tellagan, A. (1988) Development and validation of brief measures of posiitive and negative affect: the PANAS scales. *Journal of Personality and Social Psychology*, 47, 1063–1070.

Watson, R., Parr, J.R., Joyce, C., May, C. and Le Couteur, A.S. (2011) Models of transitional care for young people with complex health needs: a scoping review. *Child: Care, Health and Development*, 37, 780–791.

Weissberg-Benchell, J., Wolpert, H. and Anderson, B. (2007) Transitioning from pediatric to adult care: a new approach to the post-adolescent young person with type 1 diabetes, *Diabetic Care*, 30 (10), 2441–2446.

Wells, A. (1997) *Cognitive Therapy of Anxiety Disorders: A Practice Manual and Conceptual Guide*. Wiley, London.

Westwood, A., Henley, L.D., Wilcox, P. (1999) Transition for paediatric to adult care for persons with cystic fibrosis: patient and parent perspectives, *Journal of Paediatric Child Health*, 35, 442–445.

White, C. (2000) Body image dimensions and cancer: a heuristic cognitive behavioural model. *Psycho-Oncology*, 9, 183–192.

White, J. (2008) The development of negative body image and disordered eating in adolescence. Unpublished PhD Thesis. University of the West of England.

Wicks, L. and Mitchell, A. (2010) The adolescent cancer experience: loss of control and benefit finding. *European Journal of Cancer Care*, 19, 778–785.

Williamson, H. (2012) The perspectives of health professionals on the psychosocial impact of an altered appearance among adolescents treated for cancer. Unpublished thesis dissertation. University of the West of England.

Williamson, H. and Wallace, M. (2012) When treatment affects appearance, in *The Oxford Handbook of the Psychology of Appearance* (eds N. Rumsey and D. Harcourt), pp. 414–438, Oxford University Press, London.

Williamson, H., Harcourt, D., Halliwell, E., Frith, H. and Wallace, M. (2010) Adolescents' and parents' experiences of managing the psychosocial impact of appearance change during cancer treatment. *Journal of Paediatric Oncology Nursing*, 27 (3), 168–175.

Williamson, H., Griffiths, C., Harcourt, D. and Cadogan, J. (2012) The development and acceptability of YP Face IT: an online psychosocial intervention for young people with a visible difference, in *Appearance Matters* 5, Bristol, UK, 3–4 July, 2012.

Zigmond, A. and Snaith, R. (1983) The hospital anxiety and depression scale. *Acta Psychiatrica Scandinavica*, 67, 361–370.

Index

Note: Page references in *italics* refer to Figures; those in **bold** refer to Tables